FEMINISM, SOCIALISM,
AND
FRENCH ROMANTICISM

FEMINISM, SOCIALISM, AND FRENCH ROMANTICISM

CLAIRE GOLDBERG MOSES

AND

LESLIE WAHL RABINE

INDIANA UNIVERSITY PRESS

Bloomington and Indianapolis

An earlier version of "Rewriting the Oedipal Triangle" appeared as
"Rewriting the Oedipal Triangle: Feminism, Psychoanalysis and
the Saint-Simonians," in *L'Esprit Créateur*, vol. 29, no. 1
(Spring 1989), 37–49.

The paper used in this publication meets the minimum requirements of American National Standard for Information Sciences—Permanence of Paper for
Printed Library Materials, ANSI Z39.48-1984.

⊗™

Manufactured in the United States of America

Library of Congress Cataloging-in-Publication Data

Moses, Claire Goldberg, date.
    Feminism, Socialism, and French romanticism/Claire Goldberg Moses and
Leslie Wahl Rabine.
      p. cm.
    Includes bibliographical references and index.
    ISBN 0-253-33889-1 (cloth).—ISBN 0-253-20818-1 (pbk.)
    1. Feminism—France—History—19th century. 2. Feminists—France—
History—19th century. 3. Saint-Simonianism. I. Rabine, Leslie W., date.
HQ1616.M67   1993
305.42'0944—dc20   92-42841

1 2 3 4 5 97 96 95 94 93

For
Merle
and
Arnold, Lisa, and Leslie

CONTENTS

ACKNOWLEDGMENTS

The authors gratefully acknowledge the assistance of Kathleen Hart, Judith Pike, and Marianne Bosshard in preparing the translations. We wish also to thank Joan Ariel, Marjorie Beale, Evelyn Torton Beck, Victoria Bernal, Charles Bernheimer, Susan Blank, Francesca Cancian, Kate Davy, Dominique Desanti, Gay Gullickson, Hilary Harris, Sara Melzer, Judy Newton, Mark Poster, Kathy Russell, Joan Scott, Sally Stein, Margaret Waller, Ann Walthau, and Linda Williams for reading various parts of the manuscript and offering many useful suggestions. The National Endowment for the Humanities "Travel to Collections" Fellowship Program and the University of Maryland's International Travel Fund and General Research Board provided financial support for research and travel.

FEMINISM, SOCIALISM,
AND
FRENCH ROMANTICISM

I

INTRODUCTION

How and why do a literary critic and a historian collaborate on a study of French feminists in the 1830s? We had been trained to read texts according to different methods and for different purposes, and to write and speak about them in languages not always easily accessible to each other. Yet before becoming aware of each other's work, our independent and divergent approaches to the Saint-Simonian feminists had taken place upon the common ground of women's studies, during the same period that this new intellectual movement was itself coming to grips with the inadequacy of traditional disciplinary boundaries and methods for feminist analysis.

When we met in 1983, therefore, each of us considered herself on the one hand part of this movement and on the other hand part of a tiny number of contemporary feminist scholars who had read the remarkable French women of the 1830s with the astonished recognition of them as our own predecessors. We were both convinced by our previous work on the Saint-Simonian movement that its influence on all subsequent political and social movements, especially feminism, could not be overestimated.[1] We thus decided on this joint effort to make them better known to an English-language audience and to explore through their writings some of the unanswered questions confronting our own movement.

Some of these questions concern interdisciplinarity as a feminist response to our ambiguous relation to academic disciplines and to the university itself as a patriarchal institution. Women's studies developed not simply to study women but to investigate the reasons for their pervasive absence from the scholarship and curricula of every discipline. Since the invisible ideological and discursive structures determining women's absence were the same or similar in every field, feminist scholars needed a meeting of collective minds across disciplines.

The Saint-Simonian feminists we were about to study called for, we believed, an interdisciplinary approach like that which had grown out of women's studies, and not only because they, like us, were both insiders and outsiders with respect to a masculine organization (the university for us and the Saint-Simonian movement for them), or because they, like us, conceived their feminism as a critique of the institution or movement in

1

which they were involved. Their critique needed a double analysis because it was itself double, in their own terminology both a *word* and an
act. Their writings were both documents of the social and cultural movement they organized and texts that were in and of themselves symbolic
acts. Where the historian had been trained to regard these writings as
documents, to be read as references to social practices, the literary critic
approached them as texts, to be read as signifying practices.

How could we combine these two aspects of the *Saint-Simoniennes'*
writings? The models of interdisciplinary research then familiar to us
were limited to one of two forms: Either a specialist in one discipline
would draw secondarily on work in other disciplines or an editor of an
anthology would draw together essays from scholars in different disciplines. Neither seemed appropriate for this project. We decided to ex-
periment instead with a different model—that of a historian and a
literary critic working closely together on a body of texts over a period of
several years in order to discover how our different disciplinary approaches could complement each other. Until recently, historians have
been trained to use documents as sources of information and tools for
reconstructing the past, and literary critics have been trained to read the
creation of meaning through textual levels and patterns. But the contemporary crisis of the disciplines, abetted and in large measure instigated by women's studies, has blurred these lines significantly.[2] Our
book can be viewed as a microcosm of this complex and unfinished process at the present time. Its structure demonstrates the extent to which
the boundaries between our disciplines still exist, but its content bears
the marks of their cross-fertilization. Each of us has had to question and
test our assumptions about the relation between text and document,
about the textuality of any document, the documentariness of any text.
But we of course came to this problem from opposite perspectives.

For the historian, Claire Moses, whose discipline had trained her to
approach these writings as documents, our interdisciplinary model offered the opportunity to reconsider early French feminism in order to
pose new questions that poststructuralist theory can help to formulate.[3]
Of particular importance to this study are questions that problematize
our notions of the "text," the "context," and the relationship between
them—a relationship which is clearly more complicated and more dialec-
tical than our training in the pre-poststructuralist world supposed.

For example, to what extent do historians, in examining texts, assume
them to be documentary representations of "experience" or "reality"?
How do such assumptions prevent them from seeing the records and
documents themselves as constructing knowledge that mediates our view
of reality? Influenced by such questions, Moses has reread the Saint-
Simonians' writings with increased interest in their language and the
structuring of their arguments; the elements of the text itself, their words
and the way in which meaning is constructed, become as important as

the "story" the text presents. The work of poststructuralists who have examined the instability and interdependence of what a culture takes to be fixed oppositions was particularly useful to her for examining the construction of such categories as "woman" and "man" and "difference" and "equality" both in romantic feminist discourse and in contemporary feminism as well.

But in analyzing the construction of meaning in these texts, Moses also asks questions that historians are especially trained to answer: why certain meanings come into being at particular moments in time, why certain individuals or groups create particular meanings, and why changes in meaning happen when they do. Following those poststructuralists who, like Michel Foucault, are the more historicist and political (in their attention to questions of power, that is), she views the construction of meaning as contested and open to redefinition by interested parties with political stakes in the outcome. People do matter: They may, of course, "receive" meanings, but they may also refuse them or transform them. Moses focuses on the struggle for meaning in the construction of gender and gender hierarchy in 1830s France, which involved contests between feminist and patriarchalist romantics, between women and men Saint-Simonians, between some men and other male Saint-Simonians, and between some women and other *Saint-Simoniennes*.

Moses looks also at the intertwining of social circumstances, political events, and long-term economic change as well as more immediate and more personal needs and aspirations with the construction of meaning, but in doing so she must take into account that poststructuralists have put into question our capacity to recover historical "experience." This is especially discomfiting to historians, especially those of us feminist historians who have used the concept of "women's experience" to challenge traditional, male-centered histories or who, in our histories of feminism, have sought to recover moments when individuals "experienced" oppression.[4] If we now abandon the goal of recovering women's experience, will we be abandoning the cause of women and feminism? Of course, to some extent the problem would not exist if, by "experience" or "the experience of oppression," we were content to identify women's roles and behavior or simply to tally up wage disparities and other statistics retrievable from censuses or the records of ministries of education and criminal courts. Traditional methods of historical research and writing are adequate for recovering this "experience."[5] But to the extent that we use "experience" in discussing subjectivity—as we do when we write about "coming to consciousness"—we have been, in recent years, humbled. And not only by poststructuralist critics. In recent feminist politics as well, we have had to acknowledge that we cannot truly know how women who are different from ourselves—women of other races, ethnicities, religions, classes, sexual orientations—experience oppression; nor can we know this for women of the past.

What then are feminist historians to do? Moses adopts several strategies to cope with the epistemological challenge. One is to let the *Saint-Simoniennes* speak for themselves whenever possible. That was her motivation for a book of this kind. But the problem does not end there: Dominant ideologies determine which "experiences" are described in texts and how they are understood. Moses therefore contextualizes even the words of the *Saint-Simoniennes*, asking what kinds of experience some meanings made "meaningful." Finally, Moses recognizes that poststructuralism challenges historians to recognize not only the constructions of meanings in texts from the past but the constructions of meanings in our own texts. Having acknowledged the difficulties of knowing the "experience" of those who lived in the past, she asks if we might not contribute more usefully to scholarly concerns by a more conscious self-awareness of our interpretive practices—not that we would or could rid ourselves of present-day prejudices, but rather that we might use these to deepen our understanding of those texts. This is what Moses has attempted here— less the recovery of the experience of women in the past than an interpretation of the past informed by the present and which self-consciously addresses present-day concerns as well.

As a literary critic, Leslie Rabine came to the above issues from another direction. If some historians have come to read documents not as transparent windows to an external referent but in terms of their discursive and representational strategies, some literary critics have sought to go beyond the notion of a text as autonomous self-referentiality. They have sought connections between text and socio-historic context that also avoid the pitfalls of historical determinism. Semiotic, deconstructive, psychoanalytic, and Foucauldian methods allow us to approach any social formation as a signifying or discursive practice that can be read much as we would read a written, literary text. Although at first glance the notion that "everything is text" might seem to return us (and for some schools of criticism has indeed returned us) to the pure autonomous text, it also opens a two-way path between text and sociopolitical formation. In this pathway, the job of a literary critic is to read not simply the inscription of the social within a text but the way in which a text, literary or otherwise, actually produces and transforms systems of social meaning, and therefore the speaking subject of those social systems.

Yet Rabine's attempt to read this process in the *Saint-Simoniennes'* archival documents posed a peculiar problem. Faced with unpublished, unedited, and in many cases handwritten historical documents, reading personal letters and journal articles in a fragmentary, uncontextualized form, Rabine could not avoid doing precisely that which contemporary literary theory has insistently warned against. From the early influential essays by Roland Barthes, Michel Foucault, and Emile Benveniste to the present, theorists have challenged in particular one form of the referent preexisting the text—that of the biographical author.[6] Ironically, though,

Rabine found that in order to be able to read the way in which the Saint-Simonian women's texts produce them as writing subjects, she first had to make coherent sense of the material by constructing preexisting referents in the form of biographical authors independent of the texts. The gaps between the fragments had to be accounted for as other than "productive silences." They had to be imagined as lives lived by real people. The interdisciplinary work put Rabine in a kind of paradox. She found that she had to violate the principles of poststructuralist theory in order to follow them, that she could deconstruct the author only by first constructing her.

The need to invent the author as a heuristic device led Rabine to understand the extent to which the author preexisting the text is indeed a fiction (since she herself was creating this fiction), but this imagined referent had a strangely conflictual relation to its text, one that posed another problem in using literary theory to read documents written by women. In their early articles, Barthes and Foucault challenged the humanist notion of Author as the essential, self-identical, and (although they did not say so) masculine master and guarantor of the text and its ultimate meaning. These notions certainly fit the Saint-Simonian feminists' texts, but not in the way postulated by theories based on male writers. The act of writing produces the Saint-Simonian women as authors by transforming them from the silenced complements of humanist Man into the subjects of their own words and acts. Since throughout their lives, French society, and to a large extent the men of their movement, continued to marginalize, impoverish, scorn, and ignore them, the women authors provide spectacular evidence that this feminine subject does not in fact exist elsewhere but in her texts.

If Rabine could not, therefore, avoid examining the relations between context and text, referent and sign, and author and textual subject, she also found that these were not simply relations between a preexisting original and its mimetic copy. Rabine found that, on the contrary—and especially in the case of author as referential person and author as subject produced by writing—the relation was one of conflict and contradiction more than representation and identity. These contradictions between the texts and the lives of the Saint-Simonian feminists are themselves productive. In their utopian vision, the women sought not only to build a new society but to build one in which their textual selves could be realized as socially recognized individuals.

If our efforts toward interdisciplinarity may seem at this point mainly influenced by French poststructuralist theory, such is not entirely the case. We have also brought American feminist theory to bear upon a disciplinary split that besets French feminist studies—the split between critical theory and social history. American scholarship has extensively analyzed the historical relation between the theory and practice of the present and those of earlier North American women's movements. By contrast, contemporary French feminist theory has not delved into its historical connections to previous feminisms, and for this reason those of us influenced by this theory remain caught in the limitations of its blind spot. This book, then, sets out to explore the historical ties between contemporary theory and one of its unmistakable predecessors.

Feminism, Socialism, and French Romanticism takes us to Paris in the late 1820s and 1830s and turns our attention to what continues to strike us as one of the most extraordinary of early women's movements. It grew out of a social movement whose members called themselves Saint-Simonians after their deceased leader, Claude Henri, comte de Saint-Simon. They pledged themselves to develop his ideas for a world order based on peace, love, and cooperation. Having first developed the more rationalist elements of Saint-Simon's ideas on social and economic justice, they had, by the late 1820s, begun to emphasize the more romantic elements of his work and especially his ideas for a "new religion" based on love. Woman and the sociosexual relationship between the sexes then emerged as the movement's central concern.

The feminism of these Saint-Simonians was at first a masculine creation. Prosper Enfantin, their charismatic leader, played a leading role in theorizing a link between the equality of the sexes and sexual liberation. This book, however, will focus on women among the Saint-Simonians. It will analyze the ambivalence of their response to theories on woman and sexuality originally conceived and practiced by men. Beginning in the early 1830s, a group composed mainly of working-class women appropriated the men's emancipatory vision for their own needs. Reacting enthusiastically to Enfantin's call to women ("appel aux femmes") to speak out on the question of the relationship between the sexes, these women nonetheless transformed the men's words and ideas by integrating them into a new symbolic context that changed their meaning.

In the process of so doing, they developed, as the texts will show, unprecedented forms of women's writing and culture which make them foremothers of contemporary Anglo-American radical and French poststructuralist feminists. Although their ideas and acts belong to the specific historical context of the romantic age, the *Saint-Simoniennes* share with our contemporaries striking similarities that set them apart from feminists after 1848 and before the 1960s. Both are sexual radicals who analyze the repression of women's bodies as structurally fundamental to a system of social and economic oppression. Both choose as a strategy of liberation the development of a separate women's cultural movement and, in particular, a feminine practice of the written word, which one of these Saint-Simonian writers, Claire Démar, called a "parole de femme" (word of woman). The *Saint-Simoniennes'* principal means to achieve the end of emancipation was a journal of theory and debate which they at first called *La Femme libre*, but then retitled several times (*La Nouvelle femme, Apostolat des femmes, L'Affranchissement des femmes*) before settling on *Tribune des femmes*. In the first issue they announced that the journal would "publish articles only by women." This was likely the first consciously separatist women's movement in history.

Our book includes a historical interpretation of the writings and activities of these *Saint-Simoniennes*, a textual reading of their works, and a selection of their writings in translation. Claire Moses interprets the story of the *Saint-Simoniennes* within the context of post-Revolutionary French society and discusses the specific social, political, and cultural forces that explain a feminism centered on a theory of difference rather than equality and on sexual radicalism rather than demands for civic rights. Leslie Rabine then reads the Saint-Simonian women's letters, journal articles, essays, and memoirs as texts. She reads them not so much for what they mean as for how they transform masculine romantic autobiographical forms, theories of woman and desire, and structures of subjectivity. The translated writings included in this volume are from Suzanne Voilquin's *Souvenirs d'une fille du people* (*Memories of a Daughter of the People*), from the many letters collected in the Saint-Simonian archives, and from the *Saint-Simoniennes'* journal, the *Tribune des femmes*. Also included are Claire Démar's essay *Ma Loi d'avenir* (*My Law of the Future*) and the foreword and preface to Flora Tristan's *Pérégrinations d'une paria* (*Peregrinations of a Pariah*), reprinted in their entirety. Many of these writings have never been published; all are previously unavailable in English.

Moses places her interpretive essay in the context of Anglo-American historiography. She has organized the essay around the question of "difference"—a question that has been much discussed among French, British, and American feminists but which became a matter of special concern to U.S. historians after it figured rather prominently in *EEOC v. Sears, Roebuck*, a court case that pitted historian against historian.[7] She begins with a discussion of the multiple meanings of "difference" in recent feminist theory and historical writings, noting that some theorists and historians use the term to refer to concepts of gender that stress the differences between women and men, while others use "difference" in referring to political organizing based on a separatist women's "praxis" or in referring to theories that explore the differences among women. Moses, finding that the Saint-Simonian feminists illustrate all three meanings, interprets their history within this framework, examining their construction of a theory of gender based on "natural" differences, their development of a separatist organizing strategy, and, finally, their blending of a political analysis based on sex difference with an analysis of the differences among women.

While the nineteenth-century experience of U.S., English, and French women alike was shaped by the discourse of difference, what is exceptional about the *Saint-Simoniennes* is their discussion of "difference" in relation to feminist politics. Examining their "words" and "acts," Moses finds, brings new insights to the "difference" question both in Anglo-American historiography and contemporary feminist politics. Although British and American historians have often studied the ways in which a discourse of sexual difference has been used to frustrate feminists' demands for equality, some historians now suggest that this discourse may have had an emancipatory potential as well. A case in point is the Owenite movement—an English utopian socialist movement of the 1830s and 1840s that was akin to Saint-Simonianism in many ways. Sally Alexander, who has studied English women's participation in nineteenth-century emancipatory politics, contrasts the "difference" language of Owenites to Chartism's language of rational individualism—a movement in which women participated significantly less. She concludes that the language of difference within the Owenite movement was experienced as welcoming by women and may explain their significant participation in that movement's politics.[8]

Saint-Simonians also favored a discourse of sexual difference. Moreover, Saint-Simonian feminists were explicit about the usefulness of this discourse in arguing for sexual equality and were well aware of the implications of choosing it over the discourse of individualism and universalism used by feminists at the time of the French Revolution. They wrote that the discourse of Revolutionary rational individualism rendered women invisible and in so doing disempowered them. In the discourse of sexual difference, they contended, the feminine was recuperated and women were inspired to claim power.

The words of the *Saint-Simoniennes* would seem, then, to substantiate Alexander's opinion. Saint-Simonians appropriated the patriarchal discourse of difference but transformed it into a discourse for arguing for equality. Moses views their interpretive activity in the context of the Saint-Simonians' valorization of feminine attributes. Love, sentiment, and cooperation were deemed necessary for the world order envisioned by the Saint-Simonians. These were, of course, traits that were considered particular to women, but among the Saint-Simonians they were also considered particular to those exceptional men—such as Enfantin—who, with women, would be leaders in the new world.

In terms of praxis, Moses places the discussion of "difference" into the current historiographical debate around "women's culture" and finds here, too, interesting points of comparison between English and American women's historical experience and the experience that is inscribed in these *Saint-Simoniennes*' "words" and "acts." The term "women's culture"—borrowed from anthropologists—is used by historians for the sex-segregated world of white, middle-class women and, more recently, of white working-class and African American women as well.[9] Although some historians have found in women's kin and friendship networks and in their shared values, knowledge, and activities (social, political, and "cultural" in the more usual sense of that term) a source of strength and even *the* source of their resistance to male oppression, other historians warn against viewing women's culture in a vacuum that denies men's power in defining women's place.[10]

The story of these *Saint-Simoniennes* throws light on this debate, for their separate culture was intentional—self-created for the express purpose of challenging men's power to define their place and role. This is an interesting reversal of the progression of the women's movement in the United States, where feminism is seen to have emerged from women's culture. Historians following Nancy Cott's lead[11] have argued that women's segregation into a separate sphere, although patriarchally imposed, created the setting for what we in the twentieth century now call "consciousness raising." In other words, the "bonds" of womanhood confined to a separate sphere led to the creation of "bonds" of support and the birth of an emancipatory movement. But in France, among the *Saint-Simoniennes*, women's culture developed out of feminism. Consciousness-raising occurred within a mixed-sex setting. After several years of political activism within Saint-Simonianism, the women founded a newspaper that would publish women's writings only and began to hold meetings that only women could attend. And this self-consciously adopted political organizing strategy was resisted by Saint-Simonian men. Significantly, like U.S. women at that same time, *Saint-Simoniennes* extolled seemingly traditional female values—such as nurturance and emotional expressiveness—but, unlike their American counterparts, they did not extol a life limited to domesticity. In the Saint-Simonian story, then, lies the possibility of deconstructing the oppression/agency opposition in the women's culture debate. Ever mindful of women's oppression, they directly challenged men's domination by asserting their cultural autonomy. In doing so, they cleared a space for self-definition.

A third point of comparison that can be drawn between nineteenth-century U.S. and English women and the *Saint-Simoniennes* is their attitudes toward religion. The significant role that Barbara Berg, Ellen DuBois, Nancy Hewitt, Jane Rendall, and Barbara Taylor grant to religion in inspiring U.S. and English feminists in the early nineteenth century finds its parallel in the Saint-Simonians' "new religion."[12] Although one usually associates French social-change politics—including feminism—with secularism, in general, and anticlericalism, in particular, these romantic feminists were deeply committed to a politics that was religious. True, they created a "new religion" that was to challenge traditional Christian theology and the organized Catholic church, but their frequent reference to their "word" or "words" and their "acts" and their self-representation as "apostles" purposely reflect the early Christians. They organized a Saint-Simonian "church" that would be headed by a "couple-pope"; they awaited a female messiah; and God became "God the Father and Mother."

Moses finds that the distinctiveness of Saint-Simonian feminism alters in a fundamental way the Anglo-American view of the history of feminism. The origins of contemporary feminism are usually traced to the organized liberal movements of the mid- to late nineteenth century. As a consequence, the history of contemporary feminism appears to develop in a straight, evolutionary line from nineteenth-century movements, theories, and strategies of narrow scope and enlarge over time until our own time, when the concerns of feminism are seen to involve all aspects of human existence. But in shifting the focus on the origins of contemporary feminism to an earlier period, Moses jars our sense of a linear progression and uncovers another striking pattern. The Saint-Simonian feminists of the 1830s have little in common with the liberal feminists of the late nineteenth and early twentieth centuries but bear remarkable similarities to contemporary radical feminists. Like their descendants, they sought a broad, multileveled restructuring of culture and society, through a transformation of sexuality, language, and networks of intimate relations, and appear theoretically more profound than liberal feminists later in the century.

Moses also finds that when one takes account of the Saint-Simonians the historical practice of tracing the origins of socialist feminism to Frederick Engels's *Origins of the Family, Private Property, and the State* no longer holds. Many of the Saint-Simonian women's writings, such as Claire Démar's *My Law of the Future* and certain articles in the *Tribune des femmes*, already—fifty years earlier than Engels's treatise—contain the most valuable elements of Engels's theory, while remaining free of its now-outdated elements. The feminists of the 1830s analyze the relation between private property inheritance, the patriarchal nuclear family, and women's oppression, but without Engels's mechanical stages or his dubious anthropology. Moreover, their theory goes further than Engels's later version in that it not only advocates an end to the nuclear family and to dominance by the father but also brings into this interrelated complex of factors women's sexual repression, analyzing its role in women's oppression in general.

For both Moses and Rabine, a study of the Saint-Simonians alters the prevailing view of the history of feminism in yet two more basic ways. It is usually assumed that the origins of feminism lie in middle-class aspirations and that working-class women, who joined feminism later, limited their demands to external issues of economic justice without concerning themselves with issues of sexuality, subjectivity, and culture. The Saint-Simonian feminists show us, on the contrary, a class-conscious proletarian movement that predates middle-class feminism and that gives sexuality, subjectivity, writing, and culture an integral role in a multileveled transformation.

Rabine's interest in the way they merge sexual, gender, and class politics led her to read the texts of this movement in light of contemporary psychoanalytic feminism, in the hope that each movement could further our understanding of the other. For these early feminists psychic and emotional forms are as much sociopolitical constructs as the state, the family, and the economy. They so clearly recognized, as psychoanalytic theory can help us to do, the generally unacknowledged but overwhelming role of desire in any political activity, whether to maintain or change the status quo.

The relation between psychoanalysis and movements for social change remains one of the unanswered questions in feminism that we referred to at the beginning of this introduction. Rabine explores this question not just by applying contemporary theory to nineteenth-century writers but by looking at debates on class and sexuality at the origins of modern feminism with an eye to bringing to our own well-rehearsed debates a different, historical, perspective. One such debate concerns the practice of reclaiming the feminine as a strategy for women's liberation. Both the *Saint-Simoniennes* and the part of second-wave feminism usually called "French feminism" engage, in historically different ways, in this strategy. Based on the assumption of sexual difference that Moses addresses, it relies in the two cases on identifying with the mother, not as the repressed support of the patriarchal symbolic order, but as the metaphoric principle of a different order.[13] For both nineteenth- and twentieth-century feminists, the project entails transforming a masculine theory, and from there leads to an attempt to transform the symbolic order itself. Since traces of this attempt can be read in the *Saint-Simoniennes'* texts, psychoanalytic criticism can help here, not to psychologize the writers, but to provide tools for such a reading.

Among these tools are the concepts of the symbolic order—the unconscious network of laws and relationships organizing language, culture, and subjectivity—and its regulating principle, the "Name-of-the-Father." This latter is the metaphoric principle governing the necessity to enter culture by abandoning an immediate relation with the mother's body for a system of signs that substitute for her absence. Suzanne Voilquin, Claire Démar, Pauline Roland, and Flora Tristan in different ways seek to overturn the "Name-of-the-Father." Because these women wrote as part of an effort to build a community that would, in the words of Suzanne Voilquin, bring about a "new Genesis,"[14] the construction of their texts bears traces of determined attempts to build a new symbolic order, and therefore permits special insights into the vexing problem of feminine subjectivity.

One controversial feature of psychoanalytic cultural theory is that it makes subjectivity, as the effect of gendered positions within the symbolic order, exclusively masculine. Articulating an often expressed criticism of the psychoanalytic narrative of subject development, Eleanor H. Kuykendall says that it "leaves no place for a feminine conception of agency" except as "a contradiction in terms."[15] But the *Saint-Simoniennes'* writing suggests that it is precisely as a contradiction in terms that a feminine subject has the radical potential for change. Early feminist writing, especially if it is by very marginalized women such as were the *Saint-Simoniennes* and Flora Tristan, has the inestimable value of allowing us to study various constructions of this paradoxical feminine subjectivity as an indispensable element of a strategy for challenging a profound repression in Western culture.

They wrote at a time when legal, social, and literary sign systems were extraordinarily explicit about denying subjectivity to women and freezing them in the position of woman-as-object. The Civil Code of 1804, systematizing family and property law, denied a woman all civil and political rights, banished her from professions, and did not allow her even to enter into a contractual agreement without the written consent of her husband or father, much less to live outside of his domicile. This position of woman finds a more idealized encoding in romantic fictional narrative, as epitomized by such classics as Chateaubriand's *René*, Stendhal's *The Red and the Black*, Balzac's *The Lily in the Valley*, and Dumas's *La Dame aux camélias*. Their narrative structure follows the trajectory of the hero's desire to transcend his essential lack and find a fullness of self and meaning in the ever-deferred union with an inaccessible, idealized mother figure.[16] Another romantic genre, romantic autobiography, less straightforward and more complex in marking the gender positions of the symbolic order, will also provide the context for studying the autobiographies of the *Saint-Simoniennes* and Flora Tristan in chapter 3. Its prototypical texts, Rousseau's *Confessions* and Chateaubriand's *Memoirs from beyond the Tomb*, preserve the masculinity of the subject but make us modify the classical feminist notion that women function in the symbolic economy of patriarchy as objects of exchange among men.[17] These canonic autobiographies suggest instead that the function of woman in the symbolic order varies with her social class. The role of prized *object* of exchange is reserved for aristocratic women, while working-class women, who in both Rousseau's and Chateaubriand's works provide the instrument through which the hero-narrator constructs his subjectivity and his text, are the *medium* of exchange among men. The feminine autobiographies analyzed in chapter 3, and especially Suzanne Voilquin's *Memories of a Daughter of the People* (presented in chapter 4), make visible this obfuscated role of women's class difference both in masculine symbolic economies and also in feminist attempts to construct new subjectivities and textualities.

Of course, an individual woman could, then as now, occupy the masculine subject position, but with immeasurably more difficulty. Therefore, the *Saint-Simoniennes*, in attempting to play a public role, to write, to preach, to teach, to practice medicine in the case of Suzanne Voilquin, and to change the course of history, confronted with greater clarity a contradiction that women face today. Both then and now a woman can oscillate between two unsatisfactory situations, either entering the masculine position and adopting its values, perspectives, and roles or celebrating the feminine and staying within its roles. In both cases women risk perpetuating the dichotomous gender structure of the symbolic order. In order to get out of this impasse, some feminists are seeking to occupy the subject position as a "contradiction in terms" and so to create dissonance in the symbolic systems of their time. Although the *Saint-Simoniennes* do not theorize this impasse in the way contemporary feminists do, they do forge an alternative model of gender beyond the traditional dichotomy.

Both contemporary and nineteenth-century feminists seek an alternative to masculine subjectivity by identifying with a symbolic mother as the principle of a feminine discourse and law. And in committing themselves to such an ambitious project, they pay a similar price. Both take on the perhaps impossible task of transforming the symbolic order only at the risk of idealizing the maternal to create a mythic identity and of essentializing the feminine. A study of the *Saint-Simoniennes* therefore allows us to consider from a new perspective yet one more issue still under intense debate in the women's movement, the question of essentialism.[18] Luce Irigaray's ideas about the necessity to "think of the mother in every woman, of the woman in every mother"[19] have often led critics to reproach her for proposing an eternal, universal, and, as Domna Stanton says, "ontotheological" essence embodied by all women.[20] But her words find an echo in the *Saint-Simoniennes'* writings. In *L'Apostolat des femmes* seamstress Jeanne-Désirée Veret writes: "The banner of women is universal, for are they not, as our sister Suzanne has said, all united by the same bond of MOTHERHOOD."[21] Elsewhere Rabine has explored the implications of this shared encounter with essentialism,[22] but a few brief remarks are relevant here. If many feminists find that the belief in an innate femininity suggested by radical and psychoanalytic feminism poses for its adherents an insurmountable problem, the problem goes both ways. For we have to consider the historical irony that such essentialism enabled the improbable emergence of the first modern feminist movement out of a very forbidding sociopolitical environment.

Furthermore, essentialism carries with it the connotation of an unchanging biological nature, but the *Saint-Simoniennes*, like Irigaray and Cixous, conceive of this maternity in a symbolic rather than a biological form, and so illustrate one of the many ways in which essentialism and anti-essentialism have the disconcerting habit of sliding into each other rather than remaining in their stable places. It is noteworthy that Suzanne Voilquin, whose words Jeanne-Désirée cites above, was biologically incapable of bearing children. Expressions such as Cixous's "écriture féminine" or Irigaray's "parler femme" designate practices that attempt to denaturalize the masculine/subject-feminine/object bipolarity as an effect of the symbolic order rather than an essential set of categories. In so doing, they ironically risk embracing feminine essence, and perhaps also demonstrate that there is no way to construct a feminine subject that strains the limits of the symbolic order except by oscillating among the various positions that make feminine subjectivity impossible. In exploring this dilemma in the *Saint-Simoniennes'* texts, Rabine will also investigate the possibility that there can be no complete, whole feminist theory. Since the symbolic order excludes woman-as-subject and structures of feminine desire and sexuality, it forces us either to reject practices that challenge this deepest level of patriarchal oppression or risk complicity with a patriarchally constructed gender essentialism. Feminists have chosen one or the other of these alternatives, and so have had to face the challenge of building together a movement composed of mutually contradictory parts which never fit into a unified whole. Tangential to this issue of contradictory parts is the way in which the *Saint-Simoniennes* make us revise our preconceptions of the way they *do* fit together, since we usually assume that theorizing feminine sexuality and subjectivity are concerns of white, middle-class, academic feminists, rather than women fighting against class oppression.

This impossibility of joining all forms of feminism into a totalized whole, hardly new to our movement, also characterizes French feminism of the 1830s. And it is for this reason that an analysis of Flora Tristan's writing has been included in chapter 3. The contrast between Tristan and the *Saint-Simoniennes* can convey some of the complexity of the differences within romantic feminism. Tristan, who acted on her own instead of joining a group or movement, did not, like the *Saint-Simoniennes*, identify with the mother but, equally profound in her challenge to patriarchy, wrote texts in which the womanly for once frees itself from being, as Luce Irigaray says, "absorbed into maternity."[23] Tristan is not an essentialist in the sense described above, and neither is she a liberal who believes that equality means sameness. A "difference" feminist in a different way, she is complexly bi-sexual. Yet in the mid-nineteenth century, she could make the important contribution of liberating the feminine from its traditional patriarchal association with maternity only at the cost of an ultimately fatal denial of the body. By contrast, the *Saint-Simoniennes'* maternal essentialism allowed them to seek the "rehabilitation of the flesh." This contrast fortifies the conjecture that since feminism must be theorized and practiced within patriarchy's construction of gender, feminists of the 1830s fell into one double bind or another.

The final part of this book introduces English-language readers to the writings of these *Saint-Simoniennes*. Suzanne Voilquin's *Memories of a Daughter of the People* recounts the life of a young working-class woman who became one of the most noteworthy Saint-Simonian organizers, gained a medical education, and practiced midwifery for poor, unwed mothers. The excerpts reprinted here offer a unique view of early nineteenth-century working-class family life from a feminist perspective and describe Voilquin's involvement from the early 1830s in both the male-led Saint-Simonian movement and in the separatist women's movement.

Claire Démar wrote *My Law of the Future* shortly before committing suicide; Voilquin published it posthumously. Taking the form of a polemic against what Démar sees as the excessive timidity of the other Saint-Simonians, she advocates women's sexual freedom "without rules or limits" and without fear of exploitation and ostracism. She also analyzes the relationship between women's sexual repression, the nuclear family, and patriarchal property inheritance.

The letters presented here offer a more intimate view of Saint-Simonian relationships. Although they were never intended to be published, they were collected—some were even recopied—in order to become part of the official Saint-Simonian archives. The letters of Claire Bazard and Cécile Fournel—the two most important female leaders within the male- and bourgeois-led Saint-Simonian movement by virtue of being married to prominent Saint-Simonian men—offer insiders' perspectives on the relationships between women and men in the movement. The letters of Voilquin, Démar, Clorinde Rogé, and Pauline Roland offer a more distanced view of the movement as well as fascinating information about the writers' experiments with the new sexual morality. Pauline Roland's letters, of which we present here but a sampling of a voluminous body of texts, trace her development from a naive provincial neophyte to one of the most daring of the experimenters.

The articles from the *Tribune des femmes* were first published between 1832 and 1834. They contain unprecedented debates on the necessity to do away with conventional, Christian sexual morality, on the role of sexual liberation in a general strategy for women's socioeconomic liberation, and on such issues as class differences among the women, prostitution, paternity, and the position of women in French law. In these articles, the writers also debate their relation to Enfantin's "new morality" and to the Saint-Simonian men. The articles were chosen for the diversity of their positions in these debates.

The foreword and preface to Flora Tristan's *Peregrinations of a Pariah* are also presented here in English in their entirety for the first time. While Tristan did not join with the other Saint-Simonian women, but acted alone somewhat later in the decade to organize the working class into a political force, she nonetheless belongs in this volume because she was influenced by the Saint-Simonians and associated with many of them. Although these memoirs of her voyage to Peru have received recognition as a significant work of literature and social theory, the recently republished French edition left out the foreword and preface, which are arguably their most important element.[24] A recent English translation, apparently based on the modern French edition, has also left out the foreword and preface which are now in danger of being lost.[25] In these pages, Tristan expounds a revolutionary theory of feminine autobiography, criticizes George Sand, and recounts the experiences of her early life up until her departure for Peru.

For Moses and Rabine, working on these texts and documents provided yet another opportunity for interdisciplinary collaboration. In coordinating the work on these translations, Rabine tried to balance two needs. On the one hand, she desired to preserve the stylistic and tonal flavor of these exalted autodidacts, who had no formal education. On the other hand, she wanted to make readable their impossibly convoluted sentences. In the interest of readability, she opted to normalize and standardize syntax and sentence structure. She unraveled the convolutions in a relatively free translation of syntax and tried to make up for that by a relatively literal translation of vocabulary.

Moses's research in the archives was crucial to the selection stage; it was she who located the Saint-Simonian women's writings among the vast collection of letters and writings of the more famous Saint-Simonian men and did the preliminary selection for including those which provide insight into the development of a consciousness among the women of the distinctiveness of their experience from the men's.

This book seeks to make a triple contribution to feminist scholarship: first, by making available the writings of an extraordinary group of working-class feminists; second, by offering different ways of reading their "words" and "acts"; and third, by presenting an unusual example of interdisciplinary collaboration between a historian and a literary critic who have worked to join and balance two different methods, points of view, and conceptual vocabularies. It has not been our intention to blend history and criticism into some new happy medium. Yet, as we approached the same material and the same questions from two different directions, we did seek to compile a book where the threads of the other's influence would show through the texture of each of our essays.

II

"DIFFERENCE" IN HISTORICAL PERSPECTIVE: SAINT-SIMONIAN FEMINISM

Claire Goldberg Moses

INTRODUCTION

On Difference

Saint-Simonian feminists of the 1830s approached the difficult question of woman's nature with a set of assumptions centering on the notion of "difference." The words and acts that sprang from these assumptions should resonate for contemporary feminists who have joined in a debate that pits "difference" against "equality." In this debate, feminists of the so-called equality perspective emphasize the similarities between women and men, affirm androgyny, and argue that an equal-rights, gender-blind strategy is the sensible way to achieve women's freedom and equality. In seeming opposition, the "difference" group stresses the differences between women and men, affirms the female, and argues that sex-differentiated policies may be necessary to achieve gender justice. Feminists aligned with each of the two perspectives have taken opposing sides on issues such as pregnancy benefits, maternity leave, and custody- and divorce-law reforms; have argued on different sides in the recent *EEOC v. Sears, Roebuck* case; and have fashioned quite different justifications for affirmative action and comparable-worth policies.[1]

The ideas of the "equality" theorists dominated feminist debate in the early 1970s. Drawing for their inspiration from Simone de Beauvoir's *The Second Sex* and Betty Friedan's *The Feminine Mystique*, feminists such as Shulamith Firestone, Kate Millet, and Elizabeth Janeway pointed to the social and historical construction of gender-distinct "roles" and advocated that these give way to a universalistic ideal.[2] Feminist historians of the same moment followed suit. Influenced by Barbara Welter, whose germinal article had identified a nineteenth-century "Cult of True Womanhood,"[3] they drew a connection between the failure of nineteenth-century feminists to challenge prevailing notions that women were innately different from men—for example, that they were more moral or nurturing—and the failure of these feminists to complete the revolution of women's liberation.

Beginning in the late 1970s and gaining momentum in the following decade, the "difference" perspective emerged as a second stage in the recent history of feminism. Theorists such as Adrienne Rich, Mary Daly, Carol Gilligan, and Jean Bethke Elshtain affirmed gender differentiation and celebrated qualities considered traditionally feminine, particularly those associated with nurturance and mothering.[4] Once again, the theoretical perspective had a counterpart among historians. Nancy Cott and Carroll Smith-Rosenberg, who examined the psychologically sustaining relationships developed among nineteenth-century middle-class women in their separate culture, reconceptualized the notions of separate spheres and women's culture, identifying them as a source of woman's power rather than an explanation for her powerlessness.[5]

The emergence of the "difference" perspective troubled many contemporary feminists. Not only was the "equality" perspective the one with which we were most familiar, but also the historical analysis in which it was embedded seemed to confirm its wisdom. The "difference" perspective seemed either a departure from the ideological tradition or a step backward.

That Americans were troubled by the "difference" perspective may explain the discomfort experienced with recent feminist theory that comes to us from France. Because early translations into English of French feminist writings emphasized writings from the "difference" tendency, Americans quickly came to the conclusion that "difference" and "French feminism" were one and the same. But actually both tendencies exist in France. Theorists such as Christine Delphy, Colette Guillaumin, and others associated with the periodical *Nouvelles Questions féministes*, the group that wrote for *La Revue d'en face* before its demise, and the group that is associated with APEF (Association pour les Etudes Féministes) have continued the tradition associated with de Beauvoir; the "difference" tendency is most apparent in the writings of Annie Leclerc, Hélène Cixous, Luce Irigaray, and the group Psych et po. And in France, as in the U.S., it is actually the "equality" group which is the more visible and the one whose ideas are most likely to underpin struggles in the political arena (e.g., abortion rights, anti-rape and anti-battering struggles, and government initiatives for equal pay and affirmative action).[6] Also in France—even more so than in the United States—the disagreements between the groups (and especially between the "equality" group and the theorists now or once associated with Psych et po) have been heated, perhaps because they are fueled not only by ideological differences (which certainly have played a role) but also by power struggles.

"Difference," then, has been of concern to U.S. and French feminists alike. In the United States, in 1979, "The Scholar and the Feminist VI" conference, sponsored by the Barnard College Women's Center, focused on "difference"; *Feminist Studies* published a special symposium that examined the significance of the work of women's culture historians such as Smith-Rosenberg; *Signs* published an interdisciplinary forum examining the significance of Gilligan's work.[7] These analyses, however, failed to answer questions about "difference"; indeed, they raised new ones. Most interestingly, the analyses revealed that the term itself means different things to different people. Most often "difference" has been used in discussing the work of those whose concern is in defining the differences between women and men. But even in these instances its meaning is uncertain, for some theorists of "difference" view the differences between the sexes as innate and therefore "essential," while others stress that these differences are socially constructed, that is, that they are explained by the differences in women's and men's lived experience. To theorists who are more interested in feminist practice than in definitions of womanhood, the "difference" that matters is the distinctive culture that feminists might create to nurture feminist ideals. But for still another group, the "differences" of key interest are the distinctions among women—the differences of class, race, religion, nationality, ethnicity, sexual orientation, age, and physical capacity. The views of this group are often—but not always—incompatible with those of others who stress the importance of difference but who typically focus on what unites rather than on what separates women from one another.

For several reasons, an examination of the theory and practice of French feminists in the 1830s can help to clarify the many meanings of "difference" used by contemporary feminists. First, feminists of the 1830s grounded their claims for sexual equality in a discourse that stressed the differences between the sexes. They did so in conscious challenge to the "equality" arguments fashioned by earlier feminists. Next, the women among these feminists deliberately developed a set of practices and institutions that allowed them to act independently of Saint-Simonian men. Declaring that "women alone shall say what kind of liberty they want," they held their own meetings and founded a newspaper that would "publish articles only by women." Through its pages, we can trace the development of a feminism that differed from an original, male-inspired Saint-Simonian feminism and we can seek to understand the significance of this "difference." Finally, Saint-Simonian feminists deconstructed the essentialist category "woman" that they themselves had originally constructed, replacing it with an analysis of the differences among women of different classes. Their blending of sex and class analysis is a model for a feminism that is both radical and socialist, sensitive to the specificity of both sexual and class experience and dedicated to the attainment of a universal ideal of equality. Thus, an examination of the feminist view of "difference" at the moment of its original articulation, in France of the 1830s, should help us to see that the positioning of "equality" and "difference" in opposition to one another is itself a construct that is open to challenge.

Saint-Simonian Feminism

In the 1830s, French feminists were active among groups that came to call themselves socialists in order to distinguish their program from that of eighteenth-century Revolutionaries. Indeed, they inveighed against the Revolution, which they associated with wars and the Terror.[8] Their concern, they patiently explained, was "social," the way humans— women and men and workers and employers—related to each other, rather than "individual." Their attention consequently shifted away from the kind of individual rights of citizenship, including political rights, that had concerned French Revolutionaries to new ways of organizing enduring social networks, intimacy, sexuality, and reproduction, as well as production. Their strategy for social change was to create alternative communities intended not only to collectivize households and the workplace but also to provide a peaceful means for change that would present a distinct contrast to the more violent Revolutionary ethos. The new world would be constructed alongside the old, and people—merely by observing the far preferable utopian life—would be won over to join with socialists in replicating these alternative communities.

The most visible of these early socialists were the Saint-Simonians. Organized somewhat on the model of a religious community, they appropriated the language and symbols of both the Catholic Church and the bourgeois family, although their "doctrine" challenged both. Prosper Enfantin and Saint-Amand Bazard were the Fathers of the Church. Then, after a schism, in November 1831, Enfantin alone bore the title of Pope; an empty seat alongside him signified the awaited Female Messiah who would rule one day as "Pop-esse." Until 1833, the inner circle of Saint-Simonians lived collectively in several *maisons de famille* (in Paris, at rue Taitbout and at rue Monsigny) and pooled their financial resources. Income needs were covered by contributions. Meals were collectively prepared and served for an even larger group of adherents.

Saint-Simonians were enormously influential not only in France but also throughout Europe and in Egypt and the Americas. One explanation for their popularity was the failure of liberals and republicans to address workers' interests. The Revolution of 1830—which in Saint-Simonians' writings was often referred to as "the three days in July" or the "July days"—addressed such issues as the appropriate size and basis for the electorate and the proper relationship of the legislature to the king. But these issues were of little concern to artisans and skilled workers whose role on the barricades had forced Charles X's abdication. In their frustration they turned to the Saint-Simonians for a vision of a new social and economic order.

Saint-Simonians published several newspapers—*Le Producteur* (1825–26), *L'Organisateur* (1829–31), *Le Globe* (distributed free in 1831–32), *Tribune des femmes* (1832–34), *Livre des actes* (1833)—and distributed, often at no charge, numerous pamphlets plus the more weighty two-volume *Exposition of the Doctrine of Saint-Simon* (1829–30). Oral propaganda was also important, especially in reaching the working classes at a time when illiteracy was still widespread. In Paris, in 1831, Saint-Simonians held nine meetings a week in large, public lecture halls to present their ideas on the economy, on religion, the arts, and science, and on the emancipation of workers and women. They organized "missions" to spread the doctrine beyond Paris—to Lyon, Toulouse, Limoges, Montauban, Avignon, Rouen, Beauvais, Le Mans, Liège, Dijon, Besançon, Mulhouse, Colmar, Strasbourg, Metz, and Nancy. Outside of France, their most successful missions were to England, Germany, and Belgium. At the height of their popularity, crowds in the indoor lecture halls usually numbered in the hundreds and, outdoors, in the thousands. In 1831, letters from readers to the *Globe* ran at more than a thousand a month. In Paris, Saint-Simonians also organized special teaching programs, cooperative workshops (one for tailors and one for seamstresses), and a health program for workers (led by one pharmacist and one doctor for each of the working-class *arrondissements*). One of the weekly Saint-Simonian lectures was delivered in Italian to reach immigrant workers.

They taught that a new, peaceful relationship between the sexes, the classes, and the nations should replace social conflict; that inheritance of wealth should be abolished; and that property was a public trust rather than an individual right (the property of owners who did not place the means of production at workers' disposal should be confiscated). The feminism of the Saint-Simonians was integral to their pacifism and to their economic program. They viewed sexual equality as a natural consequence of their project to reorganize the globe by replacing the rule of "brute force" with the rule of "spiritual powers." Women, who represented peace and love in their cosmology, would have a special leadership role to play in the "new age." In contrast to the so-called military age of the past and present—which was seen as having sacrificed the interests of all women and also male workers—the "new age" would open public life to both.

DEFINING WOMAN

The feminism of Saint-Simonians was grounded in a view of women that stressed their difference from men—a difference that is presumed to be "natural"; that is, derived from a pre-social state of "nature" and embedded in human "nature." Throughout Saint-Simonian writings one finds the recurrent image of the male who represents "reflection" and the female who represents "sentiment." Men were rational—the time of their leadership in the Saint-Simonian movement is likened to "the phase of the doctors" (meaning intellectuals). It is men, for example, who have made the theories.[9] But men are "dismal like *solitude*, . . . heavy and cold like the marble of a tomb, . . . harsh like a cross" (*Tribune* 1: 193). In contrast, "*nature* [emphasis in original] provided [women] a soul that is tender, sensitive, exalted" (*Tribune* 1: 131). Women have "emotions that are gentle and poetic, a warm imagination, and fire in their hearts; they announce the reign of peace and love" (*Tribune* 1: 160), the "phase of sentiment" (*Tribune* 1: 106).

One recognizes in this Saint-Simonian view of women something rather close to the dominant, patriarchal ideology of womanhood and is puzzled. Was it not, after all, this very view of women that had led patriarchalists to exclude women from the various rights of "citizenship" that the Revolution had bestowed on men? In the words of the 1793 report of the Committee of General Security recommending that women's participation in political clubs be prohibited, "the social order results from the difference between men and women."[10] Certainly, it was this view of women that was expressed in the treatments prescribed for women in the Napoleonic Code. By recognizing the equal rights of all citizens, but excluding women from the definition of citizenship, the code enshrined not only the subordination of women to men but also the rigid differentiation of the two sexes. And it was this view of women—self-sacrificing, subordinating themselves to men's interests—that was expressed in romantic literature.

When I first examined the feminism of Saint-Simonians, I judged it "conservative." I assumed that the failure of Saint-Simonians to challenge patriarchal definitions of woman related in some way to their lack of sophistication. The 1830s were, I reasoned, an early moment in the long history of feminism; later feminists, I thought, surely understood "better." But this linear and progressive view of the history of feminism did not provide a satisfactory explanation for how the Saint-Simonians came to construct this theory of difference, for I soon discovered that feminists of an even earlier moment, active during the years of the French Revolution, had held a view of women that stressed their essential similarities to men. Furthermore, Saint-Simonian feminists were well aware of the perspective of French Revolutionary feminists and deliberately chose to challenge it. A comparison of these two feminist perspectives seemed in order.

Feminism in the French Revolution

In examining the "equality" tendency embedded in French Revolutionary discourse, I found the writings of three important feminist publicists from the early years of the French Revolution, Condorcet (Marie-Jean-Antoine-Nicolas Caritat, marquis de Condorcet), Olympe de Gouges, and Etta Palm d'Aëlders, the most illustrative. All three were Enlightenment rationalists. Arguing that individuals of both sexes were born similar in capacity and character, they ascribed male and female differences to socialization.

Condorcet's "Essai sur l'admission des femmes au droit de cité," which appeared in 1790, called for the same rights for both sexes. "Either no individual of the human race has genuine rights, or else all have the same." In this short document (about the length of a speech), Condorcet specifies the right to assist "in the making of laws," the "right of citizenship," and "the franchise" for women as well as men. He goes on to state that the "tyranny of the civil law," which "subjected wives to their husbands," should be destroyed.[11]

Condorcet bases his argument on the claim that women have the same "natural" rights as men. These so-called natural rights, or "rights of man," derive from our human capacity to reason and acquire moral ideas. Women have "these same qualities," but people have become so accustomed to women's oppression that "nobody thinks to reclaim [their rights]." Sexual inequality, then, is the triumph of the "power of habit" over reason (99). To those who would deny that women have the same capacity to reason as men, Condorcet replied that educational disabilities and legal discrimination alone explain the seemingly different reasoning capacities of the sexes.

> It is not nature, it is education . . . which is the cause of this difference.
> . . . Banished from affairs, from everything that is settled according to rigorous justice and positive laws, the matters with which they occupy themselves are precisely those which are ruled by natural amiability and feeling. It is hardly fair, therefore, to allege as a ground for continuing to deny women the enjoyment of their natural rights, reasons which only possess a certain amount of substance because women do not enjoy these rights. (100–101)

The differences are not natural, then; indeed, they are more apparent than real, for both sexes use their reasoning capacities to secure happiness. Women may, perhaps, "aim at a different end," but "it is not more unreasonable for a woman to take pains about her personal appearance than it was for Demosthenes to take pains with his voice and his gesticulation" (100).

Olympe de Gouges constructed similar arguments to support similar reforms. Her *Déclaration des droits de la femme et de la citoyenne* was based on the *Declaration of the Rights of Man and of the Citizen* (in French, the masculinity of *citoyen* is clearer than in English), to which she demanded the inclusion of the word "woman."

All women are born free and equal to men in rights. . . .

All female citizens, like all male citizens, must participate personally or
through their representatives in the formulation [of laws]. . . .

All female citizens and all male citizens, being equal in the law, must be
equally eligible for all dignities, positions, and public offices, according to
their abilities, and without any other distinction than that of their virtue
and their talents.

Woman has the right to mount the scaffold; she must equally have the
right to mount the rostrum.

Property belongs to both sexes . . . ; for each it is an inviolable and sacred
right.[12]

Gouges was, of course, specifying just those gains that the Revolution
had conveyed to men: equal rights of citizenship, equal access to political
offices and public employment, liberty to speak out publicly, equal property rights. In a postscript, she also called for women's access to public
education, which was at that moment being debated in the National Assembly, and legal equality between wife and husband (a "social contract
between man and woman" [94]).

Like Condorcet, Gouges based her arguments on natural rights theory.
Equality was not something to be granted, like a gift; equality was "natural" and had only to be recognized ("Woman, wake up; . . . discover
your rights"). And the law "must be the same for all" because natural
rights are the same for all: "What is there in common between [women]
and [men]? Everything." Only "prejudice, fanaticism, superstition, and
lies" and perhaps also some "non sequitur in contradiction to principles"
have denied women their "inalienable" rights (92, 89).

The same claims were advanced by Etta Palm. She wrote that "justice . . . calls all individuals to the equality of rights, without discrimination of sex; the laws of a free people must be equal for all beings. . . . The
powers of husband and wife must be equal. . . . Girls [must have] a
moral education equal to that of their brothers; for education is for the
soul what watering is for plants."[13] According to the reporter for the
Archives parlementaires, when Palm addressed the Legislative Assembly in
1792, she asked "that women be admitted to civilian and military positions and that the education of young people of the feminine sex be set
up on the same foundation as that of men."[14] And always she too based
her claims on a "natural" equality: "Nature formed us to be your equals."
Equality is "a natural right of which [women] have been deprived by a
protected oppression."[15]

The language of these Revolutionary feminists—two hundred years old now—is familiar. It emphasizes values—equality, fairness, property rights, education, and sovereignty vested in an independent citizenry—that were codified in both American and French eighteenth-century Revolutionary documents and that are fundamental to contemporary Western thought. Placing this discourse back into the moment of its original articulation helps us to understand its appeal. Not surprisingly, the views of Revolutionary feminists partook of the broader Revolutionary discourse of the late eighteenth century, which, in turn, was rooted in long-term historical and social changes. Both the American and the French revolutions were the culmination of a centuries-long process by which sovereignty was redefined in public rather than private terms. With the growth of national bureaucracies and the economic transformations we associate with mercantile capitalism, people came to value education and independence, in part because, unlike those who held power in feudal times, the new bureaucrats, diplomats, and merchants found that these attributes were critical to their success. Equal rights of "citizenship," as defined in the new *Declaration of the Rights of Man*, and equal access to newly promised national educational programs were important, then, to Revolutionary feminists because the intense political debate of that historic moment had made these goals important to all French people.

The feminists borrowed more than their goals from the dominant culture; the very stand upon which they based their claims—their belief in the "essential" or "natural" equality of all humans—was also shared by other groups in the society. It is important that we keep this in mind. Although feminists drew a conclusion from universalistic theories—that the sexes were equal—which few Revolutionaries shared, the feminists' certainty that females and males were "naturally" similar was actually a widely held opinion. In fact, from the time of the ancient Greeks, "science" had held the view that women's and men's bodies, skeletal frames, and reproductive organs were essentially the same "under the skin."[16] True, most scientists in the eighteenth century probably had no trouble squaring their "knowledge" that the sexes were physiologically rather similar to the view that women were inferior to men (even physiologically, since their reproductive organs, although identical, were interior and therefore cooler).[17] But seventeenth- and eighteenth-century feminists—Erna Hellerstein identifies Chevalier de Jaucourt, Claude Adrien Helvetius, and Antoine Leonard Thomas as well as Condorcet;[18] Londa Schiebinger identifies Poullain de la Barre[19]—cited "scientific" evidence to support their claims for women's rights. Just as there was no basis in nature for inequalities among men, nature provided no basis for the inequality of man and woman. Thus, by appealing to the dominant culture's professed beliefs in "natural" equality and "natural" rights, feminists made their case as had other political outsider groups—peasants and Jews, for example—and hoped, not unreasonably, for the same successful outcome.

But not surprisingly, at about this time "science" shifted to an alternative view of the sexes—called "the biology of incommensurability" by Thomas Laqueur—which seemed to more decisively justify the exclusion of women from citizenship.[20] Interestingly, feminists also shifted their view—although with a different end in mind. By the 1830s, the belief that the sexes were essentially or "naturally" similar had been superseded in science by a different view that stressed sexual difference. Erna Hellerstein has studied the medical texts of Pierre Roussel and Antoine Camus; Thomas Laqueur has discussed the work of F. A. Pouchet and Achilles Chereau, as well as the work of several German researchers, on spontaneous ovulation; Londa Schiebinger has examined the drawings of the French anatomist Marie-Genevieve-Charlotte Thirous d'Arconville and the German anatomist Samuel Thomas von Soemmerring. All of these scientists advanced the view that women were different from men—not just inferior, "an incomplete man,"[21] as had been taught since the time of Aristotle, but different in the sense of "a being apart,"[22] organized around their reproductive systems which were no longer viewed as identical to men's.

It is interesting to note that in the seventeenth and eighteenth centuries the scientific view emphasizing difference had existed alongside the contradictory view emphasizing the inherent similarity of the sexes, but that the "difference" view came to predominate only in the nineteenth century. Hellerstein, Laqueur, and Schiebinger conclude from this that science was not transformed simply by the force of its own "objective" research but rather by the *need* to reconstruct a new justification for sexual hierarchy: It was as if scientists were agreeing with equal rights feminists that the logical conclusion to the view stressing the inherent similarity of women and men in nature was sexual equality; but rather than argue for equal rights, they opted for a new view of nature. Hellerstein, Laqueur, and Schiebinger are convincing in locating the explanation for a new construction of scientific meaning in politics. The newly predominant view of woman served well to "prove" that women and men were governed by different natural laws and that women's natural role was not intellectual work or the exercise of public rights but child-rearing.

But if the dominant discourse of sexual difference served to justify sexual inequality, what possible appeal could it have had for feminists? To answer this perplexing question requires a reexamination of that discourse in the context of a historically specific moment, for the feminist appropriation of the discourse of difference is best understood by tracing the particular meaning of that discourse in the romantic era and by illuminating its explanatory power for a historically specific social reality.

Feminism in the Age of Romanticism

Romanticism brought a new orientation to a world that had been dominated by the concept of universalism. Unlike rationalists, romantics valued difference over sameness, the particular and the unique over the uniform or the universal. That romanticism may be conservative is widely understood. There was, after all, a reactionary strain within romanticism that longed for the old feudal order, the old religious order, and, of course, the old sexual order. But romanticism was also exploited for its emancipatory potential. For example, socialists of this period, borrowing from romanticism its valorizing of difference, held that the French Revolution's espousal of universal rights had actually masked a policy of entrenched inequality. It was necessary, they believed, to recognize the differences between classes. This, rather than some false sense of shared universal interest, would emancipate workers from employers. As one *Saint-Simonienne* warned: beware "a unity that will merge [*confondre*] the worker and the master; we must recognize that both have their particular interest" (*Tribune* 1: 166). Understandably, it was feminists associated with these socialists who developed the new kind of sex analysis based on "difference." To these feminists, socialist class analysis held out the promise of a more effective challenge to inequality than the universalizing that they associated with the dominating classes. However, as we shall see, this new analysis was not immediately and universally accepted by all Saint-Simonians. Rather, it was the subject of considerable debate and discussion.

The Saint-Simonian archives include a striking record of such a debate. The occasion was the creation of the ruling hierarchy for the new Saint-Simonian "church." In question was Prosper Enfantin's proposal that the church be headed by a woman and a man—a "couple-pope." Philippe-Joseph-Benjamin Buchez argued against the proposal: "I know of no being who has deep feelings, [whose feelings are] not accompanied and served by the greatest rational strength. . . . Then, why have two individuals compete in order to obtain an integration of that which each possesses integrally?" Buchez's feminism—and his words do seem incontrovertibly feminist—is within the familiar rationalist tradition which argues for equality from a position stressing "sameness": "Truly great revelations . . . are neither male nor female. . . . It matters little if [the pope] is . . . male or female. . . . " " . . . [I]t is unnecessary that the sexes share in [the papacy]."[23]

However, when viewed in the context of the circumstances of this particular debate, Buchez's argument takes on a meaning by no means so incontrovertibly feminist. Buchez was in fact arguing for one head of the Church to be chosen from among the current leadership of the movement, which at that moment (1829) was entirely male. It was Enfantin, therefore, who was actually advocating women's participation in the governance of the Saint-Simonian movement. He carried the day: Over the New World Order was a reconceptualized God, now both male and female. In keeping with this theology, the Saint-Simonian hierarchy was to be headed by a couple-pope incarnating the attributes of the male/female God. And similarly, each of the institutional structures of the new Church was to be directed by a female and male couple—the *maisons de famille* by a "sister" and a "brother," and the workers' associations by a "directress" and a "director."

Saint-Simonian women welcomed this politics and theology of "difference":

> [Woman] is no longer drawn from a rib of man; she no longer is confounded with his glory; she descends, like him, directly from *her* God, father and mother of all men and all women [*tous et toutes*]. . . . In the future, she will find her own place; she will have her own life . . . ; she will no longer, as in the past, be merged into another's existence. (*Tribune* 1: 222)

They clearly found this recuperation of the feminine inspiring. "Woman, discovering her model and guide in *her God* [emphasis in original], can now develop *active* virtues; no longer will she be reduced to a passive role as was the ideal of Christian perfection."[24]

In the debate that led to this male/female structure of the Saint-Simonian Church—and in other changes in the movement to be discussed in the following section—we can trace out the influences of romantic thought on a new feminism. This influence was multifaceted. For example, romanticism not only valorized difference, it valorized—even idealized—women and qualities traditionally thought to be feminine. Male romantic writers and artists claimed a "feminine" sensibility; the male leaders of Saint-Simonianism were loving "like women." Indeed, Saint-Simonian women, in constructing their feminism of "difference," were recuperating the feminine not only from women's detractors but from those men who would appropriate female virtues for a new kind of male dominance.[25]

Admittedly, there were limitations to the romantic valorization of women, which extended only to certain settings and certain roles, and dangers beyond that of appropriation. Nevertheless, women—feminists included—responded positively to the ideal woman depicted in romantic literature. Doubtless they recognized in this idealization a means of challenging the negative views of women that permeated the eighteenth century and especially the Revolution. As Joan Landes has so skillfully described it, Revolutionary discourse was not simply patriarchal, it was also strongly misogynist. Revolutionaries associated the aristocratic state with women: Power, they claimed, was exercised in private settings where women had undue influence and where "men were unmanned."[26] Thus, the Revolutionaries' aim of making power more "public," less "private" and therefore less elitist, assumed, through the logic of their own misogynist discourse, the complementary aim of "empty[ing] out the feminine connotations (and ultimately, the women as well) of absolutist public life."[27]

Although Revolutionary feminists protested the Revolution's exclusion of women from public life, they did not seem to understand and certainly did not challenge the misogyny embedded in the new discourse of public rights. They too associated the aristocratic state with some illegitimate, manipulative "empire" of women. Condorcet, for example, was reflecting this misogyny in holding out the promise that "this empire would diminish if women had less interest in preserving it; if it ceased to be their sole means of defense and of escape from persecution."[28]

Unlike the Revolutionary feminists, Saint-Simonians specifically sought to allay the fear of women's power, and to do so they drew heavily upon the romantic idealization of women. After all, the power of women who are attractive, charming, conciliatory, and inspiring (*Tribune* 1, no. 1: 1, 3, 6) could be neither threatening nor illegitimate. In fact, the future direction of the new age could be entrusted only to those who were especially endowed with the particular quality of women—sentiment—for only sentiment and not reason could provide a strong and solid bond for a peaceful society. "In a religion that is completely about *love*, the most *loving* becomes the most capable" (*Tribune* 1: 107).

This belief in women's capacities is not, of course, what romantics intended. Their ideal woman was domesticated—literally confined to the domestic sphere—and powerless. But Saint-Simonians empowered women and called for their full participation in public life. This faith in women's capacities runs like a leitmotif through their writings: women should recognize "the power that is in them"; "they should sense their force." "Let us understand our power"; "women . . . have a great power to exercise" (*Tribune* 1: 43, 1: 156, 1, no. 1: 2–3).

Influenced by romantic thought, Saint-Simonians came to espouse a new vision of women's nature, one that eventually led to the development of new practices among Saint-Simonian women. But as exemplified by the 1829 debate on the structure of the Church, this vision of difference and of women's power was not simply a passive assimilation of romanticism. In part, it also evolved out of a variety of tendencies and views within the Saint-Simonian movement itself. It is important then to describe the various discourses that Saint-Simonian women struggled with in order to understand the oppositional language they constructed in the process.

MAKING A DIFFERENCE

In the early years, it was Saint-Simonian men who determined the direction of the movement. Even the feminist aspects of Saint-Simonian theory and practice were developed first by men. Only in 1832—at a moment when the male-created movement was in disarray—did a separate women's movement emerge. Given these two distinct stages of the evolution of the movement, it is possible to examine two quite different moments in the history of Saint-Simonianism and, in the course of that examination, to explore the difference that women's politics made in an ideology originally conceived by men.

"The Phase of the Doctors" (The Men)

We begin our examination of the first of the stages of Saint-Simonianism in June 1825, just ten days after the death of Claude Henri de Rouvroy, comte de Saint-Simon, when the Saint-Simonian "school" (only later did it become a "society," and, later still, a "religion") was created to popularize his ideas. The initial group of adherents—all men—was small, and, among them, Olinde Rodrigues was the only one who had actually been close to Saint-Simon. Raised in a Jewish—although not observant—family, Rodrigues held an advanced degree in mathematics from the Ecole polytechnique. However, because of his religion he had been frustrated in his desire to attend the Ecole normale supérieure to prepare to become a university professor.[29] By 1825 he had turned to a career in banking. His brother Eugène, the brothers Emile and Isaac Pereire, and Gustave d'Eichthal—also part of the initial group—were relatives or family friends and from similar backgrounds.

In contrast, the backgrounds of Saint-Amand Bazard and Philippe Buchez were more specifically radical and political. In 1821, they had founded the French Carbonari, a clandestine revolutionary republican group. Bazard, at the age of thirty-four, was the oldest among the original group and was married (although, it soon became known, in a not entirely satisfying relationship) to Claire Bazard. It was through her that her niece Cécile Fournel—one of the earliest women to join the group—and Cécile's husband, Henri—at the time the director of one of France's major industrial enterprises, the Creusot Iron Works—were recruited to the movement.

Prosper Enfantin became a member of the group in the fall of 1825, at the age of twenty-nine. He was the son of a banker and had attended the Ecole polytechnique. In the early 1820s, while working in the Saint Petersburg branch of a French investment banking house, he had begun to read and discuss social and economic theory with a group of former polytechnicians. It was only after his return to Paris in mid-decade that he was introduced to the ideas of Saint-Simon by his former teacher, Olinde Rodrigues.

According to the historian Robert Carlisle, all of these men had aspirations that had been frustrated by a series of obstacles associated with the social and political culture of the times. First, there was their youth. At a time when power and influence were increasingly the privilege of age, most of these men were young—in their twenties or early thirties. A decade of retrenchment in government administrative positions and, indeed, in most other kinds of employment that university-educated men such as these had been trained for—education, medicine, and law—limited their opportunities. Furthermore, political office was restricted by the Restoration Charter to men over the age of forty.[30] Second, many of these first Saint-Simonians were in business and engineering—careers that were devalued in the traditionalist atmosphere of Restoration France. Third, some of them were Jewish. Full political rights had been granted to Jews only during the Revolution, and they were justifiably concerned about their status at a time when not only the monarchy but also the Catholic Church had been restored to power. Fourth, many of the Saint-Simonians had experienced other indignities: Both Bazard and Enfantin were of illegitimate birth (although Enfantin was later legitimized). Enfantin's father had been forced to declare bankruptcy, which, in turn, forced Enfantin to withdraw from the Ecole polytechnique, denied him a commission in the army, and led the parents of a youthful love to reject him as their daughter's marriage partner. Individually, each fits the conclusions Carlisle draws from their biographies:

> Saint-Simon's attraction was to those—businessmen, engineers, Jews suspect in a revitalized Catholic world—who were finding it difficult to make a place for themselves in the Paris and France of 1825 and whose own hidden injuries of class and occupation would sensitize them to the injuries, injustices, and potentialities of that most numerous and poorest class that had filled the Paris stage to overflowing during Saint-Simon's lifetime.[31]

The prophetic quality of Saint-Simon's writings appealed to these men. They were tired of Enlightenment rationalism, seemingly dull when contrasted to romantic emotionalism, but tired also of the conservative romanticism of Chateaubriand, Louis de Bonald, or Joseph de Maistre that looked backward to some golden age. Saint-Simon offered hope for the future, a belief in progress, and human and social regeneration. As Gustave d'Eichthal wrote:

> We were told that we must . . . take on old world roles, to become . . . merchants, doctors, engineers. . . . Such a paltry life, such a narrow life, such a life without poetry was for us an unbearable burden. We dreamt of something better, something great. . . . [32]

At first, this "something better, something great" was interpreted in economic terms. The goal was to organize production in ways that would assure progress through the expansion of industry and human and social regeneration through the fulfillment of material needs. "Unproductive wealth," by which was meant all forms of wealth that were not mobilized to further industrial expansion, was identified as the fundamental cause of poverty. These ideas led the Saint-Simonians to examine the problem of capital formation—to look at the role of the state in minimizing the risks of investment, at the role of banks in mobilizing capital, and, most daringly, at the role of inherited wealth in discouraging productive work by creating a class of "parasites." Although Saint-Simonians never imagined a classless society, they wished their upper—or "directing"—class to be based on talent and productive work and open to individuals regardless of birth.

It was this Saint-Simonian conception of "class politics" that differed most markedly from later socialisms. Saint-Simonians held that cooperation—or, to use their word, "association"—among the classes was crucial for industrial expansion. They opposed any form of class struggle (their word was "antagonism"), including demonstrations or strikes, and it is for this reason that Marx labeled them "utopian." They did regard the working classes with compassion: workers were not to blame for their condition; social and economic disorganization caused their misery; the transformation of society would benefit workers by eliminating poverty and providing socially useful employment. Still, workers' role in the transformation of society would be a secondary one, and their place in the new social order would be subordinate to that of the "directing" class—at this time (1826–27) identified as bankers, engineers, and industrial entrepreneurs.

By 1828, however, Saint-Simonians were interpreting their desire to accomplish "something better, something great" in religious terms. Their theory and practice contain many elements borrowed from literary romanticism—for example, their glorification of beauty, love, and sensual passion and their fascination with the Near and Middle East. But for most historians, it is the religious aspects of Saint-Simonianism—its mysticism, emotionality, and fantastical elements—that link the movement to romanticism and separate it from later, more rationalist or "scientific" socialism.

The New Religion. The source of the Saint-Simonian impulse to create a new religion and church was Saint-Simon's final work, *Le Nouveau Christianisme*, in which the onetime Enlightenment philosopher declared that religion was an essential social bond and that a clerical elite was necessary to lead the masses. But it was only in 1828 that Saint-Simon's followers came to focus on his words—"belief will provide the incentives to make the transformations that truth requires of society"[33]—and in the process shift their attention from practical economic matters to the task of inspiring and persuading society to work toward a new order. Enfantin, writing to his cousin Thérèse Nugues, stated the problem: "before the possibilities of the material universe can be realized through the agency of technology, technocracy, and planning, people must *feel* and *want* the attraction of the new world." He criticized the Saint-Simonians' initial writings on the economy for encouraging a narrow materialism devoid of feeling: "There is more, and it is to the understanding of the 'more' that religion devotes itself and by its understanding converts not only the intellect but the . . . emotions as well."[34]

That year—1828—and the next were spent addressing the role of religion and the nature of God and of priestly authority. The culmination of this stage of the movement came on Christmas day, 1829, when Saint-Simon's followers constituted themselves as a church under the authority of the dual papacy of Bazard and Enfantin. Their "new Christianity" was organizationally not unlike the "old": the most influential members constituted a "college"; there were "brothers" and priestly "fathers" as well as a "papacy" (but in this case, as noted earlier, not one but two "popes"), "dogme," "prédications" and "enseignements" (that is, dogma, sermons, and teachings), and, in time, "confessions," "missions," and "apostles."

Borrowing from freemasonry, the hierarchy was organized by "degrees." The first level was the "second degree"; in 1830, a "third degree" and a special workers' degree were added. The "faithful" were expected not only to accept the "dogma" but also to submit to the authority of the hierarchy, which was invoked both for "revelations" of the doctrine and also for more personal matters. The creation of this religious hierarchy was consistent with earlier stages of Saint-Simonianism, which, as we have observed, had never been either egalitarian or committed to the leadership of workers. The change was that the movement had shifted its conception of appropriate leaders from *industriels* to priests. If "feeling" was to be the foundation of the new social order, those who had the strongest emotions must lead. Saint-Simonians would put their faith in the new priests (that is, themselves), who were more sentimental than rational. As we shall see, by the early 1830s, by the force of this logic, they would put their faith only in a woman.

Members of the hierarchy wore a special color-graduated costume for the Sunday ritual; those who lived at the rue Monsigny probably wore this costume every day. Women wore white; Enfantin and Bazard wore the lightest shade of blue; the lesser disciples wore royal blue. At the Sunday meeting, the disciples were seated on a raised dais, in ascending rows and with increasingly darker hues of blue according to their "degree." The scene would have been striking and certainly aesthetically pleasing, but we should keep in mind that for nineteenth-century audiences this aspect of the "new" religion—like the structure itself—would not have seemed truly new: Church officials, masons, and members of a variety of fraternal orders all costumed themselves for symbolic rituals and ceremonies.

What *was* new in the Saint-Simonian religion was its metaphysics. Two central principles of this system became crucial to Saint-Simonian feminism. The first was the concept of an androgynous[35] God—"Father and Mother"—that we encountered in Enfantin's and Buchez's debate on the papacy—a debate that apparently was the occasion for Enfantin's first explorations of this new vision. Buchez, in objecting to the dual papacy, had written to Enfantin: "Is not the pope the representative of God on earth? Now, tell me, is God divisible into two people, . . . male or female? . . . no, of course not."[36] Rather than assenting to Buchez's assumption, Enfantin took up the challenge and responded simply, "yes, God is male and female."[37] The concept, however revolutionary, was evidently warmly received by the Saint-Simonians. Frequently we find them verbalizing this formula: "GOD . . . is not only *good* like a FATHER, but also *tender* like a MOTHER . . . ; for HE *is* and SHE *is* the FATHER and the MOTHER of all men and all women [*tous et toutes*]."[38]

The second metaphysical innovation fundamental to Saint-Simonian feminism was the denunciation of the traditional Christian separation between spirit and matter. For Saint-Simon, this "rehabilitation" of the material world, denigrated by the "old" Christianity, had involved a revaluation of work and workers and even (as the historian Carlisle so aptly puts it) of "machines, canals, factories, banks."[39] For his followers, however, this new doctrine also involved a revaluation of the physical expression of love and a rejection of the Christian concept of original sin, changes that, in turn, the Saint-Simonians connected to the revaluation and ultimately to the emancipation of women. Saint-Simonians did not reject the traditional view that women—like Eve, who is held responsible for original sin—are quintessentially temptresses. But what they did do was to regard this doctrine with changed attitudes—in effect turning it upside down—by elevating sexual passion to a virtue. In a letter to his mother, Enfantin wrote:

> Until now coquettishness, frivolity, fickleness, beauty, and grace have given rise only to guile, trickery, hypocrisy, wantonness, adultery, etc., because society has not been able to . . . satisfy . . . [these] human qualities. They therefore have become sources of disorder, instead of being, as they should be, sources of joy and happiness. People who are *inconstant, fickle, volatile* are therefore damned by the law of Christ (and notice well that woman, more so than man, possesses these qualities). . . . This explains very well the anathema pronounced against *physical* pleasures and against *woman.*[40]

On November 19, 1831, in a "teaching" to the Saint-Simonian family, Enfantin set forth a new morality for the new Christianity. The realities of human affections, he declared, require three different but equally valid moral codes: (1) that of the "constants"; (2) that of the "mobiles"; and (3) the synthesizing love of the couple-pope charged with harmonizing all social relations by "rekindling the numbed feelings" of the first and moderating the "unruly appetites" of the second. The papal priest and priestess would combine unity and variety ("limited to a single one but belonging to all"). In plain language, it seems that what Enfantin had in mind was simply monogamous, lifelong marriage for some and divorce and remarriage for others—hardly shocking, even in nineteenth-century France. But the role he envisioned for the couple-pope—and certain ambiguous statements which left unclear whether this so-called synthesizing love would be possible only for one couple-pope or for an indefinite number of priests and priestesses—did shock. This couple (or these couples) would form one lifelong union with each other but also experience variety in their sexual partners—a kind of "open marriage" that condoned adultery. The example of their enduring relationship would teach constancy to those among the "mobiles" who might otherwise become dissolute. But they would also teach the joys of sexual pleasure to the "constants"—both by their example and by their willingness to have affairs with these "constants." ("I can conceive of CERTAIN CIRCUM-STANCES where I would judge that my wife [the priestess] alone would be capable of giving happiness, health, life to one of my sons in Saint-Simon; to recall him to social sympathies, to warm him when some profound sadness demands a diversion, when his broken heart would bleed with disgust for life," Enfantin wrote to his mother.)

How did Enfantin arrive at such a daring position? Were there precedents for his views? Do they relate to other aspects of the contemporary political and social debate? Do they reflect the life experiences of the Saint-Simonian ideologues in particular or, more generally, of French men and women in the early nineteenth century? In seeking some explanation for Saint-Simonian radicalism, it is fruitful to look for answers to all of these questions. What we find, however, is that there is no simple explanation for the development of these new views. The historical moment at which Saint-Simonianism was born was filled with a variety of discourses that had placed family issues at the center of political debates; similarly, the times were permeated with social and economic analyses that relate to Saint-Simonian concerns. And, not surprisingly, there were the individual life experiences of these men that helped to shape their views. In seeking to trace the origins of Saint-Simonian sexual morality, we shall consider each of these general areas of influence.

Discourses on the Family. One indication that the Saint-Simonians' attention to family matters was not an isolated concern of their particular movement is that the occasion for their initial discussions of sexual morals was a legislative proposal to reestablish divorce. That proposal was, in turn, part of a broader political discussion of family matters in general and of divorce in particular that had gone on since at least the eighteenth century. To understand the Saint-Simonian views on sexual morals it is useful to review some of that history. Rousseau, for example, was engaging in a politics of the family in linking his arguments favoring democracy among men to a glorification of bourgeois women's newly time-consuming maternal occupations as well as their role as men's companions. His are the "family politics" that the Committee of General Security expressed in 1793.[41]

But there was also precedent for a more radical stance dating back at least to 1792 when, within days of the establishment of the first French Republic, the Legislative Assembly passed a divorce law that was extraordinarily liberal even by late twentieth-century standards.[42] Divorces were permitted simply by mutual consent, so long as both spouses petitioned jointly to dissolve the marriage. The procedures for these mutual-consent divorces were inexpensive and informal—before 1796, they did not even come before the courts. Divorce could also be obtained at the request of one spouse, if the other did not contest the action. Alimony was granted to the financially worse-off partner; child support payments were also established, and custody was determined by the parents themselves. In cases when custody could not be agreed upon, the family courts granted mothers custody of children younger than seven; for older children, mothers were granted custody of daughters; fathers, of sons.

Although women and men were treated equally under this 1792 divorce law, these Revolutionaries believed it favored women because divorce restored rights to them—for example, to live where they chose and to manage their own financial affairs—that they lost upon marriage. Indeed, the subjugation of wives to husbands gave women no recourse, other than divorce, to escape from a husband's physical or emotional cruelty or mismanagement of the family's financial resources. Husbands, of course, were not subject to a wife's authority; moreover, because men had greater opportunities to find employment, they were freer to simply leave unhappy marriages and even form new liaisons.[43]

Rousseau's view of marriage and women's place in the family[44]—or that of the 1793 Committee of General Security—was not the only republican view, then. For others, divorce was a self-conscious attempt to "republicanize" the family by undermining the authority of the husband over wives and children. Revolutionary-era feminists such as Olympe de Gouges and Etta Palm favored divorce for this reason; Gouges, who had called for a "social contract between a man and a woman," viewed divorce as an important step toward equality. Feminists were joined in their demands for family reform by many republicans who in all probability would not have entertained the thought of granting women political rights. In keeping with the values that prompted this interest in divorce, legislators also passed other self-consciously "republican" family reforms in the early years of the first Republic: the abolition of *lettres de cachet de famille*, the private warrant that permitted men to have their wives and children imprisoned; the requirement that all children—regardless of sex, birth order, or, briefly in 1793, legitimacy—be treated equally in inheritance; permission for married women to control the property they brought with them into marriage and to enter into contracts without their husband's authorizations.

But the liberal divorce law did not outlast the Revolutionary era. In 1803, under Napoleon, the grounds for divorce were reduced in number; most significantly, incompatibility could no longer serve as a ground for divorce by mutual consent. Worse, a double standard was introduced: a woman could be divorced for adultery, but adultery was now ground for a woman divorcing her husband only if he brought his mistress into the family home. A year later, the property rights of women, which had only recently been obtained, were rescinded and husbands' authority over wives was made explicit in article 213 of the Civil Code (" . . . the wife owes obedience to her husband"). Yet even these restrictions did not satisfy the traditional Right, which resumed power in 1815. Not surprisingly, the Right identified divorce with the Revolution's undermining of the authority of both Church and king. In 1816, Louis XVIII abolished divorce.

Divorce may have been the catalyst for the Right's attention to family matters after the Restoration, but it was not its only concern. Conservative thinkers such as Louis de Bonald and Joseph de Maistre had come to believe that it was the family lifestyle of eighteenth-century aristocrats that had brought down the *ancien régime* and that the strength of the restored monarchy depended on "the authority of the husband, the subordination of the wife, and the dependency of the children."[45] No less so than those republicans who had advocated a "republicanized" family, conservatives also saw themselves as reformers: the subjugation of wives to husbands and the confinement of wives to the domestic sphere—practices that we might call "traditional"—were espoused as reforms to an aristocratic way of life that, according to Bonald and Maistre, had permitted the undue prominence of women in public life. The Right's family "reform" politics was an attack, then, on the growing prevalence of independently minded women—a trend they associated with the eighteenth-century aristocracy.[46] At the same time, their "reforms" were a way of opposing Revolutionary individualism. Thinkers such as Bonald and Maistre defined one's place in the family, like one's place in the State, in relation to the whole rather than as a means of achieving individual well-being or fulfillment.

Interestingly, the "family reform" politics of utopian socialists were also an attack on individualism, also in favor of a more collective or communitarian approach to life. Unlike Rightists, however, the utopian socialists—at least the sexual radicals among them—viewed the family as individualistic and the exclusive love of married couples as isolating, separating couples from the larger community. Charles Fourier set the agenda. His *Théorie des quatre mouvements*, written in 1808 but not generally known until decades later, envisioned an ultimate stage of human progress when women and men would live in agrarian communities—phalanxes—based on associations that would organize production, households and housekeeping, and even sexual experience in new ways. Fourier held that isolated households and monogamous marriages enslaved both women and men. Among the numerous problems he associated with isolated households and monogamy were risk of misfortune, great and unnecessary expense, monotony (which Fourier said was worse for women), sterility, the loneliness and isolation of widowhood/widowerhood, and cuckoldry. The work of the home, including both socialization of children and housekeeping tasks, should be collectivized. Love alone should bind couples to one another, and their union should last only so long as their attraction joined them.

It is important to note how much farther Fourier was willing to go than even the more radical of the republicans—those who had advocated divorce and rights for women within the family but who had never intended to abolish marriage, simply to revitalize it. Radical republicans had argued, for example, that it was the indissolubility of marriage that encouraged celibacy, but that the easy availability of divorce would encourage men to marry. In contrast, Fourier scoffed at divorce—a "timid . . . half-measure"[47]—and advocated the complete destruction of the institution of marriage. His intentions were also more far-reaching than the reforms called for by republicans—that women be liberated and that women and men be equal and equally free and productive.

Fourier also went farther than earlier radical Republicans in addressing—even glorifying—sexuality. Central to his thought was his Law of Passionate Attraction—a "law" that he claimed was as fundamental to understanding human nature as Newton's law of gravity was to understanding physical nature. "Passionate attraction," in Fourier's writings, referred to a host of instincts or feelings, including but not limited to sexuality. He described twelve—the five "luxurious" passions of the senses, the group passions (honor, love, friendship, and parenthood), and the three "distributive" passions (the cabalist, the composite, and the butterfly)—which would operate in work, family, and friendship. In love relationships, the cabalist or competitive passion stimulates interest in the other, the butterfly passion (a flitting from one to another) kills boredom, and the composite regulates the extremes.

In Harmony, Fourier's utopia, all of the passions would be satisfied. In any case, according to Fourier, constraints, even self-imposed constraints, were to no avail in controlling these passions, for, when repressed, they simply express themselves in some other, destructive way. His most recent biographer, Jonathan Beecher, provides this example (remarkable not only for the modernity of its depiction of repression but also for its acceptance of homosexuality) from Fourier's notebooks:

As Lady Strogonoff, a Muscovite princess, saw herself growing old, she became jealous of the beauty of one of her young slaves. She had the slave tortured; she herself pricked her with pins. What was the motive for her cruel behavior? Was it jealousy? No, it was lesbianism. Madame Strogonoff was an unconscious lesbian; she was actually inclined to love the beautiful slave whom she tortured. If someone had made Madame Strogonoff aware of her true feelings and reconciled her and her victim, they would have become passionate lovers. But remaining unaware of her lesbian impulse, the princess was overcome by a counterpassion, a subversive tendency. She persecuted the person who should have been the object of her pleasure.[48]

Others before Fourier—Diderot, Restif de la Bretonne, the Marquis de Sade—had also celebrated a more diverse and a more open expression of sexuality. But Diderot, who appreciated polygamy in Tahiti, could not imagine its adoption in France. And Restif and Sade focused on the destructive possibilities of the erotic. Fourier's originality lay in his optimistic view of an erotic love that is the foundation of human happiness and social cohesion.[49]

The similarities of Fourier's moral views to those espoused by Enfantin are striking. Although Fourier considered a variety of sexual experiences permissible, he, like Enfantin, also imagined a system of "regulation." In his notebooks we read that he had even envisioned a Court of Love, a Female Pontiff, and priests and priestesses who would assure that everyone experiences at least a modicum of sexual happiness.

In many ways—explicitly opposing marriage and in being more certain that sexual variety would benefit everyone—Fourier went farther than Enfantin. In one respect, however, Enfantin was more innovative in his thinking than Fourier, and that was in connecting his theory of sexual liberation to the economic and social concerns that underlay his socialism. For Fourier, sexual liberation was a goal that paralleled his dream of economic cooperation and freedom from poverty, but aside from his description of the waste inherent in individual households, he posited no cause-and-effect relationships between sexual and economic issues.

Saint-Simonians, however, placed sexual liberation at the center of their economics by drawing connections between repressed sexuality, economic considerations in marriage formation, inherited property, and the exploitation of women and workers. They linked their attack on marriage and the family to their attack on inheritance and the accumulation and transmission of wealth through the family. They linked the poverty of workers—itself the result of "unproductive wealth" and economic "disorganization"—to prostitution. They considered bourgeois marriage simply another form of prostitution because it was formed on the basis of property claims rather than love. Such marriages, they said, enslaved women (the "purchase of women") and made both women and men miserable. In turn, these unhappy relationships led to adultery and prostitution.

The Social and Economic Context. Just as a review of the multiple discourses on family matters and sexuality of the late eighteenth and early nineteenth centuries helps us to understand the context for Enfantin's views, so those views are also illuminated by an examination of the historically specific economic and social context in which they were developed. Notably, demographic factors had an impact, even if subtle and indirect, on the era's family and sexuality debates in general and on Enfantin's ideas in particular. France was the first country—indeed, was then the only country—to experience the dramatic drop in the birthrate that signaled a widespread acceptance of family limitation.[50] Traditionally children had been born at regular intervals of from twenty-five to thirty months. The only processes that had held down the average number of births per family to four or five were late marriages and the fact that one or the other partner commonly died before menopause.[51] But in the space of just one generation, beginning in the early nineteenth century, this traditional pattern changed suddenly and completely.[52] By the middle of the nineteenth century, the two-child household was commonplace throughout France. The effect was a breaking of the link between sexuality and reproduction—a revolution in human experience.

Demographers do not agree among themselves on the explanations for this abrupt fertility decline; nor is there consensus on why it occurred first in France. They are certain, however, that the change was not accidental, that it resulted from a conscious desire to limit family size, which appeared in French married life first among the wealthiest classes—perhaps as early as the late seventeenth century—and which spread to other classes in the first decades of the nineteenth century. Some theorize that people came to believe that they could improve the quality of their lives by limiting the size of their families. Philippe Ariès relates the phenomenon of family limitation to cultural changes that made childhood a distinct and important phase of life: As each child became a more important individual to the parents, remained at home for a longer number of years, and represented a more severe financial burden on them, the desire to limit the number of children increased.[53]

These theories could, of course, apply to other European countries and do not explain why France was so precocious. Perhaps inheritance patterns played a role in French demographic trends, although there is evidence that primogeniture was already rare at least 100 years before it was abolished by the Napoleonic Code.[54] Roger Price theorizes that the contacts made by army conscripts during the period of the Revolution and the Empire may have speeded the diffusion of family planning values.[55]

Alfred Sauvy speculates that it was the collapse of the power and influence of religion—unique to France at this time—that explain the special French experience.[56]

Demographers are also uncertain about whether women and men had similar attitudes on these matters. Ariès presents evidence that women were already expressing approval of limiting births at a time when references to the new practice by male writers were invariably negative.[57]

We are also uncertain which methods of contraception were used by marriage partners. Abstinence was likely the most common method for limiting family size, but there are indications that *coitus interruptus* was becoming more and more popular already in these early decades of the nineteenth century. (One letter in the Saint-Simonian archives refers to "withdrawal" in a rather matter-of-fact way.)[58] It is doubtful if these particular methods of limiting births were adequate to enhance women's sense of sexual autonomy, and other methods that were less dependent on men were as yet uncommon. Angus McLaren has hypothesized that induced abortion became popular in the nineteenth century, but likely only later in the century.[59] Artificial devices that were for women's use, such as the pessary, were expensive and still rare.

Family limitation, the possibility that one could choose whether or not to have children, resulted in a new consciousness about sexuality. Once sexuality could be sorted out from reproduction, it became more possible to view the pursuit of sexual pleasure as an end in itself. By promoting experimentation in sexual relationships beyond the confines of the traditional, monogamous marriage, Saint-Simonians—at least the men among them—reflected this view.

This is not to suggest that the sexual and family debates described earlier were a simple and direct reflection solely of the demographic revolution. In fact, the attention to these matters drew upon multiple sources. For example, the linking of family to property and inheritance in many of these discourses was in part a reflection of the intensity of the debate on property that took place in the 1830s and 1840s. A new conception of property, writes the historian William Sewell, was born with the French Revolution and, in turn, "gave rise to a new set of social conflicts that culminated in an attempt to abolish private property in the Revolution of 1848."[60] It is useful to view the Saint-Simonian attack on the family in this context—as one challenge among several to the institution of private property. It is also useful to view the sexual and family politics of the Saint-Simonians in the context of their own lived experiences. We must keep in mind that these Saint-Simonians were young men, mostly single, and that sexual matters and questions of marriage and economic status quite naturally figured prominently in their lives at this time. As is clearly shown by the biographical information provided by historians Robert Carlisle and Barrie Ratcliffe, many Saint-Simonian men had themselves suffered from the sexual repression or the marriage/ property connection they attributed to the bourgeois moral order. We have already taken note of the rejection of Enfantin as a prospective husband on the grounds of his family's financial situation and of the ignominy suffered by Enfantin and Bazard as "illegitimate" children. Enfantin himself fathered an illegitimate son whom he later legitimated. He remained in a lifelong relationship to his son's mother, Adèle Morlane, never abandoning her—certainly never abandoning her financially—but never assenting to her desire to marry. Many who knew him declared that the situation tortured him. The Bazards' marriage was troubled by sexual incompatibility, and most Saint-Simonians knew of Claire Bazard's adulterous relationship with another Saint-Simonian, Charles Hippolyte Margerin. Several letters that Gustave d'Eichthal wrote in the early 1830s spoke of his "powerful," but unmet, sexual desires; in all probability he was not alone in these feelings.[61] One could generalize from Carlisle's characterization of Enfantin to most of the Saint-Simonians: "He hardly needed lessons . . . on the connections between sex, economics, politics, and morality. He had lived these connections."[62]

We have examined the social and economic context in which Enfantin's new morality was embedded and we have also seen that there were precedents and parallels for his critique of contemporary sexual morals and family life. None of these factors, however, should allow us to underestimate the extremity of the views that he set forth in his teaching of November 19, 1831. They scandalized the general public, and, even among Saint-Simonians, there were those who felt that Enfantin had gone too far. Bazard was his most formidable opponent, but having suffered a cerebral hemorrhage in late August, he was unable to mount an effective challenge to Enfantin that fall. He had in fact left the rue Monsigny residence before the November 19 meeting; Enfantin was now the "chef unique" of the Saint-Simonians. Pierre Leroux, Hippolyte Carnot (a future minister of public instruction), and Jules Lechevalier (who was later to join the Fourierists) protested Enfantin's position, and, failing to change his mind, they publicly resigned from the movement.

To avoid further challenge, Enfantin retreated from his radical position and announced instead a new policy under the banner of "l'attente de la femme." It should not be presumed, Enfantin now stated, that his description of a new morality was the last—and best—word on the matter, and certainly the new morality should not yet be put into practice. Only a woman could announce a new morality. Because it was woman whose nature is love, only she could speak to matters of love. The visible sign of the "Wait for the Woman" would be an empty seat next to Enfantin's at Saint-Simonian meetings.

Bazard was not satisfied, however. In January, he published a pamphlet explaining his side of the dispute: "Twenty months ago an important debate broke out between Enfantin and myself on one of the great questions of morality. . . . From the first moment that this question of promiscuity was introduced I opposed it vigorously. . . . The distinction between individuals as mobile or immobile corresponds to the notion of antagonism."[63]

The power struggle between Enfantin and Bazard persisted for months after the publication of the pamphlet. Enfantin's admission that his words were "incomplete" certainly did not silence him. He took over the "exposition of the doctrine" and presented five lengthy "teachings" on the new morality. All of them were reprinted immediately in the *Globe* and later as separate pamphlets and were widely distributed. In response to Enfantin's arguments, Bazard hosted frequent meetings and carried on a vigorous correspondence with potential sympathizers. The public, once supportive, was now thoroughly confused by the fathers' charges and countercharges of immorality and wrongdoing and became less generous with donations to Saint-Simonian coffers. In April, the *Globe* ceased publication and the communal dining halls were shut down.

The government hammered the last nail in the coffin. On January 22, 1832, the police shut down the Saint-Simonian lecture hall and residence on the rue Taitbout and began a grand inquest into charges of "corruption of public morals" against the Saint-Simonian leaders. In August, a trial was held: Enfantin, Charles Duveyrier, and Michel Chevalier were found guilty and sentenced to one year's imprisonment;[64] Olinde Rodrigues and Emile Barrault were fined.

Forty of the Saint-Simonian men moved to Ménilmontant, Enfantin's country home, in a celibate retreat intended, at least in part, to allay the public's fears that Saint-Simonians were engaging in "immoral" activities. There they devoted themselves to acts of symbolic communalism (such as wearing clothing that buttoned down the back, thus necessitating assistance from a "brother"), to creating new religious rituals and ceremonies, and to labor. In part, the retreat was also intended for men to "gain insight into women's lot" by doing housework and renouncing sex. Interestingly, the men were ridiculed as much on the grounds of their domesticity as on their celibacy. According to Carlisle, cartoons depicting the men "washing dishes, scraping carrots, polishing kitchenware, and emptying laundry tubs" appeared everywhere.[65]

In early 1833, the year they declared "The Year of the Woman," some of the Saint-Simonian men created a new group—Le Compagnonnage (or Les Compagnons) de la Femme—and set off in "search" of "the Woman"—now also referred to as the Woman Messiah—first to Constantinople, then to Egypt. Other "missionaries" ventured out of Paris into the provinces or to England, Germany, or Belgium in search of "the Woman." Calling themselves "apostles" or "apostles of the Woman," they preached that their search must take precedence over all other efforts at social regeneration. In a letter to Paul-Mathieu Laurent, who protested the neglect of workers' concerns, Enfantin wrote that although he experienced all the suffering of the people, he remained "calm enough" to wait for "the real saviour of the people, woman."

By 1832, then, Saint-Simonianism was at an impasse. Saint-Simonian men had obviously gone too far in their doctrine of sexual liberation and in the process had frightened not only the general public but also themselves. The "phase of the doctors was ended"; it was now time for women to speak.

"In a Different Voice"[66] (The Women)

As indicated by the history just reviewed, Saint-Simonian feminism was a masculine invention. From 1828 to 1830, Eugène Rodrigues, Charles Duveyrier, Pierre-Joseph Buchez, and Prosper Enfantin—all middle-class men—debated the role that women should play in the Saint-Simonian movement and in the new age; in 1831, Bazard and Enfantin debated the new sexual morality. After the November 1831 crisis, however, Saint-Simonian women, responding to Enfantin's "call" to define the appropriate relationship of the sexes for the new social order, began to speak out on the full range of issues that affected their lives. Ultimately, they transformed Saint-Simonian feminism.

Women had come to Saint-Simonianism a bit later than men, but, in time, they came in sizable numbers. Although the first women activists were all relatives or close family friends of the male leaders of the movement, other women were recruited to the cause after the Saint-Simonians began their propaganda work. Already in late 1829-early 1830, about 100 women were attending the weekly expositions of the Saint-Simonian doctrine.[67] Later in 1830, when Saint-Simonians began to present almost daily lectures, Enfantin estimated that 200 women regularly attended, indicating that women constituted between one-third and one-half of the estimated total audiences.[68] Some women were brought to these lectures by male friends, husbands, or husbands' friends, some of whom were employed in workshops where Saint-Simonianism was much discussed. Suzanne Voilquin first attended a lecture with her brother-in-law, Charles Mallard, who had heard of the Saint-Simonians from his fellow workers at the printing house of Firmin Didot.[69] Jeanne Deroin was brought to her first lectures by her future fiancé, the engineer Desroches. Other women came alone. Eugénie Niboyet, who was active in the Société de la Morale Chrétienne, a group which in 1830 shared its lecture halls with the Saint-Simonians, stayed one day to hear the Saint-Simonians speak and was won over to their cause.[70] Many women were recruited to Saint-Simonianism by reading the Saint-Simonian newspapers. Pauline Roland, for example, was introduced to Saint-Simonian ideas when her tutor gave her the *Globe* to read. Other women, especially working-class women, more typically became familiar with Saint-Simonianism through the outreach programs to the working-class quarters of Paris. Indeed, some of these programs, such as the medical and pharmaceutical service, the free vaccination program for children, and the cooperative workshop for seamstresses, reached out directly to women. In late 1831, following the creation of special groups for workers, 110 working-class women were inscribed as "faithful adherents."[71] A Lyonnaise woman, who corresponded with Claire Démar, claimed that in 1833 about 100 women in her city were adherents.[72]

During the first years of the decade, before the disbanding of the hierarchy, the women who wielded power within the movement were all close to the male leaders of Saint-Simonianism—spouses, sisters, cousins, or old family friends. Their work was for the movement: writing short propagandistic pieces published as pamphlets or in the Saint-Simonian newspapers, corresponding with potential women recruits, hosting the *soirées* where new ideas were discussed, organizing among workers in their neighborhoods and at their workplaces, and running (as codirectors with Saint-Simonian men) the various outreach programs.

The most prominent women leaders were Claire Bazard, Aglaé Saint-Hilaire, and Cécile Fournel. Bazard was a member of the "college," the superior degree of the hierarchy. She was also part of the Conseil Privé, sharing responsibility with Olinde Rodrigues and Charles Hippolyte Margerin to advise the two "fathers" (Enfantin and her husband, Saint-Amand Bazard) and to represent them in their absence. Finally, with Henri Fournel, she oversaw the general administration of the Saint-Simonian enterprises. Called the "mother," Bazard was charged with the indoctrination of new women adherents. In late 1830, she became the first woman to officiate at a Saint-Simonian ceremony, presiding over the "reception" to the second degree of the hierarchy. And when, also in late 1830, the Sunday ritual ceremony was moved from the Salle Taranne to a larger hall on the rue Taitbout, she became the first woman to be seated on the dais with an otherwise still all-male hierarchy. Other Saint-Simonians described her, respectfully, as especially intelligent, but also as ambitious, proud, and not particularly likable. Her letters to Enfantin complain of her difficulty in obtaining the same respect from the "daughters" that Saint-Amand Bazard and Enfantin could expect from their "sons."

Like Bazard, Aglaé Saint-Hilaire and Cécile Fournel were members of the college. They were chosen to defend Enfantin at his trials in August 1832 and April 1833. (The decision to have them fulfill this responsibility was frustrated, however, by the judge's refusal to accept women as legal counsel.) Saint-Hilaire had been Enfantin's friend since childhood. She directed the salon at the rue Monsigny residence three evenings a week and, after Claire Bazard resigned from the church, took over the indoctrination of new female adherents. Fournel, along with Charles Duveyrier and Jules Lechevalier, directed the second degree. The best-liked of the prominent Saint-Simonian women, she was especially influential, partially as a result of her personal popularity but also because of her relationship to the Bazards (she was Claire's niece) and to the financial administrator of Saint-Simonian affairs, her husband Henri.

Bazard and Fournel supported Saint-Amand Bazard in the controversy over the new morality, and both left the movement in November 1831. The aftermath of this decision was particularly difficult for Fournel because her husband joined the men's retreat at Ménilmontant. In his absence, she suffered both loneliness and financial hardship—the Fournels, as noted earlier, had donated their entire fortune to the Saint-Simonian movement. Finally, unable to bear these burdens, she moved back to the rue Monsigny residence. There she discovered that the Saint-Simonian women who remained were also dispirited. Their husbands, like her Henri, were at Ménilmontant. Earlier that spring, Saint-Hilaire had tried to organize the women for independent activity but had failed. The Saint-Simonian funds that were supporting them were low: "We need to work *materially*," Cécile wrote to her friend Elisa Lemonnier, "for several of us whose husbands have donned the apostolic costume are without resources." Although she declared that she welcomed the challenge— "Truly this will be our first step toward independence and freedom"— her "step" was unsteady. She was frequently ill and almost always depressed during the entire time of her separation from Henri. She floundered, searching for some suitable work before determining to publish Enfantin's defense from his two trials under the title *La Parole de la père* (*The Word of the Father*). In January 1833, she began to publish the monthly *La Foi nouvelle: Livre des actes* (*The New Faith: Book of Acts*), which recounted the activities of the male apostles who were traveling to the Middle East in search of "the woman." But these projects were both "to praise the acts of men" and did not take her very far "toward independence."

A more far-reaching project was undertaken by a group of Saint-Simonian women from the Saint-Simonian "workers' degree." In April 1832, they founded a newspaper that "would publish articles only by women." The first issue, undated, was entitled *La Femme libre* (*The Free Woman*), a poor choice, it turned out, because it evoked the controversy over the sexual morality and subjected them to public ridicule. They next used the title *Apostolat des femmes* (*Apostolate of Women*) with the words "La Femme libre"—then "La Femme de l'avenir" ("The Woman of the Future") or "La Femme nouvelle" ("The New Woman")—in small type above *Apostolat des femmes*; later issues placed "La Femme nouvelle" above *Affranchissement des femmes* (*Emancipation of Women*). Finally, the editors settled on *Tribune des femmes*.

In signing their names to articles, the editors used only first names, a symbolic gesture of female emancipation from masculine control: "We [who] give birth to men . . . should give them our names and take our own only from our mothers and God. . . . If we continue to take the names of men . . . we will be slaves" (1: 70). The first issue identified Jean-Désirée (Désirée Veret) as the founder and Marie-Reine (Reine Guindorf) as the director. Both were young seamstresses, ages twenty-two and twenty, respectively. In September, Suzanne (Suzanne Voilquin) joined Guindorf as codirector. Some months later, Guindorf gave up her administrative responsibilities to have more time to teach in a night school for poor women that these Saint-Simonian women founded, but she continued to write articles for the journal. Voilquin continued to direct the publication, sometimes alone, sometimes with a codirector.

Among the other regular contributors to the journal were Isabelle (Isabelle Gobert) and Céléstine (Céléstine Montagny), occasional codirectors; Marie-Pauline (Pauline Roland); and Joséphine Félicité (Joséphine Milizet) and Jeanne-Victoire (Jeanne Deroin). Many others cannot be identified— some signed their articles with their first names only (Angélique, who was also an occasional codirector, Sophy-Caroline, Amanda, Nancy, and Christine-Sophy), while others simply designated themselves "femmes nouvelles" or "new women" (1: 62, 63, 69). Other writers, clearly sympathizers, nonetheless distanced themselves from the regular contributors by signing two names—Caroline Béranger, Angeline Pignot, Adèle Miguet, Louise Dauriat, and Adèle de Saint-Amand. Women like Fournel and Saint-Hilaire who had been prominent in the former hierarchy did not write for the *Tribune des femmes*, however. Nor did Claire Démar, although her works were publicized and discussed there and although she wrote *My Law of the Future* in response to a *Tribune des femmes* article.

Most of the regular contributors to the *Tribune des femmes* were young and unmarried and living on their own or, if living with a man in either marriage or "free union," were with men who held no power within the Saint-Simonian establishment and had played no role in the development of its ideology. The contributors were either urban lower middle class or upper working class. Suzanne Voilquin labels them all *femmes prolétaires*, as does Pauline Roland in an 1834 letter to Charles Lambert.

We do know that Reine Guindorf and Désirée Veret were seamstresses. They were both from workers' families associated with Saint-Simonianism and had been apprentices in a Saint-Simonian workshop. Voilquin, another contributor for whom we have biographical information, also came from a working-class family (one not associated with Saint-Simonianism, however). Her father, a hatmaker, had once unsuccessfully attempted to establish a manufacturing business, and after its failure, the family faced real destitution. Voilquin herself had been an embroiderer before her association with Saint-Simonianism. The circumstances of Roland's childhood had been a bit more easy and secure. Her father, who had been the postmaster of their small Norman town, died when she was quite young; but her mother was permitted to assume his position. In 1832, Roland became an instructor in a Parisian girls' boarding school; in 1834, she began her always-uncertain career as a freelance journalist.

The *Tribune des femmes* reflected the uncertain economic situation of its editors and contributors. Although expenses were limited to printing and mailing—authors and editors were not paid—it was difficult for the editors to cover even these costs and especially difficult to bring the publication out on a regular schedule. Guindorf described their work as "a sacrifice" and lamented that they were so "restrained by [their] pecuniary means" (1: 43, 42). She wrote that she had "no financial resources other than the product of [her] needlework," indicating that her work for the journal was an addition to a full workday elsewhere.

It was easier for Suzanne Voilquin to direct the journal. For the first six months of her association with the *Tribune des femmes* she was married and supported directly by her husband and indirectly by more well-to-do Saint-Simonians. The Voilquins lived in a comfortable two-room apartment rented to them by a Saint-Simonian sympathizer, who also assumed responsibility for finding enough clients for Voilquin's husband, an architect, to assure that they could make their rent payments. In May 1833, the Voilquins separated. However, Suzanne's means of support were uncertain for only a month or two, after which a wealthy Saint-Simonian, Alexandre de Berny, at the urging of his mother who had befriended Suzanne, began to subsidize the journal. And "to satisfy [her] personal needs," Suzanne worked as a housekeeper for still another Saint-Simonian, Madame Prud'homme, three days a week, receiving room and board for those days plus 3 francs 75 centimes—enough, she wrote, to rent an apartment for the other four days of the week. These four days were for the journal, her correspondence, and to prepare for a Saint-Simonian meeting she hosted once a week.

The relationship between the women's publication and the Saint-Simonian family was complicated. The journal received no direct financial support from the Saint-Simonian group, although later letters between Enfantin and Lambert (expressing guilt over the matter) suggest that this had been considered and rejected. There are also indications in Voilquin's later letters that she had felt some hurt that the family had been willing to support Fournel's publication but not the *Tribune des femmes*. Still, the periodical did enjoy a certain success. Its initial print run was 1,000—and this was certainly due to the Saint-Simonian movement's extensive communications networks, including bookstores and reading rooms, which secured the journal readers, subscribers, and authors.

At first, the *femmes nouvelles* stressed their sense of connection to Saint-Simonianism. ("We are *Saint-Simoniennes* . . . [1, no. 1: 7]). Like the men missionaries, they too were "apostles." ("This publication is not a commercial venture; it is an apostolic work for the freedom and association of women" [1, no. 1: 6]). They declared that they were acting according to

Saint-Simonian principles and especially in response to Enfantin's "call" to women to "speak." ("Women . . . you are called . . . " [1, no. 1: 2]). They were lavish in their praise of Saint-Simonian men: "Honor to these generous men. A halo of glory awaits them in the future" (ibid.). " . . . [T]hey have forseen humanity's future better than anyone and are the most advanced men of our era" (1: 69). And toward Enfantin, they expressed deep gratitude: "It is for women, their emancipation and their future happiness, that FATHER ENFANTIN endures injury, poverty, and prison. It behooves women to . . . glorify him" (1: 192).

Their decision to concentrate on the sexual issue reflected both their respect for Enfantin and other Saint-Simonian men and their understanding of Saint-Simonian theory. Not only had Enfantin "called" them to speak to the sexual issue, but, more generally, the Saint-Simonian equation of women/love made this issue a central women's concern more so than, for example, "the material poverty of women."[73]

It should not be assumed, however, that all Saint-Simonian women accepted Enfantin's views. From the first, his new morality had created a storm of controversy among women as well as men. At the November 19, 1831, meeting of the Saint-Simonian family, Cécile Fournel and several of her female colleagues publicly protested Enfantin's pronouncement.[74] Fournel and other women from the original inner group— Eugénie Niboyet, Elisa Lemmonier, and, of course, Claire Bazard—then left the movement. And even though Fournel later returned, she remained convinced of the correctness of her initial reaction. In 1834, Fournel, later described as a "model of conjugal love" (Suzanne, in *Tribune* 2: 180), wrote that she rejected "these so-called novelties that are in fact only a pale copy of society seen from its sad side."[75] There must have been other Saint-Simonian women who shared Fournel's views and yet remained active in the movement after the November 1831 schism. The editors of the *Tribune des femmes* acknowledged their sensitivity to conservative women within the movement in agreeing to publish several articles by a non-adherent, Gertrude, in defense of conventional morals ("[Christian] morals are divine; for centuries people have been content with them . . . take care that you not deliver a sacrilegious blow to them").[76]

Among the *femmes nouvelles*, however, there was more willingness to consider a new "law of the future."[77] Apparently they met regularly to discuss and try to reach consensus on the sexual issue. They clearly struggled with many differences of opinion, which were aired in the pages of the periodical, but did arrive at certain shared understandings. They agreed that love, rather than financial considerations, should be the basis for forming personal unions. Also, they shared a view of contemporary morals as "disorderly." Although the government, in its prosecution of the movement's leaders, charged the Saint-Simonians with fostering "mobility" and the "community of women," these women in-

sisted that both already existed in adulterous relationships and in prostitution and that these had been fostered by the old Christian morality.
("The disastrous effects of the moral system in effect until now are adultery and prostitution." " . . . [T]his mobility that you claim to banish exists everywhere . . . ").[78]

There was agreement, too, that the problem with the old "law" was
that it did not value "the flesh": "For us, the spirit is holy and so is the
flesh; for us, Christian asceticism is completely ridiculous."[79] The old law
failed also in not recognizing "variety" ("the most beautiful work of
God") in human nature. The "moral law . . . is much too strict and absolute to satisfy all individuals. . . . " A new morality would end the "conflict" which now exists "between different natures"; "those who find
happiness in a lasting union would not have to fear . . . adultery; . . .
those with a lively nature can change, but without dishonoring their
families [or] bringing disorder into homes." Finally, the old law had
failed because men alone had made it. Lacking women's contributions,
the moral "constitution" was "dry and arid"; even men could not live by
its terms.[80]

A careful reading of the *Tribune des femmes* reveals this common
ground; but the opinion pieces and manifestos also make it clear that the
femmes nouvelles often disagreed with one another, describing different
plans for women's futures and holding different expectations for
women's behavior in the present. Voilquin was among the more cautious
of the *femmes nouvelles*. It mattered very much to her that future sexual
relations be regulated in some way—that there be a "law of the future"
to "sanctify new bonds" and a "superior" couple "to whom we will
grant the right to unite and separate us" (1: 63). Even in the future, there
would be marriages—"I cannot conceive of a society that is possible
without marriage"—albeit "more social" than now ("feeling a part of the
great [human] family"). After all, society is founded not on "absolute
independence" but upon the "social individual, united one to the other
although not identical" (1: 236–37). She recognized the need for divorce:
"As long as *marriage* exists . . . *divorce* will be the *necessary complement*" (2:
169). But here, too, she was cautious. "Good variety," but not "much
variety," was possible; "progressive unions"—and, she explained, she
carefully chose the word "progressive" over "successive"—but not free
love, were possible (1: 237).

One can't help wondering about the connection between Suzanne
Voilquin's personal life and her theories. Although divorce was illegal in
France, she created for herself a kind of Saint-Simonian divorce. (A legal
divorce was obtained six years later in the United States where Eugène
went to live with his new "wife.") Suzanne described her separation
from her husband rather frankly and at some length in the *Tribune des
femmes*; for her, this act of "publicity" constituted a religious sanctification of the divorce. The public discussion of her experiences also may

have helped her through an emotionally difficult time. We know from her *Memories* and later letters that she had actually been quite hurt by Eugène, but in the article she wrote for the *Tribune des femmes* her humiliation becomes an experience of religious transcendence and a "great act" (2: 171). She says nothing of the venereal disease that she caught from Eugène and which caused her frequent miscarriages and certainly marred their sexual relationship. Nor does she dwell on Eugène's infidelity. She simply explains that she had never passionately loved him and claims that she had resolved soon after accepting Saint-Simonian principles to be only a sister to him, "because the most intimate relations had demanded . . . a constant dissimulation" (2: 174). It was only after discovering that Eugène loved another woman that she decided on their divorce; still, she declares it "an act carried out under the inspiration of a very elevated social feeling, in accordance with my very strong desire to emancipate women from the necessity of *falsehood, moral adultery,* and *legal prostitution in marriage* by my example" (2: 171).

For the next several years she remained alone. Once again her theory and practice coincided. She argued that it would "result in disorder" if women were to immediately practice "freedom without rules or limitations" and stressed the necessity of waiting for the woman to whom "we will grant the right to unite and separate us." Until then, women should "remain subject to Christian rules" (1: 63).

Désirée Veret, Reine Guindorf, and Isabelle Gobert agreed with her on this. Veret wrote that she would practice the "ancient moral law . . . until a new and less exclusive law replaces it" (1, no. 1: 6). Guindorf wrote that we women "are not *practicing* but simply *demanding* a *new moral law."* She reminded readers that the new morality "has not yet been formulated"—that it was up to the *"woman powerful* enough to make it accepted by others"; in the meantime, if women acted precipitously, they could be accused of acting "in [their] own personal interest" (1: 203). Isabelle Gobert promised "to conquer [her] passions and silence [her] desire until that time, perhaps still far off, when love will no longer be a crime for women" (1: 130).

There were other *Saint-Simoniennes,* however, who took a much more radical stance. Among the *femmes nouvelles,* Joséphine Milizet offered the clearest expression of the radical philosophy. She wrote that she had never believed in Christianity, and certainly never in its moral teachings. "To me who wants to love, it [Christianity] has said: do not love; to me who wants pleasure, it has commanded suffering; to me who values . . . the body as much as the spirit, it anathematized the former and exalted the latter." She wrote of her lover and her decision to "love without a marriage." "I do not want to bear the name [wife]. . . . Since I don't have any wealth to regulate, it would be nothing but a contract of sale" (1: 64–65).

There may have been other sexual radicals among the regular contributors to the *Tribune des femmes*, but it is hard to be certain. Jeanne (-Victoire) Deroin also refused "to marry under oppressive conditions." We have little information about her personal life, but we do know that she had a "friend" (the engineer Desroches) whom she later married. Although she claimed to prefer celibacy to slavery (1, no. 1: 2), perhaps she chose neither. Christine-Sophy complained about being confined "within the limits of Christian morality" and especially of the double standard (1, no. 4: 4). And a woman calling herself Unita (who may have been Désirée Veret), writing from London, also clearly stated her opposition to marriage (2: 153–57).

We should keep in mind that the sexual debate that we follow through the pages of the *Tribune des femmes* was enlivened by the views and experiences of other sexual radicals who attended the meetings that the authors described. Only some of these other women left a record of their views, however. The Saint-Simonian archives include a letter to Enfantin from Clorinde Rogé, written more than ten years after the schism and the publications of the *femmes nouvelles*, in which she recalls that she had asked her husband for "all her liberty" in order to be able "to act without lies or remorse." In this letter, Rogé confesses: "I threw myself onto this new path of the woman apostle without placing any barrier before my heart or my acts. . . . Never did woman seek with so much zeal the secret of the freedom of women!"[81] The archives also include a slender pamphlet, which was probably never published, Eugénie Soudet's *Une Parole de femme*, in which the author defends the radicals among the *Saint-Simoniennes*, proclaiming: "There are no laws in the heart."[82] It may be that even Aglaé Saint-Hilaire, a *Saint-Simonienne* whose letters seem critical of the new radicals, experimented with the new morality. Robert Carlisle cites a letter she wrote to Enfantin, informing him that she intended to "play the role of priestess" to one of his "sons."[83]

Pauline Roland's attempt to "put the words of the Father into practice" can be followed in greater detail than the efforts of most other *Saint-Simoniennes* because of the survival of the many letters that she wrote to Aglaé Saint-Hilaire and Charles Lambert.[84] When she first took an interest in Saint-Simonianism, she was expressing horror at Enfantin's new morality. She had promised the man she loved—who was married—to remain celibate forever. However, after several years among the Saint-Simonians in Paris, she changed her mind. She determined to take a lover (Adolphe Guéroult) and expressed this decision in words that gave no hint of what is clear in other letters—that her self-imposed celibacy had become truly burdensome for her. Rather she represented herself as a new priestess: "I have committed an act of the future . . . sacrificing myself to a work that I believed good and great—to make of a *child* a *man*."[85] She soon broke off the relationship with Guéroult and took up with Jean-François Aicard, with whom she remained "in a love without marriage" for twelve years.

Claire Démar was the most daring of the sexual radicals. Her ideas are spelled out in two theoretical treatises, a privately published pamphlet, *Appel d'une femme* (*Call of a Woman*), which was publicized in the *Tribune des femmes*, and *My Law of the Future*, a pamphlet published posthumously by Suzanne Voilquin.[86] We have very little information on Démar's life before she joined the Saint-Simonians, but it is evident from the personal information she discloses in these pamphlets that she was sexually experienced long before the Saint-Simonians encouraged women to explore love. In writing about her in the *Tribune des femmes*, Voilquin informs readers that Démar had some kind of compromised past. Voilquin refers to Démar's "courage to accept poverty and to cast away from herself a life of ease, but ambiguous and without respectability" (1: 205). This is, of course, Voilquin's own characterization; Démar herself expressed no particular concern for lost respectability. Still, there is some evidence that Voilquin was not entirely off the mark. In a letter to Enfantin, written in December 1832, Démar confessed that her parents were "immoral" and that in spite of "loathing . . . their world," she was exploited by it, "for I had a great need to love."[87] And in an 1833 letter to a Lyonnaise *Saint-Simonienne*, Démar wrote that she had "violently broken my ties to the Old World in order to join the Saint-Simonians, renouncing by this act of free will a life of luxury and idleness in order to regenerate myself in a life of work and industry."[88] Unfortunately, we have no further information that would clarify these titillating allusions.

In *My Law of the Future*, Démar challenged Saint-Simonians to consider "a liberty without limits" (50). She attacked Enfantin for assuming that people could be placed into categories (his "mobiles," "constants," and "priestly synthesizers"): "show me the point of *separation* between *constancy* and *inconstancy*, between *mobility* and *immobility*, the point where *one ends* and the *other begins*. In truth, my weak and myopic eyes could not distinguish it" (42). It was clear to her—and she makes it clear to us that she is writing from experience—that sexual relationships are often ephemeral. But this was not because a person has some categorically "mobile" nature; it was simply in the nature of relationships. If someone is open to sexual relationships in the first place, she or he is bound to experience relationships that feel potentially lifelong at the start but that turn out otherwise: "It often happens that, on the threshold of the bedroom, a devouring flame dies. For more than one great passion, the perfumed bed sheets have become a death shroud. Perhaps more than one woman who will read these lines came to the marriage-bed throbbing with feeling and desire, only to wake up in the morning frigid and icy" (37). Démar was convinced that relationships demanded "a *totally physical trial of the flesh by the flesh*" (ibid.) and that therefore any constraint on women's sexual freedom was unacceptable: "It is by proclaiming the *law of inconstancy* that woman will be liberated, and only that way" (49). Even something as seemingly innocuous as the Saint-Simonians' insistence on openness about sexual behaviors with their sort of public confession—"la publicité"—was intolerable: "Association will one day be based on a liberty without limits, surrounded by mystery. . . . May woman keep to herself the secrets of her heart; may she confess to God alone" (50).

Sexual radicals such as Démar and Roland lost the Saint-Simonian debate, however; in time, the more cautious views like Voilquin's prevailed. One hundred fifty years later, we are likely to regret this outcome: The sexual radicals experimented with many of the same views and behaviors that interest contemporary feminists and we therefore identify with them. The rise and fall of their sexual radicalism assumes special interest for us, helping us to think through the connections between sexual liberation and women's liberation and between radical sexual politics and radical feminism.

The Relationship between Context and Text. As we have seen, Saint-Simonian sexual radicalism was first conceived by men whose new discourse on sexual matters and family structure had an explanatory power for their own experiences. The male theorists borrowed from the discourses available to them—from the emerging workers' movement and its challenge to property; from the various family "reform" discourses from Right (Bonald) to Left (Fourier); from the romantic valorizing of emotion, love, and the erotic—to fashion a particular, and even original, set of views that addressed their concerns and fit their perceptions of reality. When they looked at sexual matters, they saw problems in the connections between property, especially inherited property, and family formation and structure that grew out of their own experience or the experience of other men of their background and generation. Similarly, their experiences with birth control promised to free them from some of the constraints of their lives.

Saint-Simonian women approached sexual issues with many of the concerns and perceptions of reality held by the men. Women, too, had experienced the consequences of the family/property connection, and there were many, especially among the unpropertied *femmes prolétaires*, who protested the way in which this connection affected their lives. They demanded that love alone should be the basis for forming personal unions—a demand to which women generally were very receptive; in fact, this principle was perhaps the most widely held and least debated feminist demand from this period. Like Saint-Simonian men, the women also responded to the demographic revolution, which was creating the possibility of exploring sexual pleasure as an end in itself. Roland, Démar, Rogé, Gobert, and Milizet were all frank in discussing sexual desire.

But if Saint-Simonian women and men shared certain views on sexual matters, they also diverged from one another in a number of important respects. To understand the meaning of these differences, we must examine the differences between the men's and women's lives. It was, for example, women, not men, who risked social ostracism by practicing a new morality; the double standard that pervaded conventional morality permitted society to forgive men's, but not women's, "mobility." The tight community that Saint-Simonians built could have shielded women from "the eyes of the world,"[89] but it was not, unfortunately, long-lasting; by 1833 the *maisons de famille* had been closed. Worse, the Saint-Simonian sexual radicals could not always count on the support of other Saint-Simonians. Claire Bazard, Pauline Roland, and Claire Démar all encountered disapproval for their extra- or nonmarital relationships or their radical views.[90]

This disapproval may explain Démar's rejection of "la publicité" in favor of "le mystère." Certainly she suffered acutely from lack of social support. Her letters are painful to read: "Thursday evening, I spent six hours in conversation at Voilquin's house. There were about fifty people present, men and women. I felt opposition from all sides. All the women rejected my opinions, and the men's reaction was about the same."[91] And later: "I suffer physically as well as morally . . . frankly, this world is killing me. Each time I close my eyes, I always see a pistol and already I can feel the bullet entering my head. This will be my end; yes, I am sure of it."[92] In August 1833, Démar turned her vision into reality. She committed suicide, shooting herself through the head.[93]

Some women may have felt it safe to transgress conventional morality only in distant places. A Saint-Simonian colony was founded in Louisiana. Julie Parsy emigrated there with Eugène Voilquin after his Saint-Simonian "divorce" from Suzanne. Suzanne's sister Adrienne, although legally married to Charles Mallard, also joined that colony with a new partner. Another group of Saint-Simonians lived in Egypt for several years in the mid-1830s. Suzanne Voilquin joined them in 1834 and—this is clear from her letters and from Charles Lambert's diaries—had sexual relationships there both with Lambert and with a Dr. Delong (father of her child who died after living only two weeks).[94] Other *Saint-Simoniennes* made their way to Egypt: Clorinde Rogé, in search of "more noise and brilliance";[95] Caroline Carbonnel, who eventually moved in with Enfantin; and Judith Grégoire, who lived with Lambert.

There can be no doubt that the pursuit of sexual pleasure was problematical for nineteenth-century women in ways that indicate further distinctions between their lives and the lives of men. Few of the women, even the radicals among them, are explicit in describing their sexual experiences, but there is enough intimate information in their writings and especially in their letters to conclude that their relative silence on sex was not due so much to modesty but to their ambivalence, if not distaste, for sex. Joséphine (-Félicité) Milizet makes clear that she rejoiced in a sexually active life, but she may have been exceptional. Claire Démar was, at best, ambivalent about sex. In her published brochures, she presents herself as a woman who is comfortable with sex, desirous of and familiar with its pleasures. But in a letter to Enfantin, she confessed that she "had dreamed that love was other than what I encountered. . . . The pleasures that men seek from women are not in the least necessary for my happiness. So I was forced to feign what I wasn't feeling. In sum, love itself was false for me, since I found it stripped of the poetic magic that my imagination had vested in it. Thus, I finished with it."[96]

We know also that Suzanne Voilquin was fearful of sex and distrustful of intimate relations with men. Reporting in the *Tribune des femmes* the repeated raping of a sixteen-year-old girl, she writes: "These events happen every day in our society" and the French legal system does not consider this a criminal act (1: 93). We read in her *Memories* that, at a similar age, she also had been terrorized by the threat of rape. The long walk home from work is described as especially harrowing: "I had a hideous fear of meeting on the way home one of those contemptible men who make it a game to accost young working girls and frighten them with their disgusting proposals" (57). For a time she and her sister lived on their own in vulnerable circumstances. One night, two drunkards almost broke down their door: " . . . isolated, unknown to any person in that house . . . we clutched each other and . . . prayed to God" (60). She was finally raped, not by a stranger, but by her fiancé, who insisted on a sexual relationship to which she was not yet ready to assent: tired of not having his way, "he became violent" (43). Years later she noted that this rape was the cause of her "mistrust of men" (112). Her relationship with Eugène Voilquin did little to dispel this distrust, for, as we have seen, he took no care to protect her from his venereal disease.

However ambivalently these *Saint-Simoniennes* experienced sexual relations with men, they do not seem to have conceived the possibility of sexual attachments with other women. Perhaps that is because these early examples of women exploring the meanings of sexuality for women occurred within such a decidedly heterosexual context. After all, the romantic movement that inspired their attention to "the flesh" was a couple-oriented movement, and the Saint-Simonian couple was male and female. We cannot even be certain that lesbian eroticism had been named for these particular women, although, already by the 1830s, the lesbian existed in French novels—as a kind of monster[97]—and in popular gossip (Marie-Antoinette had been "maligned" for her supposed lesbianism).[98] And we know, too, that lesbianism existed as a possibility for Flora Tristan. Although in the early 1830s she had not yet associated with these *Saint-Simoniennes*, by the mid-1830s she had begun to attend their meetings. It is therefore significant to this reconstruction of the history of women's sexual discourses to note that by 1839, at least, Tristan was aware of and open to lesbian eroticism. From London, writing to Olympe Chodzko, she ventures:

> You say that you love me . . . be careful . . . for a long time now I have had the desire to make love passionately to a woman—oh! how I have wished to be a man so that I might be *loved by a woman.*—I feel, dear Olympe,

that I have arrived at the point where the love of no man will satisfy me—that of a woman, perhaps? . . . But you will tell me that the attraction of the senses cannot exist between two persons of the same sex, that the passionate and exalted love of which you dream cannot be realized between women.—Yes and no. For me, love, I say *true love,* can exist only between similar souls, and it is easy to conceive that two women can love each other—the same for two men.[99]

This is, however, the only explicit expression of lesbian desire in Tristan's preserved correspondence. And since her letters to Chodzko turned cool once she had returned to Paris, one assumes that Chodzko did not encourage her.

Pauline Roland's letters bring our attention to yet another matter that is crucial for understanding these women's sexual lives and concerns— pregnancy and motherhood. She is explicit in her letters in discussing what she termed her "ardent nature," but this tendency was most pronounced (sometimes it even reached the level of obsession) when she was celibate. After she became sexually active, sexual desire virtually disappeared from her correspondence and was replaced with discussions about pregnancy and motherhood.

Many of her colleagues shared her concerns; the question of motherhood was a pressing one for all of these women. Although they had been touched by the demographic "revolution," clearly for them it was incomplete, the link between sexuality and reproduction not yet fully broken. To lessen the probability that they would become pregnant, women had to persuade their male partners to agree to use contraception—most commonly *coitus interruptus*—for these practices were almost exclusively controlled by men. Statistics on fertility rates for single and married women suggest that men were most likely to acquiesce in the use of contraception within marriage. The impact of the demographic revolution was felt less among single women who chose to "love without marriage." They were likely to face single motherhood.

In France of the 1830s, this was a common enough occurrence. The number of nonmarital births was actually increasing at the very moment that the overall birthrate was falling. Until 1750, "illegitimacy" had been essentially unknown in France; but by the mid-nineteenth century, it accounted for between 5 and 10 percent of all French births, and in certain areas, including Paris and Lyon where Saint-Simonians were active, illegitimacy accounted for between 30 and 50 percent of all births.[100] And although many of these births occurred within stable, long-term heterosexual unions, the status of mothers and children was insecure unless fathers chose to legally recognize their children (paternity claims were forbidden in French law).[101]

Among the working classes—the class of the *femmes nouvelles*—even the marital birthrate was higher than the overall birthrate, in part because higher infant mortality rates and the continuing custom of sending infants to a wet nurse in the countryside permitted subsequent pregnancies at shorter intervals. (Bourgeois women more commonly nursed their infants and therefore remained infertile for longer intervals.)[102]

The debates of Saint-Simonian women on sexuality were played out, then, against the background of an increasing possibility of illegitimacy and the more general inability of women to control their reproductive lives. Roland, for example, never mentioned birth control in her letters; we do not know what she thought of it or even if she understood how to practice it. She simply assumed she would get pregnant with Guéroult. It is certain that she never sorted out sexuality from reproduction—and that left the matter of illegitimate children. In time she had four, one with Guéroult and three—one of whom died in infancy—with Aicard. Her solution was to take sole responsibility for her children: "I alone was the *family* of the children."[103] She gave her surname to all of them: "I desire to be a mother—a *mother*, but with a mysterious paternity."[104] Hers was a strategy that was much discussed among the *Saint-Simoniennes*.[105]

The work of James de Laurence (James Lawrence) may have influenced the *Saint-Simoniennes'* approach to illegitimacy; both Démar (frequently, in *My Law of the Future*) and Voilquin (in the *Tribune des femmes*) cite his *Les Enfants de Dieu ou la réligion de Jésus réconcilié avec la philosophie* (*God's Children or Jesus' Religion Reconciled with Philosophy*), published in Paris in 1831,[106] in which he insists that the "family should be based on *maternity*; . . . that *paternity* is a *belief*, and *maternity alone* is a certainty" (*Tribune* 1: 190). The theme was echoed by nearly all the *femmes nouvelles*: "God entrusts the *certitude* of the family to the mother *alone*" (Suzanne, in *Tribune* 1: 127). "We should no longer torment ourselves for a doubtful title of paternity" ("A. I." [perhaps Angélique and Isabelle Gobert], in *Tribune* 1: 198). "Be off, Man!—and with you the principle of paternity!" ("Unita" [perhaps Désirée Veret], in *Tribune* 2: 155). Démar referred to paternity as "the monstrous power" and echoed the other *femmes nouvelles*: "No more paternity, always doubtful and impossible to prove. . . . All certitude and presumption of paternity meets its doom against my theory of trial and mystery. . . . A mother who has several lovers can suspect, but cannot demonstrate, who is the father of her child" (*My Law*, 58, 55).

It is important that we notice that the *femmes nouvelles* had introduced a new element into Saint-Simonian discourse. In movement rhetoric as originally constructed by Saint-Simonian men, "mother" sometimes represented any and all women and sometimes more specifically the priestess (or priestesses). "The family" was reconceptualized to include all of humanity—in Saint-Simonian discourse, this is the family "made social"—and "the mother" was the "tie" that binds us all: "All men are brothers and sisters [*sic*] united with each other through our motherhood" (Jeanne-Désirée, in *Tribune* 1: 70). Sometimes this motherhood is plural—*our* motherhood. Sometimes it is singular—"the Mother" who is "the Woman" and "the Messiah," destined to rule the new order alongside "the Father" (Enfantin). Saint-Simonian women rejoiced in this representation of woman as a social or religious mother. It appears as often in their writings as in the men's; in fact, this is the predominant way they discuss motherhood. Nevertheless, motherhood was not simply social or religious for these women. Unlike the men, they were forced by circumstances to explore a more concrete conception of motherhood that included pregnancy, birth, and childrearing.

Reine Guindorf and Claire Démar both considered new ways of raising children. Guindorf endorsed the Fourierists' proposals for a "new organization of the household" that called for children to be raised collectively. Démar proposed that women should head families and men raise children: "I truly have faith that the Saint-Simonian Religion will have power only when these two points are accepted by the Family."[107] Some months later, she was offering an alternative suggestion, that the child be taken "from the bosom of the *blood mother*" at birth "to the arms of the *social mother*."

> . . . woman must create a work and fulfill a function.—And how could she, if she is always condemned to spend a more or less long period of her life attending to the upbringing of one or more children? Either the work will be neglected and poorly done, or the child will be badly brought up and deprived of the care that his weakness and lengthy period of development demand. (*My Law*, 58–59)

She intended her conclusion—"no more maternity"—to shock; and it did.[108] Still, however outrageous her rhetoric, her point was well taken. In addressing sexual liberation, women would need to address not only issues of maternity but also those of economics.

In fact, just as Saint-Simonian women and men faced different sexual circumstances, so they lived under different—often starkly different— economic circumstances. As we have seen, the male theorists of Saint-Simonianism were generally from the business and professional classes and their ideas and beliefs reflected their material circumstances: industrialists, scientists, economic planners, and credit managers would replace the aristocracy of birth and inheritance in the new age. The expectations of the *femmes nouvelles* were never so lofty, not only because they were women but also because they were from a lower class than the movement's leaders. In France of the early 1830s, even ideologies of and about women did not challenge the assumption that the women of this class would work for wages.[109] However, in comparison to men, working-class women had to contend with far more restricted employment opportunities and wage-earning potential. Like Reine Guindorf, Désirée Veret, and the young Suzanne Voilquin, these women worked in the

garment-making trades, in the *ateliers* or small workshops (large industrial enterprises were extremely rare in Paris at this time), or, like
Voilquin after her divorce, as domestic servants. Only Roland was sufficiently well educated to find work we might think of as "professional"
(although certainly not in the strict sense of the term; the teaching
post—*sous-maîtresse sans appointement*—she held before her pregnancy
was marginal in that it was outside of any system that required certifica-
tion. After she became pregnant, she was able to support herself by
writing cultural and literary reviews and short, historical pieces for the
socialist *Encyclopédie nouvelle*—work that was also marginally professional).

Apparently most of these working-class women were able to earn
enough to support themselves. Unemployment, however, could be deva-
stating. When the young Voilquin lost her job in an embroidery workshop, the only employment she was able to find was piecework, which
she did at home for half her former wages. Démar was unemployed in
the early 1830s and had to borrow money and "sell [her] last two pieces
of furniture in order to pay [her] debts."[110] But for the most part, at least
at the height of their participation in the movement, the *femmes nouvelles*
seemed to manage economically. Paris was a rapidly growing city and
jobs for working-class women were plentiful. The *Saint-Simoniennes* were
young and had no dependents. Their involvement in the movement also
helped: they lived or took their meals in the *maisons de famille*; Guindorf
and Veret participated in the movement's apprenticeship programs;
Roland found freelance work through Saint-Simonian contacts; and, as
noted before, after Voilquin's divorce, Saint-Simonians saw to it that she
could support herself.

It is likely that if this financial independence had continued over a
number of years, these women would have come to believe that they
could indeed carry out the principle of being "alone the family." However, their independence did not outlast the collapse of the movement
and the closing of its "enterprises." Within a few years, Guindorf, Veret,
and Roland were all living with men. (Guindorf and Veret married;
Roland remained true to her original radical politics by living in a "free
union.") All continued to work, but none was the sole support of a
family. And although there is no evidence that they felt driven into relationships by economic considerations, we do know from Voilquin's and
Roland's later experiences that it was difficult, if not impossible, for
women of this time to construct an independent life, especially if they
had dependents.

In 1834, Voilquin left Paris to join some Saint-Simonians in Egypt and
to find work among them. She earned some money by doing their laundry; she also assisted a Dr. Dussap in caring for plague victims and then
took a course in midwifery. In 1837, she returned to Paris to take the

Faculté de Médicine examinations in midwifery. Once in Paris, she also studied homeopathy.

Voilquin had great difficulty supporting herself as a midwife—she evidently assisted at many births at no charge—and, finally, in 1839, left for St. Petersburg, Russia, where she had been able to arrange to practice her new profession. But life in Russia was lonely, the work uncertain, and the winters hard; in 1847, she returned to Paris, still struggling to support herself—and now, also, her elderly father and a young niece. She wrote to Enfantin for help in setting up an establishment for wet nurses and, later, in obtaining a tobacco concession in a railway station.[111] During the Revolution of 1848, recognizing that poor women were unable to pay midwives, she organized the Paris midwives to demand that the government put them on salary, but this effort failed. Her struggle for subsistence continued until 1873, when she accepted an annual pension provided by former Saint-Simonians.

Roland's struggle for subsistence began in 1847, when she left Aicard. She unsuccessfully sought a financial settlement that, she claimed, would have merely recouped the funds she had brought with her into their union, plus her earnings, minus half of the couple's joint expenses and debts. She then wrote several letters to Charles Lambert, first asking for his support, but then begging for it. She explained, "I can no longer sit down at my table and dispatch articles as I used to do. In any case, the field of journalism is so overcrowded, book-selling at such a low point, that no matter what I did, I probably could not find a job." Her circumstances were even more dire in 1851 and 1852 when she was imprisoned, first in Paris and later in Algeria, for her involvement in Revolutionary activities. Again she had to beg money from old friends. This time, she wrote to her former lover, Adolphe Guéroult, although in 1832, determining to "alone be the family," she had promised herself she would never do this. He did not, however, answer her letter.

Women who, like Guindorf and Veret, had been employed as seamstresses also saw their economic fortunes worsen in the 1840s. The restructuring of the garment-making industry from dressmaking and tailoring to ready-made production resulted in more jobs for women, but the new jobs were mostly unskilled and poorly paid. Garment-making was depressed in the 1840s, and although the industry later recovered, female wages never rose to a level that would support a woman on her own.

Young women who worked as servants could at least count on a subsistence living, which may explain why throughout the century domestic service was the fastest growing and largest employer of Paris working women. Often, according to Theresa McBride, servants' wages were supplemented by room and board and such perquisites as an annual bonus, cast-off clothes, and bribes paid them by shopkeepers for patronizing their stores. But these benefits came at the cost of fifteen- to eighteen-hour workdays, limited vacations, miserable accommodations, frequent mistreatment, and vulnerability to sexual exploitation.[112] Perhaps most significant was the servants' almost total lack of independence; this was not "liberating" work.

Given the life circumstances of French feminists that we have just reviewed, we should not be surprised to discover that sexual liberation ceased to be a priority for them. The stigma attached to free love for women was severe, birth control still too unreliable, the possibility for women's sexual pleasure too commonly limited by bodily injury incurred through childbirth or venereal disease, and women's ability to support themselves too fragile to sustain their sexual radicalism. Isolated once the Saint-Simonian community dispersed, the sexual radicals ceased to speak of a "love without limits." Although Voilquin had originally declared that women must *first* address the moral issue, a year later she was saying that "for the time being, the question of the relationship between the sexes must be a postponed question." She explained why: "Before being morally free," women must be "materially self-sufficient" (*Tribune* 1: 91). Guindorf repeated this theme in several articles: "As long as a man provides us our material needs, he can also demand that in exchange we submit to whatever he desires, and it is very difficult to speak freely when a woman does not have the means to live independently" (1: 204). Claire Démar wrote in a similar vein: "once woman is delivered and emancipated from the yoke of tutelage and protection of man, once she no longer receives from man her food or wages, once man no longer pays her the price of her body, then woman's existence and social position will derive only from her own ability and her own works" (*My Law*, 58). The inspiration for these important insights was not Saint-Simonian men. Their "inspiration" was from the meanings they gave to women's experiences.

While male Saint-Simonian theory did not offer the women a basis for their economic analyses, another contemporary movement was helpful in this regard. Reine Guindorf and Désirée Veret credited the Fourierists with providing them with a discourse for their economic politics. In his writings, Fourier had insisted that the right to work was as essential for women and children as for men. In proposing the collectivizing of households, Fourier sought to create a system that would not only add variety to people's intimate lives but that also would liberate women from private domestic responsibilities, enabling them to participate in every social and economic function, "even medicine and teaching."[113] Fourier even proposed a kind of "affirmative action" plan: if it were to happen that one or the other sex came to dominate some category of work, one-eighth of the jobs would be set aside for the other. In 1832, in the aftermath of the Saint-Simonian debacle, the followers of Fourier (who called themselves "associationists") were stressing these economic aspects of their master's teachings and avoiding any mention of sexuality. By the fall of that year, this seems to have suited the *femmes nouvelles;* they placed the Fourierist slogan, "Liberty for women, liberty for the people through a new organization of the household and industry," on their masthead and declared that Fourier's theories were "the most complete of any that have yet appeared . . . " (*Tribune* 1: 33, 38–39).

It is instructive to note the very different kinds of influences that Fourier exerted on Saint-Simonian men and women. To Enfantin, Fourier provided a discourse for sexual liberation; to the *femmes nouvelles,* he provided a discourse for economic liberation. In part, men and women had different interpretations of Fourier because Enfantin had actually read his works, while the women interacted only with his followers at a point when they were downplaying his sexual theories. But in part the differences occurred because the men and the women each read or heard that which best explained their perception of reality.

It fell to the Saint-Simonian women, then, to work out their own meaning of women's liberation. For Saint-Simonian men, the concept had been limited to women's "moral" liberation; but for the women, "liberation" came to be "triple"—"moral, intellectual, and material" (Suzanne, in *Tribune* 1: 62). We have already examined how the women viewed the "moral" and economic aspects of liberation; the concern for intellectual freedom was introduced into their discourse somewhat later. Beginning in late 1833, questions of intellectual emancipation took up more and more space in the journal. That winter, a series of conferences was held to discuss women's education and the *Tribune des femmes* devoted most of its second volume year to covering its various reports and speeches. The occasion for all of this attention to women's education was the general political discussion of education that had been prompted by the legislature's consideration of a law to establish public elementary schools. The *femmes nouvelles* were angry that the law made no mention of female education except to say that "girls schools can be founded if there is a need."[114] The editors exclaimed: "If there is a need! Do not women everywhere need an education?" Christine-Sophie declared: "the first and most important question is the question of education" (1: 44). Marie-Reine Guindorf linked the intellectual issue—as she had the sexual issue—to economic aspirations. In calling for a "complete reform" in women's education, she complained that their lack of a serious education closed scientific careers to them (1: 114; repeated 1: 204).

Again, the *Saint-Simoniennes* were as much provoked by the social barriers they had encountered as inspired by the discourses available to them. None of the *femmes nouvelles* had had much of a formal education. Voilquin, who had been taught to read only the most basic prayers, had improved her skill by reading newspapers to her father. Roland had been privately tutored by a local boys *lycée* teacher. Jeanne Deroin was entirely self-taught: In the 1840s, she failed the primary school teaching certificate examination twice—because she could not write in cursive or do simple arithmetic—before finally passing.

As the women began to address the practical issues associated with education and economic self-sufficiency, their rhetoric began to change from the utopian and visionary, becoming more grounded in material concerns. The emancipation of women will be when "their means of existence will no longer depend on their fathers or their husbands" (Angélique and Christine-Sophy, 1: 95); when a new organization of the household will permit them to devote "themselves to all the careers for which they might have talent" (Guindorf, 1: 204); when they will earn better wages ("as soon as it is noticed that we can do a job, the wages there are lowered" [Marie-Reine, 1: 113]); when women will have the same property rights as men (Marie-Reine, 1: 114); and when the law will grant them the right to enter any profession "that suits [them] without requiring their husband's authorization" (ibid.). Voilquin protested the Civil Code—"civilization's masterpiece . . . that men impose upon us"—and drew readers' attention to its "arbitrary and depraved" character. Married women are enslaved by Article 213—"The wife must obey her husband"—and Article 214—"The wife is *obligated* . . . to live with the husband, and to follow him wherever he judges it appropriate to live." The laws are even more "malevolent" for mothers: "(Art. 373): The *father* alone exercises [parental] authority over his children." She cried out in frustration: "What then is the mother in the family? *Everything*; her influence is immense. And her rights? *None*. O, justice of men!" (1: 123–25).

The women were energized to undertake some practical activity, to turn theory into practice. Angélique and Sophie-Caroline proposed a house of "artists' and workers' association, where young girls . . . and widows whose husbands have died or are absent . . . [would find] safe asylum from poverty, hunger, men's brutality and seductions, or the lure of gold that commands such power over those who suffer from cold, thirst, and hunger." Their proposal, detailed in the *Tribune des femmes* (1: 92–98), with a full estimate of income expected from the women's pooled earnings and of expenses, never came to fruition. They did, however, organize the Society for Popular Instruction to teach poor women; Reine Guindorf gave up her editorial work for the *Tribune des femmes* to devote three to four nights a week to this activity. The school, founded in 1832, was still in existence in April 1834 when Voilquin referred to it in the journal's final issue (2: 182).

A Feminist Practice. In becoming more oriented to the practical, Saint-Simonian feminists were in some sense following the same path as the men, who, at least until 1832, had engaged in concrete activities.[115] Once again, however, there was a difference—one about which the women were increasingly self-conscious. The difference was in the process that the women used to create their practice. Gradually that process was becoming more and more separatist and egalitarian, and as those changes unfolded, the meaning of the Saint-Simonian ideal represented in the word "association" was becoming subject to challenge.

To Enfantin, association had meant women and men—and workers and employers—working together in harmony; but, as we have seen, his "association" was by no means to be a democratic collective. People would be classified according to their "capacities," and harmony would be achieved because those with special talents for leadership would direct the social order.

Furthermore, sex was no disqualifier for leadership in the Saint-Simonian association. In addition to artists, poets, "priests," and technocrats, Saint-Simonian theorists had identified women as potential leaders. And women's particular capacity for "sentiment" was, of course, especially valued in the most religious phase of the movement's history. But women who were encouraged by their elevation in the Saint-Simonian vision of a new world order were frequently disappointed with the actual practice of Saint-Simonian internal politics. Working-class women were the most disappointed; although one's sex did not *theoretically* disqualify one for leadership, class was another matter—*le degré des industriels* was never intended to be a "directing" one. *Saint-Simoniennes* struggled against a devaluation that they sensed but that the men denied. In so doing, they not only exposed the hypocrisy of Saint-Simonian men's behavior toward them but also that the men's conceptualization of "association" was fundamentally flawed.

To better understand the struggles of the women, we should review an aspect of the Saint-Simonian story that we have thus far only touched on—the relationship of women to its leadership structure. Before late 1831, some women had been integrated into the Saint-Simonian hierarchy, but not without a contest. In October 1830, Enfantin and Bazard had proposed to Claire Bazard—the "mother" of the increasing number of Saint-Simonian "daughters"—that she have a special seat in the new meeting hall that would honor her position. She demanded instead that she be integrated into the all-male hierarchy and seated among them on the dais:

Ah! enough, my Fathers, enough of these temporary elevations from which we always fall back so painfully; enough of these illusory distinctions that have never brought us closer to you and have always distanced us further from our sisters. . . . I would see [my brothers] all gathered together, all at your side. . . . Is it not there [at your side] that you should be able to offer me to the incredulous eyes of men? . . . [T]hrough my presence in your midst have the women become used to seeing me thus in order to make them desire to join me up there soon.[116]

Bazard's demand was granted, and in early 1831, when the hierarchy was reorganized, other women joined her. Fournel and Saint-Hilaire were named to the "superior degree," four other women were named to the second degree, and five to the third, bringing the number of women represented in the hierarchy to twelve out of a total of seventy-nine—a number too small, however, to change the male-dominated character of the Saint-Simonian movement.

Furthermore, while women shared the directorships of all the "practical enterprises," they were marginalized in "religious" work. In Paris, no woman ever became a *prédicateur*, responsible for an "exposition of the doctrine" at a Sunday ceremony. Although a letter from Claire Bazard to Jules Resseguier suggested that Eugénie Niboyet was being considered for that office, the appointment never materialized.[117] (Niboyet did become codirector of the *degré des industriels* for the fourth *arrondissement*.) In 1833, Louise Crouzat wrote to Claire Démar that she had preached in a small town near Lyon but lamented that she was "the only *femme Saint-Simonienne* . . . from Lyon who has preached ['done a teaching'] to men." Démar responded that the problem was even more pronounced in Paris: "You are the first and only woman, not only in Lyon, but also in Paris, who has preached to *men!*"[118]

One could expect, then, that the Saint-Simonian women, especially the more radical among them, would have cried out in protest when, at the November 1831 meeting, Enfantin dismissed women from the hierarchy and announced "our apostolate which is *the call of the Woman* is an apostolate of men."[119] Enfantin's pronouncement surely represented a most extreme example of practice contradicting theory: although only a woman could complete the doctrine, there would "NO LONGER [be] ANY WOMEN IN THE DEGREES OF THE HIERARCHY."[120]

But women did not object: Those most affected had either resigned the movement over Enfantin's sexual views (Bazard, Fournel, Niboyet) or, like Saint-Hilaire, were unpracticed in questioning Enfantin's pronouncements. And *femmes prolétaires* actually welcomed this strange turn of events. Voilquin sheds light on their reaction, reminding us that none of these women had been in the hierarchy in the first place: "If . . . Father Enfantin had not . . . dissolved the female hierarchy, I would have remained forever in the preparatory degree" (*Memories*, 81). She re-presents Enfantin's directive as an empowering one: He had placed women in a "state" or "level" of equality (ibid; also *Tribune* 1: 107). All women—and for the first time this would include *femmes prolétaires*—were "called to speak."

The acquiescence of the *Saint-Simoniennes* was not, however, long-lasting. Following Enfantin's declaration, the Saint-Simonian "family" in Paris was governed by an all-male general assembly. Within a year, Voilquin was protesting this arrangement and demanding that women who, like the *femmes nouvelles*, had formed some kind of group "under the Saint-Simonian inspiration" participate in the assembly's deliberations and have a role in the initiation ceremonies. Voilquin also proposed new governing structures—a mixed-sex "court of justice" to judge injuries against Enfantin, the male disciples, and "the people"; and a "court of love," presided over exclusively by women, which would judge all injuries committed against them (*Tribune* 1: 99–102).

But the men were evidently uninterested in the women's demands. Voilquin commented that they feared "the revolution that has taken place. . . . They think they see a tendency toward usurpation on our part when we dare to demonstrate our *will*. In general, men, even somewhat those in the [Saint-Simonian] family, act toward women the way governments act toward the people; they fear us and do not yet *love* us" (*Tribune* 1: 107).

It is possible to view the *Saint-Simoniennes'* separatist activities, as some Saint-Simonian women did, as encouraged by the men. Voilquin, for example, credits Enfantin for encouraging "the uttering of our word" (*Tribune* 1: 220). However, this interpretation almost certainly gives too much credit to men who in all likelihood believed that the women would—or could—do little without them and/or seemed fearful of the women's initiatives. But regardless of whether the source of the new feminism was the encouragement the women felt in Saint-Simonian doctrine or the anger they felt in Saint-Simonian men, it is clear the experience of being in the movement had energized them. The exposure to a community committed to change made inactivity unthinkable.

They presented their decision to create "women-only spaces" as a well-thought-out strategy to attract more women to the movement. Women would feel most comfortable talking about personal matters such as sex and morals in meetings that were for women only, or writing "according to our heart" (*Tribune* 1, no. 1: 7) in a journal "edited entirely by women" (1: 99). The poverty of women's education even more so than their modesty, said Voilquin, made them timid: "under the charm of the brilliant theories that these gentlemen have made . . . , [the women] dare not make their weak and timid voices heard" (1: 106). The journal's editors promised to take into account the level of women's education: "We will hold less to science and the elegance of style than to frankness of thought. For what we want above all is for women to shake off the state of restraint and discomfort in which society holds them, and to dare to say from the complete sincerity of their heart what they foresee and want for the future" (1, no. 1: 7).

But while the call for separatism was couched in terms of helping women feel comfortable within the movement, it actually encompassed a broader goal: the creation of an autonomous women's movement. Voilquin, complaining that women are too much "under the influence or will of men," called upon women "alone" "to resolve all questions; . . . in a religion that is completely about *love*, the most *loving* becomes the most capable" (1: 106–107). Désirée Veret obviously agreed. In October 1832, she was writing that women should "rid themselves of their overly great preoccupation with Saint-Simonianism which prevents them from having their own ideas."[121]

In November, Veret announced she would no longer call herself a Saint-Simonian. She claimed that this decision was not based on opposition to the Saint-Simonians—"they have foreseen humanity's future better than anyone"—but that she had "different work to carry out. For me, all social questions depend on the freedom of women; it will determine them all. It is therefore . . . to the banner of the *femmes nouvelles* that I will relate everything I am doing for our emancipation" (1: 69). Joséphine Milizet underscored the new direction that the *femmes nouvelles* had taken: "Women alone will say what freedom they want. . . . Men have advised, directed, and dominated us long enough. It is now up to us to advance along the path of progress without tutelage" (1: 45–46). Voilquin went even further, asking men to defer to the women's initiatives: "temporarily the action of man [should be regarded] as secondary to that of woman" (1: 254).

Although the women did not intend any break with the Saint-Simonian movement, one was in fact occurring. The "universal association of women and men" collapsed in the clash of women's and men's interests. One *Saint-Simonienne* complained that Saint-Simonian men wished that women were "free from obeying our parents, free from the duties imposed on us by religion and society's opinion . . . [but] slaves to your desires. . . . When we want to break away from the slavery imposed on us . . . particularly by you . . . you invoke immorality. You say that we are lost, that we have lost our morals. . . . Is it because we are opposed to your exploitation?" (Joséphine-Félicité, 1: 127–28). Although Enfantin had declared that the emancipation of women would be the work of "the couple, male and female," women were coming to the realization that they would have to "work for our liberty by ourselves" (1: 46).

Their "association" would be separatist and egalitarian; it would also be inclusive. The *Tribune des femmes* pledged itself to a new openness. "We call to all women, whatever their status, religion, or views" (1, no. 1: 7). "We call on all women to participate. In our hearts, we exclude no one and no one will be rejected" (1: 62). "We [who are] women Saint-Simonians . . . turn away no one, but, on the contrary, call . . . " (1: 130). The decision to change the name of the journal of the *femmes nouvelles* from *Apostolat des femmes* to *Tribune des femmes* was intended to encourage more women who were not Saint-Simonian to become contributors. ("Several ladies have refused to write in this newspaper, because the title *Apostolate* it bore signified a solidarity that they could not accept . . . we have decided that in the future this little paper will be entitled *Tribune des femmes*. A *free* place will be accorded to each opinion and each woman's thought. With us, no censorship. Under this new format we call upon women . . . " [1: 169–70].)

There was no model for "this new format." Saint-Simonian men had always insisted on a unified belief system; disagreement, which was equated with "antagonism," was not tolerated, with the result that divisive issues were settled only by schisms. Beginning with this legacy, the women, not surprisingly, "dream[ed] of a common language."[122] "Our goal is association" (1, no. 1: 7), to make "trivial rivalries" (1: 42; also 1: 92) disappear; "let us form a *unity* of sentiments" (1: 138). Again: "our strength is in Association . . . forget all that divides us . . . let us form a single corps having *all* the *same desire*, the *same goal*" (1: 199).

The response to their call, however, was not a common language, but a cacophony of voices. There were meetings almost every night—small discussion groups, "balls" (Démar organized three), and "general" meetings of the Saint-Simonian family. Encouraged to express themselves, women did not resolve their disagreements; on the contrary.

Voilquin represented her yearnings for resolution and unity in the figure of "the Mother" (the "Woman" "called" by Enfantin): "The WOMAN ELECTED by God will bring forth the *general* thought . . . this woman will be the MOTHER!" (1: 235). She was unreserved in her expression: "My heart *desires* her, my faith *hopes* for her and *waits* for her" (1: 235); "Alas! The French people have a queen, but women have no mother!" (1: 253). Still, there is a sense in which Voilquin's "mother" seems to be more a means to an end than a definitive figure. Her function is to sustain tolerance in the women's debates: "Until a sublime woman comes . . . let us all act according to our own conscience, but without reprobation or anathema" (2: 183).

A contributor, writing from London, who signed herself "Unita, a new mother," but who may have been Désirée Veret, went a step further: "The *Mother* . . . is not one woman; she is all women" (2: 153). While these were not the terms Suzanne Voilquin used to express herself, they may well have captured her true sentiments. In her *Memories*, written decades later, Voilquin claimed that she "only saw the 'call' as a symbol":

> Women should first reveal themselves to each other, outside the sphere of masculine influence, through a show of their feelings or the acts of their free will. . . . These women will seek each other out in the natural course of things so that they may create among themselves a council where each of them can contribute her stone to the moral edifice of the future. It is this *completely feminine* feeling that will create what the Saint-Simonians call the Mother. (*Memories*, 187)

Saint-Simonian women were, in other words, working toward an agreement to disagree. "Every woman . . . must act and . . . from the multiplicity of these acts, we will rise to the unity of their principle. GOD is ONE and MANY at the same time" (*Tribune* 2: 183). In the debate on sexuality, for example, they reached no consensus but declared their "association" nonetheless. Voilquin, writing for the women "who would wait," suggested they wear a deep violet-colored ribbon (*le ruban dahlia*); Joséphine-Félicité proposed a flame-colored ribbon (*le ruban ponceau*) for the women who would "love without marriage." And they promised each other "respect and silence": "The femme nouvelle does not make herself into a judge of her companions; it is not for us to praise or blame" (1: 63–64).

Saint-Simonian women never reconstituted a hierarchy. In the months immediately following their dismissal from the integrated hierarchy, some of the bourgeois women who had been leaders evidently tried to impose their authority on the other *Saint-Simoniennes*. Voilquin reported that Saint-Hilaire tried to organize the Paris women in a hierarchy: "this lady . . . had the vexing idea of placing herself in our midst as a supreme being, claiming the name of *Mother*, and of wanting to establish a hierarchy among us. . . . " Voilquin objected: "My heart and independent spirit rejected . . . these pretensions" (*Memories*, 89). In Lyon, Clorinde Rogé apparently attempted a similar assumption of power. Louise Crouzat, writing to Démar, reported that she had been impressed by Rogé's closeness to Enfantin and urged the Lyonnaise women to acknowledge her as their leader, but then "I realized that Mlle Rogé was only telling us that which I had known for a long time and was not helping us to progress at all. I announced that I no longer acknowledged her as a leader because I felt in myself the strength and the power to go forward and that I did not want to regress."[123] Crouzat's words point to what was happening in the second phase of Saint-Simonianism: The *Saint-Simoniennes* were creating a distinctive political movement, at once separatist and collective.

Moreover, as the women's movement unfolded, it developed not only a feminist agenda but also a concern for class issues. We have already examined some aspects of this concern in noting the *Saint-Simoniennes'* practical interests and activities—their instructional program or their proposed home for single women. These concerns stand in contrast to those of the Saint-Simonian men who, after 1832, seem to have been frightened not only into celibacy but also into avoiding workers' projects.[124] Their plans now were for railroads, canals, and banks. At some level, of course, the men's movement had never been a "workers' movement," although its concern for workers' interests and compassion for their poverty were extraordinarily advanced for the times. But the women were indeed building a workers' as well as a feminist movement. As we turn to the issue of how *Saint-Simoniennes* regarded differences among women, we shall also be tracing this development.

THE DIFFERENCES AMONG WOMEN

Perhaps the most original aspect of the politics of the *femmes nouvelles* lay in their blending of sex and class analysis. Saint-Simonian men had, of course, set forth analyses of both sex and class, but in their theory only men were "classed." Women, on the other hand, were a uniform category, and what mattered to Saint-Simonian men about them were their differences from men. The *femmes nouvelles* likewise thought, spoke, and wrote about the differences between women and men. They felt themselves empowered by a theory that valorized these differences because it valorized the particularity of women.

Still, from the very first, it was clear that the *femmes nouvelles* understood that "woman" was not one, and that the unity of women was more aspiration than reality. Women were divided by economic class into rich and poor and were divided by "moral" class into "submissive slaves" and "rebellious slaves" ("never free") (*Tribune* 1, no. 1: 3) or into married woman and prostitute (both "sold"). The first article of the first issue of the *Tribune des femmes* included a plea to "privileged" women: "Let us no longer form two camps, one of women of the popular classes, and another of women of the privileged classes. Let our common interest bind us together" (1, no. 1: 2). The second article recognized "two . . . opposed camps, one of which is as exclusive in its regularity as the other in its disorder," and promised that "we will use all of our conciliatory power to end the antagonism between them and to make them appreciate each other's virtues and valor, until their mutual progress allows them, not to form a single and identical camp, but to be seated together in the new temple and be united by the same love, desire, and harmonization of personal interest in the social interest" (1, no. 1: 6).

This was not, however, the same kind of class analysis that Saint-Simonian men presented in their "science of society."[125] In the late 1820s and early 1830s when class analysis was still new, the meanings of class were very much in flux, of course; but for the middle-class men, who were the movement's ideologues, "class" was at least linked to work and work was always linked to men. Sometimes classes were designated as simply "producers" (or *industriels*), in which they included capitalists and workers alike, and *oisifs* (both the unemployed and—of particular concern to Saint-Simonian economists—holders of "unproductive" wealth, that is, property not invested in ways that would encourage industrial growth). Sometimes they spoke of the "directing" class, in which they included bankers, engineers, and entrepreneurs, and "the most numerous class" or workers. Saint-Simonian men had much to say about these groups—their role in the social and economic order, their place in the "new order." But women found it hard to locate themselves in these analyses.

Femmes nouvelles do tell us that they also were *workers*, oftentimes identifying themselves by their actual trade (e.g., needlework), sometimes more generally as "proletarian women." According to Judith A. DeGroat, who has examined women's work identity in Paris of the 1830s, this was not uncommon: Women in the manufacturing trades typically identified themselves by their work. Many even designated their particular skill: among shoemakers, for example, women identified themselves as *bordeuses* or *joineuses* or *cordeuses*. Even among homeworkers in the shoe trades, DeGroat found women who gave their occupations as "edger" and "piercer."[126] And Joan Scott reminds us that working-class men, too, recognized that women "worked."[127] The new class analysis, then, was a decidedly bourgeois analysis, reproducing the ideology of the idealized bourgeois family in which only men "worked."

Femmes nouvelles not only identified as workers; they also contested their absence from the discourses of class. Nonetheless, when they undertook a key task of class analysis—defining their status in terms of "the other"—they identified themselves as "poor women" and the "others" as "women of the privileged classes" or "wives and daughters of the rich." In part, their attempt to create a woman-centered analysis discouraged them from identifying themselves, *in their class analyses*, as workers. Had they viewed themselves primarily as workers, they would have defined the "others" not as women of wealth but as *employers*—in other words as men. They also might have been prompted by the class analysis of the male Saint-Simonians to probe the employee/employer relationship of domestic servant and household mistress. But since they did not pursue these lines of analysis, their theories of class focused on economic relationships that were less directly exploitative and assumed a less oppositional cast than those of their male counterparts.

One article in the *Tribune des femmes* comes close to describing a relationship that was oppositional, although not directly exploitative. Suzanne had observed two women—one poor and one rich—and from their brief interchange fashions a drama of "two mothers." They encounter one another in front of a commercial establishment: the rich woman descends from her carriage and prepares to enter the store. The poor woman approaches her, withdraws, and then moves forward again, entreatingly. The rich woman dismisses her. Suzanne imagines their motives, their character, even what actually transpired between them—that they are both mothers, that the poor woman lives with her children in an unheated room, and that she assumes a mother, however rich, will have compassion for her. "You, mother, have not deigned to help end the sorrows of a mother." Suzanne laments that the rich, "whose souls are too narrow to understand [the concept of] association," will not even "practice philanthropy." "Let me remind you, rich woman: to each according to their works."[128]

Such bitterness was not unusual but did not lead to a theory of class struggle. We read of "privileged women . . . puffed up with self-importance . . . [who] do not understand the cries of distress of their suffering companions. . . . They know not at all how to extend a helping hand" (1: 94). But the logic of a Saint-Simonian politics of association, which, as we have seen, had assumed a particularly collective spirit among its female followers, directed them away from "antagonism." Rather, they reinterpreted rich women's lives in ways that could create a commonality of interest. "A stock market reversal, a fire, a bankruptcy—one of those strokes of fate which reoccur so frequently—could throw [rich] women rudely off their silken sofas, out onto the streets. . . . I would like the wives and daughters of the wealthy to imagine themselves for a moment in such a predicament" (1: 94). Or: "Women of the privileged class . . . you reign, but your reign is of short duration and ends with the ball. Back in your own home, you become slaves again; you return to find a master who makes you feel his power" (1, no. 1: 2). Surely, then, rich women would join the common struggle: "I strongly believe that one day all women will feel their solidarity and that those who are most favored by their birth and fortune, touched by the fate of our less fortunate clients, will join with us proletarian women" (1: 36).

But to the *Saint-Simoniennes*, the differences among women were not only economic. They held that the conventional (or "Christian") moral order did as much to divide women from one another as did "fortune." Their interest in these two strains of difference converged in the figure of the prostitute, who represented both class and sex oppression and is featured prominently in their writings.

The focus on the prostitute was not wholly motivated by theoretical concerns, however. Vulnerable themselves to the prejudice that women of their class, especially those who lived independently, were casual prostitutes or "kept" by a man, the *femmes nouvelles* had a personal stake in creating meanings for the nature and causes of prostitution.[129] The emotional tones of their explanations were mixed. At times, perhaps somewhat defensively, the *femmes nouvelles* distanced themselves from the prostitute. (Jeanne-)Désirée Veret, for example, described prostitutes as "unfortunates who got carried away," not like "us who had the force to resist."[130] But Veret refused to advance a simplistic theory of individual responsibility to explain the prostitutes' plight. The culprits were "circumstances" or poverty or men: "wretchedly unhappy [prostitutes] have been lost by . . . *husbands* . . . *brothers* . . . *sons*" (1, no. 2: 2).

In fact, the *Saint-Simoniennes* were moving toward a general rethinking of sharply defined moral categories. Démar, fearing that dualisms result inevitably in the domination of one over the other, argued that Enfantin's system of "constants" and "mobiles" would deteriorate into a morality of good and bad—"and soon we will have . . . original sin."[131]

This rejection of easy dualisms surfaced in other challenges to prevalent assumptions. The *femmes nouvelles* raised questions about the conventional "good woman/bad woman" stereotypes, particularly when they permitted the automatic equating of the "bad woman" with the "poor woman." The *Saint-Simoniennes*, for example, condemned "disorder"—a state that was represented both by prostitution, presumably implicating poor women, and by adultery, implicating the rich. Or prostitution was compared to marriage, still typically arranged among the bourgeoisie: "[I] wanted neither to be prostituted or sold," explained Isabelle Gobert (1: 130), while Claire Démar defined marriage as legal prostitution.[132]

All women, then, not just poor women, were vulnerable to prostitution. Christine-Sophie spelled out this belief by, in essence, deconstructing the category of "prostitute." Although it was claimed that there were 35,000 prostitutes in Paris, she wrote, this number included only those registered by the police. But prostitution, she continued, was everywhere. An unfortunate girl turns to prostitution "for a piece of bread . . . [to bring] home to her old, sick mother" because her wages are insufficient. Young, beautiful, ambitious, pleasure-seeking women from families without fortune or rank prostituted themselves simply to satisfy their desires for "glory." And among the privileged classes, women are sold into marriages, "condemned to bestow [her] caresses on a stranger whom [she doesn't] know and who, perhaps, will never be able to really understand [her]." And even the "noble daughter of the king . . . slave of some diplomats" is a prostitute (1, no. 3: 2–4).

Thus, in analyzing how women differed from one another, the *femmes nouvelles* found that women were, despite apparent distinctions, fundamentally united in their subjugation to sex oppression. And while there seemed to be possibilities for healing the breach between rich and poor women, it was nevertheless true that many women suffered from economic oppression. The answer to this dual oppression would have to be a politics that challenged both of its sources, those of class and those of sex. "Emancipation for the people; emancipation for woman" (1: 47). Workers have a stake in women's liberation; women have a stake in workers' liberation: "Only by emancipating woman will we emancipate the worker" (1: 37). "Women, understand this well: Our fate is always improved with that of the people."[133]

It was a challenge, however, to bring together a workers' politics and a women's politics into a unified movement. The women had no precedent to turn to in trying to meet this challenge. In Saint-Simonian discourse, the two kinds of politics were distinct. Women's emancipation required a new moral order; workers' emancipation required a reorganization of the economy. *Femmes nouvelles* recognized the insufficiency of Enfantin's vision: women were empowered "religiously," raised up from the damnation of original sin; but the problem of their dependency on men had not been addressed. Workers were promised that the productive investment of wealth that would spur industrial growth would provide them with sufficient work at sufficient wages to lift them out of poverty; the problem of women's poverty was ignored. The abolition of inheritance would usher in a new meritocratic order that would provide workers the opportunity to enter the "directing classes"; opportunities for women in the new order were undefined. Thus *femmes nouvelles* were in a position of double jeopardy—as women, dependent still on men; as workers, disempowered even within the Saint-Simonian new world order.

It is clear from the women's discourse that they did not easily challenge the construction of women and workers into differentiated social categories. Revolutionary and socialist discourses, in constructing a "people's" identity and a "workers' " identity that excluded women, hindered the development of women's politics grounded in their identity as workers. Only as the feminism of the *Saint-Simoniennes* evolved were there signs that at least a few of the women were moving beyond the discourses available to them. Guindorf's and Veret's repeated declarations of their work status in passages that are intended to have political significance can be seen as a beginning in the construction of women's political identity as workers and "women proletarians." Démar also broke some new ground. In addressing her *Appel d'une femme* (*Call of a Woman*) to "the people," she addressed "the *women* like . . . the *men*, for it is common to forget to mention women when speaking of the people—the people of which women make up the largest part."[134]

Reine Guindorf took another tack: not so much challenging prevailing views that excluded women from the class of workers, but offering a different vision for the future. In Fourierist plans for "reorganizing the household and industry," she located the potential for "reconciling the material interests of the people and women" (2: 167). Women's emancipation required that they be workers; the reorganization of the household and of industry was in their material interest, for this change alone would permit them careers and independence from men. "If we respond to women who plead for a remedy for their sufferings and those of children, for women often suffer more for their children than for themselves, by saying to them: 'demand your moral freedom,' do we not resemble those who tell the people when they are hungry: 'demand your political rights,' as if those rights could satisfy them and reorganize their work? Both women and the people need 'material emancipation' *and* 'social emancipation' . . . one cannot be established without the other" (1: 204–205). Angélique and Caroline, echoing Guindorf's views, declared that "association is the only means to emancipate women and men at the same time." Their proposed "artists' and workers' home" would emancipate "women, because their means of existence will no longer depend on their fathers or their husbands; [and] men, because they will be able to devote themselves more freely to their vocation, knowing that their daughters and wives will no longer depend on them for food" (1: 95).

In their new self-awareness, these women not only recognized their difference from men (this was their legacy from earlier Saint-Simonian theory), not only saw the significance of that difference to practice (this is their original contribution to Saint-Simonian theory), but, finally—and again, this is original—understood their difference from bourgeois women, including those of the former Saint-Simonian hierarchy.

CONCLUSION

The Denouement

After 1834, feminist activism in Paris became less visible. The *Tribune des femmes* ceased publication in the spring of that year. All of the Saint-Simonian collective ventures, including the men's retreat at Ménilmontant, had collapsed. Claire Démar was dead. Many of the other Saint-Simonian feminists had left France. Désirée Veret was in London, Clorinde Rogé and Cécile Fournel in Egypt.

Voilquin left in June, traveling slowly south to visit with Saint-Simonians along the way, before also embarking for Egypt. Although she went there for "practical" purposes, it is likely that she expected to be able to continue some kind of "apostolic" work among Egypt's fairly substantial Saint-Simonian community. But from her account of her years in Egypt in her *Memories* and also from what can be pieced together from her unpublished letters, it seems that in this respect, at least, the Egyptian years were a disappointment to her. Clearly, a collective—of a kind that did not exist in Egypt—was necessary to sustain women's feminist activity.

The feminists who remained in Paris continued to meet. They became close to the associationists, the followers of Fourier, and found among them encouragement for their aspirations for economic independence. But, as noted earlier, associationists became timid after the Saint-Simonian tangle with the law and were soon downplaying not only a radical sexual politics but, more generally, a politics of women's independence.

The *femmes prolétaires* were still in contact with each other when Voilquin returned to Paris in 1836. She lived for a while with Reine Guindorf-Flichy, who was now married, before taking on some freelance writing assignments—adequate, evidently, to support living on her own and her medical studies. In 1836, she proposed the establishment of a "maternal society" for young unmarried mothers. Twenty-eight women agreed to support it with monthly payments, but evidently this funding was not enough to sustain such an institution.

Another venture, this one successful but short-lived, was undertaken by a group of former, mostly bourgeois, *Saint-Simoniennes*, Eugénie Niboyet included. They came together, in 1836, in support of the publication the *Gazette des femmes*, a journal that proclaimed itself "for the exercise of POLITICAL AND CIVIL RIGHTS FOR WOMEN." It focused its attention primarily on legal issues and encouraged the writing of petitions to the legislature—a new strategy for feminists, borrowed from the American and British antislavery movements. Some of these petitions, especially those arguing for the reestablishment of divorce ("not only as it was under the Empire of Napoleon but for INCOMPATIBILITY OF TEMPERAMENT, and for IMPOSSIBILITY OF LIVING TOGETHER IN THE STATE OF MARRIAGE declared by one or the other or both of the spouses"), show evidence of a continuing Saint-Simonian influence.

In 1838, the journal's editor, Herbinot de Mauchamps, and his companion, Poutret de Mauchamps, were sentenced to prison for "corruption of morals," recalling the fate of Enfantin, Chevalier, and Duveyrier six years earlier. In describing the *Gazette des femmes*, the prosecutor claimed it "exalted everything that is disgusting to good morals." Two historians, Evelyne Sullerot and Marie-Louise Puech, have closely examined the court records and concluded that the charges against the de Mauchamps (which included Herbinot's alleged seduction of a servant) were fabricated, reminding us how dangerous the espousal of feminism could be in France of the 1830s.[135]

It is in the context of these years that we must place Flora Tristan, the most celebrated of all French feminists of the nineteenth century. Too often, Tristan is treated as exceptional; but we can now see that this view robs feminism of its collective history. We do not minimize Tristan's significance, but rather enrich our understandings of her, in pointing out the influence that Saint-Simonian words and acts had on the development of her politics. In 1835 and 1836, after returning from a two-year voyage to Peru, Tristan began attending the editorial meetings for the *Gazette des femmes*. Her earliest writings were of the kind discussed and supported in their meetings and publicized in the pages of their journal: petitions to reestablish divorce and abolish capital punishment, and the pamphlet "On the Necessity of Welcoming Foreign Women." Her last political activity before her untimely death at the age of forty-one—a tour of France undertaken to garner support for her ideas on workers' and women's emancipation—followed the path of the Saint-Simonian "missionaries." She died at the home of Elisa and Charles Lemonnier.

Tristan's background was similar to that of the Saint-Simonians. Like many of them, she had experienced the full harshness of the bourgeois moral order that connected inheritance and other economic considerations to marriage formation. Born to a wealthy Peruvian father, who died when she was four, and a French mother, she was raised in poverty because the government, refusing to recognize the legality of her parents' marriage—a religious ceremony in Spain—confiscated her father's property as "alien property" after his death. Tristan was thus declared "illegitimate," an injury that rankled.

At sixteen, she went to work in a lithography workshop and at eighteen was forced by economic necessity into an unhappy marriage with her employer, André Chazal. She gave birth to three children, one of whom died in early childhood, before she left him in 1826. During the next nine years she traveled as a "ladies' companion" to London and independently to Peru. (Chazal had custody of their son; their daughter was sometimes with Tristan, sometimes boarded out, sometimes with Chazal.) Her experiences in Peru are described in her autobiography (*Peregrinations of a Pariah*) and are the background for her novel, *Méphis*, both published in 1838.

It was Tristan's exceptional talent that distinguished her from the *Saint-Simoniennes*. She had extraordinary self-confidence and perhaps even an inflated sense of self-importance. In her later writings, both the *Union ouvrière* (*The Workers' Union*) and her diaries from her tour through France, she created roles for a "Defender of the Working Class" and a "Woman-Guide." Although she avowed that the "Defender," who should be able to represent workers in the legislature, would therefore have to be a man, she clearly saw her own role in a workers' revolution in these kinds of lofty terms. The spiritual quality with which she imbued both positions shows the influence of the "Woman Messiah" of the Saint-Simonians.

Contemporaries remarked on her forceful personality, her daring, her beauty, and her indefatigable energy. Between 1838 and 1843, she published four books—two travel books, one novel, and a political treatise—and several brief pamphlets, all of which are noteworthy for their remarkable social commentaries. She devoted her final years to the cause of workers and women, and although she held herself aloof from organized movements, preferring to work alone, she built enduring ties to workers' groups. In 1848, four years after her death, Bordeaux workers, honoring her memory, erected a monument at her gravesite.

In general, however, socialists of the 1840s were moving away from feminism and becoming more exclusively a male workers' movement. As they looked back on Saint-Simonianism, they began to create a history for the predecessor movement—a history that this study challenges. In the *Communist Manifesto*, Marx had called Saint-Simonians "utopian," not because they were impractical dreamers but because they supported a model of class "association" rather than "struggle." But the label "utopian" stuck, imbued with all the negative connotations that the term implies.

Even more important, the later socialists mocked or ignored the feminism of Saint-Simonians. The religious aspects of the movement—the rituals, the costuming, the celibate retreat, and the search for a Woman Messiah—have particularly been held up to ridicule. Is this only because later socialism became more intensely secular and therefore uncomfortable with romantic spirituality? Perhaps. But we should keep in mind that the socialists mocked only the quasi-religious rituals of these feminists, not the rituals of Catholics (whom they may have found detestable but never ridiculous), nor those of fraternal orders, especially not workers' fraternal orders. Ridicule, we know, is a weapon commonly used against women who are considered "uppity"; Saint-Simonians were almost certainly condemned for their defense of such women.

In fact, feminism was *the* significant legacy of the Saint-Simonians to later socialists—at least as significant, if not more so, than their class analysis and studies in banking and credit. Saint-Simonians traveled to England and influenced the direction of Owenite feminists. Engels borrowed directly from Saint-Simonian theory in making connections between the institutions of inherited property and the family and the oppression of women. We should bear in mind, however, that in the 1880s, when Engels wrote, few socialists were questioning traditional familial and sexual relationships; his work had little impact, therefore, on the politics of his own time. The politics—if not the anthropology—of *The Origins of the Family, Private Property, and the State* are actually better understood within the context of the politics of the earlier period, the period of their original articulation.

Beginning in the later nineteenth century, socialism and feminism diverged more decisively from one another. In the 1970s, feminists, who aspired to bring these two ideologies together again, came to call themselves "socialist-feminists." Saint-Simonians could be called the first socialist-feminists, but this designation, which suggests that two separate movements—a socialism of workers and a feminism of women—have been combined, does not capture the aspirations of these women for a more holistic kind of politics. Perhaps we should remember them as they named themselves: *femmes nouvelles*.

Deconstructing Equality-versus-Difference

Let us return now to the question of difference with which we began. Within the U.S. feminist movement, theory and practice grounded in analyses that have privileged difference have been viewed with suspicion and have seemed to call out for explanation. Of particular concern is the apparent conflict between a politics grounded in difference and demands for equality. The political discourse most familiar to Americans, the basis for our Revolution, comes to us from the Enlightenment and valorizes universalism. Our unfamiliarity with a revolutionary discourse that valorizes difference may explain why we have assumed a dichotomous relationship between "difference" and equality. This discussion of Saint-Simonian feminism is intended to challenge that view—to deconstruct the equality-versus-difference debate and to offer an alternative understanding of difference and particularity, of sameness and universality, and of the relationship of each of these concepts to equality.

Feminists have tended to overlook the fact that, like all ideologies, feminism varies across time and place, that it is shaped by historically specific forces—some social, some economic, some intellectual. Hence, there is no one unified feminist discourse. At various moments, under one or another set of circumstances, feminists' preoccupations have shifted. And when feminists have reordered their priorities, their view of the causes of the status quo and their strategies for change, including their rhetorical strategies, have also shifted.

Given these dynamics, it is of interest to compare the feminism of the Saint-Simonians to that of the French Revolution. During the Revolution, it was the universality of rights that preoccupied feminists. Challenging the *ancien régime*'s caste-like "estates," the Revolutionaries stressed the universality of rights, proclaiming that one's membership in the human race determined one's rights. What mattered was that which all humans have in common and that separate them from the animal species—not their reproductive organs but their brains, not their different procreative roles but their shared capacity to reason.

Historians tell us, however, that this Revolutionary vision of feminism is not our only historical tradition. Writing in 1964, Aileen Kraditor, in *The Ideas of the Woman Suffrage Movement, 1890–1920*, examines "two major types of suffragist arguments"—one of which she calls the justice argument, based on "the ways women were the same as men and therefore had the *right* to vote"; and a second, the expediency argument, based on "the ways [women] differed from men, and therefore had the *duty* to contribute their special skills and experience to government." More recently, Denise Riley, in *"Am I That Name?" Feminism and the Category of "Women" in History*, identifies these same kinds of arguments in English suffragism. Karen Offen, in her recent article "Defining Feminism: A Comparative Historical Approach," seems to concur with Kraditor and Riley in identifying "two distinct modes of argumentation or discourse"—which she terms "individualist" and "relational"—but she suggests that these two schools of thought differ from one another not only in mode of arguments but also in goals. ("Instead of seeking unqualified admission to male-dominated society, [relational feminists] mounted a wide-ranging critique of the society and its institutions.")

These studies, however, do not resolve the concern over difference. This is especially the case with Offen, even though it is clearly her intention to do so. By identifying the "relational" tendency as "couple-centered"—one which endorses traditional family structures and accepts the sexual division of labor—she does little to dispel fears that the difference perspective is essentially conservative.[136] Kraditor and especially Riley are more convincing in uncovering the emancipatory potential of "difference," but their perspectives are limited by their subject matter. Kraditor focuses exclusively on suffrage; she makes no attempt to reflect on the many other issues feminists have addressed. And Riley, a philosopher, concentrates on theory, paying much less attention to the practice associated with this theory.[137]

A discussion of Saint-Simonian feminists takes us farther. Grounding their politics in an understanding of women and men that stressed their difference from one another, *Saint-Simoniennes* self-consciously constructed a practice that was different from that of Saint-Simonian men, even creating a separatist culture to nourish their politics. At the same time, they examined the differences among women, developing perhaps the earliest blending of class analysis with feminism. Most significantly, they offered a far-reaching vision of liberation that resembles the feminism we today call "radical."

In this last respect the French historical record is different from the U.S. tradition. Although there have been U.S. feminists characterized by a "difference" perspective, only the French historical experience includes a tradition of *radical* "difference" that challenged the doctrines of separate spheres and the traditional nuclear family and that permits us to understand that a recognition of "difference" need not pose a threat to our claims for equality.

Certainly, Saint-Simonians never viewed equality and difference in opposition to one another. Having claimed that women and men were "naturally" different, they also claimed that they were equal. A commitment to equality permeates the writings of these women: "we are free and equal to man. . . . Let us take our place in the public forum, in the new temple which recognizes rights for woman equal to the rights of man" (*Tribune* 1, no. 1: 2). "We, women, must make [everyone] understand our equality with men" (1: 199). "We preach the equality of man and woman" (1: 132). "Equality . . . must extend to everyone" (1: 148). Several issues of the *Tribune des femmes* carried the words "Equality of rights and duties for all" on the masthead.

But, of course, such pronouncements do not by themselves tell us how Saint-Simonians interpreted the concept of sexual equality. Did their focus on the differences between the sexes lead them to imagine a different role for women—a role that perhaps undercut their claims to equality? An 1829 letter from Enfantin to Duveyrier suggests that this may have been the case initially:

> Would woman be more powerful than man? Yes, religiously; no, politically. Yes, when it comes to reminding us of our goals; no, when it comes to conceptualizing or administering the means of attaining our goal. Yes, as prophet revealing the future; no, when we must administer the social movement which will bring that future into being.[138]

But by 1831, Saint-Simonians were proclaiming that women and men must share power and all public functions, even the administration of their social movement: "All law should be made by man and by woman."[139] Having already reviewed the history of the Saint-Simonian movement, we know, of course, that Saint-Simonian practice regarding equality was less advanced than its theory. Still, the very fact that Saint-Simonians subscribed to a belief in sexual equality emboldened the women to expand its meaning in perhaps unintended ways and, no less important, to challenge hypocrisy inside the movement.

Most significantly, *Saint-Simoniennes* never accepted the ideology of separate spheres. Women should work, have careers, "fill all functions" (1: 114). "Women . . . are not all born good housekeepers" (1: 37). "Wouldn't men be happier if they had wives . . . who shared his rights and also his work?" The merchant family, wife and husband working together, was the model they held up for emulation (1, no. 3: 7). There even was some exploring of a domestic role for men. Démar wrote to Enfantin that men should raise children. And on the men's retreat at Ménilmontant, which was intended to realize the feminine within men, one strategy was to introduce them to housework.

What then do we make of the binary opposition of equality and difference among today's feminists? I suggest that this sharp dichotomy is inadequate to capture the complex meanings of feminist discourses. Revolutionary feminists, for example, did not deny the biological differences between women and men. They did not even challenge the sexual division of labor. But they considered these differences irrelevant to the claims of women to citizenship rights. These rights were based on the capacity to reason, and, because there was said to be no biological difference between women's and men's brains, there could be no difference between their capacities to reason.

Saint-Simonians, on the other hand, never denied the importance of equality. Still, as part of a generalized challenge to Enlightenment values, they did challenge the universalizing of human experience in Revolutionary discourse—not, however, to reinstate the feudal order of particular rights, but, rather, to extend the very notion of equality. Forty years after the Revolution, the priorities of feminists had changed. Social relationships of intimacy, reproduction, and production now claimed their attention rather than the formal rights of citizenship. Although the universalistic discourse of Revolutionaries had been useful for arguing for the rule of law, it was inadequate to the tasks of reordering relationships of production between workers and employers and of reordering the sexual relationships between women and men. For this work, it was necessary to pull apart the component parts of relationships and to identify the particularities of class and sex.

The 1830s were an extraordinary moment in the history of feminism. Although later in the century, feminists who valorized difference were often rather conservative, particularly in their unwillingness to challenge the doctrine of separate spheres, this was not the case in the 1830s. Saint-Simonians used "difference" to argue for social transformation.

Theorizing an essential difference between the sexes led them to new understandings about repression and to articulate a politics of sexual liberation—a politics, that is, which today we would view as radical—and they used it to demand that women be involved in all of the kinds of activities that were usually reserved for men.

The comparison to radical feminists of the 1970s and 1980s—those who valorize difference (I think especially of Hélène Cixous and Luce Irigaray, Adrienne Rich and Mary Daly)—is striking. These women also have privileged sexual matters and, like the *Saint-Simoniennes*, have shifted their attention to that which is indeed innately different between women and men, our bodies. Their discourse grounded in "difference" both reflects and constitutes experience—interpreting sexual/bodily difference and encouraging the development of a consciousness of women's sexuality.

Further, the Saint-Simonians' analysis of "difference" served to create the collective consciousness that we today call sisterhood but which the *Saint-Simoniennes* called motherhood.[140] That all women—defined by the biological fact of being born women—share an experience of political significance is basic to this kind of feminist analysis. This is what *Saint-Simoniennes* meant when they exhorted women to recognize their common maternity—not a call to attend to the duties of childrearing or even an appreciation of women's concrete roles as mother, but rather a metaphor to identify the unity that exists already among women; it also calls women to unity.

In a frequently cited article, historian Elizabeth Fox-Genovese has linked the concept of sisterhood to liberalism and Revolutionary individualism,[141] but this is now shown to be incorrect. The language and reality of sisterhood was important to Saint-Simonians—socialists not liberals—and, contrary to the view of Fox-Genovese, their belief in sisterhood did not preclude class analysis. A fuller explanation of the origins of the concept of sisterhood would recognize its historical specificity and place it in the moment of the creation of an autonomous women's movement. Sexual antagonism shaped sexual solidarity, creating a sense of "we" distinct from "they."

Given what we have learned about the use of a "difference" discourse by a group of socialist and radical feminists, we may wish to ask if there is no intrinsically conservative tilt to the theory. Certainly the similarities between this kind of analysis and traditional patriarchal analyses of womanhood raised a threat of cooptation of feminists. But this threat was realized only later in the nineteenth century and into the early decades of the twentieth century, when "difference" was used to extol a separate role and place for women as mothers. Among the *Saint-Simoniennes*, "difference" was not a conservative doctrine. Also, the "difference" perspective, which in its essentialism would seem to unify women, at a later time actually divided women when it denied the very real differences of women's lived experience. But, again, this was not the case among the class-conscious *femmes nouvelles*.

Nancy Cott has recently written that "feminism is nothing if not paradoxical":

> It aims for individual freedoms by mobilizing sex solidarity. It acknowledges diversity among women while positing that women recognize their unity. It requires gender consciousness for its basis, yet calls for the elimination of prescribed gender roles. These paradoxes of feminism are rooted in women's actual situation, being the same (in a species sense) as men; being different, with respect to reproductive biology and gender construction, from men.[142]

Two recent and important feminist works, Denise Riley's *"Am I That Name?"* and Joan Scott's "Deconstructing Equality-versus-Difference: Or, the Uses of Poststructuralist Theory for Feminism," also examine these paradoxes. Perhaps, then, we are witnessing the emergence of a new consensus that feminists must learn to live with these complexities. An appreciation of the Saint-Simonian experience can support the building of that consensus: Saint-Simonian thought and practice allay the qualms of Americans, whose political tradition predisposes them to view theories of "difference" suspiciously, because, as they developed their ideas on difference, the Saint-Simonians were able to identify and explore its emancipatory potential.

III

FEMINIST TEXTS AND FEMININE SUBJECTS

Leslie Wahl Rabine

REWRITING THE OEDIPAL TRIANGLE

Among the romantic feminists of the 1830s, Suzanne Voilquin, Claire Démar, and Pauline Roland have left a substantial body of texts that both theorize a transformation of the social and sexual order and also practice a challenge to the symbolic order. The *Saint-Simoniennes* seek a maternal principle to replace the paternal principle of language, law, and subjectivity. Their original contribution to Western women's writing of the nineteenth century, in going beyond the tradition that aligns public discourse and theorizing with masculine identification and feminine identification with the silenced maternal body, becomes discernible when we place this study of them in the context of other psychoanalytic-feminist studies of nineteenth-century feminine writing. In one recent, important work of the subject, *The Mother/Daughter Plot: Narrative, Psychoanalysis, Feminism*, Marianne Hirsch shows us "the thoroughness with which the figure of the mother is silenced, denigrated, simply eliminated, or written out of . . . Victorian fictions" by women. "Maternal absence and silence," she says, "is . . . the condition of the heroine's development, . . . the basis of the fiction itself."[1] In the one nineteenth-century French work Hirsch examines, Valentine, the eponymous heroine of a novel by the *Saint-Simoniennes'* contemporary George Sand, does not manage "to survive and to construct a life outside of the debilitating dichotomies of the maternal and the sexual, the maternal and the creative" (p. 64). At best, heroines of the Victorian period can, like Jane Eyre, find "multiple and surrogate mothers" (p. 46). Wholly other are the mother-daughter relations in the theoretical and autobiographical texts of the *Saint-Simoniennes*. Although Voilquin, Démar, and Roland do separate from a biological mother, whom they regard with hostility or ambivalence, they cannot act, write, organize, or create without inventing and identifying with a powerful maternal ego-ideal who epitomizes the nineteenth-century maternal qualities of love, nurture, and sentiment. For them, as opposed to the heroines in the fictions of their contemporaries, the maternal *is* the sexual and the creative. Pauline Roland, writing to her own maternal ego-ideal, Aglaé Saint-Hilaire, of her desire to be a sexual pioneer, says: "I desire to be a mother—a *mother*, but with a mysterious paternity. . . . I will be proud of my maternity."[2]

The maternal structures the writing of the *Saint-Simoniennes* in a manner far different from that formulated by Margaret Homans in her analysis of nineteenth-century women's fiction, *Bearing the Word*. For Homans, culture and literature are structured by a "dominant myth of language according to which women's experiences are unrepresentable and women cannot perform acts of representation."[3] In this myth, the symbolic order is organized around the repression of the mother's body, which functions as its absent referent, the "literal," outside of symbolization. While the son enters the symbolic order by abandoning the mothers's body for substitutive signs, women remain in the pre-Oedipal, pre-symbolic communication with the mother. Feminine Victorian writers, according to Homans, can bring their experience with the literal mother into language only through the creation of textual aporias, which she calls the "literalization of figures," and which usually involve the death of heroines, especially as mothers. In the *Saint-Simoniennes'* texts, the maternal represents not a return to the pre-Oedipal mother, but a going beyond the Oedipal to a new symbolic principle after the father, not the literal but the metaphoric principle governing a new order. Démar, for instance, speaks of "the word of the WOMAN REDEEMER," which will be "A SUPREMELY REVOLTING WORD, for it will be the most expansive, and consequently the most satisfying to every nature and every want."[4] This word will bring about a new order, without patriarchal (or indeed matriarchal) filiation, as the basis for a symbolic, sexual, and social economy, because in it "each and every woman and each and every man will be the daughters and sons of their works and only of their works" (p. 59). Likewise, Suzanne Voilquin describes a new order in which the maternal/corporeal is the metaphoric principle of myth: "[Saint-Simonianism] is beginning to be embodied in women and the people. The phase of the doctors is over; all the theories have been made; let the phase of sentiment, of women, in a word, arrive and give birth to the new Genesis."[5] This chapter will trace the textual figures that make that attempt.

A third work of feminist criticism, Sidonie Smith's *A Poetics of Women's Autobiography*, a transhistorical study with one chapter on a nineteenth-century writer, provides the closest parallel to this study as it concerns not only autobiographic writing but, in particular, memoirs of nineteenth-century feminist Harriet Martineau. Faced with the necessity to negotiate between the polarized maternal and paternal narratives, Martineau wrote in perhaps the only way available to her. Smith says: "Giving her allegiance to the ideology of male selfhood, she silences the 'feminine' story of her identity as daughter."[6] Within this context, the Saint-Simonian feminists offer us special interest. Although they do not formulate explicitly self-conscious critiques of the genres and language in which they must write, they resemble less their own contemporaries than the twentieth-century writers that Hirsch and Smith study, and especially the "French" feminists, in that they attempt to forge mother-daughter structures beyond the dichotomies of the Oedipal son and the eternally pre-Oedipal daughter, beyond the impasse that opposes mother/body/silence to father/symbol/discourse, and to create a language that prefigures this beyond.

Like most women writers, they fit into a double literary history—that of a hidden, discontinuous, and nonlinear "female affiliation,"[7] and that of the male tradition to whose influence they relate with ambivalence. Like psychoanalysis, the Saint-Simonianism of Enfantin elaborates a theory of feminine sexuality as pivotal to Western culture, but in a way that both offers necessary tools for dismantling oppressive structures and also perpetuates these same structures.

At least one recent history of Saint-Simonianism, Robert B. Carlisle's *The Proffered Crown*, sees Enfantin as a precursor of psychoanalytic thought. His practice of encouraging confessions in the movement, for instance, "more closely resembles the famous 'talking cure,' which would revolutionize psychotherapy two generations later, than it does the confession and forgiveness of sins."[8] After the death of Claude Henri de Saint-Simon in 1825, Enfantin, as the new leader of the Saint-Simonian movement, gradually changed the founder's emphasis. Saint-Simon's rationalist doctrine of economic cooperation, in which the emancipation of women played a minor role, coexisted with a social romantic doctrine which sought to build a new order cemented by bonds of love rather than greed and exploitation. By emphasizing this second doctrine, Enfantin transformed Saint-Simonianism from an elite corps of young, idealistic bankers and engineers into a multi-class social movement. In the early days of the July Monarchy, the Saint-Simonians attracted thousands of men and women to one of the earliest forms of socialism.

Saint-Simonianism would be a new religion, whose members would unite into a new form of the family. By emphasizing "love" and morality rather than economic reform, Enfantin appealed to unconscious desires for personal fulfillment that early capitalism had engendered but could not satisfy. Enfantin drew recruits not to a mere social movement but to the inspiring warmth of a new liberating religion and a new liberated family, both governed by a new sexual morality. Since the reason/sentiment, mind/body oppositions that governed post-Revolutionary ideology placed woman on the side of sentiment and the body, the new religion, preaching love and "the rehabilitation of the flesh," placed the emancipation of women at its center. Its god was bi-sexual, "God . . . father and mother" (*Tribune* 1: 254), and it decreed that the basic social unit was not individualist man but the couple: "Woman and man form the social individual" (*Tribune* 1: 191). Saint-Simonian enterprises, like the communal dining halls and a publishing house, were managed jointly by a man and a woman.

The earthly leaders, formed in God's image, would be a "couple-priest," a Father and a Mother. Enfantin and Saint-Amand Bazard became the Fathers of the new Religion and the new Family, but the position of Mother posed problems. The two men had classified the male members of the Saint-Simonian family into an elaborate hierarchy and attempted to organize a parallel hierarchy for the women, with Bazard's wife Claire as its mother. Her tenure did not last long. Claire lacked leadership skills and inspired merely resentment among her working-class charges. In 1831, an intense debate on sexual morality and its role in a movement of social and economic reform would lead both to the demise of Saint-Simonianism as a widespread social movement and to the birth of the first modern women's movement.

During this debate, Enfantin redefined the Mother as a mystic Woman Messiah who alone could liberate her sex. Although he called upon women to speak their own needs, he also announced that women were not yet ready to assume equality with men, much less to assume the august role of Mother. She could not be any woman present within the group but the absent object of a quest. Her future coming was to be desired with great fervor.

Some scholars have insightfully analyzed Enfantin's call to the women and his emphasis on women's emancipation as a tactic to silence his male opponents and to wrest power from Bazard.[9] But as significant for the nascent women's movement as Enfantin's motivations are the contradictory, unconscious ideological structures surrounding his concept of the Woman-Messiah. The debate on women and sexuality culminated in an emotional meeting on November 1, 1831, where Enfantin decreed that the Saint-Simonian movement had entered "the wait for the woman,"[10] and excluded the women from the Saint-Simonian organization:

> Before passing to the state of equality with man, she must have her liberty. We must therefore fulfill, for the Saint-Simonian women, this state of liberty, by destroying the hierarchy established up till now for them as well as for the men, and ushering them into the law of equality among themselves. THERE ARE NO MORE WOMEN IN THE DEGREES OF THE HIERARCHY. Our apostolate, which is the call of the woman, is an apostolate of men." ("Séance," 120).

The (absent) Ideal Woman as object of male discourse replaces real women. During his proclamation, Enfantin pointed to an empty chair next to his as "the symbol of this call," a visible symbol that "Woman is lacking to the doctrine" ("Séance," 120).

Enfantin's proclamation is remarkable both in the way that it transposes the desires which structure romantic fiction into the realm of social action[11] and also in the way that this transposition renders obvious the unconscious workings of Oedipal subjectivity that are usually veiled in romantic writing. It would be difficult to think of a more explicit political or literary expression of the entry into the symbolic order and its trajectory of desire than his "call of the woman." Speaking as the "Father" to his sons, Enfantin tells them to separate themselves from the women in their movement and to take on the task of desiring and questing this absent Mother. And in true romantic fashion, they decide to seek her in Egypt, the mysterious "Orient."[12] Enfantin's lieutenant Barrault declared 1833 "the year of the Mother" and organized "the Companions of the Woman," a group of Saint-Simonians who left Marseilles for Egypt on March 22, 1833, to seek the Mother (and, incidentally, to investigate building a canal at Suez).

They bring into "real life" the quest of nineteenth-century romantics like Chateaubriand's René, Balzac's Félix de Vandenesse, Stendhal's Julien Sorel, and the hero of Nerval's *Daughters of Fire*, whose plots move them along the trajectory of a desire to transcend their inherent sense of lack and incompletion. Like the fictional heroes, the Saint-Simonians sought an absent ideal woman who would act as the mirror that could unify and complete them. In Balzac's *The Lily in the Valley*, Stendhal's *The Red and the Black*, and Flaubert's *Sentimental Education*, the heroine is an object of erotic desire who is implicitly a mother substitute. Enfantin's literal version of the romantic quest also literalizes its object as Mother.

But by reformulating romantic desire as a social strategy, Enfantin puts into play the contradictions of gender inherent in the workings of the symbolic order. Unlike romantic novelists and poets, he has to contend with real women who refuse to be simply metaphoric substitutes for the absent referent of the sign system. His contradictory gesture, joining his "call of the Woman" with a "call to women"[13] to say what they want, opens the irresolvably ambiguous relation between male theories about the role of sexuality in culture and feminism.

Enfantin's declaration that "Woman is lacking to the doctrine" fatally echoes in the mind of a contemporary feminine reader Lacan's notorious statement that "there is woman only as excluded from the nature of things which is the nature of words."[14] Lacan's sentence reformulates in poststructuralist linguistic terms the notion implicit in Enfantin's statement: "Woman" is the name given to the necessary lack in the Oedipal subject as well as in his discursive or theoretical systems. "She" is that unsymbolizable energy that produces the system but must be repressed from it if it is to function as an organized, coherent, rational whole. As repressed productive energy, "woman" is that which is both needed to complete the lack in the system and that which threatens its coherence. In order to bring together sexual and social politics, the Saint-Simonian movement had to exclude women and create the image of Woman as visible absence, so that "She" could be both kept away and desired. Enfantin's Saint-Simonianism articulates this contradictory role of woman with rare explicitness.

Psychoanalysis also makes this contradiction explicit, and so for Luce Irigaray, it has the inestimable value of making accessible to critical inquiry the hidden repression of the feminine "by which the truth of every science and the logic of every discourse supports itself."[15] The problem, according to her, is that psychoanalysis does not distance itself from this mode of structuring scientific and philosophical discourse.

In its poststructuralist form, psychoanalytic discourse shares a salient element with romantic socialism. Both valorize the feminine not so much for any essential quality, but as the devalued, marginalized term of a symbolic bipolar structure whose meaning, despite the similarities, is different in the nineteenth- and twentieth-century discourses. Where the Saint-Simonians value sentiment, love, and harmony, poststructuralists value the disruptive margin or outside of phallocentrism, difference, the Other. But in giving woman a privileged relation to the Other, that no-place of the law which generates the signifying order, psychoanalysis places her in the position of being, as Irigaray says, "absent as a subject" from that relation.[16] Like Enfanfin's "call of the woman," the poststructuralist discourse about feminine difference and jouissance is a discourse of men, and according to Irigaray: "To speak *of* or *about* woman can always come back to or be understood as a recuperation of the feminine inside of a logic that maintains its repression . . . " (*Ce sexe*, 75, emphasis in original). Both the nineteenth-century Saint-Simonian feminists and the twentieth-century psychoanalytic feminists adopt the men's discourse of woman but incorporate it into a different logic.

The Saint-Simonian feminists begin this work by responding to Enfantin's exclusion of women from the family. A group of young proletarian embroiderers, seamstresses, and laundresses, which eventually included Suzanne Voilquin, found themselves relieved to get away from the tutelage of the bourgeois "mothers," and from the very notion of hierarchy. They took the opportunity to establish a journal, *Apostolat des femmes*, later called *Tribune des femmes*, published from 1832 to 1834. Enfantin never really responded to them or recognized their endeavor. But in adopting his quest for the Mother, they transform it beyond recognition.

They could relate to Enfantin in this ambiguous way because his doctrine both clarifies and obfuscates the mutual exclusion of Woman and women. In romantic desire real women are in a double bind, placed in the position of substitute for Woman but necessarily failing to fill that position by their very presence. By joining the quest for the Woman with its contradictory other, the idea of women's freedom and equality, even if practiced by men, Enfantin lets the genie out of the bottle. As Suzanne Voilquin says: "It was in this year [1833] that the feeling for *woman* was deeply incarnated in the hearts of a host of men who had adopted the theory of equality between the sexes, but without being aware of the consequences of this principle" (*Tribune* 2: 181).

By claiming the Woman as a principle that women actualize, the *Saint-Simoniennes* follow a strategy that most contemporary feminists, even the "French" feminists, would consider dangerous, preferring instead to play with the double bind that for them always connects women to Woman.[17] Whatever its very real dangers, Démar, Voilquin, and Roland incorporate the concept into texts that make women into subjects of structures that exclude them, and thus transform the structures. In their writing, the *Saint-Simoniennes* begin by miming the male quest for the Mother. Claire Démar, for instance, writes to Enfantin of her intention to go on her own quest, not to the mysterious Orient but to America, the land of freedom: "And now, I will search for *my Mother*."[18] She never does go to America, but her writing will soon upset the subject/object structure of desire on which the masculine subject and his discourse depend. One elementary illustration of this complex change appears in her essay *My Law of the Future*. Démar, scolding the editors of the *Tribune des femmes* for their timidity, says: " . . . but I . . . doubt ourselves, poor women, who believe ourselves so strong, and who, weak, timid, and Christian, would perhaps remain silent and insensitive to the call of the WOMAN REDEEMER . . . "(*My Law*, 27, emphasis in original). An almost imperceptible shift drastically transforms the "call of the Woman": from object of the men's call, She becomes the subject of a call to the women not to remain silent, and as such the model for the women as subjects.

In order to become such subjects, they rewrite the Oedipal triangle. Any symbolic act needs a triadic structure in which the Name-of-the-Father intervenes in the immediately dual union between mother and son, replacing it with the mediation of names and signs,[19] and also instituting the desire to transcend this mediation. Women are excluded from the subject position, and not only because the symbolic triangle codes the object as feminine. In addition, many feminist revisions of Freudian psychoanalysis, including those of both Nancy Chodorow and Luce Irigaray, find that women's separation from the mother and their entry into the Symbolic Order remain incomplete and unstable.[20] To the extent that women have not lost the early union with the mother, they would have no desire to quest it, and no means to symbolize the mother-daughter relation. Given this exclusion from desire and discourse, what form can feminine subjectivity take? While women's texts of different times and periods provide different answers to this question, those of the *Saint-Simoniennes* trace the outline of a different symbolic system, governed not by the father but by another, symbolic, mother. Their texts, then, house the figures of two different mothers, one, the real mother, whom they separate from and reject, and a second, symbolic mother, who makes possible this separation. This substitution of a purely symbolic family for the real, biological, and socially constituted family lies at the core of Enfantin's strategy. His ability to attract a large and devoted following to socialism through his mythology of the Family in which he is the Father seeking a Mother, and they are the sons and daughters, suggests how deeply post-Revolutionary society imprinted in its subjects a new ideology of the family and motherhood, and how little that ideology represented their lived experience. Although post-Revolutionary ideology conceived the bourgeois family as the private arena of an intense affective drama, with the mother in a new, and newly idealized, role at its emotional center, it remained an economic institution.[21]

Enfantin's purely symbolic family, removed from its network of oppressive socioeconomic roles, could draw precisely those people who had suffered most from what the Saint-Simonian d'Eichthal called "family afflictions" (Pelosse, 187). Their painful experience in the bourgeois family led not to a rejection of the family but to an even stronger longing for its ideal form. Enfantin intensified this contradiction between the longed-for ideal and the real family as an institution regulating greed through inheritance. He used the bourgeois ideology of the family to create an anticapitalist movement that undermined the family, promising to replace the sordid reality with its idealized representation.

Far from idealizing their own mothers, Roland, Démar, and Voilquin all feel stifled by the pressure to imitate their mothers' passivity. The daughters are anxious to break away from feminine complicity to a patriarchal system that makes motherhood for proletarian women "a surplus to her woes and afflictions!" (*Tribune* 1: 36). Roland's letters to Aglaé Saint-Hilaire express with the most spontaneous fervor the rejection of the biological mother for Enfantin's ideal family. Trapped in the provincial town of Falaise, she enters a voluminous correspondence with Saint-Hilaire, whom Enfantin has chosen as "mother" to women recruits. Roland begins her correspondence to this woman she has never met by writing: "It's to my mother I want to write today, it's to her I want to reveal my atrocious sorrows, it's her whom I ask to sooth them, because I know that she won't abandon her daughter. . . . "[22] Pauline writes to a "mother" because in nineteenth-century ideology the "soothing" and "consolation" she needs are archetypically summed up by the word mother. Yet her "sorrows" themselves result from an "eternal separation [between Pauline and her beloved tutor M. Desprez] pronounced five days ago by the caprice of my mother" (no. 1, Jan. 31, 1832). With apparent disregard, Pauline uses the same word "mother" in the same letter with two entirely different, and even opposed, denotative and connotative meanings. In the course of the *Saint-Simoniennes'* writing this use of the same signifier for the negative, smothering figure and the positive, distancing figure of their subjective universe will reveal both its liberating potential and its dangers, but for now let us see how the opposition between the two mothers takes shape.

Saint-Hilaire represents the absent symbolic mother who liberates Pauline from immersion in her own hateful mother, about whom she writes: "she does not think, she loves nothing. Hate! That's her whole life. . . . We have therefore abandoned her for a long time" (no. 16, Oct. 24, 1832). Having abandoned her all-too-present mother, Roland clothes her second symbolic mother in the essentially maternal quality of love, but transformed into a symbolic mediation: "Farewell my mother, my true mother, receive the tender kisses of your daughter, love her and pity her" (no. 14, Oct. 10, 1832). By her absence, the in fact rather mediocre and dry Saint-Hilaire becomes at once object of desire, model of identification, and symbolic source of Pauline's writing, and so engenders Pauline as subject.

Claire Démar also calls for abandoning the biological mother, but on a theoretical level and in more general terms. Her scandalous essay, *My Law of the Future*, not only advocates women's unconditional right to sexual pleasure, but links this to a call for abolishing the family:

No more property, no more inheritance.
Classification according to ability, compensation according to work.
Consequently:
No more maternity, no more law of blood.
I say no more maternity. (*My Law*, 58)

The "Woman-Messiah" as governing principle of a new society will replace the blood mother.

This Saint-Simonian Mother does not, then, represent a simple regression to the pre-Oedipal Mother. She in her turn replaces the paternal instance, ejecting him from the Oedipal triangle and taking his place. But the daughter's separation from the real mother differs from the Oedipal son's castration crisis in that the resulting triangle is not the stable configuration of filial subject/maternal object/paternal mediator. Instead the ideal mother is both object of desire and mediating model of identification for the daughter-subject. This rewritten triangle, although highly unstable, generates a new form of desire, a new logic, and a new structure of subjectivity.

First, *Saint-Simoniennes* do not desire, in the manner of the male romantic subject, a return to fusion with the archaic mother or her substitute. They desire instead a new form of mediation between desiring subjects, or in other words, a new way of desiring. Suzanne Voilquin, who ardently sought the Mother, explains this in an account written in 1865 of her vision of the Mother in 1833:

Therefore, I have seen only a symbol in the call of Barrault. In my opinion, women should first reveal themselves to each other, outside the sphere of masculine influence, through a show of their feelings or the acts of their free will, no longer weighed down by the prejudice of their Christian upbringing; these women will seek each other out in the natural course of things so that they may create among themselves a council where each of them can contribute her stone to the moral edifice of the future. It is this *completely feminine* feeling that will create what the Saint-Simonians call the Mother![23]

Voilquin makes it clear here, first, that she conceives the Mother as a symbolic principle and, second, that in her conception, the maternal principle, contrary to the concept of Roland but similar to that of Démar, will always be absent. Voilquin here explicitly contests the Saint-Simonian men's notion of the mother, contesting also the structure of male desire. By placing the mother in an alternate structure, that of women's collective action, Voilquin dissolves the romantic unitary chain of phallocentric desire connecting dominating subject to dominated object and replaces it with a network of desiring chains, in which multiple subjects mutually quest (seek out) and desire each other. Desire does not end with the fusion of the object into the subject but with the subjects engendering the Mother.

The rewritten Oedipal triangle also generates a new logic. The Oedipal triangle composed of son-subject, Father, and Mother generates the hierarchical bipolar oppositions of the Symbolic Order, organized around the analogous asymmetrical dichotomies of Father/Mother, Male/Female, Subject/Object, Mind/Body, Spirit/Matter, Language/Silence, and so forth, in which the first term dominates the second and reduces it to an inferior mirror of itself. The feminists' triangle, formed not by the opposition between the Mother as object of desire and the Name-of-the-Father as object of identification but by the difference within the Mother who is both at once, generates not an endless series of oppositions but an unstable difference. Just as the *Saint-Simoniennes*, in their writings, demand an end to mind/body, subject/object, masculine/feminine oppositions, so do these writings, as multileveled texts, trace figures of the birth of this new symbolic triangle.

One such textual figure from each of the three writers will serve as an example, while a contrast among the three examples will suggest the varied forms this figure can take and the significance of this variation. Voilquin's writing attempts to establish a triangular relation among women in an article in the *Tribune des femmes* appropriately entitled "The Two Mothers." But neither of these mothers is the ideal Mother. They are a rich woman and a poor woman, whose encounter Voilquin reports having seen in the street. In fact, her outraged account represents the scene as significantly bereft of the Woman-Messiah's influence. As she says to the poor mother: "What expressive looks you give this brilliant carriage and the tattered clothes that barely cover you; and then, raising your eyes to heaven, you seem to question the justice in the mystery of this inequality!" (*Tribune*, 1: 117). The rich mother does not even heed the other's plea for alms and "informs the servants . . . that they must hasten to push away the troublesome solicitor" (1: 117). Voilquin organizes the essay around a rhetorical triangle between herself and these two women. In a world deprived of the Mother, she places herself in the mediating position of the triangle, and apostrophizes each of the other two women in turn, in an attempt to have them address each other. Voilquin of course addresses most of her apostrophe to the poor mother, saying at one point: "Like you, this woman is a mother. She must sympathize with your misery. . . . Poor woman, hasten to present your mother's request" (*Tribune* 1: 117). Voilquin first addresses the rich mother as a member of her class: "Oh, rich people! since your souls are too narrow to understand association, then at least practice philanthropy" (1: 117), and ends by excoriating her for refusing to complete the triangle by refusing to recognize the poor mother as a mother and as a subject.

The class difference between the two mothers bears on the image of the ideal Mother of the Saint-Simonian men, who is implicitly upper class. As one writer in the *Tribune des femmes* says: "They will not find the ideal they seek so long as their narrow view does not expand to see it in all women" (2: 153). Like the rich mother in this essay, the Saint-Simonian men refuse to recognize any embodiment of the Mother in the proletarian women within or outside their movement. Voilquin's essay, like much of her activity as a midwife and organizer, counters this ideology that can see maternity only in the bourgeois stereotype.

Her use of the figure of apostrophe traces a triangle around the potential space of a different ideology. Unlike the ideology generated by the paternal triangle, in which the Name-of-the-Father mediates the relation between superior subject and inferior object, her maternal triangle would mediate relations among equal subjects. The textual figure of an incomplete triangle acts out the class conflict that prevents the utopian space of a new symbolic system because the rich mother refuses to make the completing connection. Voilquin addresses her at the end of the essay not to complete the triangle but to mark in anger and frustration its disintegration. One mark of the failure to engender a maternal symbolic law is that Voilquin addresses the rich mother not in the loving mother's voice she uses for the poor mother but in the discourse of paternal law, specifically that of Old Testament vengeance: "Yes, rich woman, your life will go on like that of the poor woman! You, mother, have not deigned to help end the sorrows of a mother. May God help you achieve progress and soften your soul by making you suffer through your children all the anguish of hunger, cold, and poverty that you have not prevented" (*Tribune* 1: 118).

Because of the rich mother, the "new Genesis" Voilquin so longs for is not "engendered." Given Voilquin's notion of the Mother as a symbol created by a "*completely feminine* feeling" among women, the completion of a feminine triangle would itself serve to generate the Mother and her law of the future. Voilquin's narrative voice, situated in the broken triangle, can only rewrite the patriarchal tradition of the biblical myth of Eve, but not write a new maternal myth. She can only invert the biblical narrative of feminine suffering, bringing vengeance down on the rich mother, not because she gained self-knowledge as did Eve, but because she refused it; not because she betrayed the male in power over her, but because she betrayed someone over whom she had power; not in order to make feminine suffering eternal and natural, but to end it; and not in order to establish a hierarchy of authority, as with Adam and Eve, but to establish equality. Without the Mother, Voilquin can only play the role of a feminine father, and without her law, she can only invert, rather than structurally transform, the paternal law.

This attempt to create a feminine symbolic triangle through the rhetorical figure of apostrophe also occurs, with significant variation, in the writings of Démar and Roland. Its use to mark a desire for a different form of desire and subjectivity is in fact one of the similarities between them and the twentieth-century French writers Cixous and Irigaray.[24]

In Cixous's classic essay on "écriture féminine," for instance, the passage from first-person to second-person voice marks the passage from analyzing feminine writing to practicing it: "And why don't you write? Write! Writing is for you, you are for yourself, your body is yours, take it."[25] Likewise, in Irigaray's *This Sex Which Is Not One*, the chapters which practice an experimental "écriture de la femme" (writing of woman) differ from those which analyze the texts of male philosophers in that they not only pass into the second person but also incorporate the shifting personal pronouns into their apostrophe: "I love you: your body there here now. I/you touch you/me, so that we can really feel ourselves alive" (*Ce Sexe*, 208). Although this similarity between past and present is marked by historical difference, especially differences in self-reflexivity about rhetoric and language, it marks in all these texts a desire for entry into a maternal symbolic space that does not exist outside their texts.

Démar's essay, *My Law of the Future*, also puts the authorial voice at the apex of a broken triangle, apostrophizing first one and then the other of its disconnected members. In the debate between Démar and Voilquin, Démar insists on the primacy of heterosexual erotic freedom, while Voilquin focuses on the importance of socioeconomic freedom and sisterly solidarity among women. Therefore, as we might expect, Démar sees the completion of this space as a result of liberated sexual love between men and women. In addition, the two addressees of her double apostrophe are a group of men and a group of women, although not those to be joined in sexual embrace. *My Law of the Future* begins with the word "You," addressing itself first to the women editors of the *Tribune des femmes*, and later to the male leaders of the Saint-Simonian Family. Like Voilquin, Démar occupies the position reserved for the not-yet-existing mother in a rhetorical figure reflecting the vision of a future utopia when the mythic Mother will mediate a harmonious union between men and women. Démar's vision frankly eroticizes Enfantin's more discrete version of the coming of the Woman Messiah:

> . . . I call in all my prayers for the sanctified hour that will establish the relation between man and woman upon the foundation of this new moral law. . . . Glorious hour when all the peoples of the earth . . . will for the first time see man and woman obey the laws of a divine attraction, fused upon each other's bosom, a sublime couple finally realizing the social individual impossible until that hour. (*My Law*, 25)

While this vision of man and woman merged on each other's bosom suggestively resembles a pre-Oedipal erotic ecstasy, it is not a regressive dual union with the Mother but a triangular relation mediated by Her: "May she therefore rise up among women, she with the branch of oak and olive in her hand, who will sign the treaty of rehabilitation, alliance, and equality" (*My Law*, 25).

In order for her "new moral law" to come about, sexuality, according to Démar, will have to be based on "a liberty without rules or limits" (*My Law*, 32), and furthermore, "a liberty without limits, surrounded by mystery" (*My Law*, 50). The term "mystery" signifies what we would call privacy and sets up a limit or barrier between the couple and the outside world, thus protecting the women from exploitation. In other words, it establishes a space around them. More explicitly than in Voilquin's essay, here the maternal triangle of desire becomes a space that encloses equal subjects, rather than a network linking male subject to female object.

Démar's image of sexual freedom without limits, surrounded by limits, fits into a maze of interconnected images in *My Law of the Future* about disintegrating old barriers, limits, and boundaries, and setting up new ones in different places. These images of limits and barriers between bodies, or of barriers prohibiting sexual pleasure, are images of repression. These images are strangely similar to a figure that Lacan uses. In his theory of the erotic repression that ushers the subject into the symbolic order, the phallus becomes a "bar" of repression, separating the subject from the unconscious, and also from the maternal "real."[26] In Démar's textual figure that bar of repression seeks transformation into the limit of mystery surrounding the couple and framing their freed bodies. The symbol of the phallus, signifier of the paternal symbolic, will be transformed into the space representing feminine pleasure. Her imagery is significant in light of psychoanalytic feminist ideas about sexual differ-ence, recalling for instance Jessica Benjamin's argument that "finding woman's desire requires finding an alternative to the phallic structures, to the symbolic mode. And that means an *alternative mode of structuring the psyche, not just a symbol to replace the phallus.*"[27] For Benjamin, the concept of intersubjectivity, in its difference from the subject-object rela-tion, organizes this alternative structure, because "the intersubjective mode of desire has its counterpart in spatial rather than symbolic repre-sentation" (Benjamin, 95). Likewise, in a discussion of the so-called *fort-da* game by which the little boy prepares his entry into the symbolic order by mastering the presence and absence of an object that substitutes for the mother, Irigaray says: "Girls do not enter language in the same way as boys. . . . They make their entry by producing a space, a track, a river, a dance, a rhythm, a song. . . . They describe a space around them-selves and do not move a substitute object around."[28] Irigaray's remarks are especially relevant to a reading of the *Saint-Simoniennes'* figures of feminine symbolism, for she is not celebrating this feminine entry into the symbolic. She is rather proposing a different symbolic in which women would no longer be placed at a disadvantage for the very struc-ture of their subjectivity. In similar fashion, given the historic difference, Démar and Voilquin figure a future symbolic which structures itself around a form of feminine subjectivity.

Roland's letters also figure this feminine space of subjectivity as a uto-pian maternal triangle, but with a significant difference from Voilquin and Démar. Unlike them, she lives in the illusion that the mother already exists, embodied for her in Aglaé Saint-Hilaire. And her writing, unlike theirs, inscribes an illusorily complete, rather than incomplete, triangle. Among the many triangular patterns that appear in Roland's letters to Saint-Hilaire, one of them can illustrate this point with economy. She typically refers to herself in the third person as "votre fille" (your daugh-ter), as in the sentence: "Mother, your daughter is happy, she loves you" (no. 23, June 18, 1833); or "even if your daughter should seem to you weak and of little faith, she will tell you all her thoughts" (no. 33, Feb. 21, 1832). This construction makes her identity oscillate between all the points of the "I," "you," "she" pronoun triangle. Rather than locate itself in a stable position like the Oedipal ego, it represents subjectivity as the shifting outline of a space. It also closes the space.

The letters repeat often the quintessential statement of metonymic de-sire: "I intensely desire to be close to you" (no. 7, June 16, 1832). But since the "you" as object of desire is also Pauline's object of identifica-tion, these two terms, which remain polarized in the Oedipal triangle, as the maternal and paternal points, are here unstable, in danger of merg-ing and collapsing the triangle into a pre-symbolic dual union. This danger hovers most clearly in one letter, where Pauline is desperately insisting that a resistant, reluctant Aglaé remain in the position of *mother* to her. In this letter a desire for proximity drifts perilously close to a demand for fusion:

> Think about it, mother, I want to be *your daughter*. . . . It's up to me to *nourish* you if one day you lack bread. But also, mother, it's up to you never to hide from your daughter the place of your retreat; you should never be separated from her except by death, and even then, mother, it's to her that you will bequeath your thoughts. (No. 23, June 18, 1833)

If Pauline's writing expresses the illusion that the Mother already exists, and figures the outline of a feminine symbolic space as complete, it also expresses the illusion that the maternal symbolic law can already govern and order social reality. She decides to put into practice the Saint-Simonian notion that the mother is the only true parent of the child since fatherhood is unknowable. The movement's anti-patriarchal beliefs held that man's desire to be certain of his fatherhood, for reasons of property ownership, created sexual slavery for women. Démar's *My Law of the Future* elaborates an eloquent analysis of this theory, but Roland collapses theory into practice in the illusion that simply living the ideal maternal order will force social reality to conform to it. She writes to Aglaé of her decision to have children outside of marriage, saying: "This will is still that society know everything except the name of the man I shall give myself to. . . . And he alone who can understand and submit to this woman's will, he shall renounce the right to *protect* me. . . . [H]e will have been carried away by me, voluntarily abdicated his masculine role, and acknowledged not only the equality between man and woman, but the superiority of a woman over him as a man" (no. 30, June 1834). Where the texts of Démar and Voilquin figure their sense of the impossibility of embodying the mother for the present, Roland's letter suggests a conviction that she can do so: "my child will be proud of his birth, and his mother will be great and saintly in his eyes."

By contrast, Voilquin's and Démar's textual figures of incompletion suggest their understanding that the maternal symbolic does not yet function as an autonomous system. To operate autonomously, a symbolic system has to become the invisible filter through which the ideological representation of social reality is experienced as natural truth. The Saint-Simonian feminists never gained such power. Yet the potential power of this symbolic mode to forge new kinds of collective sociopolitical practice is demonstrated by the original forms of action the Saint-Simonian feminist movement could initiate in the face of a complete lack of moral and material support. If Pauline Roland, who became one of the most noted socialist organizers of the Second Republic, and one of its most celebrated prisoners of conscience, had to face dire and constant poverty as a single mother, her fate cannot be attributed to her illusions. So hostile was their environment that no stance could have saved these early socialist feminists from isolation and tragedy. Claire Démar, having sold all her furniture in order to continue writing, committed suicide after completing *My Law of the Future*. Suzanne Voilquin, having finally received her medical certificate, never did succeed, as a midwife to poor unwed mothers, in gaining recognition for them as real mothers. Divorced from her husband in order to be a free woman at a time when divorce was not legal, she too was forced by poverty to spend many lonely arduous years in Russia and America to make a living.[29] Succeeding social movements gained acceptance and power only by fragmenting their vision.

In the intervening century and a half, those other feminist movements have improved many women's position within the still fundamentally oppressive socio-symbolic order, and this improvement accounts for much of the difference that sharply distinguished Saint-Simonian from poststructuralist feminists. Yet the affinities between the *Saint-Simoniennes* and the poststructuralists are striking enough to alter our view of the history of feminism along the lines set forth in the introduction to this book. If we take the *Saint-Simoniennes* into account, the history of feminism does not follow a linear and progressive widening but begins with a vision similar to our own and then narrows after 1848. What happened in this interval?

Margaret Talbot and Barbara Taylor find that later progressive political movements, in rejecting the utopian breadth of vision, also lost the connection between struggles for class and gender liberation, as well as the connection between economic struggle and personal life.[30] But what future social movements lose is not so much the relation between class and gender as the role of sexuality and desire in tying them together. Post-1848 socialist and liberal movements, to which feminists have been in large measure allied, repress the idea that social struggle is fought by gendered subjects of desire, whose own desire and subjectivity are constructed by the social order they fight against and so have to be changed in the course of struggle. This notion does not again play an influential role in social movements until 1968. In the period between, questions of sexual equality and difference do not disappear but are reduced to the "women's question," seen as exterior to the subjects who theorize it and who do not therefore have to examine the role of their desire in repressing from this theory issues of masculine subjectivity and its relation to the feminine.

For examining this neglected sexual component of politics, psychoanalysis, whatever its pitfalls, offers resources well deserving feminist transformation. So transformed, it can even provide an analytical distance from the quest for feminist origins implicit in this study of the *Saint-Simoniennes* as its precursors. A major theme of poststructuralist theory has been a critique of the myth of origins as the basis and guarantee of the Oedipal subject's stable identity. Feminist psychoanalytic theory, and especially the work of Luce Irigaray, has amplified and transformed this theme by criticizing the ways in which this masculine model of identity entails "the impossibility, the prohibition against woman . . . imagining, figuring, representing, symbolizing, etc. (none of these terms being adequate since they are all borrowed from a discourse complicitous with the impossibility and prohibition) her own relationship to her beginning."[31] Without a representation of origins, however mythic and fictive, women cannot construct an identity. But such a representation would need a symbolic mediation between women and their mothers that differs from the Oedipal model of symbolizing the son's break from the mother and his identification with the Name-of-the-Father, not only in the symbol used (i.e., the phallus) but in the structure of symbolization itself. The *Saint-Simoniennes* engaged in this quest for another form of symbolization, and because they saw their effort as collective, their writings retrace not only the emergence of a feminine subjectivity but, beyond that, the quest for a feminine symbolic order.

This study of the *Saint-Simoniennes'* attempt to collectively engender the mother as symbol of a new order itself participates in another, late twentieth-century, quest to establish the possibilities for a feminine genealogy. Although the quest has led not to a mythic origin as pre-lapsarian plenitude but to other feminists as problematic and contradictory as ourselves, it does suggest that the notion, at the core of both romantic and poststructuralist French feminism, of a "bond of motherhood" uniting women, implies not only joining women in solidarity but linking them across the generations. Like the symbolic Mother Herself, this genealogy would not simply substitute, as Claire Démar puts it, an "umbilical succession" (*My Law*, 56) for a paternal succession; it would have a different structure.

Taking up the problem in another generation, Luce Irigaray writes: "But how can we persuade the world of men to rule peoples poetically, when they are interested primarily in money, in competing for power, etc.? And how can we run the world as women if we have not defined our identity, the rules of our genealogical relationships, our social, cultural, and linguistic order? For this task, psychoanalysis may be of great assistance to us, if we know how to use it in a way appropriate to our bodily and spiritual needs and desires."[32] In her analysis of Irigaray, Elizabeth Grosz likewise says: "To be able to trace a female genealogy of descent entails new kinds of language, new systems of nomenclature, new relations of social and economic exchange—in other words, a complete reorganization of the social order."[33] In order to pursue in more detail and complexity this early attempt to forge those new rules, nomenclatures, and exchange systems of feminine genealogy, we now turn to Suzanne Voilquin's autobiography, *Memories of a Daughter of the People*.

SUZANNE VOILQUIN AND ROMANTIC AUTOBIOGRAPHY

Romantic Autobiography

Although Suzanne Voilquin's autobiography *Memories of a Daughter of the People* was not actually written until 1865, it remains one of the most valuable accounts of working-class life and of the Saint-Simonian movement in the 1830s. Its narrative describes in detail the family life, working experiences, and inner feelings of a proletarian girl who rebelled against the prescribed womanly role of submission and abnegation to assume active responsibility in the Saint-Simonian movement, act as editor of the *Tribune des femmes*, gain a medical education, and create an independent living as a professional midwife. But as text, on another, implicit and self-referential level, it recounts the difficult, precarious process by which Voilquin succeeds in becoming the subject of her autobiography. Written in bare and simple language, the *Memories* nevertheless have the power to make us revise our view of romantic autobiography as a genre. In so doing, it also suggests the need to revise Philippe Lejeune's influential theory of the "autobiographical pact,"[34] as well as an important principle of feminist theory, according to which the exchange of women among men constitutes the basis of Western culture.

Lejeune's notion of the "pact" defines autobiography in opposition to fiction as an "implicit or explicit contract proposed by the *author* to the *reader*" (44), specifying that the author, narrator, and character are identical. In other words, the author-reader pact guarantees that the "I" within the narrative refers to the empirical author who is telling the true story of his life. Yet this empiricist definition falls apart when questions of sexual and class difference enter into consideration, as when Voilquin's autobiography is read in the context of the romantic autobiographical canon, as represented by its masterworks, Rousseau's *Confessions* and Chateaubriand's monumental *Memoirs from beyond the Tomb (Mémoires d'outre-tombe)*.[35] Such a reading suggests that autobiography is defined not by the reader-writer relation external to the text but by the author's ability to inscribe the structure of a particular kind of reader-writer relation within the text. In the texts of Rousseau and Chateaubriand that ability depends on the author's membership in an institutionalized masculine community, and Voilquin must transform their textual structure through a writing practice very much akin to the feminist social practice through which the *Saint-Simoniennes* sought to transform society.

Lejeune's model can help us understand the import of Voilquin's work to a different vision of romantic autobiography, especially if his model is filtered through feminist revisions of autobiographical theory, such as those of Nancy K. Miller and Domna Stanton. According to Miller: "[H]is notion of a contractual genre is dependent upon codes of transmission and reception. It relocates the problematics of autobiography as genre in an interaction between reader and text."[36] Linguistic codes always depend on what Domna Stanton calls "the set of stable conventions in a community that help define what is permitted a writer and expected of a reader."[37] It follows from this that truth and referentiality in a reader-writer relation are not simple givens but cultural constructs. The obstacles to Voilquin's becoming an autobiographical subject lie precisely in the codes governing this interaction, or for her, no such community, no such conventions exist. That which Lejeune takes for granted in his notion of the pact, namely the codes internalized by the reader, is what confronts her as the problem. The self-referential level of *Memories of a Daughter of the People* concerns a quest to answer the questions: Who will consent to be the reader? Who will allow her to tell her story of masculine injustice? Who will listen to it? And how? Finally, how will she construct the community that will create its own readerly and writerly conventions?

If, according to Lejeune, autobiography is a "retrospective prose narrative that a real person makes of his/her own life" (14), then again, that which he takes as unproblematic, the meaning of the word "real," presents to Voilquin the problem. Being a real person means being recognized as real by others. It implies a priori membership in a community, which encodes the "real" through ideological means of representation. The texts of Rousseau and Chateaubriand construct powerful representations of the real through a process that deprives women like Suzanne of the means for such recognition.

This recasting of Lejeune's speech-act theory as a question of social codes and the shared conventions of a community, as well as the premise of nonidentity between the I of the autobiographical character and the I of the author, occurs in the context of recent feminist debates about autobiography. They set a humanist notion of the autobiographical subject as preexisting the text and revealed through it against a poststructuralist notion of the subject as itself a fiction, product of language and textuality.[38] Wary that poststructuralist theory can obliterate sexual, class, and cultural differences (as indeed it sometimes can), some feminist critics resist giving up completely the referential subject and the notion of language as a vehicle for recounting her experience.[39] Yet Voilquin's autobiography demonstrates powerfully that the textual production of feminine autobiographical subjectivity concerns sexual and class difference on a deeper level that underlies and plays a major role in producing social experience in empirical reality. The internal workings of autobiography are every bit as much a historical and political process as the "experience" represented in its pages. If, as poststructuralist critics have been saying, experience is a linguistic construct, textuality is just as much a social construct.

The reader-writer relation that engenders Voilquin as textual subject is a variant of the self-other relation fundamental to the existence of any subject. Following Roland Barthes, Michel Foucault, and Jacques Lacan, Candace Lang and Shari Benstock maintain that no self can exist outside of a relation to that Other which is the social system of language and meaning preexisting the subject and speaking through it.[40] But men and women relate differently to this self-estrangement in language. Benstock says: "It may be that female autobiographers are more aware of their 'otherness' " (16); and Lang observes briefly that "the vicissitudes of an autobiographical project emanating from a subject who is designated a priori by its social context as Other offer material for a highly interesting critical text" (8), but she does not here elaborate. A study of Voilquin's text in contrast to those of Rousseau and Chateaubriand can bring precision to this observation. While many feminist critics may wince at a return to these two masters of the genre, it is only in contrast to them that we can understand not only the challenge of Voilquin's text to the autobiographical genre but also the contribution her text can make to the problem that so preoccupies feminist theory: that of feminine subject formation in a symbolic system that represses it. In this case the texts of Rousseau and Chateaubriand establish that system.

In the *Confessions* and the *Memoirs* the critical point informing the autobiographical subject arrives at the moment of late-adolescent sexual awakening. Rousseau's character Jean-Jacques and Chateaubriand's character François-René enter a self-other relation with a man who can confer recognition upon the subject as "real," and who figures the ideal reader and the representative of the legitimating community and source of language. As guardian of the social system of codes and language, he also represents the Name-of-the-Father within the text and transmits to the autobiographical hero the power of this guardianship. This self-other relation is mediated by an eroticized feminine figure who enables the hero to wrest such recognition from the other man.

Like the romantic quest for the absent Mother analyzed at the beginning of this chapter, this struggle for recognition is also a triadic relation. It resembles the structure of exchange of women among men, which, according to Claude Lévi-Strauss, "accomplishes the passage from nature to culture."[41] He sees the prohibition of incest as fundamental to the institution of marriage as a relation between men of different clans cemented by the exchange of women. The romantic quest for the Mother analyzed at the beginning of this chapter also results from the paternal prohibition against mother-son incest, which dictates that the son repress the maternal body and enter the order of signifiers, there to take his place in the position of the subject. The exchange of women and the quest for the absent Mother are two faces of the Oedipal triangle that structures subjectivity, symbolism, and desire in Western culture. Where the theoretical writings of the Saint-Simonian feminists (including Suzanne Voilquin) radically redraw the quest version of this symbolic triangle, Voilquin's autobiography restructures that of the exchange of women.

This exchange, according to Gayle Rubin's synthesis of Lévi-Strauss and Lacan in "The Traffic in Women," ensures the transmission of the Name-of-the-Father, as paternal heritage, power and prestige, from generation to generation.[42] The scenes of autobiographical subject formation in *Confessions* and the *Memoirs* retrace such a passage of the hero into the symbolic order and such a transmission of culture. In Voilquin's *Memories* a similarly structured episode of sexual desire occurs, but on the level of subject formation it narrates a disastrous failure, and so generates additional episodes to forge an alternate economy of symbolic exchange. Voilquin's difference from Rousseau and Chateaubriand takes shape within a striking similarity among the three autobiographies. The three scenes of subject formation repeat the structural elements of an early childhood episode of Edenic bliss, and also repeat, or, depending on how one views it, are repeated in, the introductory paragraphs of the autobiography itself. The adolescent scene acts as a kind of textual knot, binding the events of the life and the form the autobiography will take into a meaningful pattern. Suzanne's adolescent scene will perform a failure to tie this knot.

Rousseau's Stolen Ribbon

Although two of Rousseau's major critics, Jean Starobinski and Philippe Lejeune, have in various ways linked the Edenic childhood scene of the "children's punishment" and the adolescent scene of the "stolen ribbon" in the *Confessions*, they have not analyzed the way in which this linkage structures the autobiography and its subject.[43] In "the broken comb," Jean-Jacques discovers erotic passion at the age of eight in the punishment meted by his tutor's sister Mlle Lambercier: "As Mlle Lambercier had the affection of a mother for us, she also had her authority, and sometimes took it to the point of inflicting upon us the punishment of children when we had deserved it" (1, 52). Discovering that "this punishment increased even more my affection toward the woman who had imposed it upon me," Jean-Jacques can barely refrain from seeking "the return of the same treatment by deserving it; for I had found in pain, and even in shame, a mixture of sensuality which had left me more desire than fear . . . " (1, 52). This just punishment indissolubly cements sexual pleasure with a mother figure to justice, judgment, pain, and shame in all Jean-Jacques's future erotic desires: "the children's punishment . . . decided my tastes, desires, passions, and myself for the rest of my life" (1, 53).

In the episode of "the stolen ribbon," seventeen-year-old Jean-Jacques restages, but in a symbolic mode, the union of just judgment, erotically charged punishment, shame, and pain. While a servant in a wealthy household, he steals a ribbon, makes almost no effort to hide it ("I hardly hid it" [1, 120]), and when caught, falsely accuses Marion, the young, pretty, and virtuous cook, of having given it to him, "to seduce a young boy" (1, 121). He thus precipitates a scene of judgment in which both he and Marion are judged by le comte de la Roque, who convenes a "numerous . . . assembly" (1, 120) to witness his shame and the presumed erotic relation between him and Marion. He has now rearranged the original scene so that Marion substitutes for the original object of desire and/or seducer Mlle Lambercier, while the judge is changed from a "mother" figure to father figure. Jean-Jacques has so arranged the scene that the judge and "numerous" witnesses are forced, whether they lay the guilt to him or Marion, to perceive an indissoluble link binding erotic passion to the crime and punishment. The erotic relation itself lies nowhere else but in that punishing perception, which thus links shame, punishment, and erotic pleasure.

Jean-Jacques controls the perceptions of the judge and witnesses, who as models for the readers of Rousseau's text receive the impossible task of deciding "which one of the two was the scoundrel" (1, 20), and so must perceive Marion as mirroring Jean-Jacques. Rousseau elaborates this mirror relation for us, the actual readers, in explaining that Jean-Jacques accused Marion because of his "amitié" (ambiguously "love" or "friendship") for her: "She was present to my mind, and I excused myself upon the first object that offered itself. I accused her of having done what I wanted to do, and of having given me the ribbon because I had had the intention of giving it to her" (1, 122).

In an analysis of this passage, Paul de Man reads the wholly one-sided, specular relation as a relation of reciprocity: " . . . the ribbon 'stands for' . . . the reciprocity which, as we know from *Julie*, is for Rousseau the very condition of love; it stands for the substitutability of Rousseau for Marion and vice versa. Rousseau desires Marion as Marion desires Rousseau."[44] De Man posits himself as Rousseau's ideal reader, and ironically, he misperceives this scene in exactly the way that Jean-Jacques sets it up to be misperceived by his textual ideal readers. De Man's ideal misperception can thus lead us to understand how this scene establishes the symbolic economy that Voilquin will have to transform. He comes close to suggesting the one-sided nature of the Jean-Jacques/ Marion relation when he calls the reciprocity a "fantasy" (283). Yet he neglects to see that there is no reciprocity in the fantasy, which is only Rousseau's. In an analysis of de Man's reading, Barbara Johnson summarizes his difficult essay in a remarkably clear way: "De Man describes the incompatibility between Rousseau's description of his choice of the name Marion as motivated by his desire for her, on the one hand, and Rousseau's explanation that the name came to him by accident, on the other, in terms of the figure of anacoluthon—a syntactical interruption or discontinuity. What is revealed by Rousseau's anacoluthon, says de Man, is the eclipse of the subject (Rousseau) by the textual machine."[45] Contrary to de Man's reading of two "Marions," however, the object of desire is no more referential than the "thing" accidentally present to Jean-Jacques's mind. The Marion of reciprocal desire exists nowhere but in Jean-Jacques's imagination, until he makes the imaginary reciprocity exist in the eyes of his judges, and so forces her to mirror him. Although she protests strongly against this mirroring position, she is powerless to free herself from reflecting, in the perception of the judges, a reciprocal desire between them.

If the two Marions of the passage illustrate not the opposition between a referential and a non-referential figure but two different forms of non-referentiality, the passage can be read not as eclipsing the subject but as *producing* the subject (both as character and as author) of his autobiography. Rousseau succeeds in establishing the self-other, reader-writer relation because he is able to make the judging witnesses, as models for the ideal readers, read the scene as he has constructed it. They must believe that either one or the other stole the ribbon to seduce the other, and in the end can only oscillate between the two possibilities. As a result: "the comte de la Roque, sending both of us away, contented himself with saying that the conscience of the guilty party would sufficiently avenge the innocent party. His prediction was not vain; it does not stop fulfilling itself for a single day" (1, 121). Le comte de la Roque's sentence is that Rousseau internalize, and eternalize, the original complex unity of crime, punishment, erotic pain-pleasure of guilt and shame, and "the unbearable weight of remorse" (1, 120). The reader-author relation takes the form of a judgment in a book that Starobinski calls a "universal tribunal" (313), but he performs the readerly misperception of assuming that Rousseau's purpose is to have "his innocence confirmed" (313). Rousseau can instead repeat forever the erotically charged shame and punishment by retelling the whole scene to an ever-expanding circle of judging witnesses who are now the readers of his *Confessions*.

The introduction to the *Confessions* situates the reader-writer relation in the ultimate scene of judgment:

> Let the trumpet of the Last Judgment sound when it will; I shall come, this book in my hand, to present myself before the sovereign judge. . . .
> Eternal being, assemble around me the innumerable host of my fellow men; let them listen to my confessions, groan at my indignities, blush at my wretchedness. (1, 44)

Growing more grandiose with each repetition, the scene now contains innumerable rather than "numerous" witnesses, the comte de la Roque has become God himself, and instead of appearing before them with Marion, Rousseau appears with his book, which, he claims, mirrors him with complete "frankness" and "sincerity" (1, 44). Also like Marion, the book cannot escape from this role of faithful mirror in the eyes of these judging witnesses, who are now readers.[46]

In the scene of the stolen ribbon, Marion mediates Jean-Jacques's passage into the paternal symbolic order, but in a way that gives a twist to the classic model of the exchange of women. Formulated in Freud's *Totem and Taboo*, this model posits a mythic horde of sons who enter into rivalry with the father for the mother. After killing the father, they form an alliance to prevent further deadly rivalry by deifying the dead father and forbidding the mother to all the brothers, instituting instead the exchange of women.[47] Rene Girard revises this Freudian model through his own model of mediated desire. According to him, the subject desires an object not because it is in itself desirable but because it is possessed by a prestigious rival. In gaining the desired object, the subject gains mastery over his rival.[48]

Rousseau's use of Marion in a way that both fits and deviates from these classic paradigms, to establish his mastery of the reader-author relation, illuminates the problem that Voilquin confronts as autobiographer. Although Marion becomes the substitute for Mlle Lambercier, Marion is herself not a mother figure but someone less sacred and idealized.[49] And although she becomes the means by which Rousseau gains mastery over le comte de la Roque, she is not strictly speaking an object of exchange between Jean-Jacques and the count, for neither is she exactly an object, nor is she exactly exchanged. The two men instead exchange her supposed thoughts, feelings, and intentions, as Jean-Jacques communicates them to the count. Rather than the object of exchange—as a cook, she does not have sufficient value in the male economy—she is the medium of their exchange. She is, moreover, represented to the count not as an object but as a quasi-subject. In order for Rousseau's strategy to work, she must be seen as an active agent of sexual desire, yet be in reality too powerless to play an active role in this scene. As autobiographer in a hierarchic world, Rousseau can reveal the double gesture by which he represents a woman as active agent of desire in the very act that represses her power of personal agency, and still maintain reader identification with his text, only if that woman is lowly enough not to elicit indignation as the butt of a false accusation, yet just high enough to warrant a "reciprocal" desire. Rousseau represents in a far different manner his sexual relation with his beloved bourgeois mistress Madame Warrens, whose sexual power he portrays with great awe. He describes himself as even more obsessed for his aristocratic object of desire, Mme d'Epinay, and, apologizing to the readers even for publishing his feelings for her, takes great care to stress that they are not on her part "reciprocal."

More to the point here, Marion contrasts to the upper-class heroines of the fictional romantic quest analyzed earlier in that she is portrayed as mirroring the hero actively rather than passively. Where the heroines who mediate the fictional romantic heroes' quest substitute for the mother as ultimate object of a desire for plenitude, Marion is instead a metaphor for the autobiographical book, mediating the hero's desire for mastery of the metaphoric author-reader relation. But in order to understand more fully the significance of Rousseau's use of a working-class woman here, we need to compare the stolen ribbon episode with the equivalent scene in Chateaubriand's *Memoirs from beyond the Tomb*.

Chateaubriand's "Solitary Life in Paris"

Chateaubriand's autobiography tells the story of the youngest son of an ancient aristocratic Breton family, who fought against the French Revolution and returned from the Emigration to become the most celebrated author of his generation—dubbed in literary histories "the Father of Romanticism"—and a political figure of considerable influence. The temporal structure of his *Memoirs* revolves around a rupture, in the form of the French Revolution, between a dream-like lost paradise, in which all time is one unified time, and the post-Revolutionary period marked by constant and repeated ruptures: revolutions, invasions, changes of government. So much does Chateaubriand identify himself with the French history of his era in the *Memoirs* that the structure of his own Oedipal subjectivity is projected onto the course of history itself. The scene of autobiographical subject formation occurs immediately upon François-René's rupture from the Edenic space/time of his childhood in the ancestral chateau of Combourg: "like Adam after his fall, I set forth upon unknown land" (1, 148). He is leaving home to begin his military career, and he stops first in Paris to be presented at the Court of Louis XVI. Coincidentally, within the Oedipal narrative of French history, the year is 1788, just before the Revolution.

Chateaubriand prefaces his scene, as Voilquin will preface her scene of (non)subject formation, with a reference to Rousseau: "Rousseau believes he owes to his sincerity, as to the education of men, the confession of the suspect pleasures of his life. . . . If I had prostituted myself to the courtesans of Paris, I would not believe myself obliged to instruct posterity on that matter" (1, 170). Thus expressing his rivalry with his literary father, Chateaubriand introduces an adventure in which François-René restages a Parisian love affair of 1606, recounted by le maréchal de Bassompierre in his own *Mémoires*.

Chateaubriand inserts within his own text a long passage from Bassompierre's *Memoirs*. The seventeenth-century nobleman had been accosted by a beautiful and passionate laundress. Arriving at their second assignation, Bassompierre finds a burning bed and the naked body of the woman with that of another man, her husband or another lover. In 1788, following the detailed directions provided by Bassompierre's *Memoirs*, François-René sets out to find the laundress, wanders around in the neighborhood described by Bassompierre, asks directions from characters that uncannily resemble those in Bassompierre's world, and ends his story by saying: "You will therefore admire the chastity and reserve of my youth in Paris . . . : I had commerce only with a 216-year-old courtesan, formerly in love with a maréchal de France [Bassompierre], rival of le Béarnais for Mademoiselle de Montmorency, and lover of Mademoiselle d'Entragues. . . . Louis XVI, whom I was going to see, did not suspect my secret relations with his family" (1, 173).

Like Rousseau, Chateaubriand presents his relation with this "gentille grisette" (pleasing working-girl [1, 173]) as existing solely in his imagination. But here, the whole account of the triadic relationship is so blatantly fanciful that it ends up precluding any thought of Chateaubriand as cruel Rousseauian exploiter of a poor, defenseless woman to mediate his rivalry with a prestigious man. The exaggerated fantasy quality of the narration serves to divert attention away from the even more outlandish fiction contained in Chateaubriand's interpretation of the story, and to make it pass as axiomatic: "What a beautiful story is this story of Bassompierre! It is necessary to understand one of the reasons why he was so resolutely loved. In that period the French people were still separated into two distinct classes, one dominant, the other semi-serf. The laundress held Bassompierre in her arms like a half-god descended to the bosom of a slave: he gave her the illusion of glory, and French women, alone among all women, are able to become intoxicated by this illusion" (1, 173). But who here has the illusion, and who is projecting that illusion onto another? More fantastic than the triadic relation itself are the thoughts and feelings attributed to the laundress. The "resolute" and "disinterested" (1, 173) quality of her passion for Bassompierre is the structural equivalent of the "reciprocal" quality in the desires of Jean-Jacques and Marion.

Chateaubriand establishes mastery over the metaphoric author-reader relation of his autobiography by making himself into the ideal reader of Bassompierre. What Bassompierre passes on to him is not the woman herself as object of exchange but her supposed thoughts and feelings, which express her active desire for his power over her. Like Rousseau, and unlike the romantic heroes who desire reunion with a lost mother figure, Chateaubriand desires recognition as the subject who transmits the paternal heritage. By accepting his interpretation and identifying with his reading, the readers of *Memoirs from beyond the Tomb* enter the role of the ideal reader and repeat the exchange of the *grisette's* putative feelings between Bassompierre and himself. Chateaubriand's post-Revolutionary version of this exchange clarifies the reasons for its imaginary quality and for its use of a working-class woman. François-René's fantasy relation to the laundress, recounted by the narrator in a tone of bantering indulgence for the naive, innocent, young chevalier, serves to represent as real another, less innocent, imaginary relation. The cruel sexual/political relations between upper-class men and lower-class women, vehemently denounced in the *Tribune des femmes*, are represented in their imaginary form as idealized and eroticized, as well as desired, sought after, even instigated by the lower-class woman, and provided for her benefit. By accepting Chateaubriand's desire for class and sexual mastery as faithfully mirrored by the *grisette's* desire, the reader can say with Chateaubriand, "What a beautiful story!" (1, 173), and find his own identity in that mirror.

The object of exchange transmitted from Bassompierre to François-René, and from Rousseau to Chateaubriand, is the "Imaginary" of patriarchal ideology, the mirror-reflection through which the male subject forms its identity.[50] This paternal legacy of ideology is passed intact from the *ancien régime* to serve the needs of a new bourgeois ideology,[51] as Chateaubriand's apparent nostalgia for a lost social hierarchy serves in fact to clothe the new post-Revolutionary hierarchy in a seductive haze of poetic eroticism.

When another "gentille grisette," the embroiderer Suzanne Voilquin, does speak, she reveals the horror of being put in this position. All three romantic autobiographies illustrate vividly, from different temporal, gender, and class perspectives, this imposition of a false subjectivity and desire on a working-class woman as a condition for the male imaginary of bourgeois society to be imposed as the real framework for social relations. Her role in ideology is to confirm that representation as real. By the 1830s, ideology demands that bourgeois women bear the image of an idealized object, but their passivity is only part of the story. Its corollary is that working-class women are pictured as giving themselves in free, generous passion. Ideology clothes them in an image of active desire through the very act that binds them to silence and paralysis. Voilquin's autobiography unbinds them as "a daughter of the people" counters the ideology articulated by "the Father of Romanticism."

Voilquin's "Intimate Drama"

Almost every element from the scenes that form Chateaubriand as autobiographical subject appears in Voilquin's *Memories of a Daughter of the People*, but in the negative register. Yet the two autobiographical texts do not symmetrically reflect each other as two sides of the same story: Chateaubriand's successful claim to universality requires the silencing of a text such as Voilquin's, and on three levels. As published book, *Memories of a Daughter of the People* is excluded from the literary canon. On the level of narration, the text recounts Suzanne's sexual relation to a representative of universal male subjectivity who forcefully represses her story. Finally, the self-referential narrative of the text's own birth explains why it cannot achieve the textual density of the *Confessions* and the *Memoirs from beyond the Tomb*.

As the title of *Memories of a Daughter of the People* suggests, the whole autobiography structures itself through the kind of metaphorical, non-biological mother-daughter relation discussed earlier. The introductory sentence explicitly encodes the reader-author relation as this mother-daughter bond: "In order for you to understand my life, I must, dear child, briefly describe its early years; the past gives birth to the future" (3). The metaphor of childbirth characterizes the writing that links Voilquin to a reader who is not her literal daughter but a niece whom she adopted in the late 1830s.

This introduction marks several differences from Chateaubriand's and Rousseau's reader-writer relation. In contrast to their claims to speak in a universal voice to a universal audience, Voilquin addresses a particular person. Second, insofar as the first sentence places any reader of the *Memories* in the mother-daughter relation, the poles of that relation, as we have seen, shift back and forth. Because the writer oscillates between being the daughter (as in the title) and the mother (as in the first sentence), so, as will later be clear, does the reader. Nonbiological and unstably shifting, this mother-child relation would render impossible the patrilineal genealogy, unbroken and based on the purity of blood lines, as represented in the "genealogical tree of the de Chateaubriand family" (*Memoirs*, 1, 121) on the wall of the father's study, that underlies and unifies Chateaubriand's subjectivity and his textual time/space.

This difference both enriches and impoverishes Voilquin's autobiography with respect to the romantic tradition. On the one hand, the reversible relation with the reader precludes the kind of fixed hierarchy that establishes Rousseau and Chateaubriand between a patriarchal God or godlike king and an imaginary other as lower-class woman at the bottom of the hierarchy. It also precludes the symbolic economy of exchange, rivalry, and mastery that structures the autobiographical subjectivity of Rousseau and Chateaubriand. And the possibility for a different economy is its potential wealth. But by the same token, on the level of text, the mother-daughter relation lends itself with difficulty to the establishment of a triadic relation necessary for any symbolic act. And on the level of the book, it signals the lack of socially established means for its transmission to future generations.

Like the theoretical and epistolary texts of the *Saint-Simoniennes*, Voilquin's autobiography necessarily situates itself both inside and outside the symbolic order, and the resulting ambiguity marks the scenes of autobiographical subject formation. The scene that takes the place of Rousseau's and Chateaubriand's childhood Eden is Suzanne's early relation to her "beloved" mother: "Though dead for more than forty years, she is as alive in me now as she was the moment of our separation" (3). But the natural, literal mother, as we have seen earlier, is an ambiguous figure, ultimately rejected. On the one hand, her mother's love provides Suzanne the pleasurable space of childhood: "In the winter, maternal inspiration was a very ardent breath to make us leave our beds at six o'clock. . . . But in return we received as compensation a very tender kiss and a very hot soup; I must admit that the former gave me as much pleasure as the latter" (2).

But on the other hand, unlike Chateaubriand's Combourg and Rousseau's Bossey, this maternal space cannot constitute a lost paradise because, for Voilquin, in patriarchal society a mother "whose intelligence ha[s] been extremely diminished by her upbringing" (2), and whose soul is "benumbed by the most complete ignorance of every idea and thing" (18), cannot fully provide one. Forced by custom and the Church to remain ignorant, the mother exemplifies the "renouncement" (7) of her own will and acquiesces to unjust convention, and as a result abandons Suzanne on more than one occasion to great physical and spiritual harm. While her warm, loving presence "illuminate[s]" (18) the path of her children, "she annihilated herself in a complete abnegation. In order to reconcile her feelings and her duties, she made herself silent and submissive" (18). Where nineteenth-century religious and secular ideologies see maternal love and abnegation, sentiment and duty, as an instinctive and indissoluble unity, Voilquin presents them as contradictory to each other. Through a writing about motherhood that is unusual, if not unique, for the nineteenth century, Voilquin separates and rearranges these elements of motherhood, so that she can conceive not only a split within what generally appears as a natural unity but also a split between natural, biological motherhood and symbolic motherhood. In order for Voilquin to choose symbolic activity instead of silence, she will have to do away with the romantic illusion of a maternal space as a lost paradise.

Where Chateaubriand presents his pre-Oedipal time/space as essentially unified, Voilquin presents the maternal figure that embodies her space as already split into a good mother and a bad mother. The bad mother takes shape not explicitly, but in scenes that oppose her to another prominent figure in Suzanne's private mythology, that of the doctor. Suzanne's double ambition is to become a mother and to become a doctor. The second is of course an impossible ambition for a French woman of the 1830s and '40s, but she does ultimately succeed in gaining medical training and establishing a practice in midwifery.

On two occasions during this childhood period, a doctor saves Suzanne from the grave harm done her as a result of the mother's acquiescence to patriarchal and Christian morality. But the text also treats this mother-doctor contradiction ambiguously. Although these two scenes implicitly suggest that Suzanne will later desire to be a doctor in order to avoid resembling her mother as accomplice to patriarchal society, Voilquin explicitly traces her medical ambition to her ardent love for her mother as victim of patriarchy. The mother dies because social rules of feminine modesty prevent a female patient from describing her symptoms to the (necessarily) male doctor: "They *all* dissimulate the gravity of their symptoms" (24). The doctor "must guess everything" without much

to go on, and so generally guesses wrong. To solve this problem, Voilquin demands that women become doctors: "To women and women
alone, the right to aid their sex, not only in the divine work of maternity,
but also in all illnesses from which chastity has so much to suffer in
divulging them to men" (24).

Voilquin's text also differs from those of Rousseau and Chateaubriand
in that the prototypical pleasurable experience of lost childhood cannot
provide her with the structural elements for forming the autobiographical
subject, because too many elements are missing. Their loss occurs not in
the Oedipal rupture but already haunts the pre-Oedipal space. The de-
fective mother-daughter relation cannot by itself provide the basis for the
reader-author relation but must be conflated with the doctor- patient relation that: (1) does not yet exist and must be created; and (2) must go
beyond maternity, as the quotation above states. In this ideal autobiographical structure, the good patient is a good writer able to make clear the
language of symptoms and of the body. The good doctor is a good
reader, sensitive to the nuances of that language, and able to interpret
them for the health of the patient. This, it will become apparent, is what
Voilquin asks of her readers. Like the symbolic mother-daughter relation,
this ideal doctor-patient relation is shifting and reversible, upsetting
socio-symbolic hierarchies.

This difference in subjectivity between Voilquin and Chateaubriand not
only emerges in the scene of late adolescence but also takes root in the
childhood family. Chateaubriand's aristocratic family structure, centered
around an unbroken patrilineal genealogy and its history of grandeur,
requires that each family member unquestioningly fill, and identify with,
his or her position in the kinship nomenclature of mother, father, sister,
brother. Chateaubriand invests much of his identity in his traditional position as youngest son. This stable identity between person and nominal
position aids his illusion of ontological unity. Voilquin's proletarian
family structure, centered around precarious survival, maintains the
same kinship nomenclature, but requires that all family members shift
into and out of the different positions of mother, father, sister, and
brother as the need arises.

In Suzanne's childhood space, the position of the mother not only is
split but alternates among different family members. Because of family
poverty and the mother's poor health, Suzanne at a very young age becomes the adoptive mother of her younger sister Adrienne; and so at a
very early age she must separate biological from metaphorical motherhood. As her mother's disease advances, she must "replace the mother
of the family" (27) for all the members of the family, and when her
father is unemployed she has to replace the father by bringing home a
wage. An earlier illness of the mother had placed the father in the position of caring for the children "with the tenderness of a mother" (34).

Given the difference between Suzanne's proletarian family and François-René's aristocratic family, the subjects that emerge in their autobiographies will take correspondingly different forms. This difference in the
shape of subjectivity also results from the contrasted forms taken by the
respective ruptures from the childhood space. Like Chateaubriand, Voilquin links her personal history with the course of French history; but
where Chateaubriand identifies his personal separation from childhood
with the Revolution, and idealizes the Restoration of 1815 as a return to
Right and Good, Voilquin identifies her personal rupture with the trouble brought by that same Restoration: "The years that followed the Restoration were very painful for working people to live through. And so
poverty, our old acquaintance, came knocking at our door again. This sad
visitor weighed primarily upon my mother . . . and the horrid illness of
which she died three years later began to exert its ravages . . . " (24).

The mother's death creates Suzanne's rupture from her childhood
space, and the period of her mourning coincides with her late adolescent
sexual awakening. The autobiographical subject of the *Memories* will not,
however, like that of the *Confessions* and the *Memoirs*, grow out of the
erotic relation in which the mirroring other acts as the screen upon
which the hero's desires are projected. In this erotic relation the position
of mirroring screen can be occupied by none other than Suzanne herself.
Like Chateaubriand, Voilquin introduces this scene of adolescent sexual
awakening with a reference to Rousseau, but as author of the *La Nouvelle
Héloise*: " . . . I preferred Rousseau, and of him I read with pleasure *Emile*
and especially *La Nouvelle Héloise* . . . and although I claimed I could remain strong against his influence, the charm worked; I no longer felt the
same after this reading" (36). This novel along with other novels "exalt-
ing love made themselves the accomplices of nature, by strongly exciting
my imagination and filling my heart with unknown desires" (36). Where
Chateaubriand refers to the *Confessions* through denial of its influence,
and an expression of rivalry, Voilquin substitutes for it a fictional work
whose narrative voice is in large part feminine.

The episode introduced by this reference to Rousseau rearranges, in-
tensifies, and repeats in a negative register the elements of the lost maternal space. Stanislas, Suzanne's first and only love, presents himself as
a promise to repeat the relation with the good mother, and is in reality
studying to be that other ambiguous mythical figure, the doctor. The
beginning of this episode echoes the metaphors of warmth and light that
began the episode of the childhood relation with the good mother:
"Through it I was lifted for a few moments into a luminous world, but
the man who had made me live in ethereal heights brutally threw me
back into an abyss" (38). This abyss suggests the absence of a mirroring
surface necessary for the establishment of Suzanne's identity. While in
the episodes of "the stolen ribbon" and "My Solitary Life in Paris" the

heroine mirrors the hero's imaginary projections, here Stanislas seduc-
tively presents himself as such a mirror but only to monopolize the position of subject and reduce Suzanne to acting out his fantasies.

In Voilquin's narrative the adolescent erotic relation repeats much more
consciously and explicitly the lost childhood structure, in all its ambiguity, than in the narratives of Chateaubriand and Rousseau. Voilquin
represents Stanislas as promising her a new good mother, in a family
situation where, like the one of her childhood, the members shift in and
out of the nominal positions: "He sought to reassure me by talking about
his mother, a sister he had lost a short while before, and the happiness
his parents would have to find her again in me, etc. My heart translated
the incoherence of his words with this sentence: he loves me!" (40).

But Suzanne cannot form her shifting subjectivity out of this repetition
of the childhood maternal space, because Stanislas controls another slip-
pery shift, that between his words and the reality of the couple's situation, which in fact repeats another element of the early childhood
structure, that of the relation between the timid mother and the inept
doctor. In the above quotation, Stanislas occupies the position of the bad
mother and Suzanne the position of the bad doctor, who fails to interpret
the incoherent words of her patient. Worse, she even misreads her
patient's bodily symptoms: "He uttered a thousand tender and delicate
things to me, taking as witness to the truth of his words the rapid beating of his heart, which he made me feel with my trembling hand" (40).

Having promised to recreate Suzanne's role as beloved daughter, Stanislas instead turns her into the bad mother of her childhood. He pressures her to let him "treat [her] like his wife," or in other words to let
him reduce her on a sexual level to the state of submissive renunciation
and resignation against which she had revolted in her heritage from her
own mother. He makes this explicit by changing his promise to make her
into the daughter of his mother into an exhortation to her to "imitat[e]
the example of his mother who before her marriage had loved his father
enough to refuse him nothing" (41).

For a period Suzanne is able to resist Stanislas's "attacks" (43) by hal-
lucinating the ghost of her mother. Since these "hallucinations" raise
complex issues in the problems of feminine subject formation (or lack
thereof) and working-class feminine sexuality, they are worth examining
in some detail. To begin with, this maternal power occupies in this episode a position analogous to that of the father-rivals in the autobiographies of Rousseau and Chateaubriand, and so clarifies the impossibility
of Suzanne's textual situation. With all her power, the mother can be
only an entirely negative force who ultimately fails as a spiritual principle
in the face of Stanislas's social and sexual masculine law.

For several months the hallucinations are Suzanne's "safeguard" and
"protection." During this time, "These repeated phenomena caused me
no fright. On the contrary, I thanked my mother for thus coming to

protect me against myself and comfort my heart for the struggle" (43). At best this maternal ghost offers a purely negative aid that Suzanne can use "against" the upsurge of her subjectivity and desire. But to complicate matters, as Stanislas's attacks become more violent, the ghost becomes correspondingly frightening:

> Toward dusk, when we were alone together in my room, he became violent, out of control, and committed such a brutal assault against me that I was seized with fright. . . . My hallucinations had come back, but this time stronger and more frightening. I saw nothing but them; everything else had become alien to me. My mother seemed to plunge her sad eyes into mine; I followed the progression of this shadow with a certain anguish, for it kept growing and growing, extending its arms and filling the room in the manner of the *vulture*, that bird of the poets with its vast wingspread. By this time, I was no longer breathing, my eyes were closed, and I was trembling; my body was convulsed, so much did it seem to me that this enormous volume was going to crush me. (43–44)

This Dead Mother, the symbolic (non)equivalent of Chateaubriand's Dead Fathers, Bassompierre and the ancestors of his august genealogy, epitomizes the ambiguity of the mother figure as the principle for creating a feminine symbolic structure. She is all the more problematic in that she is no longer the immediately present, weak, submissive mother of Suzanne's childhood but a spirit possessed of more power and intelligence than she ever had in life, and even more powerful than God himself: "I had sworn, in laying my last kiss upon her cold brow, to be forever worthy of her! This thought was stronger in me than the fear of God himself" (42). Yet, mighty as this deified maternal spirit may be, and much as she seems to resemble the internalized paternal super-ego, she does not, within the constraints of patriarchy, have the power to usher her daughter into subjecthood, but only to "crush" it. For Voilquin, then, the symbolic mother around whom she will eventually organize a feminine symbolic economy cannot simply be the spiritual equivalent of the symbolic father, but will have to take a different form altogether. She will also have to come into existence through a different narrative path.

The other troubling aspect of this maternal hallucination concerns Suzanne's sexuality. For nineteenth-century working-class women, sexual freedom was not simply a liberation from passivity and repression into sexual activity, but a more complex liberation, as we have already seen, from an imposed, constrained activity. Its path is not unified or clear. Forced to enter the public space forbidden to women, "when, confronting daily necessities, work must provide for their needs" (53), women workers found that prostitution and rape were often a condition of work.

Suzanne's internal conflicts, as recounted in this episode of the *Memories*, as well as the conflicts between different Saint-Simonian women recorded in the *Tribune des femmes* demonstrate that in the nineteenth-century, working-class feminine sexuality takes a multiplicity of forms. In the debates between the women who choose a "flaming red ribbon" as sign of their freedom to enjoy "love and pleasure" (Joséphine-Félicité, *Tribune* 1: 66) and the women who adopt "as a symbol of our devotion and waiting, the [deep violet] color of the Dahlia" (Voilquin, *Tribune* 1: 63) in the *Tribune des femmes*, Voilquin unambiguously represents the latter tendency. Her reserve in talking about her own sensuality is one of many positions that include the vivid evocations of desire and pleasure in the writings of Claire Démar and Pauline Roland. In her essay *My Law of the Future*, Démar writes: "What! because a woman might not have confided to the public her womanly sensations; . . . because her nights of love might not be transparent and illuminated; because she might not open her doors and windows when she wished to abandon herself to the arms of a man and lavish upon him her kisses and caresses: it would thus necessarily follow that she would be the toy or slave of a man . . . ?" (31). Démar's rhetorical questions find an equally passionate echo in Pauline Roland, who in a letter to Aglaé Saint-Hilaire expresses her decision to engage in free love: "I am a woman of love, but not of mystical love, love of the flesh as well as the heart, complete love in sum. The celibacy I kept for so long, and which I reentered more than two months ago, has been painful for me. . . . I have suffered physically and morally atrocious pains, and even since I've been here, desire has so raged within me that I have rolled around in my bed screaming" (no. 28, March 21, 1834).

By contrast, Voilquin speaks of desire in a vague, abstract, and collective way: "Let us thus acknowledge that whatever our secret desires may be . . . we must remain subject to the law of the world" (*Tribune* 1: 63). Here in the pages of the *Tribune des femmes*, as in her letters and her autobiography, Voilquin is more concerned with solidarity among women than with their individual sexual pleasures. Yet although Voilquin's French critics have tended to qualify her as traditionalist and conservative in opposition to Démar as radical,[52] her sexuality may be more complex, especially if seen as one possible response among many to the hypocrisy surrounding the enforced sexuality of proletarian women. The choice for sexual "virtue" *and* the choice for sexual "freedom" both placed working-class women in a double bind in the context of the nineteenth-century double standard. Because of this, each could be endured as a path of oppression or chosen as a path for freedom. The meanings of sexual chastity or activity fluctuate constantly.

In the *Memories* Voilquin seems much more indignant about the affront to women's "modesty" and "chastity" in the doctor-patient relation than in the stigmatizing of their sexual desires. And when she does talk about freedom, both in the *Memories* and her article on her divorce from her husband in the *Tribune des femmes*, it seems to connote rather a bodily integrity which does not do away with passion, but which protects her from masculine constraints and allows her to throw herself into public activity, to study, to practice medicine, to be free to go all over the world and do everything. In the article on her decision to divorce Eugène at a time when divorce did not exist and women were required to live under their husband's authority and in his house, she says: "I can teach *everyone* about the new route that I was the first to dare travel. Placing myself above the narrow, petty customs that men *alone* have transformed into law, raising my thought to a universal conception—the freedom of woman—I have rejected as antihuman a law which oppressed me" (*Tribune* 2: 171). It is no coincidence that in defining feminine freedom, Voilquin uses the metaphor of a journey, speaks of transcendence, and rejects as law, not that which represses feminine sexuality, but that which enforces feminine sexual activity while repressing women's passion.

Voilquin's account of the Stanislas episode also bespeaks a sexual dilemma that is more complex in many ways than a simple sexual conservatism. The correspondence between the escalation of Stanislas's violence and the escalation of the maternal ghost's violence, whereby the latter almost directly reflects the former, suggests first that Suzanne's hallucination results not just from her fear of Stanislas, but from her fear of her own sexual arousal: "I was in love, and if I could resist my own emotions for so long, . . . it was only the memory of my mother that gave me strength" (42). Typically, Voilquin here speaks of her sexual desire in more reserved and tepid terms than she uses to express her passion for freedom from constraints of her body's integrity. Thus the passage suggests secondly that her fear is not just that of losing respectability, but of losing the game of the double bind tying nineteenth-century working-class women to the identity of Woman. All women were defined as women by the dictates of chastity and passivity, but working-class women *also* lived under the dictates of sexual activity. Suzanne's terror comes in part from her fiancé's demand that she perform this double bind and thus lose her identity in its abyss. Her reaction to this confusing and terrifying plight is partly to take refuge in the traditional morality that deprives women of freedom and partly to resist submission to a man's will by using the maternal hallucination to protect her autonomy.

Yet this maternal power, a copy of patriarchy's paternal principle, can only lead Suzanne to an impasse. She can maintain her identity only by losing consciousness, and this loss of consciousness also exhausts her resistance: "I was at the end of my strength and could not think any more; therefore that man's new attempts obtained all the success he desired. From that moment on I was his! . . . " (44, ellipses in text). She is reduced to what the text several times calls "silence" (cf. 71, 73) not only because her erotic scene is a rape but because a rape in the nineteenth century cannot be named. This cause for silence provides one connection between nineteenth-century proletarian and African American women's autobiography, where, according to Domna Stanton, "even the violence of rape was consistently silenced in nineteenth-century narratives" (13) Although the *Memories* narrates the overcoming of this silencing, it cannot pronounce the word "rape," so that modern historian Valentin Pelosse can still misread it as a "seduction" and Suzanne's "first adventure."[53] In the quotation above, Voilquin's description of her lack of thought, as well as the ellipses, suggests that instead of forming her subjectivity, the episode annihilates it. And where Rousseau and Chateaubriand form their autobiographical subjects though an erotic relation in which the sexual relation is imaginary, Suzanne fails to form her autobiographical subject because she cannot prevent an erotic relation she had enjoyed in imagination from becoming terrifyingly real. Because she is forced to sustain sexual relations with Stanislas on a regular basis, and to hide her tears about this from him and from her family, her silence is not that of the simple passivity associated with the nineteenth-century bourgeois stereotype, but an exhausting activity.

Narrating on the self-referential level her failure to form the relation of recognition that confirms her as subject of her autobiography, the episode, like the childhood experience, superimposes the writer-reader, mother-daughter, doctor-patient relations, but without the former ambiguity. Stanislas is now the bad doctor who cannot read Suzanne's bodily symptoms, the bad reader, who reduces Suzanne as writer to "silence" (45), having to play an active role in but unable to talk about "the secret of our intimacy" (49), and finally, the bad mother of her childhood, who abandons her. And so she *has* succeeded in forming the metaphorical mother-daughter relation that will eventually structure her autobiography, but in a completely negative version. The original childhood space is reconstituted, but in order to structure the autobiography it must be repeated in additional episodes so that a new kind of symbolic economy can form itself.

Establishing the author-reader-mediator triangle means finding someone who will accept the role of imaginary other and someone who will play the role of ideal reader and recognize the subject as mirrored by an other. For Rousseau and Chateaubriand, the ideal readers are already included in the episode of subject formation: for Rousseau, le comte de la Roque; for Chateaubriand, himself in relation to Bassompierre. Voilquin's episode narrates instead the striking absence of its ideal reader, since Stanislas, to put the finishing touch on his plan, sends away from the apartment Suzanne's last protector, her beloved sister and adoptive daughter Adrienne (the future mother of the adoptive daughter to whom the *Memories* are finally addressed). He exerts his masculine power to break up the triangle in which two women had formed an alliance to control his behavior. In order for Voilquin to become the subject of the text addressed to a reader, she must rebuild the triangular relation. In contrast to Rousseau and Chateaubriand, Voilquin must repeat the adolescent scene by telling it to an ideal reader. This repetition, however, also repeats the failure of the Stanislas episode on a symbolic level, since the ideal reader in the second episode turns out to be anything but ideal and rejects her story. But this failure itself leads her to an understanding of the author-reader relation she needs.

The additional episode in the self-referential narrative occurs in 1832. Suzanne has married and joined the Saint-Simonian movement led by Father Enfantin, but has not yet organized the separate women's group. She decides to confess her past to an ideal audience remarkably similar to the God of the *Confessions* and King Louis XVI of the *Memoirs*: "I want to make my whole past known to my husband, but I want to tell it to him in the presence of the *Father*" (83), emphasis in original). This father, the negative of the mother, hears the Stanislas episode, but instead of helping her to create a new form of symbolic triad by recognizing her as subject, he reconstructs the old one by recognizing the husband in a relation mediated by Suzanne: "Voilquin threw himself sobbing into the arms of the Father, but, in these first moments, *neither of them extended a hand to me!*" (84, emphasis in original). This episode illustrates the problem of forming the autobiographical "pact" discussed earlier. This audience cannot recognize Suzanne as a "real" person, cannot include her in its community, cannot recognize any common codes or conventions in her story, and can interpret it only according to the codes and conventions of patriarchal morality.

Indignant over this "iniquitous distribution of male justice," especially from the man who had infected her with a venereal disease that prevented her from being a mother, Voilquin rejects this mode of autobiography. She will no longer conform to its Rousseauian code of confession and justice. She tells her adoptive daughter that she decides to seek another mode, and in so doing she discovers her future ideal reader:

> From this moment on I vowed never again to speak of my thoughts or the intimate acts of my apostolic life to any man whatsoever and to confess myself thenceforth to my conscience alone, reserving myself the right, if I met a woman great and loving enough to appreciate with her heart all the acts of life, to explain to her the motives that would have made me act. (84–85)

This "great woman" resembles the Saint-Simonian Great Mother, as well as Suzanne's own good mother, who is "great among all women for her heart" (18); and this explanation is what Voilquin will eventually offer to every reader of her book, who thus reads as a mother—and at the same time as a daughter. But Suzanne must still find the "great woman."

The father-daughter relation, in which Suzanne had recounted her episode to Enfantin, does not allow for this reversibility of roles but locks her in the position of subordinate daughter in a fixed hierarchy. Within this static relation, Suzanne cannot achieve the shifting form of subjectivity needed for her autobiography. In order to achieve this, her text must differ from those of Rousseau and Chateaubriand in one more way. Their episode of subject formation repeated for an audience representing the ideal reader the Edenic moment of childhood before the rupture. Voilquin, in her second repetition of the childhood structure before her husband and Enfantin, repeats not the childhood moment, which was never a lost paradise, but the rupture itself, which she incorporates into the self-referential narrative. Here it separates the Father and husband (non)-ideal readers within the text from the mother/daughter ideal reader to whom the narrator addresses the text. Instead of providing a model for reading, as they do for Chateaubriand and Rousseau, the reader figures in the text encode a model for misreading.

This is because no positive model is available to her. The reading model encoded in the texts of Rousseau and Chateaubriand is inherited from the past and transmitted to the future along the lines of patriarchal descent, and it is also in itself the model of patriarchal transmission. Voilquin cannot inherit her model, and in order to establish one, she must sever herself from rather than repeat and transmit the fixed institutions, not only of family, motherhood, marriage, and class, but also of idealized childhood and idealized erotic relationships. The contradiction between textual reader figures and the ideal readers also suggests that there never is a critical point in the *Memories of a Daughter of the People*, as there is in the two men's texts, when the reading model falls into place and the autobiographical knot binds the form of the text. Suzanne never meets THE Great Woman, but she contributes to establishing the first modern feminist movement, and through her experiences comes to the conclusion, quoted earlier, that the Great Woman is "only a symbol" and a "completely feminine feeling" among women, in relation to whom they can "reveal themselves" to each other and "seek each other out," "outside of the sphere of male influence," in order to collectively build "the moral edifice of the future" (187).

The mother, then, mediates the relation between author and reader but not as object in an economy of exchange. More important, the symbolic mother is not a symbol or a maternal figure at all. By contrast to the Name-of-the-Father, she is not represented by a genealogical line of dead fathers. She instead figures a kind of empty space that each of the women in the relation can temporarily occupy in turn, as writer or as reader. Like the rewritten Oedipal triangle of the *Saint-Simoniennes'* theoretical essays, the symbolic triangle structuring the autobiographical text is an extremely precarious one, risking collapse, but also fertile with promise for feminine writing. By contrast, another romantic feminist autobiographer, Flora Tristan, to whose memoirs we will now turn, turned away from the mother to devise an entirely different strategy for transforming fundamental symbolic structures.

FLORA TRISTAN: THE NAME OF THE FATHER
AND THE BODY OF THE MOTHER

The feminine subject that takes shape in Flora Tristan's writing differs significantly from that of the Saint-Simonian feminists of the *Tribune des femmes*. She is also, and not coincidentally, unique among feminist and socialist organizers of the July Monarchy. Her biographers credit her with having posited first and most lucidly among pre-Marxist socialists the principles of class struggle and solidarity among all workers,[54] as she traveled through France in 1844, exhorting workers to unite in a "Workers' Union" and to "constitute the working class" as a political force.[55] She is today the most famous of the 1830s feminists, probably because she wrote a significant body of texts: the autobiographical *Peregrinations of a Pariah* (1838), her novel *Méphis* (1838) (considered the first proletarian novel), her pioneering sociological study of the industrial revolution *Promenades in London* (1840), and her socialist manifesto *Workers' Union* (1843).[56]

Tristan's biographers and literary analysts have tended to write of her in an uncritically celebratory or admiring way, brushing over troubling and discomforting contradictions in her work. The one notable exception in this respect is Sandra Dijkstra's book, but her critical approach takes the form of seeing Tristan's contradictions as the result of her individual psychology, citing "her confused feelings for her mother" or "the internalization of guilt feelings."[57] Rather than psychologize Tristan, we could see the disturbing aspects of her work in more social and political terms. Her contradictions would then appear to arise from a dilemma that all feminists confront, that of having to struggle for change within and through the very socio-symbolic structures they are trying to change. As a brilliant pioneer feminist indispensable to an understanding of our history, Tristan reflects back to us, as do the *Saint-Simoniennes*, a historically different version of contradictions that also tear at us. Instead of using psychology to examine her individual psyche, we can instead examine women's relation to those symbolic and cultural structures.

Tristan's *Peregrinations of a Pariah* begins with a summary of her position in the 1830s, which epitomizes the oppression of women by the political economy of that period. Her situation has two symmetrical irregularities, both of which stem from the Civil Code of 1804. It had attempted to stabilize that political economy by ensuring that the fathers could transmit their capital to their "legitimate" sons and keep the property within the family. Wives were strictly placed under their husband's authority so as to prevent ambiguity in the relation between husband and son. The Code decreed: "The wife owes obedience to the husband" (article 213), and forbade her from living outside of his domicile. All children born in marriage were the father's children over whom the mother had no rights. All children born outside of marriage were the mother's children, to whom the father had no duties. "Paternity claims are forbidden," decreed the Code.[58]

Having fled from the conjugal domicile, Flora is, on the one hand, in 1833, when the account in *Peregrinations* begins, the outlaw, runaway wife of André Chazal. She travels around France, living under the false identities of "fille-mère" (unmarried mother) or widow, as she tries to prevent her husband, the courts, and the police from taking her daughter away from her. On the other hand, she is also, in the eyes of the French law, an illegitimate child, unentitled to anything from her paternal inheritance, because the marriage between her French émigré mother and her Spanish aristocratic father, which Tristan insists was contracted during the French Revolution, had never been registered in France: "as a result of this lack of a formality, I was considered a child born out of wedlock. Until the age of fifteen, I had been ignorant of this absurd social distinction and its monstrous consequences" (*Peregrinations*, 92). Thrown into the working class, and living in dire poverty, she goes to work as a colorist in the shop of printer André Chazal at the age of sixteen, and is, as she says, "*obliged*" by her mother to marry the boss in order to alleviate the family's poverty (xxxvi).

Peregrinations recounts Flora's voyage to Peru in 1833 to regain her inheritance from her father's brother don Pio de Tristan. In order to win familial recognition, she must pretend she really is *not* married, while pretending that her mother really *is*. This ironic chiasma makes her a double pariah: "Pariah in my own country, I had believed that by putting the immensity of the seas between France and me, I could recover a shadow of liberty. Impossible! In the New World, I was still a pariah as in the other" (77).

The Name-of-the-Father

The autobiographical subject formed in the course of this pariah's peregrinations might seem troubling in the way it relates to the feminine and in the particular way it reorganizes the masculine and feminine poles of the gender system into a form of bisexuality.[59] Where the *Saint-Simoniennes* attempt to replace the symbolic father with a symbolic mother, Tristan's writing emphatically does not. Where Suzanne Voilquin must find alternatives to the paternal symbolic economy, in order to become the writing subject of her autobiography, Tristan devises a strategy of playing with it in an explosive way. *Peregrinations* connects the symbolic economy as a system of semiotic exchange and production much more clearly and intricately to the capitalist political economy as a system of commodity exchange and production than do the texts of the *Saint-Simoniennes*.[60] Yet while Tristan seeks to do away with patriarchal economies, she seems to do so with a disconcertingly paternal identification.

Tristan would seem to fit Alice Jardine's description of women writers of the past who wrote within a masculine economy, "identified with the Father and rejected the Mother."[61] Tristan certainly rejected her mother— "I have pardoned her for the harm she did me . . . , but I can never forget it"[62]—and identified with her father, describing "the idolatrous love with which I had loved my father, a love which preserves his image alive in my mind."[63] At the beginning of *Peregrinations*, during her voyage to Peru, where her father's family reigns as aristocratic colonialists, she tells a fellow traveler: "I was born in France, but I am of the country of my father" (68), although she has never been to Peru. Along with this attachment to the father, Tristan's text manifests other qualities that suggest masculine writing.

First, she emphatically claims a kind of truth which poststructuralist theory associates with "phallogocentric" writing. This truth consists of the claim to an exact mimetic reproduction of a preexisting, original referent whose status is unquestioned.[64] In the preface to *Peregrinations*, she says: " . . . we can no longer act upon opinion except with palpable truths and irrefutable facts. . . . Hatred may rise up against me; but, as I am a person of faith before anything else, no consideration whatsoever can prevent me from telling the truth about people and things."[65] Second, her attachment to the father and to this form of truth accords with the figure she cuts in the above quotation. Here as elsewhere, Tristan often engages in an exaggerated imitation of male romantic egotism, which casts her autobiographical self in grandiose roles. She does this not only in *Peregrinations* but even more so in her later autobiographical *Tour of France*, a private journal she keeps in 1844, while organizing her Workers' Union.[66] In the later work, she identifies herself with the mythical "Woman Guide," reminiscent of the Woman Messiah sought by the Saint-Simonians in the early 1830s, and composes such modest self-assessments as the following: "In 2 or 400 years the poets will sing 'Flora Tristan, the first woman' who went throughout the world 'bearing the new law'" (*Tour of France*, 179). So much does her autobiographical self imitate a stereotypically masculine ego that one of Tristan's most astute readers, Phyllis Zuckerman, concludes that in spite of her challenge to capitalism and patriarchy, Tristan's writing perpetuates the values of the Father, God, and identity.[67]

A third mark of Tristan's writing, in which she differs from Voilquin and is much closer to Chateaubriand, concerns the relation she establishes with her predecessors in the autobiographical tradition, and specifically with Rousseau and Chateaubriand. If Voilquin places herself outside of the Oedipal rivalry that transmits patriarchy from generation to generation, Tristan even out-rivals Chateaubriand: "These days, our leaders arrange to have their testamentary revelations published immediately after their death. That is the moment they choose to have their shadow bravely rip the mask off those who preceded them to the grave.

. . . So did the Rousseaus, the Fouchés, the Grégoires, the Lafayettes, etc. . . . ; so too will the Talleyrands, the Chateaubriands, the Bérangers, etc. . . . "(*Peregrinations*, xix). Where Chateaubriand, as we have seen, seeks superiority only over Rousseau, Tristan seeks superiority over everyone, including Chateaubriand, and on much more global grounds. Her entire project will supplant theirs. If Rousseau's stated project in the *Confessions* is "to show to my fellow men a man in all the truth of his nature,"[68] Tristan will expose his inadequacy by being more truthful still. According to Rousseau's readers Jean Starobinski and E. S. Burt, Rousseau presents this notion of truth only to undermine it.[69] While Tristan does not exactly undermine a notion of truth, she does use a phallocentric identification with truth to turn it against itself.

Although Tristan imitates a masculine subjectivity, she does not, as an ardent feminist, identify herself as "masculine"; on the contrary, she portrays herself in the various guises of the romantic heroine. Her "truth," moreover, consists in imitating masculine subjectivity to such excess that it goes to its outer limit and reveals its underlying fiction. Although Tristan differs from the *Saint-Simoniennes* in their affinity with poststructuralist "difference" feminists, her writing does recall the feminine strategy that Luce Irigaray terms "mimeticism," but taken to a monstrous dimension. For Irigaray, mimeticism is only a beginning strategy and consists in an effort of women to "stake their claim to speak as (masculine) 'subjects.' " From this position, according to Irigaray, a woman writer can repeat men's discourse on woman in order to "make 'appear' . . . that which must remain occulted: the recovery of a possible operation of the feminine in language. This would also 'unveil' the fact that if women mime so well, it is because they are not simply reabsorbed in this function. *They also remain elsewhere.*"[70] The mimeticist narrative voice of *Peregrinations*, with its belief in mimetic truth, does succeed in inscribing the unsymbolizable "elsewhere" of Tristan's autobiographical subject, but not in the way Irigaray might have meant.

This pariah clings tenaciously to the mimetic notion of truth because the structural opposition between truth and lies is not hers to subvert or displace. Her position imprisons her between its two walls. In this way, she is like the prostitutes she observes in *Promenades in London*, who, "through paternal power or despotism and the indissolubility of marriage, are put in the alternative of submitting to oppression or infamy!" (*Promenades*, 125). Patriarchy's systematic rule decrees that she must either adopt its socially constructed roles of wife and daughter as absolute truth or else remain caught in the "horrible despair" (*Peregrinations*, 62) of living a constant lie about her marital status. Before her own truth as mimetic relation of sign to referent can be deconstructed, it first has to be constructed through a particular writing that frees her from this opposition and from the relentless "constraint" of having to resist constant temptation to "reveal the truth" (62) about her social identity. This liberating writing pushes to an extreme and then reappropriates otherwise an exorbitant form of this phallocentric opposition between truth and falsity.

Tristan recounts feeling the constraint of this opposition most strongly in relation to ship captain Chabrié, who sails her to Peru and falls in love with the beautiful "demoiselle." She first meets Chabrié in Paris in 1829, when she has her daughter Aline with her. Because she cannot tell him she is married, when, she meets him again in Bordeaux in 1833 and becomes his passenger, on pain of being sent back to her husband, she tells him she is a "fille mère" and so wins his sympathy. During the voyage, when, according to the account in *Peregrinations*, she has provoked, or at least been complicitous in inspiring, his passionate love, he insists on marrying her. Flora, in need of a protector, must walk a tightrope. Her actions toward Chabrié, like the narration of the episode, are wildly contradictory. Both seducing and repelling him, the character uses a rhetoric of motherly and sisterly love, couched in exaltedly passionate tones, while the narrator describes her physical gestures of affection that could be interpreted as both seductive and defensive. Of her entanglement with Chabrié, Tristan says: "Oh! how poorly does he who resorts to a first lie, in order to get out of trouble, know the dead-end road on which he sets forth! He must continue to lie, and he cannot get out of the inextricable sinuousities of that dark labyrinth except by coming back to the truth" (61).

Tristan's seemingly naive and simple opposition between truth and lies turns out to follow an equally labyrinthian strategy to get beyond the opposition. In fact, the labyrinth is a fitting metaphor for her indirect strategy of transforming the symbolic order. A first twist in this tortuous strategy postulates that if apostolic writing can bring about reforms for women only by telling the truth, then George Sand is to be criticized: "But this writer, who is a woman, not content with the veil behind which she had hidden herself in her writings, has signed them with the name of a man. What reverberations can there be from protests enveloped in fictions? What influence could they exert when the facts that prompt them are stripped of their reality?" (xxvii). But in a second twist, Tristan's own insistence on writing under her "real" name does not so easily sort out fact from fiction.

In explaining her desire to free herself from lies, Tristan says: "In separating from my husband, I had abandoned his name and taken back that of my father. Well received everywhere as a widow or *unmarried lady*, I was always shunned when the truth came to be discovered" (xxxvii, emphasis in text). The truth discovered in these circumstances, the very truth that she unveils in *Peregrinations* and which requires that she write it under her real name, is that Flora Tristan is not her real name. Her principle truth is also her principle fiction, and worse, her principle deception. She too signs her writing with "the name of a man," the name of her father. And she will show in the course of *Peregrinations* how this paternal name is connected to the Name-of-the-Father as governing principle of the symbolic order. The text will also show that anyone who claims to have the Name-of-the-Father, which is not a name someone can have, but the "support of the Symbolic function," the dead "authority" of the symbolic economy, commits a deception.[71] Tristan will thus arrive through her indirect strategy at the point to which the Saint-Simonian feminists arrive by a more direct route. For them, Tristan, by insisting on the use of her patronymic, would be hiding behind the name of a man much more than Sand. Understanding the deception involved in claiming to hold what psychoanalytic theory calls the Name-of-the-Father, they refuse to sign their patronymic to their articles in the *Tribune des femmes*. In an article entitled "By My Works You Shall Know My Name," Jeanne-Désirée [Veret] explains this refusal:

> Leave to men these distinctions among names. . . . Their minds, more systematic than ours, need to attach the progress they make to a name or an individual to act with order. But we, as people of feeling and inspiration, leap over these rules and traditions that men deviate from only with great difficulty. We should see in the human race only the children of a single family. . . . All men are brothers and sisters united with each other through our motherhood. . . . We should give them our names, and take our own only from our mothers and God. . . . If we continue to take the names of men and doctrines, we will be slaves without knowing it of the principles they have engendered and upon which they exercise a kind of paternity to which we will have to submit in order to be consistent with ourselves. We will thus have fathers; their authority will be milder and more loving than in the past, but we will never be the equals and mothers of men.[72]

These two different attitudes, that of the *Saint-Simoniennes* and that of Flora Tristan, toward the name of the father condense two radical feminisms—one based on Jeanne-Désirée's above-stated assumption of sexual difference, the other on bisexuality—and two divergent strategies for freeing women from the doctrines and principles ruled by patriarchal authority, be they Christian, capitalist, Saint-Simonian, or socialist. In the conclusion to this chapter, I will return to this contrast between the two feminist forms of identity, which in this case are linked to maternal and paternal identification. For now, let us go more deeply into the radical implications of Tristan's attachment to the father's name (and the Name-of-the-Father as the law of referential language) since it is so alien, and perhaps even a bit discomfiting, to the views of modern radical feminism.

Her attachment to this name, which includes a fierce court battle won in 1839, one year after the publication of *Peregrinations*, to win it back legally for herself and her children,[73] does not result simply from a bitter aversion to her husband's name, although this aversion does play a role. In this one aspect, Tristan resembles the Saint-Simonian feminists, who refuse the husband's name even more than the father's. As one of the *Saint-Simoniennes*, Jeanne Deroin, says: "The . . . dispositions of the civil code prove well enough the extreme dependence of woman on bearing the name of her husband; is this not the burning iron which imprints on the brow of the slave the initials of the master so that he can be recognized by everyone as his property?"[74] Yet as critics Sandra Gilbert and Susan Gubar and Nancy K. Miller have pointed out, the flight from the husband's name has not historically led women writers back to the father's name. They have generally followed one of two strategies to "circumvent the problem of the patronymic,"[75] either using a fictional man's name, like George Sand, or using only a first name, like Mme de Staël's character Corinne and the *Saint-Simoniennes*. Flora Tristan offers the more unusual, if not unique, example of reclaiming the patronymic to turn it against itself and to attack the institutions of family, property, self-identity, and meaning it supports. She follows a third and more labyrinthine strategy to a similar end, transforming what turns out to be perhaps the most fictive name of all.

If Tristan's use of the father's name to support a claim to truth does not call into question the relation between sign and referent, it does call into question the relation between the referent as social image and an essential reality underlying it. If she presents her ego as exaggeratedly unified and grandiose, she will ultimately call attention to the emptiness that underlies all self-images. If Tristan's writing does not hint at the abyss of non-meaning that would accompany the collapse of the paternal triangle, as do the precarious maternal triads of the *Saint-Simoniennes*, she does hint at another abyss, that underlying the social and self-images designated by language. To begin with, Tristan's truth recounts, not her essence, but what she calls throughout *Peregrinations* her position, "the position that laws and prejudices have made for me" (xxviii). Positions not only are arbitrary and changeable but exist only by virtue of their relation to other positions within an organized network, "the correlation existing among all individuals of a single coherent whole" (xxxviii).

The only difference between Flora's "false positions" (xxxvii) as Flora Tristan, "widow or unmarried woman," and her true position as André Chazal's wife and as mother to *his* children lies in their status as fictions. The lie of her own invention differs from the lie invented by a patriarchal society only in that the Fathers have the power to impose their representations. People are so universally forced to live by them that they become commonly accepted not as representations but as the essential law of God. Tristan's truth consists in representing her groundless fictions and ruling groundless fictions as having equal status. This radical fictionality combines with her strategy of labyrinthine indirection.

Tristan's criticism of Sand for veiling herself in fictions has yet a further labyrinthian twist: in the preface, the author of *Peregrinations* announces her intention not only to represent truthfully her previous deceptions but also to add a whole new level of deceptions within the writing practice itself: "But if . . . religious or other prejudices recognize a class of PARIAHS, oh! then, the same devotion that leads us to denounce the oppressor with loathing must make us cast a veil over the conduct of the oppressed who is seeking to escape the yoke" (xxiii). Among the classes of pariahs that Tristan mentions are black slaves, Russian peasants, Jews in ancient Rome, and women: "to publish a woman's loves is to expose her to oppression" (xxv).

What then, is the reader to make of her subsequent narrations of her relations with men, specifically with Chabrié, which she characterizes as "the portrayal of a true love on one side, and a pure friendship on the other" (*Peregrinations*, 60)? The constant slippage between veiling and unveiling, which takes place both on the level of narration and on the level of event narrated, disorients the reader. Is she reading the true representation of a previous deception or the deceptive representation of a previous sincerity? But in the course of *Peregrinations*, this question is transformed as the shifting between truth and lie moves toward a different symbolic economy.

In the entanglement with Chabrié, the character Flora differs in one respect from the narrator Tristan. While the narrator leans heavily on a rhetorical opposition between truth and falsity, the character, in her treatment of Chabrié, creates a much more tortuous relation that blurs the border between them. In following her narrator's advice to "not get out of the inextricable sinuousities of the dark labyrinth except by coming back to the truth," the character Flora does not simply tell the truth but goes deeper into the labyrinth of lies. For both the character and the author, the labyrinthian strategy involves not only twists and turns, but going in the opposite direction from the destination in order to arrive at it.

In taking lies to their outer limit to arrive at truth, Flora parallels the author's strategy of taking phallocentric truth to its outer limits to overturn it. This particular structure of exorbitance seems to remain stable in Tristan's strategy for change throughout her life. Later, when she is organizing the Workers' Union, she repeatedly expresses implacable abhorrence for the bourgeoisie singularly and collectively. She reminds herself in her journal that she has "sworn to destroy all property—and to do that by pillaging and killing all property owners if there is no other way to reach this end" (*Tour*, 265); and she writes to a group of workers: "are not *all* the bourgeois by their *position* against the union of workers!" (*Lettres*, aux ouvriers membres du cercle de l'Union ouvrière à Toulon, Sept. 9, 1844, 211, emphasis in text). Yet in every city she goes to, she insistently visits the local factory owners and bishops, pressing upon them her book *Workers' Union*, and in all sincerity asking for their moral and financial support. The pattern for this lifelong practice seems to form itself in her entanglement with Chabrié.

Having first lied about her marital status, Flora lies again more dangerously by giving in to Chabrié's insistent demands with a false promise to marry him. To subsequently disentangle herself, she does not then tell the at least partial truth that she cannot marry him because she is already married, but instead invents a more grandiose, more atrocious deception, calculated to make her appear an evil woman. Its purpose is to "detach him from me forever," to "lose his esteem and love" (*Peregrinations*, 152). But why such an elaborate scam? Flora's false role as *demoiselle* has imposed a "painful task" not only because she has to deceive those for whom she cares the most, Chabrié and Uncle Pio, but also because to do so she has to repress her own ardent, passionate nature, characterized by "an extreme frankness," "the ardor of my imagination" (72), and "the impulse of my mind" (73). The elaborate deception that Flora perpetrates for Chabrié has the unexpected effect of freeing her "true" character, her "impulse" and "ardor," from a repression caused by simpler deceptions.

The staging of such elaborate deceptions, not only for Chabrié but for don Pio, to whom her voice is the most sincere and impassioned when her words are the most manipulative, leads to a different kind of truth from that in the system of opposition between truth and deception or truth and fiction. The chapter of *Peregrinations* which treats these elaborate and emotional scenes with Chabrié and don Pio are also full of apparently unconnected references to the theater. As a foreigner in Arequipa, Tristan experiences the estrangement whereby a social ritual which would seem natural in one's own culture takes on the appearance of "a theatrical scene" (125). She also observes with increasing interest that "the Arequipians have a great deal of fondness for all sorts of spectacles" (163), theatrical or religious. The naive enthusiasm for spectacle is both cause and effect of "the stupefaction of this people" (146), who believe in the reality of the spectacle they see. Tristan reserves special disdain for people she meets who have no critical distance from theatrical representations.

She suggests that like the audience and actors of a theater, the members of a society fill roles and witness scenes, and further, that only the most naive believe in their essential reality. So, instead of having to "sustain a role" (xxxvii) assigned by others in their social theater, why not stage one's own theater, a theater in which Flora herself will create the scene, write the roles, and assign them? She can exit, albeit temporarily, from her false position within the network of positions governed by the law of the Father by creating her own network of false positions. By staging these scenes she establishes a fiction that can compete with the patriarchal fictions called society.

If Tristan can escape from an externally imposed false position more especially in her scene with Chabrié, she can give vent to her "true char-

acter," sincere and passionate, more especially in her scene with Uncle
Pio, played before an audience of family and friends. This spectacle con-
forms strictly to the formula of domestic melodrama, in which Flora
plays the role of the pathetic "orphan" (187) denuded of her rightful
place in the family fortunes, "an innocent victim of the guilty negligence
of the authors of her life" (196). In what she calls "the scene that I have
just had with don Pio" (189), she is able to express with abandon, even
"exaltation" (198), that which she had to repress before: "the pride and
frankness of my character . . . , the freedom of my mind" (198).

This sincere and free character consists not in the content or referent of
her words, which hide the truth as much as before, but in the energy
used to produce the scene. The energy produces an excess in language
beyond content or meaning, and in this energetic excess resides the
"elsewhere" of a non-symbolizable feminine subjectivity, one that does
not have the illusion of permanent status, ontological grounding, and
transcendental identity signified and guaranteed by the proper name. In
this exaltation of tone, Tristan can temporarily produce herself as a subject, which is true and real in the sense that it exists outside of the
network of "positions" that imprison women, and is unsymbolizable. Yet
it is nothing but a burst of force and power to intervene in a patriarchal
situation and change it to her advantage. She describes her "scene" with
don Pio:

> . . . the state of sensitivity I had been in from the beginning of this conver-
> sation was immediately followed by such a violent attack of indignation, a
> commotion of feelings so strong, that I thought I had come to my last
> second. . . . Sparks burst from my eyes; my muscles were tensed. . . . I
> was in one of those moments when the soul communicates with a super-
> human power. I stopped before my uncle, squeezing his arm with great
> strength, and talking to him with a tone of voice he had never before
> heard from me. . . . (188)

Her fiction gives birth to the truth of the subject as the nonidentity of
pure energetic excess. As such, it contrasts to the disunified subject
Suzanne Voilquin constructs in her autobiographical writing in a way
that illuminates the class differences that complicate sexual difference.
Voilquin's disunified subjectivity is grounded in the proletarian family,
where the subject shifts in and out of the various family positions with
their names of mother, father, sister, daughter, etc. Tristan constructs a
subjectivity of non-symbolizable energy from her position in the gap between aristocratic and working classes, in the absence of a family and
without membership in any class or institution. Where Voilquin anchors
her subjectivity in a shifting, fluid relation to institutionally defined networks and nomenclatures, Tristan's subjectivity is not anchored at all.
Where Voilquin and the other *Saint-Simoniennes* trace figures of a mater-

nal symbolic order that are figures of incompletion, Tristan's radical fictionality traces no textual figures at all, but makes visible the void behind the apparent substantiality of patriarchal images.

As the above-quoted passage suggests, this production of a kind of truth outside of symbolization and mimesis occurs on two levels of the text: the level of event represented and also the level of writing the text. As Tristan writes of these events, the narrative voice also adopts the exaltation Flora expresses in the scene. The same energy which marks the production of a theatrical scene in the events recounted in *Peregrinations* also bursts forth in its writing. It expresses itself not only in tone and style but in printing marks that exceed any signified, such as triple exclamation points and frequent italics. In remembering her deceptive plan to make Chabrié hate her, Tristan exclaims: "Very well! I had this courage!!!" (*Peregrinations*, 152). In reviewing her drama with don Pio, her voice carries fiery indignation and sarcasm: "I did not dare tell these gentlemen [the lawyers] that I had counted on *the affection, the gratitude, and the justice of my uncle*" (191, emphasis in original). When Tristan expounds her theory of mimetic truth and feminine writing in the foreword to *Peregrinations*, her choice of metaphor is perhaps not purely ornamental: " . . . may every individual . . . make it a duty to recount in all their truth the events in which he has been an *actor* or witness" (xxviii, emphasis added).

The publication of her work of "truth" also stages a monstrous theatrical fiction within the society in which it will be read. And this second theatrical spectacle, the one produced by the writing and publication of the book, will appropriate the name of the father so as to turn it against itself, thus transforming (temporarily) the male symbolic economy and creating the possibility for, if not the actuality of, a feminine economy. Tristan maintains in the foreword not only that apostolic women writers should write under their real name (which is their fictive name), "but above all let them name" (xxvii) those who have committed injustices against them. The combination of naming herself with the name of the father and naming don Pio with the same name produces a theatrical effect. By signing this name, Tristan commits not only a deception but a theft, for in his legal documents, don Pio, who now represents the Law of the Father, makes it clear that Tristan is not her "real" name: "In them I was not designated as the daughter of don Mariano, but only by my name of Florita" (101). But the broader deception involved in writing under the Name-of-the-Father also becomes clearer. Tristan's referential truth of naming don Pio de Tristan calls into question his notion of the truth in which this name signifies his essential identity as patriarchal authority.

Naming makes the book into theater, because it makes the readers of 1838 into actors who in the act of reading leave their roles within patriarchal society to play roles in a competing spectacle staged by Tristan. Don

Pio, and even more importantly Chazal, read the book with the knowledge that the public is also reading it. Don Pio, as reader, sees that the other readers, who by being drawn into this position are also actors, see him and the name which identifies him not as he is in "reality" (the male fiction) but as he is in Flora's writing, or in other words, in her competing fiction. She takes his name out of the "position" it occupies in the social network of signs designating positions and places it in another linguistic network, that of *Peregrinations*. A similar process occurs with Chazal. Each man must now act his role in her drama, express his outrage, take steps to reestablish the link between his name and his identity within the masculine "reality." By the very act of taking visible steps to reestablish its fiction as the only, universal reality, he reveals its nature as a social construct produced through power relations. Tristan's act of naming has as much a performative function as a mimetic function, since it pushes the patriarch to act on a belief in the mimetic power of the proper name to reflect a real identity, thus showing that belief to be illusory.

This is what happens when don Pio seeks legal means to deny Flora her pension, and gives his tacit consent to the people of Arequipa and Lima who, in another "drama" (*Letters*, Dec. 1, 1838, 89), burn her in effigy along with her book in the public square. Saying that the book was written "by a certain Flora de Florez, etc., etc.," they take back the name she has stolen: "they did not dare name me because of my uncle *Pio de Tristan*" (*Letters*, 89, emphasis in original).[76] This happens in a more complex way when an enraged Chazal, having drawn a picture of a tombstone inscribed with "La Paria," buys a set of pistols and shoots his wife in the street, precipitating a spectacular trial, where Flora can play her part to the hilt, and stage yet another theater of truth about social relations for the public and the press and, through it, at least win her freedom from the marital institution.[77]

By displacing and multiplying the name of the father, making it both the name that signs the book and the object of the book's naming, Tristan strips from it the illusion of eternal essentiality and demonstrates it as a relation of power between *positions* in the social network. In the economic system of this network, the symbolic Father holds the phallus, and the legal father holds the money. Money as universal equivalent and the phallus as master signifier play analogous roles in their respective economies—that of centering and regulating the play by which all other exchange values or signifiers can enter into relations of equivalency and difference with each other.[78] In their mythic state, each appears as the essential thing in itself, haloed with the double illusion that someone— whoever can claim to embody the Name-of-the-Father—can (1) actually have it; and (2) control thereby the entire system of economic and sexual exchange. In this state, money and the phallus mask the social relations of economic, sexual, and symbolic production.

By displacing the paternal name, Tristan also reveals as a socio-historic process the system where women are objects of exchange (and as Don Pio's beautiful niece, she is a valuable object of exchange) among men for the purpose of transmitting the name of the father. By writing a text which as published book becomes an exchange object bearing the name of the father, Tristan displaces all the elements in this circuit of exchange. She has placed herself, the seemingly essential object of exchange, in the position of exchanger and made the name of the father into an object of exchange, a signifier just like any other. By changing the positions of exchangers, objects of exchange, and regulators of exchange, Tristan's writing reveals that they are social relations subject to change and governed by arbitrary law. Don Pio and Chazal, finding their law unveiled, are forced to exercise power visibly in order to whisk it back under its veil.

The name of the father is the one signifier in the male economy that is not supposed to circulate. By putting it into circulation, Tristan explosively, if temporarily, disorganizes the system, which has been naturalized into invisibility. She also shows the name of the father as a crucial link between the symbolic economy and the political economy. The stability, or noncirculating status, of the name of the father guarantees and is guaranteed by the marriage and family laws that keep the property passing from father to "legitimate" child, and that have "property as their object" (*Peregrinations*, 74). By reclaiming as an illegitimate daughter the name of the father and his patrimony, Tristan has endangered the family name and the system it designates.

By her provocative misuse of the name of the father, Tristan weakens a crucial link between the symbolic economy and the political economy. If her writing appears to situate itself in a male symbolic economy, it is because she constructs the beginnings of a feminine economy not within the literary text itself but along the border between the text and its socioeconomic context. Her writing shows how an outsider's, or pariah's, repetition of the order of truth can spectacularly, if only temporarily, disorder it.

The Body of the Mother

The masculine violence disturbingly unleashed by this feminine repetition of the order of truth does not allow Flora to change the patriarchal order, but it does expose its arbitrary injustices. *Peregrinations* also marks a crucial turning point in Flora Tristan's development. One of the reasons that the book seems constantly divided against itself by contradiction is that the content recounts the character's quest to be reintegrated with and recognized by the patriarchal family, while the writing of the book and its publication mark the author's voluntary rejection of patriarchal institutions as a "liberated pariah," who in the words of Denys Cuche cuts "her bridges definitely with the aristocracy and the bourgeoisie. From now on she will be in solidarity with all the pariahs of the world without any ambiguity."[79] She does thereby succeed in transforming the relation between sign and referent signified by the name of the father, making of "Tristan," as Stéphane Michaud says, "a rallying symbol for all obscure and excluded people."[80]

After the publication of *Peregrinations*, Tristan, never losing confidence in the power of the written text to transform social relations, takes her last published work, *Workers' Union*, as a prop and sets out to organize the workers of France, collecting her impressions and experiences in a journal that records notes for another, future book she will never publish. Although the *Tour of France* lies outside the scope of this study of French feminism in the 1830s, I would like to trace briefly the development of certain contradictions inherent in Tristan's identification with the father and rejection of the mother from *Peregrinations* to the *Tour of France*, in order to compare her feminism to the *Saint-Simoniennes'* maternal feminism.

In *Peregrinations*, Flora's social theater produces a true self as unsymbolizable energy through a particular process. The energy that creates a real violence of emotion also affects the material reality of her body, sweeping it to the border between life and death: "The morning [after the scene with don Pio], my body was exhausted from fatigue, without my feeling any desire to eat or sleep. The exaltation of my brain sustained me that way for five days" (190). By contrast to the *Saint-Simoniennes'* program of the "rehabilitation of the flesh," Tristan portrays her actions so as to suggest that in order to intervene as a feminine agent, she has to deny her body. She must act as if there is no face behind the theatrical mask.

This is how the feminine self as unsymbolizable energy is born from taking a paternal identification to its farthest limits. If Tristan does not anchor her subjectivity in the material networks defining family and class, she also denies its anchorage in the materiality of the body. As she travels through France organizing her Workers' Union, Tristan arrives at a point of extreme idealism, like saints who have gone beyond the traditional Western forms of patriarchal idealism, where the name of the father so blots out any identification with the maternal body that the subject as pure energy exists only at the cost of material life itself. In assuming the role of a pure force of life to change the world, Tristan literally destroys her body in 1844 and, although she dies of an illness, in a sense kills herself. Living in squalid hotels, running around strange cities from meeting to meeting in filthy, airless rooms, giving herself totally to her fervent passion, she describes in almost every journal entry the worsening sickness, and then denies it: "stomach pains, dysentery, a headache that raises the fear of putrid fever. . . . I alone do not notice it" (*Tour*, 183; see also 44, 180).

She describes herself as a force of soul, of "will perhaps without example in humanity" (265), and of passionate but nonsexual love, a "delirious passion of the soul" (150) for the workers: "I am content with these workers, but how much life I give them! I must have a great deal to be able to dispense it with such profusion" (96). In this sense, Tristan does arrive at a kind of negative version of the feminine economy discussed earlier. Hélène Cixous describes it as the "desire-which-gives," the alternative to the phallocentric dialectic of return, profit, and obsessive balancing of debt and credit:

> Elsewhere, she gives . . . she does not measure; but she gives neither a bill of goods nor something she doesn't have. She gives more, with no assurance that an unexpected benefit will come back to her. She gives life, thought, transformation. That economy can no longer be talked about in terms of an economy. Wherever she loves, all concepts of the old management are outmoded.[81]

Nothing could more accurately describe Tristan's transformative theory and practice of love than this passage—except that Cixous's feminine economy frees the body and its sexuality, while Tristan's practice of this utopian feminine economy within the social structure of a capitalist economy finally exacts a dire cost from her body.

Earlier we saw the *Saint-Simoniennes* coming to terms with the structure of analogous bipolar oppositions—mind/body, spirit/matter, subject/object, masculine/feminine—that organizes the phallocentric symbolic order. This analogous series associates men with the mind, women with the body. To act and write as feminists, the *Saint-Simoniennes* had to mend this mind-body, spirit-matter separation. They tried to do this by constructing a maternal symbolic order. Tristan, by contrast, tries to create a feminist subject by exacerbating these bipolar oppositions to a point that exceeds their structure.

She differs from a masculine subject of the phallocentric symbolic order, who, split as he is by the mirror stage and by his relation to language as coming from the Other,[82] can at least relate to his body as an alienated symbolized object across the chasm of symbolic castration. By contrast, Tristan's strange construction of a feminine subjectivity through paternal identification leaves her without a way to identify with her feminine—and maternal—body. The two autobiographical texts, *Peregrinations* and *Tour of France*, deny both the pleasure and the pain of the body. On the one hand, Tristan says that her continuous exertion of enormous energy to organize the workers "evidently proves that the martyrs did not feel their pains" (*Tour*, 44). On the other hand, she says of the love she and the workers demonstratively express for each other in their enormous meetings: "even in moments of amorous ecstasy, I never feel the slightest movement of my senses" (196; see also 159). While both the

Saint-Simoniennes and Tristan develop theories of love out of an ambivalent reaction to Prosper Enfantin's doctrine (as well as to Charles
Fourier's),[83] the *Saint-Simoniennes'* theories of sexual liberation contrast
strongly with Tristan's disembodied revolutionary love.

If, in order to develop their theories of sexual regeneration, the *Saint-
Simoniennes* had to reject their own biological and social mother in favor
of a symbolic mother with whom they identified, Tristan successively
rejects not only her mother but her own maternity. In the 1830s, she
detaches herself from her son, and leaves her daughter behind to go to
Peru, where she is haunted by guilt-ridden visions of Aline's death. In
Tour of France, she records a growing feeling of distance toward her now
grown-up daughter (20, 131, 277). Strangely, some of Tristan's readers
have seen her as trying to embody the Great Mother, neglecting an important aspect of her contribution to feminism, which comes from her
effort to separate the womanly from the maternal, however fraught with
contradiction the effort may be. Sandra Dijkstra says that "her self-righ-
teous assumption of the role of saviour allowed her to . . . perfect her
image as Mother."[84] Laura Strumingher, who, like Dijkstra, attributes
Tristan's motives to personal psychology, says: "Tristan sought to resolve
the dichotomy of her personal needs for autonomy and for intimacy
. . . by becoming the mother of the working class."[85] Margaret Talbot suggests Tristan's distance from this image, but conflates the role of the
"Woman Messiah," with which Tristan identifies, with that of the
"Mother Apostle."[86] Although, during her Tour, one newspaper calls her
the "mother apostle" of the workers,[87] there is no record of her referring
to herself this way. She does see herself in the guise of "Woman Guide":
"There I was, completely without premeditation, the Woman Guide, just
as I too, in my own way, had dreamt her" (*Tour*, 71). But this figure
transforms Enfantin's Mother figure even more drastically than writings
of the Saint-Simonian women. The Woman Guide appears in Tristan's
own novel *Méphis*, and far from being a mother figure, this daughter of
the proletarian revolutionary Méphis and his mistress Marequita does
not take after her mother, but rather compensates for the mother, who is
too attached to bourgeois convention to act out her principles, and re-
incarnates the dead father. As Woman Messiah, Tristan sees herself in
the *Tour of France* not as a mother but as the rival and supplanter of
Jesus Christ. The only time in this journal that she does describe herself
in terms of a mother-child relation to the workers comes in one of her
rare moments of self-denigration: "I am acting exactly like those mothers
who, attentive only to their passionate love for their children, stuff them
with food in the hope of seeing them grow more quickly, and by dint of
giving them too much, smother them by weakening them and making
them sick" (*Tour*, 67).

If Suzanne Voilquin can become an autobiographical subject only
through reconstructing the author-reader relation as a symbolic mother-

daughter relation, Tristan becomes an autobiographical subject only by neglecting, ignoring, and wishing away her own maternal body. It is also notable that in contrast to Voilquin's text, and indeed to most autobiographies, Tristan's autobiographical text does not encode a single author-reader model, and for many interrelated reasons. Since, for her, all social personae are changeable, fictional roles, sustained by no essence, there are many different, ephemeral author-reader encodings. Second, her writing strategy requires that there be at least two reader positions, that of the oppressors named in the book, like Chazal and don Pio, and that of the actor-witnesses in the social drama the book provokes. Third, this writing strategy pushes the reader into *performing* a certain role through the act of reading rather than *imitating* a certain ideal reader within the text. Finally, because the feminine autobiographical subject Tristan constructs is an unsymbolizable energy, and because in *Peregrinations*, and even more clearly in the *Tour of France*, her stereotypically masculine self-aggrandizement is at the same time a stereotypically feminine self-negation, there is, strictly speaking, nobody for the reader to identify with as author-within-the-text.

Tristan's contradictions concerning feminine freedom, maternal slavery, and the body are concentrated in a group of images that in one sense distinguishes her from other romantics. In romantic rhetoric, as used, for instance, by Claire Démar, the nude body stands as metaphor for a language of truth, authenticity, and freedom, clothing for a false language used to oppress others.[88] Tristan, whose soulful love contrasts sharply with Claire Démar's "trial of flesh by flesh" (*My Law*, 36), provides an original twist on this tradition. In her metaphoric imagery, one cannot present oneself in a more authentic mode than through one's clothing. *Peregrinations* very rarely uses images of nudity, and instead opposes two kinds of metaphorical clothing—that which oppressively weighs a person down and that which frees a person by veiling her—as if there were no body behind the clothing. Two contrasting scenes present Tristan's ideal of liberty as a costume with no body and her nightmare of enslaved motherhood as a naked body.

In *Peregrinations*, a chapter on Lima, the capital of Peru, focuses on the upper-class women, describing them as the most free and powerful women of the world, because of a costume, called the "saya," which completely covers them, hiding the shape of the body and even the face, leaving exposed only one eye. Eminently suitable to enter Tristan's symbology, the saya is physically uncomfortable and constricting but socially liberating. All upper-class women wear this identical garment when they go out, so that in anonymity they can go wherever they want, do whatever they please, initiate love affairs, and even engage in politics.

This costume becomes a metaphor for the language of *Peregrinations* as a language of truth which blurs the opposition between truth and falsity. Once a Limanian woman adorns herself with this "impenetrable disguise" (*Peregrinations*, 338), her body and her social identity (that is, the identity of her husband) disappear and she becomes authentically herself: "under the *saya* the Limanienne, if *free*, enjoys her independence, and rests with confidence upon that true force which every person feels when he can act according to the needs of his organization. The woman of Lima is always *herself* in every position of life" (*Peregrinations*, 338, emphasis in text).

Like the metaphorical veils with which women writers hide their loves, the saya is not a garment that hides the true woman, whose element of "truth" is her "strength," but rather makes her into a different woman: "she is no longer the same woman" (333). The Limanienne can be at the same time truly "herself" and many different women in different guises, because, as Tristan suggests in the preface to *Peregrinations*, people have no essential identity but only positions in a patriarchal nomenclature. Flora has succeeded in slipping into the spaces between and outside these positions, but at the cost of becoming a pariah. The saya symbolizes for her a unique and almost magic method whereby women can step outside these positions without being pariahs.

Tristan, in her enthusiasm, claims that a Limanian woman, because of the saya, is as free as or freer than her husband. But of course, he has the freedom to engage in amorous and political intrigues without the veiling saya and without having to lie. The difference between husband and wife, which could be stated as the male enjoying his freedom under his "true" identity, while she must enjoy hers under a "false" one, could also be stated as a difference between the male enjoying freedom under his proper name and social titles, while she enjoys hers in the absence of name and title. *Peregrinations* uses the same language to describe the pariah and the saya: the pariah is "placed . . . outside of everything" (xxxvii), while the saya is "a garment outside of all garments" (331). It transforms the pariah's status by permitting women to act outside of the positions in the networks of social organization, outside of all the positions then available to women, but still enjoy the benefits of acceptance in society. The saya, which even changes the wearer's voice, is itself a language of power and seduction and, as such, works as a visible blank, a nonidentity in that male dominant social structure, through which women can manipulate it. Beyond this liberating veil, there is no more essential self to expose. The saya, as a feminine self seemingly not anchored in the materiality of the body or the network of social relations, figures in *Peregrinations of a Pariah* as a potentially liberating language if only it could expand its power not simply to play the game but to change it.

A stark contrast to this freedom of nonidentity comes in the form of two African American feminine bodies, "entirely naked" (*Peregrinations*, 352), whose nudity signifies their status as slaves and the guilt that colonial, patriarchal society has placed on them as mothers. Flora visits in prison two slave women who have killed their children by refusing to nurse them. She interprets their actions as a gesture of excessive maternal love:

> . . . the other [woman], young and very beautiful, trained her great eyes upon me; her gaze seemed to say to me: "I let my child die, because I knew he would never be free like you; I preferred him dead to enslaved." The sight of this woman made me ill. Beneath this black skin can be encountered great and proud souls; the blacks pass abruptly from the independence of nature to the state of slavery, and some indomitable ones can be found who die without being bent to the yoke. (352)

If Flora is in the process of taking paternal identity to an extreme limit where it goes against patriarchy, the slave mothers, like the heroine Sethe in Toni Morrison's novel *Beloved*,[89] have taken maternal devotion to the furthest extreme where it destroys itself. In a rare identification with motherhood, Tristan sets up in this scene a mirror relation between these mothers and herself, and so through this portrayal presents the extreme boundaries of her own thought, on the one hand its potentially advanced amplitude and on the other its ultimate limitation. On the one hand, Tristan expresses through this most marginalized of others, a person even more a pariah than herself, the rejection of conventional opinion and the recognition that the institutions of motherhood and the family are luxuries of the bourgeoisie, all of which she herself does not yet have the courage to articulate openly. Although she has left her children in the care of others, it is not until *Tour of France* that she will be able to say:

> This family life appears to me atrocious and what immorality!—to forget humanity in the concern for one's daughter or son. . . . These three little children [of the Goin family] eat more among themselves alone than 30 children of workers—with everything that they waste, throw away, and lose, ten workers' children would live off the fat of the land. This luxury for some at the expense of necessities that the masses are deprived of is a monstrous immorality. (123)

In addition to Tristan's identification with these mothers, there is another striking element of this portrayal. It is emblematic of Tristan's contradictions that her description of these enslaved, infanticidal mothers marks the only time in her autobiographical texts that she describes, in however mystified a way, a mother who, as mother, is a powerful agent of her own actions.

On the other hand, Tristan's representation of the slave mothers only, in the end, situates itself within the confines of the phallocentric structure whose hierarchical oppositions, as demonstrated in Rousseau's *Con-*

fessions, invariably make the other into a mirror of the self. If, even in *Peregrinations*, Tristan has the courage to side with the slave women against conventional morality, she necessarily speaks about the slave from the structural position of the master. Tristan can describe the black slave only through a typically phallocentric gesture of projection and appropriation: she projects onto the slave's silent body her own imaginary discourse so that she makes the slave's silence speak her own concerns. Then, returning to the typically romantic rhetoric she had rejected in talking about herself, Tristan makes the slave's black skin into a kind of second clothing that hides a Western-fashioned "soul." Her confrontation with this Other suddenly displaces her from the position of the Other, and so necessarily puts her in the position of the Western self. Her representation of the slave thus offers a different, and this time unconscious, kind of evidence for the notion that positions in the social and symbolic network determine subjective identity. It also shows the impossibility of talking about the other—be it a man talking about woman, or a white European (or North American) talking about Africans or African Americans—without appropriating their voice, and without confronting the limits of our own thought.

When Tristan writes about herself, her writing, in a different way than that of the Saint-Simonian feminists, upsets this self-other structure, as well as other structures of the symbolic order, because in this case the speaking subject *is* the silenced other. Like the *Saint-Simoniennes*, Flora refuses to abandon that paradox. However significant their differences, they have in common a desire to write while at the same time explicitly upholding their position as other, and so they upset the rigid network of positions which organize the symbolic order. The paternal law of this order dictates that individuals enter it as men or women in accord with the law of gender, by identifying either with the Father or the Mother within the Oedipal triangle, and by associating with one side or the other in the series of analogous bipolar oppositions (see above). This Law produces an ideology which can claim biology as destiny, because it decrees that male children identify with the Father, and female children with the Mother. Both the *Saint-Simoniennes* and Tristan refuse this form of symbolic identification, Tristan by scandalously combining a paternal identification with a feminine identification, and the *Saint-Simoniennes* by refusing to identify with the imaginary, biological, social, or ideological mother and inventing a symbolic mother to replace the symbolic father.

CONCLUSION

In contemporary Western feminism, theoretical work has explored the path begun, unbeknownst to us, by the *Saint-Simoniennes*, almost to the exclusion of the path blazed by Tristan. Yet both kinds of feminism, that of the *Saint-Simoniennes* and that of Tristan, are aspects of our feminism in many of us as individuals. Paternal identification seems repugnant to us, a perpetuation of life-destroying forces we are trying to change. By contrast, the ideas of forming a new self, new social relations, and a new ethics based on maternal relations has overwhelmingly directed feminist research, as suggested by the pervasive influence of the work of Nancy Chodorow and Carol Gilligan[90] on one form of North American feminism, and the influence of Luce Irigaray, Hélène Cixous, and Julia Kristeva on another, as well as the central role all these women have in our feminist debates. This urgency to investigate a maternal replacement for the now life-threatening and planet-threatening Law of the Father perhaps also explains the widening feminist interest in psychoanalysis, as attested not only by Chodorow, and the French feminine writers, but by a host of works too numerous to mention, including the collections *The (M)other Tongue, Between Psychoanalysis and Feminism, Feminism and Psychoanalysis,* and *Engendering the Word,* as well as individually authored works such as Marianne Hirsch's *The Mother/Daughter Plot* and Margaret Homans's *Bearing the Word.*[91] But the identification with the Father also works within feminism, albeit as a denied and a very little theorized force. Janice Haney-Peritz, Katherine C. Hill-Miller, Elaine Showalter, Carolyn Heilbrun, as well as several of the authors, including Nancy K. Miller, in the recent (1989) collection *Refiguring the Father,* are among the few contemporary theorists to have explicitly articulated this ambivalently enabling element in our feminist psyches.[92] Significantly, feminist poets from ethnic minority communities, such as Adrienne Rich, Sandra Cisneros, and Ana Castillo, have been able to identify with their fathers in seeing him as a member of an oppressed and struggling minority.[93]

As long as we have no choice but to speak, act, and write within the present symbolic order, it is through our paternal identification that we as intellectuals and activists can articulate on a theoretical level our maternal identification and make it into a powerful political force for change. The three *Saint-Simoniennes,* in violating the law of gender and recombining its poles, also had to assume the paradox of entering the masculine position in order to speak as women and to trace their incomplete figures of a maternal order. They had to alienate their maternal identity in order to make it the object of a theoretical discourse rather than a mutely assumed "instinct." The work of Chodorow and Gilligan, as well as that of Irigaray, demonstrates that the maternal self is only a potential force for a new ethics and social system, but in the present political structure perpetuates women's oppression, if not placed in a new theoretical and political context.

What these nineteenth-century feminists, as well as some contemporary feminists, are seeking to do, it seems, is to reintegrate the Father differently into a different symbolic and social law, where he is no longer in a position of symbolic and political dominance, and no longer the centering force of a unicentered system. That there are many different ways of reordering a multi-sexual symbolic mode is perhaps what we can learn from these nineteenth-century feminists of desire.

Texts

IV

SUZANNE VOILQUIN, MEMORIES OF A DAUGHTER OF THE PEOPLE

[Excerpts from: Suzanne Voilquin, Souvenirs d'une fille du people ou la Saint-simonienne en Egypte. Paris: Chez E. Sauzet, 1866.

Suzanne Voilquin, born Suzanne Monnier, was the third child of working-class parents. Her father, a hatter, was an enthusiast of the Revolution; her mother was devoutly Catholic. Voilquin became a Saint-Simonian adherent in late 1830, one among many working-class women and men won over to the movement at that time. Her Memories were published in 1866, decades after the events described; but her unpublished letters in the Saint-Simonian archives indicate that she was usually faithful in reporting the events accurately, although in some instances she did omit information—perhaps because she found it too painful or embarrassing, perhaps because temporal distance had lessened the distress. Addressing herself to her niece, whom she had raised as a daughter, she described her childhood and young adult years (1801–30), her experiences within the Saint-Simonian movement in Paris (1831–34), her tour through France (1834), her sojourn in Egypt (1834–36), and her return to Paris (1836–38) before departing to Russia to practice midwifery. The excerpts that we present are from the Paris years to 1834.]

[Chapter I: Childhood]

In order for you to understand my life, I must, dear child, briefly describe its early years; the past gives birth to the future; logic wills it thus.

Turning my mind back to this bygone time, I see first of all the sweet face of your ancestor, my beloved mother; though dead for over forty years, she is as alive in me now as she was the moment of our separation. Through her, the years of my youth were devoted to the most exalted practice of the Christian faith.

My father, although very revolutionary, left our moral upbringing up to her, smiling at our extreme devotion and treating it as one of those childhood maladies of no consequence for the future.

My mother, who had a great heart, but whose intelligence had been extremely diminished by her upbringing, never argued with what the Church had prescribed; she believed in it, and I imitated her. Nothing was so glorious to my eyes as the ceremonies of the Catholic faith. [. . .]

[Chapter II: Adolescence]

When my mother brought her last child into the world, we were allowed to go kiss the newborn a few hours after her delivery. At that moment, my mother, presenting me a delicious little creature, told me: 'This is not a sister I am giving you, but a daughter; from now on she belongs to you." I was barely nine years old; the rather solemn gift of this little person, given to me in the presence of the family, caused me immense joy. I took it so seriously that from then on I allowed my mother only the right to be her nurse. [. . .]

This precocious maternity, which like all exclusive sentiments brought me both joy and sorrow, became a salutary stimulant for my youth and food for my heart. Such a pure sentiment made me understand duty. And even later, in a very sorrowful circumstance, it saved me from suicide by forcing me to live for this child. Therefore, until the time of her marriage, she never left me, not even for school or apprenticeship, but everything that the straitened circumstances I experienced in my adolescence allowed me to assimilate, and this was, alas! precious little, I learned in order to share with this dear adopted daughter.

Here I leave my childhood and begin my adolescence under the influence of this sorrowful era that saw our France diminished, and her children dispersed by death and exile, after having seen her so great and mighty under the hero acclaimed by the people.*

It is in the family environment that the nuances of a child's character are formed. My mother reigned over my early years through her tenderness, for my excessive devotion was in part her doing. But the strong will of my father, whose intelligent nature was open to generous ideas, was grafted, so to speak, onto my adolescence. To him I owe my first practical sense of social life.** [. . .]

Our revolution, which had succeeded in emancipating the people and destroying antiquated abuses, found my father steadfast, happy to see

---

*Reference to Napoleon, defeated in battle in 1815.
**Saint-Simonians used the word "social" instead of "political" (a word they considered too narrow for the full scope of their concerns) or "public" (a word that presumes a "public/private" split which their ideology challenged).

feudal rights and powers of all sorts fall with the Bastille. He came to Paris with his wife and two boys. There was no longer time for him to study, since he had to provide for the needs of this young family. Young Raymond Monnier thus remained to his great regret in his initial state of ignorance. Even if his financial means had enabled him to do so, how in the course of those thrilling years could one find a moment to study? It was for everyone a time of action. The aspirations of social life burned so strongly that individuality was forgotten for the advantage of the collectivity.

Oh, indeed! It was much more exciting to be present at the diverse phases of this social renovation, sometimes quite somber, alas! but always great in its goal, to dedicate one's leisure time to the activities of the clubs, to fraternize every *décadi** with warm and energetic comrades; and these activities spoke more to the heart than all the books in the world. [. . .]

My sweet mother was in every way the opposite of her husband. Timid and fearful before the emotions and clamor of social life, whose principles in any event disturbed all of her religious beliefs, she annihilated herself in a complete abnegation. In order to reconcile her feelings and her duties, she made herself silent and submissive. She was, in a word, the Christian wife of the Middle Ages. Raised in a small town by a cold and rigid mother, she entered marriage with a soul benumbed by the most complete ignorance of every idea and thing. She thus had vague aspirations, but no initiative. As the product of her circumstances, this Christian mother was hardly suited to develop us intellectually. But I still see her great among all women for her heart. It was always the light of her angelic goodness that illuminated the painful road I had to travel, and which prevented my heart from turning to ice upon contact with the selfishness and false affections of society.

Much as I venerate her memory, I still congratulate myself on having been swept into the current of my father's feelings and ideas. His energetically social character produced this latent, so to speak, seed of the future that later on made me love the religious idea of indefinite progress.** But let us not anticipate, for many troubles and tears separate me from this time of regeneration.

When I was about fifteen, my character developed spontaneously. That love of independence and feminine dignity that showed itself in me at all times was not in the least inspired by Saint-Simonian theories. No, it was part of my being. Let me cite for you a single example: One day, my father addressed to his wife some brusque and disdainful comments on the subject of religion, which made my brothers smile. I was indignant.

---

*The tenth day of the *décade*, of which there were three in each month of the revolutionary calendar, was a holiday.
**Reference to the "theology" of the Saint-Simonian movement.

"Truly," I said to my mother, shedding an angry tear, "you are too patient, dear mother; why let yourself be treated that way?" "Ah! my daughter, one must buy peace with the weight of gold." "It is too expensive," I said bitterly. "Oh! little philosopher, never forget this proverb: where the goat is tied, there she will have to graze." But I was angry and daringly replied: "No, no, the goat can break her rope and go graze elsewhere."

Although I could not sense the whole import of my act, my mother was terrified by this repartee in a child of fifteen. She made me be quiet and forced me to go kiss my father.

After that altercation, our roles changed; my mother depended on me to gain respect for her sweet, weak nature, and my intervention often served to reestablish the frequently troubled moral equilibrium between her sons and husband.

From that time on, I felt that a human soul was coming to life in me and transforming a mind long obstructed by the mysticism of my childhood years. My character became gay and open. Everything interested me and took on a cheerful glow in my eyes. But since the social position of my parents was on a very lowly level, I remained, despite my aspirations toward the beautiful, a poor child of the people, very naive and ignorant. [. . .]

If, in the restrained circle of my life, an unknown word struck my ear, I would quickly run to my brother's dictionary to learn its meaning so that I could assimilate it. At public concerts or in museums, I oftentimes felt my tears flow. There was, in these tears, happiness in aspiring to the unknown and despair in never being able to attain it. "Happy, very happy," I said, "are the children of the rich, who can traverse at leisure this immense garden of human knowledge and gather the fruits of these divine trees!" [. . .]

My desire to learn attained some satisfaction in my family; Philippe, the youngest of my brothers, had wanted to become a priest at the time of our extreme devotion. To this end, he had taken classes at the seminary of Saint-Merry* until the age of seventeen. At that time he threw away his frock, telling my mother to console her that he would rather be an honest worker than a bad priest. This young cleric, who had quit at the moment of his tonsure, was thus the scholar of the family. It was he who initiated me into the history of the Greeks and Romans and somewhat into contemporary history. I had found the road but was lacking the time and books to follow it.

I passionately loved reading and was allowed to abandon myself to this penchant in the evening beside my mother, on the condition that while she worked I read to her the entire contents of the nearby book-

---

*The neighborhood church where Suzanne had undergone many formative childhood experiences.

shelf. Instead of the solid instruction that young girls are now beginning to receive, I extracted from these novels false notions about real life. [. . .]

The years that followed the Restoration were very painful for working people to live through.* And so poverty, our old acquaintance, came knocking at our door again. This sad visitor weighed primarily upon my mother, who out of devotion for her loved ones took upon herself the greatest share of it. From this moment on, therefore, her health declined, and the horrid illness of which she died three years later began to exert its ravages, without any complaint coming from her to awaken our concern.

When education is given equally to both sexes, and women with a studious bent compete like men to deserve and obtain medical diplomas, how many victims will be spared a cruel and premature death! They will not wait, as my mother did, for the last stages of this horrid disease to put their trust in science. During the long practice of my art, I have noticed the same thing everywhere: women hesitate to speak of certain symptoms. Everything in them recoils at disclosing to the doctor those details that are repellent to imagination and modesty. They *all* dissimulate the gravity of their symptoms or talk about them too late. In Russia, where I practiced my profession for seven years, I saw a great lady hardly allow herself to be questioned by her doctor. There, as in Egypt and America, he must guess everything, while the hideous *cancer* has already marked its imprint on the victim's features, and inexorable death is ready to pounce.

To women and women *alone*, the right to aid their sex, not only in the divine work of maternity, but also in all illnesses from which chastity has so much to suffer in divulging them to men.

[Chapter III: Death of Suzanne's Mother]

When my mother died, I escaped to a dark room to cry without restraint over my dear lost one, for the modesty of a true feeling is so strong in me that ordinary consolations are words empty of meaning. But my [sister] Adrienne incessantly came to dry my tears with hugs and kisses. "You are now my only mother," she told me, "why do you want to abandon me?" [. . .]

Reading became the only distraction I felt I could enjoy. [. . .] Negative philosophy was in fashion. Young people borrowed their slogan from Voltaire: *Let us destroy evil!* Under this general influence, I avidly read everything that had to do with this destructive breath of the past.

---

*Reference to the period 1815–30, when, following the defeat of the Napoleonic Empire, the Bourbon Monarchy was "restored." It was a time of conservative reaction.

The works of Voltaire, Rousseau, Volney, and others were a little indigestible for a mind as uneducated as mine. From Voltaire, I read only the theater with interest. I preferred Rousseau, and from him I read with pleasure *Emile* and especially the *Nouvelle Héloïse*. Despite the shudders of terror that his terrible preface had caused me, and although I claimed I could remain strong against his influence, the charm worked; I no longer felt the same after this reading. I still consulted my good authors, but I was forced to admit my preference for works of fiction, as they seemed to speak more to the imagination. Mesdames Cottin and de Genlis, the charming storytellers of that age, were my favorites. From the wise Madame de Staël, I read with pleasure *Delphine* and *Corinne*, the new Sappho in which, it is said, she tried to depict her own triumphs and sorrows.

[Chapter IV: Disillusionment in Love]

[. . .] This isolation [of my mourning] weighed upon me. That melancholy which follows great sorrow had joined with the ardor of a soul questing the mysteries of life. The friendship of my adoptive daughter was no longer enough for me. My heart needed another love, and this great unknown threw my inner self into turmoil. Housework absorbed well enough all my time, but not all my thoughts or desires. [. . .]

My moral state led me to return to those joyous meetings [at the home of my sister-in-law]. It was there that I encountered the man who was to shatter everything in me, my heart and my belief in a vow sworn before God!

Let me briefly paint for you this first love. Through it I was lifted for a few moments into a luminous world, but the man who had made me live in ethereal heights brutally threw me back into an abyss. This descent changed a person full of life and love into a miserable creature, endlessly crying out to God: "Lord, Lord, take me! By saving me from myself, you save me from a suicide which I still hold in horror, for it would separate me from my mother; my heart has become like those fruits which maintain their appearance but are already full of ashes and bitterness. Dear God, have pity, withdraw me from this world unto you!"

These moral sufferings weighed upon my heart for many years. It was Saint-Simonianism, which I encountered in 1830, that alone had the power to regenerate me.

Dear daughter, my hesitation to enter into the details of this intimate drama proves to you my horror of scandal. Just as solitary tears and a sincere confession to God raise a woman up, so, in my opinion, does a useless disclosure of a fault or weakness, even one she regrets, diminish and depoeticize her.

But this is not a case to remain silent about. The sequel to this story will let you know by whom and at what time this adventure was revealed, quite against my will and expectation. I therefore have the duty to reestablish here the facts just as they happened. You and womankind will judge me. [. . .]

When I saw Stanislas at my brother's house . . . I was already predisposed in his favor by my sister-in-law's accounts. He would suit me, she said, in every way; to arrange this marriage was to work for my happiness. He was given the same treatment through my sister-in-law's exaggerated praise of my qualities. I shall not tell you that this drama of my sister-in-law produced a love at first sight between sympathetic souls. It did seem to me, however, that my heart was waiting for him. His distinguished looks and witty good humor made a strong impression on me. He was then almost twenty-four years old. [. . .]

He had only one more exam to pass before being accepted as a doctor. His father, a medical doctor himself with a practice in a small city in the South, had sent his only son to Paris to study the same profession, so that he could later take over his father's practice.

Listening to my sister-in-law tell me these details, I should have thought about my lack of education and the poverty of my family and fled. But the thought did not enter my mind. Happy to be openly distinguished by him, I immediately felt the aristocratic instincts I owed to my mother's delicate nature awaken within me and designate him to me as the man I had been dreaming about for a long time.

That evening, he obtained permission from my brother to walk me home. On the way he held my hand and pressed it tightly against his chest. He uttered a thousand tender and delicate things to me, taking as witness to the truth of his words the rapid beating of his heart, which he made me feel with my trembling hand.

Then, seeing my agitation, he sought to reassure me by talking about his mother, a sister he had lost a short while before, and the happiness his parents would have to find her again in me, etc. My heart translated the incoherence of his words with this sentence: he loves me! And this thought made me tremble with joy and surprise! Although charmed by this brusque declaration, I could only translate my emotion into tears, without being able to stop or explain them. Was this happiness? Was this a portent of the future? Joy had been a stranger to me for such a long time that it could not enter my heart without finding it full of doubt! The only answer I could give was to lightly squeeze his hand. Then I escaped to my room to hide this happiness and these inexplicable fears.

I could not sleep that night. I prayed to God and my mother to show me the road to follow. . . . Then, the next day, fatally swept away by my heart, I went back to my brother's. After that we saw each other every day, for upon his request, my father authorized him to visit our home. The whole family liked him, because he seemed so open and had such sincere and pleasant manners.

When we had reached the point of confiding in each other, I told him about my mother and the power her memory still exerted over my mind, to the extent that after any slightly strong emotion I experienced hallucinations that made me see her alive again. [. . .]

He wanted to know, in his turn, the reason for the tears that had welcomed his declaration. It was through his repeated insistence that, overcoming my shyness, I arrived at making him understand my fears, at first confused and instinctive, but later justified in my mind by the difference between our respective social positions; what future was reserved for our love? "Won't your parents reject me?" He interrupted me with these words, and was tender and persuasive: "My father is liberal," he told me. "He would never set himself against my happiness over a question of dowry. But my father has said many times that until I obtain my medical diploma and reach my twenty-fifth birthday, he does not want to hear any talk of marriage. This is a year of waiting, but the present is glorious. Let us love each other while waiting for better days."

What did these conditions matter to me? I had faith in his word. To love for the sake of loving—I did not desire more than that. I felt the present so radiant that I would have wanted, like the prophet, to stop the sun on this moment of my life!

In the course of this enchanting summer, everything helped to consolidate my trust in the loyal intentions of my beloved. Our good times and outings took place only with the family; the books he brought me were about syntax and history; he was preparing, he said, my triumphant entrance into his dear little town.

For five months this happiness was unmixed with tears or anxieties. A few increasingly ardent but still chaste caresses were not always refused, and my heart held his interests too dear to refuse him all the time.

But these innocent tokens of my affection were already no longer enough for him. Already he complained of my insensitivity. My self-control was, he said, the indication of a cold heart, incapable of true love. His sulks and reproaches made me cry; I did not know then that this was the usual tactic men used to reach their end. I was in love, and if I could resist my own emotions for so long during the long and frequent hours we spent alone together, it was only the memory of my mother that gave me strength. I had sworn, in laying my last kiss upon her cold brow, to be forever worthy of her! This thought was stronger in me than the fear of God himself.

When Stanislas had suitably passed his last exam, he hurried to impart this happy news to his parents, and selected this favorable occasion to let them know about his love for me. I was, he told them, the woman chosen by his heart. He understood no happiness except with me; in his Suzanne, his good mother would find again the sweet daughter she still mourned. He begged them, in concluding, to send their authorization for him to take me as his wife as soon as his thesis was finished. I read this letter in its entirety; he asked me to mail it myself. I did this toward dusk. Before slipping it into the mail box, I covered it with kisses, and letting it flee like a carrier pigeon, I prayed to God that it would bring me blessings and happiness.

Stanislas, feeling strong because of this step that my family knew about and approved, wanted to treat me like his wife. He became more and more pressing; weren't we united by our love and the consent of our parents? He had no doubt that his would consent. Furthermore, he told me, in yielding to him, I would be doing nothing but imitating the example of his mother who before her marriage had loved his father enough to refuse him nothing. This confidential information struck me; I could see in it only a proof of the strength and truth of his love; without this excuse, would he have had the audacity to so accuse his mother, whom he appeared to love with great tenderness?

However, I still had the strength to refuse. I cried and suffered from his bluntness, and our meetings became stormier and stormier.

I have told you above about a phenomenon created and perpetuated by my overexcited imagination. It was still my safeguard for a few months. Every night, after a similar scene in which my heart and head seemed ready to submit, I would again see my mother in every corner of my room. She would float above me, and the more my eyes focused upon this dear shadow, the more she seemed to expand and fill the space to cover me with her protection. Without seeking to understand these visions, I believed in them! These repeated phenomena caused me no fright; on the contrary, I thanked my mother for thus coming to protect me against myself and to comfort my heart for the struggle.

Toward autumn my father went on one of his tours of the provinces, which he was in the habit of doing every year. All four of us, my brother Philippe, Stanislas, my sister, and I, decided to accompany him past the city barriers; the weather was beautiful; this outing was for me like the Saint-Martin summer that comes just before the cold and cloudy days. When he was just about to leave us, my father, after kissing us all, warmly recommended his two daughters to these gentlemen. My brother as well as Stanislas reassured him with hearty protestations. Well then, this man, who had in the morning shaken the hand of a too trusting father, chose that very day to renew his attacks. Toward dusk, when we were alone together in my room, he became violent, out of control, and committed such a brutal assault against me that I was seized with fright. I screamed out; my brother and sister came in; I don't know what Stanislas told them to explain my state; I was staring rigidly into space, for my hallucinations had come back, but this time stronger and more frightening. I saw nothing but them; everything else had become alien to me. My mother seemed to plunge her sad eyes into mine; I followed the progression of this shadow with a certain anguish, for it kept growing and growing, extending its arms and filling the room in the manner of the *vulture,* that bird of the poets with its vast wingspread. By this time, I was no longer breathing, my eyes were closed, and I was trembling; my body was convulsed, so much did it seem to me that this enormous volume was going to crush me. They put me to bed; my brother, my sister, and Stanislas spent the night near me; I did not recognize them and had no consciousness whatever of what was going on.

This state lasted all night long; toward the early morning, thanks to some sedatives given to me, the hallucinations stopped; I fell asleep more calmly; when I awoke, I was shattered, but the ghosts had disappeared and taken away with them the memory of what had happened the night before. My brother, seeing me improved, went back to work; my sister was sent by Stanislas to get some provisions for the day. At this moment, a vague fear, a fear I didn't even realize I had, made me call this dear child back; but, upon an entreaty from Stanislas, who used my health as a pretext to give her a reason for going out, my Adrienne went quickly away. That was my last sign of resistance; I was at the end of my strength and could not think any more; therefore that man's new attempts obtained all the success he desired. From that moment on I was his! . . . On the following days, he dried my tears with his kisses and calmed my conscience with the vow to marry me as soon as possible. Only then did he admit to me that his parents' answer had arrived a long time ago; it contained no refusal of his dearest desires, but his father insisted upon the necessity of his son waiting to reach his majority before getting married; he pointed out to him that this was not a long delay, that this postponement of six months should not hurt his fiancée in any way. His trust in his son's judgment was complete and he could not have made a choice that would be unworthy of them and himself, etc. In spite of the circumlocutions he used to translate this letter to me, I felt a deep sadness, but without letting him see it, for my trust was too complete to doubt his truthfulness. I was afraid that he would take for mistrust my acute desire to read the letter from this parents. He said to me: *Let us wait.* I resigned myself in silence.

About two months later, toward the end of December, Stanislas asked me what I wanted for Christmas. An engagement ring, I answered, looking at him tenderly. On Christmas day, he brought me a ring with a date and our initials engraved on the inside. I lovingly kissed this ring as a sign before God and my conscience of my rehabilitation.

That day was completely given over to joy; my father proposed that we have Christmas supper after we came back from midnight mass. He stayed home, wanting to preside over the preparations for this family ritual. Stanislas whispered to me: "This is the perfect occasion to have your ring blessed, my dear little religious fanatic; entrust this ring to me for a few moments." The four of us went back to the Church of Saint-Merry; it was already lit up for the great Christian festival. I can still see myself placed in the middle of the nave beside Stanislas. When everyone rose, he took my left hand, and while they all sang the hymn *O salutaris*

Hostia, he slid his ring on my finger, and swore once more, taking God as a witness, that he would never have any other wife but me. Who could still doubt, after a vow made in these terms and on this solemn occasion?

Since then, I have often asked myself if at that moment he was acting in good faith. I wanted to convince myself he was for the honor of humanity, because this impulse came from his own free will. I had belonged to him for two months; so to what end and for what good would be this useless sacrilege? What would profit him this refinement of ignominy? And yet when I reconsider all the acts of this intimate drama, doubt, I confess, has at times come to turn my stomach with disgust and contempt for this man!

I am not making up a romance, believe me, dear daughter; *everything* I have just written is as true as truth itself, true in *every* detail! I attest to it here upon the memory of my mother; the memory of her is still the most powerful force there is in my life. I needed to affirm for you this story before I could continue it, for I must have your complete faith in order to find the courage to do so.

Toward the beginning of March 1823, Stanislas's visits became less regular. Therefore a gnawing anxiety worked upon my imagination. He often found me with my eyes reddened from crying; then he would scold me; and sometimes he still *deigned* to give me a few reasons to justify his absence. Could I, despite my strain, find once more the serenity and gaiety I had had in those early days of our relation? No; a sad foreboding weighed upon my life, and I did not always have the strength to hide the thought of it. He no longer commiserated with me, but became more and more irritated and restrained himself less and less. One time among others, after a few days of absence, he suddenly burst into my room. He found my face decomposed by tears; he became furious, angrily threw his hat to the other end of the room, and yelled in an imperious voice: "Always, always tears! I *do not like Madeleines*." I was devastated by this violence and these bitter words. Each of us bears inside ourself the mysteries of our heart; I was and still am both proud and shy; a harsh word represses in me any expansion toward the outside; in such cases silence becomes the safeguard of my dignity.

After a few moments that were painful for both of us, Stanislas seemed to come to a resolution and said to me without any preparation: "Listen, my love; come live with me, my courses are upsetting me and my thesis isn't finished yet; come and share my life; that will force me to work; aren't we united? You will take my name; if you love me, *nothing* should hold you back."

The proposition, which no previous word had led me to expect, caused me a sorrowful commotion. "Me, leave my father's house?" I said to him without hesitating; "me, abandon my sister? my adoptive child? at her age, where would such an example lead her? No, no a hundred times no, that is impossible for me! I already feel guilty without adding scandal to my sin. . . . " He went away cold and disdainful, saying that I did not know how to love, since he had to wring everything out of me.

Obviously this man sought a pretext to break the bonds that had become too heavy. He visited me a few times more, but was no longer the same. Finally, before this fatal month had ended, he went away without any prior explanation and without taking into account the vows formerly offered before God with so much love. From that moment on, I never saw him again! Never!

This drama had lasted six months!

From the moment I became convinced of his cowardly abandonment, I was killed in my faith and love: nothing remained at the bottom of my heart but contempt for him and his sex. [. . .]

[Chapter V: Life as a Young Working Woman]

The two years from 1823 to 1825 (the year of my marriage) will acquaint you with the life of women workers and their tribulations when, confronting daily necessities, work must provide for their needs. Love them, too, my child, and protect all those whom you meet along the way, for they are not without merit, these daughters of the people who, proud and worthy, know how to resist every kind of temptation, and demand from work alone their daily bread. [. . .]

The first house of embroidery which accepted us as workers was located on rue Saint-Martin, and run by a lady who was very devout, but not in the same way as my three Norman sisters whose religion was so true and pure from all human self-interest.* Here, on the contrary, it was a matter of outward form and self-serving hypocrisy. Mlle Marie, a spinster around thirty-five years old, had quite recently united her establishment, her savings, and her person to Monsieur Martin, an old employee, crippled with rheumatism, with a salary as thin as his person. These two spouses, bored with a celibacy infinitely too prolonged, joined themselves to each other and complemented each other perfectly. Thus I soon understood the cheerfulness of the six young girls composing Madame Martin's workshop. Her devotion, ridiculous in its concern for minutiae, combined with the simperings of a new wife, sufficiently justified the jokes of which our strict employer was the object.

Because of my Adrienne, I congratulated myself for having fallen in the midst of this swarm of silly young girls. My sister in fact came back to life as a result of this contact. [. . .]

Our task, however, was rude; we had to be at work at seven o'clock sharp, and, before undertaking the long race to arrive on time, we had

---

*As a child, Suzanne had been apprenticed to work in Normandy, in the home of a very devout family, which included three young girls close to her in age. Her daily regime of work and prayer (no play and no exercise) eventually made her physically ill.

to hastily complete all our housework. If some details made us late, Madame Martin did not allow excuses and did not grant any mercy, and we had to pay in kind, that is to say, remain some minutes after the workday. When our days were thus prolonged, I had a hideous fear of meeting on the way home one of those contemptible men who make it a game to accost young working girls and frighten them with their disgusting proposals. In such cases, my nerves are always agitated and physical courage fails me completely. It was otherwise with my proud and pretty Adrienne. Laughing at my cowardice, she would say: "Dear sister, am I not there (she was hardly fifteen years old)? Let the occasion arise, then you will see that *valor does not depend on age! . . .* " One evening, she in fact proved it to me. Toward nine o'clock, we were on rue Temple, near the Church of Saint Elizabeth; we were stopped by the vulgar words and disgusting gestures of a miserable creature. As usual, I remained trembling and speechless before this insulting man. Adrienne on the contrary had a moment of sublime energy; she succeeded in managing a tone so resolute while brandishing an enormous key before his eyes that he recoiled and, at the end of the boulevard, we were delivered from his insolent remarks. [. . .]

My father, disappointed in his desire to have us both married and so gain his liberty of action and spurred on above all by a feminine influence that was the evil genius of my mother and ourselves, saw fit, despite his tenderness for us, to leave Paris, but not *alone*, in order to go and tempt his fate again in the city of Amiens where he still had a few friends. Before his departure, he found us a little room on rue Michel-le-Comte, decorated it with our old furniture, poor wreckage left from the ruin of our family, and set off, leaving me an authorization to preside over the marriage of my sister whenever I saw fit.

This abandonment, whose result, alas, was to greatly increase our poverty and isolation, did not, however, afflict me unduly. Misfortune had already taught me to count on myself alone. My sole concern was to preserve my sister, that frail and charming creature, from any overly harsh contact with reality.

The lodging that we then occupied was centrally situated to our work; that was its only advantage. The house was ugly and without a porter, and our single room on the third floor had only one window overlooking the narrow, dark courtyard. The sight of this house made our hearts ache. In the evening, coming home from work, when we had to cross that dark alley and go up that evil-smelling staircase hand in hand to reach our dwelling, we experienced wild terrors and felt that there was no protection whatever to ensure our security.

One scene that took place a few days after we moved in explains well enough our fearful panic. Allow me to recount it in a few words. These diverse little mishaps can strike all poor, young women workers, deprived, as we were at this time, of any moral and protective guarantees.

One Sunday, my young sister's fiancé came to call upon us with his younger brother to go for an outing in the countryside. That evening, around nine o'clock, these gentlemen drove us back to the door of our house. Once inside, occupied with our prayers and preparations for bed, we suddenly heard furtive footsteps halt at our door; people were speaking in low voices, seeming to consult one another; "it's here," said one, "this is the only lighted room"; then they softly knocked. At first, terror seized us. "Who is it?" I said with a trembling voice. "It's us," the strangers replied mysteriously. "You have the wrong door, go somewhere else, we do not know you." "Really," replied these men with a kind of anger, "you do not know us? Did you not just leave us with some silly pretext a few steps from here and come into this house? Ah! we have been your cavaliers all day, and now you dare to say: go away, we don't know you; come on, lovelies, open up! because we don't expect to be made fools of like that."

Judge, dear child, the cruel dilemma these men put us in. Two timid young girls, isolated, unknown to any person in that house, and so vulgarly addressed out loud! Trembling, we clutched each other and, throwing ourselves on our knees, prayed to God without answering further. But these men continued to knock louder just as they had threatened. . . . Luckily, after a fervent prayer, my energy came back to me. Climbing upon a piece of furniture, I knocked with a stick on the ceiling with all my strength. I made such a racket that finally the upstairs and downstairs neighbors began to stir. The place reverberated with the footsteps of many people, and we heard voices rebuking our persecutors. These men, however, continued to say that they wanted to see us and speak to us, that they knew us, all four of us having spent the day together. Our neighbors responded to our denials in vain: "Open your door, don't be afraid, show yourselves." But we paid them no heed; nothing could overcome our fright. All we dared do to confound this impudent lie was to open our window and approach it together, a light in our hands; our illuminated faces could thus be seen perfectly from the landing. Everyone was then certain that these young people were in good faith; for hardly did they see us than they were beside themselves with excuses, not only to us but also to all of our neighbors, for the noise and the scandalous scene that they had just created, recounting, in order to justify this ridiculous prank, the hoax of which they were the victims.

To finish this story, the next day we told Mallard* about our panic the night before, and begged him to obtain information. He ascertained in fact that the imprudent frivolity of two young women had justified the nocturnal uproar of our young men; they had merely gone to the wrong house.

"These two vigorous chaps," Mallard told us, "admitted to me, laughing like fools, that having met these two young provincial fellows on an

*Adrienne's fiancé.

outing, the women had been quite happy to play that risky game of accepting their attention for a whole day, but that night, wanting to restrain them within certain limits, the girls had found it amusing to escape their pursuit."

This strange coincidence was not of a nature to reassure us. But we had to live in this sad house for two more months until Adrienne's marriage.

During this lapse of time, we were to know that most distressing situation in the life of the worker: *unemployment*.

It was the end of the reign of Louis le Désiré;* everywhere conditions of luxury came to a halt, for the decorum of the court demanded sadness. Balls and festivals were prohibited; no more of those dresses of gold and silver lamé, nor those delicious whimsies which, while adorning the beautiful privileged women, at least provided the woman worker a living. Madame Martin's workshop was reduced by three quarters; having come last, we were the first to be let go. That was fair, but the turmoil Adrienne experienced compromised anew her health. I had to look elsewhere, and just about everywhere, for work. I found only some very poorly paid embroidery of shoddy goods with some exporters, which I had to accept or else die of hunger. We rented frames and worked in our room. During these two months, our best daily wages came to *one* franc each, with us beginning at six in the morning and often prolonging our workday until midnight.

This tedious existence could not last long without danger; already the forced work, together with an insubstantial diet, was exhausting my poor sister physically and mentally. Because of this austere diet, her delicate and pure beauty began to fade. The dear child had a horror of real life; her exalted nature, always rising to the summits of the ideal, could not adjust to the mean, unpoetic life we led. This instinctive revolt of all her sentiments made her reject the mundane struggle, doubtless honorable, but full of misery. She languished and yet could not decide to say yes to the solicitations of her fiancé. [. . .]

[Chapter VI: Marriage]

[. . .] Marriage without divorce as a corrective is a serious thing in its consequences, even when this indissoluble bond is contracted with love by the naive and pure young girl; but I, whose withered heart could open up only to the feeling of maternity, had to wage cruel struggles against myself before daring to unite with the man whose name I have loyally born.

*1827

I made Voilquin's acquaintance in a circle of modest bourgeois and honest workers to which my brother-in-law belonged. [. . .] Voilquin was one of the handsomest men in the place; he had a gallant turn of phrase, as they used to say then; his facility with words was inexhaustible; his vivacity and gaiety were dazzling; his frank and lively features predisposed people in his favor.

Therefore, before our arrival, all the young ladies of the circle had begun a systematic flirtation to capture his attention. But, as it often happens, it was I, who troubled myself little to attract his compliments, whom he noticed. [. . .]

For the past two and a half years my heart had been able to throb only for the dream of the rosy little angels maternity promised me. Oh! to have children and give them this immense need to love that tormented my life was, for me, the only enviable happiness. I thought of it constantly, but I wanted to confer upon these dear little creatures all the conditions of happiness possible. They needed for this an acknowledgeable name and father. With this in mind, I felt no repugnance whatever in taking as spouse this kind and confident young man. "As compensation for the love I cannot possibly give him, can I not," I asked myself, "embellish his life and make him happy through my constant and devoted care? His inconsistent, unstable character leaves his heart open to all impressions; everything therefore makes him need an affectionate support. Thus this quasi-maternal sentiment I feel for him will eliminate every harmful obstacle from his path and give wing to his good instincts."[. . .]

The marriage took place.

For every young girl marrying under the protective wing of a tender mother, this day is full of a mysterious and charming turmoil. For me, as a poor orphan, it was only a day of anguish. This anxiety grew to an indescribable point; when our friends had left us and we found ourselves finally in that dreaded tête-à-tête, the specter of the past rose up anew before me. Under this pressure I was almost going to give up my secret in a wave of honest frankness, when I was overcome by such suffocation that I completely lost consciousness. For how long? I do not know. As I came to, I was touched by the care that Voilquin lavished on me and by his acute emotion. I understood that it was too late to trouble his complacency. I swore to myself again, as compensation for an unknown wrong, to dedicate myself to his happiness.

A few days later, yet another intimate drama took place between us, a drama in which I was called to my roles of abnegation and consolation all at once. Alas! it had quite fatal consequences for me, for it shattered in full flower the happiness I had reserved for myself in this union, the hope of being a mother. [. . .]

When I complained of various symptoms a few days after our marriage, I found Voilquin interrogating me with a certain intensity; my answers visibly troubled him. A short while later, he claimed he had an errand to run and left immediately; he did not come back until rather late that night. When we had retired to our bedroom, I pressed him with questions without realizing my anxiety. Instead of answering me, I saw him go pale, tremble, become nervous and agitated, stiffen, and finally lose consciousness completely. This totally unforeseen effect made me divine all the gravity of our situation, but my compassion for his condition made me take him to my heart above any other consideration. Even while seeking to revive him, I told myself that only a good and loyal person could feel so keenly a wrong that doubtless had to be involuntary on his part.

When he came to, I let him hear only words of tenderness and encouragement. He admitted to me in effect that an inexperienced doctor had declared him cured, for several months, of a rather grave affliction. Unfortunately, this malady still persisted. That very morning, following our conversation, he had gone to consult another practitioner, and it had been proved. This certainty had driven him almost mad. He had thought to calm down by spending the whole day in the countryside.

In the end, I accepted everything! This shared misfortune tightened our bond by serving to increase a reciprocal devotion.

Never during the eight years our union lasted did I let him hear a reproach or complaint on this subject.

I must however, to be precise in my statements, mention here one exception. Yes, a single time, in 1832, the cry of an unknown and rebellious heart escaped in a reproach addressed to Voilquin in the presence of Father Enfantin. [. . .]

As for me, during the first five years of my marriage, I had to abandon the hope of being a mother as a result of this sad cause. Yes, during this lapse of time, I felt three times a dear little being stir in my womb and die there before having seen the light of day! How many tears did I shed in the silence of the night, seeing each time my hope disappointed anew! Oh! to have felt so close to my heart this young life I was harboring with such love decline and expire, and not to have heard that long desired first cry! . . . Believe me, one has to go through similar griefs to appreciate all their bitterness!

Words are powerless to express to you the weariness and disgust for life that each of these crises left in the depths of my heart. I had come to doubt divine justice! "What!" I thought, "can I accept the loss of my health, the more precious loss of my child, as expiations of a transgression *against* social *rule* and *not* against divine grace? If God is just, why these new sufferings?" Was it not I who had been basely deceived just a short time before? And besides, had I not cried and prayed enough? If there was a transgression, had I not morally rehabilitated myself through work, courage, and devotion?

Oh, holy maternity, my cherished ideal!! Why have you always fled me? What can I cleave to? Is this union, to which I have given so much of my life for so many years, and from which I receive so little happiness in return, not then blessed? [. . .]

[Chapter VII: Life with the Saint-Simonians]

Such was my turn of mind when the Saint-Simonian doctrine found me. When I learned about the notion of indefinite progress, eternal like God, and came to appreciate the fundamental idea of our liberty and the religious future in these words of Father Enfantin, "God, Father and Mother of all men and women," I experienced a sort of bedazzlement. I felt an immense joy at rediscovering my mind, heart, and action free by virtue of those holy formulas. God had spoken to me and was truly bringing me back to life! From then on, I felt myself again capable of loving God and men with a new love.

I designate as my apostolic life the period between 1830 and the end of 1838. It is therefore, dear child, these eight years of exceptional existence that I will recount, this period of time when I no longer thought of the material interests in life, and dispensed quickly with worldly opinion. Yes, I, formerly so timid and fearful of what people would say! Judge by this alone how much the new faith had transformed me.

In the last months of 1830, at a time when the people, as vengeance against the deceptions inflicted by the quasi-legitimacy,* sang along with their poet: "Poor sheep . . . ," etc., we were all four equally tired of the disavowals of the ex-republicans, advocating in concert with the liberal bourgeois the tiresome maxim of *Each for himself, each to his own* [*Chacun pour soi, chacun chez soi*]. Very saddened by all this cowardice, especially after the great aspirations of July, and hearing the clamor of society, we were waiting for—what? We had no idea! . . .

It was then that we heard about Saint-Simonianism from the typography workers of Firmin Didot. Many of them were attending the meetings that elaborated these social theories. Mallard, stimulated by his colleagues, persuaded us to go hear these new apostles, for since our marriage we were never apart from each other. Thus all four of us went together, and then went back, more and more interested in this crowd of young apostles.

I, who in my mistrusting spirit had so dreaded meeting some middle-of-the-road duplicates of the Jesuits, could not hear enough of the eloquent demonstrations of those young, wise, and religious minds.

---

*Reference to the rule of Louis-Phillipe of the Orleanist branch of the royal family. In July 1830, a revolution brought down the reactionary Charles X, the last of the Bourbon kings. Although republicans and workers played significant roles in these events, a compromise—to which key republicans agreed—established the "July Monarchy" of Louis-Phillipe, a liberal bourgeois regime, instead of one that was more democratic.

From that moment on, we bid farewell to the friends who did not want to follow us, farewell to the societies of pleasure that no longer spoke to our hearts, and finally, to everything that was not this new and powerful doctrine. No, never was the life of four individuals more completely transformed. We gave ourselves body and soul to this new family, whose social, economic, and religious principles were *ours* from the first moment.

Its teachings attracted crowds in the various places opened for that purpose. The ones we attended most regularly were those at the Athenaeum, in the Faubourg Saint-Germain, and then at the Grand Center, in the Salle Taitbout.

Each branch of the doctrine's teaching had its own day of exposition. In those two lecture rooms of the Athenaeum, questions of finance and the religious use of public credit* were treated with order, grandeur, and clarity by the P[ereire] brothers. Social criticism was vigorously expounded by Leon Simon and Laurent; when they recalled the abuses that weighed upon women and the people, their fine and biting criticisms never lacked applause. Then on Sundays, in the Salle Taitbout, the words of Beau, Guéroult, Charton, and young Retouret, all so engaging, succeeded in thrilling our hearts with hope and joy for the future they envisioned and promised to the next generation.

But the orator who later contributed most powerfully to my moral resurrection was our excellent Charles Lambert, to whom the theological development of the new dogma was entrusted. Every Saturday, which was his day, he spoke of God with all his heart, in such an elevated, convincing manner that he even stirred the atheists! This was no longer Christianity, but its development and splendid transformation. Therefore my religious fiber was strongly moved by it; "so I can," I thought, "reconquer my place in social life."

The Salle Taitbout, in which the Saint-Simonian family presented itself every Sunday to the public gaze, offered a delightful sight. Those who saw it and heard the speeches and the sermons of this youthful elite left feeling enthused, and remembered it for a long time.

The Saint-Simonian hierarchy consisted of three degrees, in which the wives and female relatives of the new apostles distinguished themselves. On the stage were seated the members of the first degree; on the benches of the periphery were placed the members of the two other degrees. The floor of this hall was filled with ladies. It has been compared, quite rightly, to a charming basket of flowers, so much did it contain young and pretty faces, adorned with fresh and cheerful toilettes.

It was there that I saw for the first time the two supreme leaders: Bazard, bearing on his austere, manly face the force and energy of the fighter, and Father Enfantin, showing in all his person the gentleness

---

*In other words, the use of public credit in accord with Saint-Simonian doctrine.

and calm of a strong will, as well as the beauty and charm of the apostle of the future and of women. Seeing him, hearing him, my heart and my feminine pride gave with joy to him, and to him alone, the sweet and august name of *Father*.

Olinde Rodrigues, the first after the two leaders, was the direct disciple of Saint-Simon. [. . .] [He] was one of the most ardent promoters of the seeds contained in that lovely motto placed, as everyone knows, at the top of the *Globe*:* "All for the improvement of the most numerous and poorest class."

Many of the young men who stood out during this era through the force and authority of their words or their writings are still alive, thanks be to God; unnecessary to name them here. Most kept the promises we had a right to expect from their beginnings. Since then, the world has opened its ranks to them, and almost all have reached the top of society where they continue to hold fast and firm to the standard of progress.

After we had spent many months following these teachings and reading the *Globe* and the other Saint-Simonian works, I was seized with the desire to belong to the family.** Voilquin knew several members; it was easy for him to have us admitted. But the mistrust of men, sad companion of my youth since 1823, weighed heavily upon me and made me approach the Saint-Simonian personnel with reserve. [. . .]

Once admitted into the assemblies of the Saint-Simonian family, we made the acquaintance of the ladies who maintained the salon on the rue Monsigny. It hosted a crowd of young and pretty women who adorned it with their presence; they were placed under the friendly tutelage of the ladies of the first degree.

Madame Bazard, a very intelligent woman, spoke at length and with facility; she knew how to talk to workers, but not at all to women. I found her too submissive to the masculine hierarchy to have any power over my independent spirit.

The second, Mademoiselle Aglaé Saint-Hilaire, a friend of the Father and his family, was a woman of true merit, greatly esteemed by all those gentlemen. She deserved it for her morality and her intelligence; but I was first of all struck by her cold and grave appearance. It was to the third woman we felt drawn; Madame Cécile Fournel greeted us with a perfect generosity and subjugated us with her gracious kindness. If, however, Father Enfantin had not later dissolved the female hierarchy, I would have remained forever in the preparatory degree, for my heart could never pronounce the name of Mother when I addressed any of these women.

In my opinion, to think of establishing a hierarchy among women, before they had performed an act of free will and before they could

*The official Saint-Simonian newspaper.
**Reference to the Saint-Simonian movement or "family."

know themselves, was nonsense. It was to say to the women: "We declare you free, but walk in our footsteps, repeat our speech, and grow, if you can, under our breath and inspiration."

Fortunately, a few months later, the Father sensed that this was a continuation of the tutelage of the past in a different form, and he put us all in a state of equality. This course was longer and more dangerous in its results for the doctrine, but it was also the only consistent one, and the only one that justified those words of the Father: "Women, like us, you are in God! Thus it is your right to be free! Show yourselves, make yourselves known, we will respect your words and your acts." [. . .]

Shortly after our admission into the family, financial contributions, either from the outside or from its own members, allowed it to expand its propagation. In several neighborhoods the Saint-Simonians created centers in which they explained Saint-Simonian principles to the workers; they then established in two or three houses some very simply served tables, where the heads of the centers and all those who had given their entire life to the family could find a frugal and sufficient meal.

Olinde Rodrigues invited Voilquin to devote himself entirely to the new ideas. "Come live among us," he told him; "your wife will run the dining hall that we want to establish on the rue Taitbout; her sister and Mallard will also belong; come, we will have enough work to give you." I certainly did not want to dampen his enthusiasm; he left without regret, but not without merit, the clientele that he had established in his profession as architect and the drawing class he directed in the evening for construction workers. [. . .]

My sister, her husband, and several other Saint-Simonians came every day to sit at this fraternal table. This existence, too happy to last very long, continued until the reversal of fortune changed the face of things. Dissolution came through the action of the authorities. The "powers that be" were moved by the force and reach of our doctrines. Judiciary proceedings were ordered against the Saint-Simonian leaders. This ended the trust that their loyalty and devotion to this work deserved so well. The financial contributions ceased; their personal fortune was exhausted; and soon it was necessary to think about liquidating the society, dissolving the dining service, reducing the rent, and finally excluding even the expenses that seemed indispensable.

But, before reaching the extremity of having neither hearth nor home to shelter ourselves, I must retrace my steps in order to tell you of two important events. I have already indicated the first in telling you of my marriage.

The Father, wanting to know the morals of everyone who surrounded him, had induced many of the family members to confide their past lives. Many had agreed to do so in the general interest. I found this measure quite logical on his part. It was even said that many women had participated.

Since I had been living in the midst of this *Family* whose devotion I appreciated by trying to imitate it, the holy passion for truth, temporarily dimmed within me, had revived at this contact. I too, I thought, need to be truthful; every lie weighs upon me and troubles me. I want to make my whole past known to my husband, but I want to tell it to him in the presence of the *Father*. From then on, if he bears up under this confidence nobly, our union, grafted on trust, will perhaps be able to rest on love.

My gaze often followed the Father in the Monsigny salon. I desired an interview with him and did not dare initiate it. He doubtless understood, for one day, taking me aside, he said: "And you, dear daughter, have you nothing to tell me?" "Yes, Father, I want to talk to you; receive me in your study, I will go there with Voilquin." He fixed a deep gaze upon me, then said: "Come tomorrow morning, I will listen to you."

But alas! I had presumed too much upon my strength. Hardly had we been brought together the next day, with me seated facing these two men who were awaiting my speech, when, in an attempt to begin the account of the extortion of which I had been the victim, I stuttered and sobs choked me, as when I had previously addressed myself to my old confessor. Through my broken words, these gentlemen could at most understand the downfall, but not that which explained it and, I dare say, excused it completely. Voilquin threw himself sobbing into the arms of the Father, but, in these first moments, *neither of them extended a hand to me*! Oh, my saintly mother, I thought, looking at them, you would have dried my tears with your caresses before turning to a man!

This iniquitous distribution of male justice stopped my tears. The memory of the six years since my marriage, as well as my wounded dignity, made me raise my brow. I looked at Voilquin severely and said: "Remember, before condemning me for the wrong of another, my sufferings over the past six years; remember that to you alone do I owe the sorrow of my incomplete maternities."

The Father looked at me in complete astonishment. Upon leaving us, he embraced me tenderly, but *it was too late*! From that moment on I vowed never again to speak of my thoughts or the intimate acts of my apostolic life *to any man whatsoever* and to confess myself thenceforth to my conscience alone, reserving for myself the right, if I met a woman great and loving enough to appreciate with her heart all the acts of life, to explain to her the motives that would have made me act. [. . .]

Around the same time, there occurred in the family a grave event, foreseen, it is true, by everyone, and of a general interest. It not only stirred our hearts and consciences but also determined the separation of the two supreme leaders. This scission did not stop at the summit; we saw many other defections before the family reconstituted itself under the paternal influence of Father Enfantin.

For six months, discussions had been focused on the moral question.

They had begun in the intimacy of the college between the two leaders. The Father wanted the woman question to be treated in the public teachings and women to be declared free and equal with men. He also wanted the terms of his call to women, as well as to the woman superior enough to epitomize her sex and to come take her place at his side, to be enunciated in terms broad enough for the minds of diverse natures* to understand it and find within it their place and happiness.

The development of his theories, which the Father set forth first in the confines of the college and then, in November of 1831, before the entire family, terrified certain natures placed more especially under the influence of Christian spiritualism. Men as well as women protested publicly against these theories at the Salle Taitbout and afterward withdrew. To our great sorrow, Madame Cécile Fournel was of this number. For seven months we no longer saw her among us. But, at the moment of the criminal court trial, August 27 and 28, 1832,** she had the noble courage to cross Paris on foot beside the Father, as did Mademoiselle Aglaé Saint-Hilaire, and to follow him to the court to affirm his morality and serve as his counsel, if this completely logical innovation could have, in any event, been granted by the tribunal. But let us return to the events of November 1831.

At the time of Jean Reynaud's protest, a very moving scene took place. He rose to reject the moral theories, saying that they would lead to promiscuity between the sexes if one dared to publish them. He denounced the Father so vehemently that the latter, to calm him, put his hand on his shoulder, and, before he could address him a friendly word, several voices from the upper galleries cried out: "*Embrace your Father! Embrace your Father!*" "The voice of the people is the voice of God," he said, throwing himself into the arms of the Father. But that changed nothing in the decisions he had already made.

At this moment I cursed the timidity that prevented me from rising to affirm the dignity of our sex; I wanted a woman's voice to respond to Jean Reynaud, but that was impossible for me. I wrote to him on this subject; the Father read my letter and had it sent to him, saying: "He will not believe it." He declined to answer, and only said: "Enfantin is behind all that."

I listened to the protests of the dissenters, without however being swayed by them. Yes, the men of an austere nature would have to withdraw in the face of this moral agitation of minds, but I understood less the profound emotion that manifested itself among us [women]. From that time on, no longer part of this family of men except through the

---

*By "nature," Enfantin meant various sexual tendencies, especially the categories of "mobiles" and "constants."

**Reference to the government's prosecution of the Saint-Simonian leaders for "corruption of morals."

voice of the call, with our sex being declared free to cooperate in the search for the truth, and feeling, moreover, supported in a milieu where we found respect and fraternal friendship, what had we to fear?

The public session of November 21 was the first and stormiest of this series; all the dissenters withdrew. The four following sessions, which ended on December 7, 1831, treated the highest questions of human morality. One can reject them according to one's nature, education, or prejudices, but nothing, for me, has ever in the world been more beautifully and grandly said since the gospels of sweet Jesus!

It was at the beginning of these sessions that the Father declared the women of the family outside the masculine hierarchy, and so put us all in a state of equality. This measure was logical, especially given the new position of the doctrine; it was especially consistent with his theories of the call, as I have said before.

Mademoiselle Saint-Hilaire, for whom I have always professed the greatest esteem, had us meet in the Monsigny salon, in an attempt to have us reach agreement and act in concert. It was a good idea. We were all, proletarians and bourgeois alike, disposed to cooperate in our activity and dedication. But this lady, who could lead a discussion without being impugned by anyone, had the vexing idea of placing herself in our midst as a supreme being, claiming the name of *Mother*, and of wanting to establish a hierarchy among us before we knew each other. It was inconsistent. My heart and independent spirit rejected both of these pretensions as contrary to her hardly sympathetic nature. I had promised myself to be sincere in everything; I therefore took the floor without hesitating. I told her how much I wished to remain under her direction, that in her I recognized all the qualities of a president, calmness, intelligence, and dignity, but that I did not sense in her the affectionate bent of a mother and could not, consequently, address her with this title. This lady, determined not to preside over a republic, and I, for my part, not conceiving hierarchy as possible given our nature, could no longer share an entente. This was regrettable, and much strength was lost through this division, for several other ladies followed my example. As the claimed title was the condition of our presence in that place, we submitted to this little coup d'état; we withdrew, resolved to act each according to our inspiration.

Near the end of January 1832, the authorities, who dreaded the immense influence that our principles were having on people's minds, declared them subversive of all order. They attacked the Saint-Simonians in their probity and morality and denied them the right to assemble to preach their religious doctrine. The Salle Taitbout was closed on January 22 with a great show of force. A long inquest was immediately begun; it lasted over seven months.

Once the leaders of the doctrine were charged with such serious accusations, slander struck all of us. Our efforts at propagation were diminished, hindered internally by a thousand financial obstacles and externally by the judiciary turmoil. The society women, no longer feeling supported, distanced themselves or no longer dared to appear, not to mention support those who had the courage to persevere along this road.

On April 23, 1832, the Monsigny house was abandoned. The Father, who had just seen his mother taken by cholera, cloistered himself with forty of *his Sons* in a vast property he still owned at Ménilmontant. The Paris family, that is to say, all the Saint-Simonians who could not live at this retreat, were not admitted to visit the forty recluses until June 6, a day that was as bloody and deplorable as any civil war! It was on that ill-fated day, under the noise of the thunder that burst over our heads, and the more terrifying noise of the canon that came right up to us, that the taking of the symbolic habit occurred. This pretty and remarkable attire signaled to the attention of society the individual who wore it as well as all of his acts.

Twice a week, our happiness lay in going to visit our friends at their retreat in Ménilmontant.

[Chapter VIII: The *Femme nouvelle* (New Woman) and the Divorce]

[. . .] Toward the beginning of August 1832, my activity received a new employment. Two young proletarian women, who had also left the rue Monsigny, were publishing a small weekly journal entitled *La Femme libre*. At their request I wrote a quite timid article for the second issue calling women to a peaceful crusade in order to combat with weapons of courtesy the abuses of the stronger sex against us.

Shortly thereafter, these two young women, fascinated by the theories of Fourier, [. . .] departed, leaving me to edit our little paper.* [. . .] From that time on, our journal took this name: *La Femme nouvelle* or *Tribune des femmes*, a more ambiguous title, but not vulnerable to the jokes of society. [. . .]

Although a large number of women entered into correspondence with us, our poor little paper, created and continued by proletarian women deprived of fortune, social standing, and an elementary education to light our path, remained without prestige and never had a real influence on society. It served to console a few hearts disillusioned by the great

*Reine Guindorf and Désirée Veret were the journal's first editors. In 1834, in her farewell article in the *Tribune des femmes*, Suzanne gave a different explanation for their giving up this work—that Guindorf had chosen to devote more time to an instructional program for poor women, which she and other *femmes nouvelles* had organized, and that Veret had left for England. Both Veret and Guindorf continued to write for the *Tribune des femmes* for at least a year after Suzanne became editor. From their articles, it is clear that they were influenced by the Fourierists, but this did not seem to cause them either to stop writing for the *Tribune des femmes* or to dissociate themselves from the *femmes nouvelles*.

Saint-Simonian disaster; it sustained in the souls of our provincial brothers and sisters the sacred fire and hope in the Father and the future; and lastly its publication encouraged society women to speak out, for shortly after our attempt there appeared several magazines edited by society women, flying the flag of light literature, fashion, etc. They succeeded, had subscribers, and by that very fact helped in the emancipation of feminine thought.

Then there appeared suddenly in the intellectual sky a brilliant star, who forced the men to salute her coming. Certainly our George Sand is worthy in her own right: she can be counted among the first writers of the century; her style is delicious music for the soul; and her heart dictates her eloquent pages. But she owes the development of her genius to the great religious ideas that were floating over the world and which will change the face of society by the end of the century. [. . .]

But, dear daughter, we have strayed far from our little paper. You must be saying to yourself that it is presumptuous of me to name George Sand in relation to *La Femme nouvelle*. I am not in the least unaware of the high esteem and admiration you profess for her. So rest assured; I am not trying to establish a parallel. If I have talked about her at this juncture, it is because there is also something of the apostle in her. This feeling forms, so to speak, a bond of kinship among all women devoted to humanity. Everyone who feels this way loves her, in spite of the homage due to her great talent. As for me, having now made my profession of faith to the intellectual summits, I come back to my modest role. [. . .]

Listen and judge with indulgence this event whose results you have seen without knowing the details.

One day [in 1833], as a good housekeeper, I was cautiously brushing my husband's city clothes, softly running the whisk along the seams out of respect for its ripe old age and also for the insurmountable difficulty of replacing this old garment. I had taken out some papers which were getting in the way of my work. They were notes about footage, acreage, etc., and while rearranging them in their proper place, I noticed the heading of a letter whose handwriting was unknown to me. It was tempting for a daughter of Eve. From the beginning of our marriage, having nothing to hide from each other, we had given each other the *reciprocal* right to open each other's correspondence. I therefore opened and read this little letter. Imagine my stupefaction! It was a very tender reply from a heart still timid but greatly in love! The avowal was complete. This letter was signed *Julie Parcy*. Chance let me know without a shred of ambiguity that my husband's heart had turned away from me. To learn all of a sudden, after possessing it without competition for eight years of union, that it was being given to another without equivocation while I remained completely trusting was a cruel moment to go through! I put the letter back and succeeded in remaining silent; but for several days I was prey to some very sad reflections, to serious fears about our future, and also to sorrowful indecisiveness. Should I prevent this passion from doing greater damage to the hearts of these two imprudent people?

Even now I doubt that Voilquin had been calculating in his feelings; his ego was no doubt flattered by the declared preference of a young woman. But, let me stress, for eight years I had always seen him behave like a gentleman; love therefore was the only seducer on this occasion.

I decided to wait and study in silence, in order to judge whether or not this passion to which the letter replied was the caprice of an over-excited imagination in my husband. In such a case, I would warn the mother and daughter and no longer receive them in my house. If, on the other hand, it was for both of them a *deep, true love*, like the one he had futilely desired to find in me, then, *in my new ideas* on unions of the future, it was up to me to perform an act of devotion, provide an example for women by giving him his freedom before God and as much as possible before men, and do it without conditions or reservations.

Ah! if our union had been blessed, if I had had children, I would not have thought I had such a right. I would instead have vied for their father against any woman who would have tried to take him away from me! For although its principles placed Saint-Simonianism way ahead of contemporary society, the familial group to which I belonged did not have enough power or organization to replace paternal protection. But I was alone, and strong in my will and religious faith; I waited for *everything* and did not provoke *anything*.

Seeing me more thoughtful than usual, my husband several times said to me: "What's the matter, my love?" "Nothing!" Characteristic answer of women who have too much to say and so find it prudent to remain silent. He did not insist. He was himself preoccupied; he wanted to speak but the first word never came.

One fine day in April, however, the lilacs in bloom were gladdening our sight; his heart was, like the birds, singing the joys of spring. He came up close to me, took my hand, and then all of a sudden said to me: "If I happened to love *with love* another girl, what would you say?" "If this love were real and shared, what could I say or do?" "What! You would not be too unhappy if I abandoned you? You would let me leave, go far away, with the woman I loved? . . . " A word from me, and my destiny could continue as it was. My heart was aching, but I looked at him calmly and told him: "Yes, be happy, you are free!" He kissed me with great emotion and quickly went out.

A few days later, the situation being less tense, he informed me of their plans, which seemed to go back several weeks, so much were they ready to be put into practice immediately.

From ten to twelve Saint-Simonians, among them my brother-in-law Mallard, had left a few months previously for the United States with the goal of forming a fraternal association in that land of freedom. This precedent had made Voilquin decide to go and establish his new family there as well. He had thus persuaded the Parcy ladies to accompany him. The mother, he said, had from eight to ten thousand francs; she would establish her daughters, and they would live happily together in this Eldorado!

This America still retained all its prestige for his sunny imagination; he kept coming back to this theme, embroidering it in every way. He told me: "We will all owe you our happiness. Julie loves you; if you let her, she will come ask from you as blessing a good-bye kiss."

Listening to him ramble on in this way was for me a real compensation. I told him: "In order to preserve this unique moment in our life, both of us should write a few words to Father Enfantin." He agreed. We wrote standing, each at the corner of a table. I don't know what Voilquin said. We sealed our missives without communicating anything to each other; but since we were both extremely exalted right then, our notes must have exuded something of our state. They were subsequently sent to the Sainte-Pélagie Prison. If the Father has saved these two letters, they can later be joined to this account in order to complete it.

Here, as far as my memory can recall them, are the last lines of my note:

"I am alone now, but I have sent forth a man into the world by deposing my rights upon the altar of humanity and making him free. From now on, paid up with respect to the past, I too want to *think, love, and act freely*. I want to live at last!"

At that moment, Voilquin activated his departure. [. . .]

Voilquin was so drunk with happiness that he had left Paris without remembering to find out about my monetary situation. It was, however, far from brilliant, since once the costs of the move had been paid, exactly *five francs* were left for me to begin my new life; but, for my ex-husband, as for the heroes in novels, money was too secondary a question to be considered. Away with it! When the sky of Mohammed had just opened its wings to receive them, how could they worry about such minor details! Therefore, in response to his request to buy him a surveyor's manual, I was forced to make him come back to earth and admit to him the amount of my fortune. This admission caught the attention of Julie, who had him send me immediately a hundred francs, the most he could. And send them he did, I am convinced, with goodwill. This little sum is the only money I have ever received from him since our separation. [. . .]

I remained for a few months in my little garret on the rue Bourbon-le-Chateau. Our dear Lambert had influenced the hearts and minds of a host of young people from the bourgeois class. They were all so attached to him that they even called themselves *the sons of Lambert*. One of the best and most religious, Alexandre de Berny, mentioned our little journal to his mother, who wanted to meet me; I responded to her invitation. This woman of remarkable heart and intelligence did not content herself with giving us some advice and inserting a few articles, but engaged her son to help our little paper financially, which is exactly what young de Berny very generously did until I left Paris.

The first time I saw her, her appearance struck me, for she so resembled my mother in face and figure that I told her so with tears in my eyes, so much was this dear memory revived by the presence of that lady. She kissed me tenderly, and our friendship was sealed. My taste was refined by my contact with this distinguished woman, who belonged to the upper classes by birth and upbringing, but whose warm heart had been completely won over to our cause. Unfortunately, she died when she was still young. This excellent woman, who had shown me such disinterested affection, had, during one of my journeys, succumbed to a nervous disease brought on by long-standing sorrows.

Thanks to the fraternal help of mother and son, I was able to leave my seventh floor and move my household with great joy to the rue des Juifs, to live with the good family Montagny, whose daughter, young Célestine, became almost my own through the honorable trust her parents placed in me. [. . .]

In spite of its modest appearance, our little journal put me into contact with a large number of women, so that I could, just as in an active correspondence, propagate our principles to a very extended audience.

Once a week we held a meeting similar to those of the rue Cadet. My pretty Célestine and a few ladies of our acquaintance adorned it with their presence.

Young Retouret, one of the preachers of the Salle Taitbout, was astonished by the animation that reigned among the thirty or forty women who crowded into the two rooms of my apartment. Therefore, he said one day upon coming in: "Well, well, well, there certainly are women here! This becomes abundantly clear from the gaiety on all these faces!" [. . .]

This was not the only regular meeting. We also had general meetings which frequently took place beyond the city limits and which all the members of the Paris family attended. [. . .]

Often, after our pilgrimage to the Father's house, we would go in groups to meet in a vast hall and make truly Spartan dinners, noted for the frugality with which we put together these fraternal meals. After dinner, two young women, artists who contented themselves with a small compensation, would take their violins and play dance music for us until ten o'clock. These were real family festivities. On the way home, we would go along the exterior boulevards following the organizational impulse of Gallé, Vinçard, Ducatel, and a few others, singing all together the lovely songs of Ménilmontant. One day, one of our friends heard this response to a startled witness to this long procession: "Oh, those are the Saint-Simonians singing their hymns. They're good folks; they love the people."[. . .]

The financial help of de Berny and his mother did not wound my proletarian dignity, for it went to protect our center of propagation and indirectly to allow women to develop without imposing any form or condition.

But to meet my personal needs, I wanted to depend only on my own labor until subscriptions could suffice to sustain this work.

One of my friends who had remained faithful in spite of the divergence in our opinions, blaming Voilquin for leaving and feeling sorry for me in spite of all the explanations I gave her, incessantly urged me to come live with her. To all this goodwill I constantly answered: "Give me work, and I will accept the daily wage of a woman worker but nothing more." Wanting to be useful, Madame Prud'homme, that generous woman, had to come around to my way of thinking.

I therefore went to work three days a week for her family, where I received board plus wages of three francs, seventy-five centimes for my expenses on the four following days—a happy arrangement that left me in complete liberty to use them for the needs of our cause, be it with the journal, with correspondence, or in helping our friends to prepare our general meetings.

[Chapter IX: Preparations for the Voyage to Egypt]

Early in 1834, the *Livre des actes** published a letter from Father Enfantin, dated from Cairo, in which he said: "We do not call upon any woman in particular, but regard all those who come to us as sent by God himself." I awaited only this call to begin preparing for my departure. [. . .]

I did not want to leave without receiving a kiss and a blessing from my old father. I went to let him know about my journey and my reasons for undertaking it. Even as he pulled me tightly to his bosom, he made a few timid observations: "Poor child! But it's madness to travel alone so far, and without an income," etc. In order to change the direction of his thoughts, which were beginning to make us both too emotional, I joked with him as I gave him a tender kiss: "Calm your worries, dear Papa," I told him. "Remember your own youthful years and the ardor with which you made the revolution. Now let me make mine. Good blood cannot lie!"

I will pass over the farewell scene with the entire Paris family and all

---

*Journal published by Cécile Fournel and Marie Talon to celebrate the deeds of the Saint-Simonian leaders.

the habitués of our private meetings, all those kind friends whose good-luck wishes were as sincere as they were moving. With a full heart and wet eyes, I wondered as I saw all their hands extended toward me if I would again find upon my return all these good friends that bid me good-bye in the same vigor of feeling, and if they would not be diminished or gone when I came back. Thanks to God, I did again find my Paris very alive after two and a half years of absence. The family meetings were just as crowded and animated, and my group of friends welcomed me as eagerly as before.

Our good proletarians had not stopped preaching in the workshops, and even in the cabarets, about progress through the union and association of the fraternal efforts of all people.

Today, in 1865, a new generation has assimilated a part of these ideas. They germinated and bore fruit not only in Paris but in all the big cities of France, where there are cooperative societies and associations of every kind.

Before dragging you along with me on this voyage, I must ask your pardon in this era of rationalism and religious negation for the somewhat outmoded expressions that I have used in this second part of my memoirs. Please accept them at least for the past I am describing.

In hearing me talk about all these young men of 1830, you must have smiled more than once at the words *apostles, apostolic missions*. . . . These phrases doubtless no longer belong to our time, but at that time they were logical. Saint-Simon had named his doctrine the new Christianity; but Enfantin, from the height of the tribunal as he stood accused in court, gave the world his religious formula in these terms: "God is all that Is, everything is in Him, everything is by Him, none of us is outside of Him; but none of us is He. Each of us lives in his life, and we all commune in Him, for he is all that Is."

From this moment on the philosophical doctrine of the Master, under the direction of the Father, took the name of Saint-Simonian Religion. Dear daughter, reread the volume that contains the trial, and you will understand the zeal and ardor of all these young neophytes. From that comes this language, the symbolic clothing, the eccentric phrases coined to strike society and attract its attention to the moral ideas and religious feelings of the Father and all his sons.

V

CLAIRE DEMAR,
MY LAW OF THE FUTURE

[*Claire Démar*, Ma Loi d'avenir *(1833). Ouvrage posthume, publié par Suzanne. Paris: Au Bureau de la* Tribune des femmes, *1834.*

In her views on the "moral question," Claire Démar went further than all the other Saint-Simoniennes and this may have contributed to the isolation she experienced even among the Saint-Simonian family in Paris. She was in her early thirties at the time of her suicide in August 1833 and had been a Saint-Simonian adherent for about a year.

In a "Notice Historique" published with My Law of the Future, *Suzanne Voilquin wrote that the manuscript for this pamphlet was discovered on Démar's desk after her suicide. A note was attached to it requesting that it be "given to M. Vincard, rue Beaubourg, # 44, to be read to the Saint-Simonian family of Paris, and then handed over to Father Enfantin." A special meeting was called for the reading and, according to Voilquin, "many people attended." Then, after the pamphlet was delivered to Enfantin, in retreat at his country estate in Ménilmontant, he suggested that it be given to Voilquin because it addressed "the women of the Tribune." Voilquin had it published in the late fall of 1834.*

Voilquin claims that she had repeatedly urged Démar to write for her journal and that, in fact, it was to attract Démar that the journal's name was changed from Apostolat des femmes *to* Tribune des femmes. *(This change made it clear that the journal was intended to be an outlet for all women, not just Voilquin's circle.) Démar evidently began this pamphlet as a response to an article by Voilquin on "the religious ideas of our times"* and determined to publish it independently only when it became too long for a newspaper article.]*

---

*Reprinted here.

Foreword

This pamphlet will perhaps surprise some people, who will be curious to know the identity of the ladies to whom I frequently address myself— I owe them an explanation, and here it is:

For the past several months, a host of weighty questions, in particular about the freedom of woman, have been raised in a journal, appearing at first in a half-page format, then in full-page, at indeterminate intervals under different names: *La Femme libre, Apostolat des femmes, Affranchissement des femmes, la Femme nouvelle, Tribune des femmes*, which reached its seventeenth issue through a series of articles signed Jeanne-Désirée, Jeanne-Victoire, Marie-Reine, Suzanne, Joséphine-Félicité, Christine-Sophie, Françoise, Rosalie, Juliette B., Isabelle, Pauline P., Emélie F., Angélique, Sophie, Caroline, Gertrude, etc., etc. Today the *Tribune des femmes*, under the editorship of Mesdames Suzanne and Angélique, continues its ever calm and peaceful course along the new paths of the apostolate.

The fifteenth issue of the *Tribune des femmes* began with an article entitled: "Considerations on the Religious Ideas of the Century."

I wanted to respond to it in a few lines, but, carried away by the immensity of the questions I raised, I composed a pamphlet rather than a letter which could not exceed the bounds [bornes] of an ordinary journal article.

Convinced that its publication might be of some use, I have decided that, while preserving its original form, I would publish it outside of the journal for which it had been originally intended, and whose columns would be quite insufficient to reproduce it in its entirety.

—Claire Démar

My Law of the Future

You have abandoned the pulpit of the apostolate for the tribune of debate. Your dogmatic words no longer speak alone of woman's needs and sufferings, no longer set with authority the limits of a certain law of the future, but call upon every woman to reveal her every need, her every suffering, to formulate for herself her law of the future.*

And you have acted wisely.

---

*Reference to the Saint-Simonian "call" to women to speak out on the relationship of the sexes and especially on the moral question. First put forth by Enfantin, it was repeated in the journal *Tribune des femmes*.

For today, every word of *woman* must be spoken and will be spoken for the *emancipation of woman*. For today, a voice of woman, be it energetic, powerful, and mightily reverberating or trembling, indecisive, and inarticulate, friend or enemy, discordant and jarring like a thousand confused noises, like the death rattles erupting from the crash of societies crumbling to ruins and civilizations laid to waste, or sweet and harmonious like the hymn of future celebrations—every voice of woman will be heard and listened to.

You have therefore taken the only appropriate and possible position: you call and no longer judge.

You have to make sure that each woman speaks about, or at least can speak about, everything she feels, loves, and wants.

And I, a woman, respond to your call.

And I, a woman, shall speak—a woman who cannot hold my thoughts captive and silent in the depths of my heart, who cannot veil their rough and daring virile forms, nor clothe TRUTH in a gauzy dress, nor stop on the tip of my tongue a frank, free, audacious word, a naked, true, caustic, poignant word, just to filter it through the conventions of the old society, or pass it through the mystical sieve of Christian prudery.

I shall speak, I who already, all alone, without support or encouragement, without the applause of any woman, have, I repeat, already called upon the people, no matter what has become of my call.*

I say alone and without the help of any woman, for it is not futile to note how slight a bond unites us.—Yes, alone; for even those who would call themselves new women [*femmes nouvelles*],** and would claim to be doing an apostolic work, did not deign to notice a pamphlet written, if not with talent, at least with conscience and fervor. Instead they went about stirring up to their advantage all the cadaverous garbage of old institutions and a powerless moral law.*** —No! Not one of these strong women was strong enough to dare explain herself! . . . And yet the writer and the writing were both known to them.

Not that I am complaining or angered. That is the way things are, Mesdames, doubtless because they must be so; I accept them just as providence or your will has sent them to me. But these are personal facts that I have experienced; I take note of them and recount them. I analyze

---

*Reference to her 1833 publication *Appel d'une femme au peuple sur l'affranchissement de la femme* (*Call of a Woman to the People on the Emancipation of Woman*). One would assume from Démar's complaint of lack of support that few people purchased or read it. Démar's death, however, likely attracted readers. Voilquin had the brochure reprinted because the demand for it in 1834 exceeded its 1833 print run.

**The group "femmes nouvelles" held regular meetings to discuss the sexual question. Their opinions were published in the *Tribune des femmes*.

***New moral law," "religious . . . love," and "sublime couple" are all Saint-Simonian terms. See chapter 2.

them because perhaps it will be good, and someday it will have been good, to note and analyze the facts and to have recounted them. They have, besides, a direct relationship and intimate connection to the thoughts and feelings I am about to reveal to you, and they bring me to it necessarily and naturally.

Yes, Mesdames, like you I am waiting, like you, I call in all my prayers for the sanctified hour that will establish the relation between man and woman upon the foundation of this new moral law, arising from the sympathetic and simultaneous conjunction of man and woman and surrounding man and woman with a bond of religious and pure love!— Hour eternally great and fertile among all the hours of humanity. Hour which will open up a new era of social life for the great family of man!— Glorious hour when all the peoples of the earth, united under the same banner of association, ready to march down the boundless paths of a future of concord and harmony, will for the first time see man and woman obey the laws of a divine attraction, fused upon each other's bosom, a sublime couple finally realizing the social individual impossible until that hour.

Then at last will fall the heavy chain of slavery that has for so long bound in a web of misery all the nations of the world and cast into the hands of a few privileged idlers the labor, liberty, even the blood, and even the life of several millions of their fellows who, strong, industrious, active, noble, and trusting, have groaned under the ruse and weakness of a fratricidal whip.

Yes, *the emancipation of the proletariat, of the poorest and most numerous class*, is possible, I am convinced, only through *the emancipation of our sex*, through the association *of strength and beauty, harshness and gentleness, man and woman.*

It is up to women, then, to make this cry of emancipation reverberate, to repudiate the injurious protection of the man who would call himself her master and is only her equal! May she therefore rise up among women, she with the branch of oak and olive in her hand, who will sign the treaty of rehabilitation, alliance, and equality.

I, too, call upon her; I will hail her with delight. I, too, immerse my gaze in this immeasurable horizon, asking the nations of the North and South, of the Orient and the Occident, where, then, is she? When will she come? . . .

And not one voice responds or can respond to these cries of a suffering soul!

For the hour has not come, the world is not ready, and long will we struggle in this pestilential atmosphere of a suffocating Christian moral law. And longer still will our wishes, words, and acts clash tumultuously in the darkness of this night, this chaos of thought, before a trembling and uncertain gleam foretells that dawn of renovation and definitive redemption, the sun that, after so many centuries, will see woman's foot crush forever the serpent's head.*

But very few of us will raise an eyelid weakened by age to the rays of this dazzling dawn. Few indeed among us will be able to join their voices in this hymn of gladness, and in the endless acclamations that from all sides will hail in sweet concert the coming of the woman messiah!**

Happier are the women who succeed us in life, for they will then form her great and peaceful procession! For us, unfortunately cast into these times of destruction, struggle, and anarchy, our role completely of struggle and action will be no less beautiful, noble, or worthy of the future songs of pious gratitude, if we can understand it and prove ourselves equal to it! Certainly, there will be some glory in having been the first women, forgetting all individuality, to sound a cry of emancipation and to march unflinchingly toward this order of affairs better than we had envisioned, in the midst of insults, outrages, slander, and the cruelest loathing endlessly leveled against us by those very women to whose happiness we devote ourselves!

I know, Mesdames, that, more trusting than I, you do not push so far into the future this limit [la borne] to the wretchedness and suffering of our sex and humanity. Already I seem to hear you protest, hear you say that the ways of providence are broad, secret, mysterious, and above our feeble mortal intelligence. I seem to hear you say that we must rest upon our faith, and that doubt is irreligious.

No, I do not doubt, I have never doubted providence and its ways of working, but I do doubt ourselves, poor women, who believe ourselves so strong, and who, weak, timid, and Christian, would perhaps remain silent and insensitive to the call of the WOMAN REDEEMER, and who perhaps would today repudiate her word, for her acts would terrify us.—No, I do not doubt providence, but I do believe that since she is immutable and assured of the unvarying advancement of humanity in its eternal development under the necessity of continual progress, she will wait for time and progress to engender in the hearts of women new ideas and forces necessary for their new situation, without deviating from her eternal laws, even were this in favor of the ladies of the Tribune.***

Now do not get angry.—I have said, I repeat, that my word is naked, sometimes harsh, sometimes an irritant, but always true.—I am about to prove it.

---

*See also Joséphine-Félicité [Milizet], in Tribune des femmes 1: 128; reprinted here, p. 309.
**Reference to the "Woman Messiah" "called" by Saint-Simonians to oversee (with Enfantin) the direction of the new religious order.
***The journal Tribune des femmes.

Ignorant as we are of the needs and will of each nature and every individuality, we have the power and the mission only to reveal the will and needs of our own personality, without seeking to enclose in the same circle, in the same constant law of movement and life, organizations which are stronger or weaker and more or less susceptible to an action apt to vary in intensity. But, at the same time that we define our own nature and need, we proclaim boldly that all natures and needs are holy, good, and want satisfaction!*

All right! Having set down my terms, I say that we must listen with respect and composure, without any possibility of judgment or blame, to every word of emancipation that rings out, however strange, however unprecedented, I would even say, however revolting [*révoltante*],** they may be.—I will go further:—I maintain that the word of the WOMAN REDEEMER WILL BE A SUPREMELY REVOLTING WORD, for it will be the most expansive, and consequently the most satisfying to every nature and every want.

Now, if this be so—and I can back up my opinion with the authority of a name that you often invoke, that of the head of the Saint-Simonian religion, Father Enfantin, who, in calling upon woman, did not believe he could determine limits for her beyond which her voice was not allowed to be heard and beyond which her language would become bad and immoral.—If therefore it really is as I have just said, was I not right to assert from the start that even the women of the *Tribune* could not speak for the Woman Messiah!!!

I must confess, I was grievously affected when, upon receiving one of your last issues, my eyes lit upon an article, actually quite remarkable, which showed us how your style could submit with such marvelous facility to all the demands of thought and clothe itself so readily in the austere formalities of argument and philosophism that one might well attribute its pages to the pen of a trained logician rather than a sensitive and impressionable woman.—Yes, I was grievously, painfully afflicted, for you cast disapproval upon a word of emancipation, and in declaring it bad, you acted thoughtlessly and frivolously, like women concerned with those ancient theories of the old society, and you erected boundaries [*des bornes*] and limits, where neither boundaries nor limits are possible.

Here is what you wrote. I copy word for word:

"The vast difference between him (Mr. James de Laurence) and the court of Rome consists in the moral freedom he wants to give us. With-

---

*For Démar, "nature" means sexual tendency, "organization" means sexual body, and "action apt to vary in intensity" means arousal. In other words, Démar is talking about sex here.

**The double meaning—revolutionary/rebellious and revolting/shocking—is even clearer in the original French.

out rules or limits, with the mystery he accepts, and with our having to account for our acts only to an entirely mystical God, it would drive us straight into a vulgar and horrid helter-skelter. In any event, this is hardly the way to create association; this is hardly the way to restore a society that is crumbling on all sides!"

And a bit further:

"The Society of the future will be based not on *mystery* but on *trust*; for mystery would still prolong the exploitation of our sex, while publicity and trust will have to form the foundation of the new morality!"*

Certainly, Mesdames, if, like you, I confused trust and publicity; if, like you, I proclaimed that mystery must prolong the exploitation of our sex, I should hail with my blessings the times we live in, the circumstances in the midst of which we are placed; I should bow my head before the law that oppresses us. For never has the union of the sexes been more boldly acknowledged than today; never less than today has love (if these days the word love has any value or can represent any idea other than a totally material, cynical idea); never, I repeat, less than today has love found refuge beneath the veil of mystery.

Listen: the Christian pulpit reverberates with publications announcing marriage. Look up: the walls of the church and the parish house are covered with them, the newspapers fill their useless columns with them.—That line of carriages parked before one of our temples or at the door of a mayor of one of our twelve *arrondissements* is there to take some noisy wedding party to the banquet room.—Before the mayor and before the priest, in the eyes of the material world and the religious world, a man and a woman have dragged along with them a great entourage of witnesses of every age and sex; and the priest with the golden stole and the mayor with the tricolor scarf have blessed or sanctioned, in the name of God and the Code, an indissoluble alliance. So much for the so-called legitimate union, that which permits a woman to say without blushing: *on such and such a day, at such and such a time,* I will receive *a man in my BED!!!* . . . The union, contracted in the presence of a crowd, is *slowly* dragged through an orgy of drinking and dancing, right up to the nuptial bed, turned into a bed of debauchery and prostitution, where it permits the frenzied imagination of the guests to follow and penetrate all the details, *all the hazards,* of the lewd drama played out under the name of the wedding day!

If the custom or law which thus subjects the young bride, trembling

*This article is reprinted here. For more information on James de Laurence, see chapter 2. In Saint-Simonianism, "publicity" was intended to regulate sexual behavior. An early form of its practice was the "confession" of adulterous or premarital sexual experiences that some Saint-Simonians made to Enfantin. However, the practice was criticized by many who feared that women would be hurt by having their indiscretions made public.

and fearful, to all the impudent stares of a large assembly and prostitutes her to the unruly desires and revolting [*révoltantes*] jokes of overheated men excited by the effluvia of a licentious feast; if, I say, this custom or law does not strike you as a HORRIBLE EXPLOITATION; if, in reflecting upon it, you have never shuddered with disgust and indignation . . . I'm getting carried away . . . then the words "woman's dignity," "woman's emancipation," no longer have any meaning for me, no longer represent any idea to my mind!!!

These, however, are only some of the consequences of this law of publicity that you claim as a safeguard and foundation for the new morality.

It is also publicity who, in the lair of Jerusalem Street, uses his vile pen to inscribe so many misled, stigmatized young girls in the red book of the police!! . . . *

It is also publicity that leads to those brutal hour-long unions, which the unfortunate prostitute begins under a corner street sign [*une borne*], and then completes in great haste in her poor hovel, on the altar of debauchery, only to begin again the very next moment!!!

It is yet again publicity when these scandalous legal debates, in our courts and tribunals, proclaim before our judges the words adultery, impotence, and rape, and so provoke odious inquests, revolting [*révoltants*] decrees! . . .

But let us leave aside this tedious enumeration—these tableaux hideous enough to turn one's stomach—and let us see if, as you claim, mystery would still prolong the exploitation of our sex. What! because a woman might not have confided to the public her womanly sensations; because, among all the men who might surround her with attentions and homages and offer her love, an eye other than her own could not distinguish her preference; because her neighbor could not spice up a malicious conversation with details about her private life; because her nights of love might not be transparent and illuminated; because she might not open her doors and windows when she wished to abandon herself to the arms of a man and lavish upon him her kisses and caresses: it would thus necessarily follow that she would be the toy or slave of a man, that no association could henceforth be possible, that the happiness of humanity would be forever destroyed? . . . What! a woman would have to be exploited and unhappy, if, without fear of seeing them tear each other to pieces and hate each other, she could satisfy the love of several men, contribute to the happiness and pleasure of all those men who thought they could find happiness and pleasure only with her! and by her!

Happy are the poor in spirit, Mesdames. All the subtlety and finesse of feeling or reason have not been able to give me even a hint of the lofty

---

*In nineteenth-century France, prostitution was regulated by the police.

considerations that have made you resolve so peremptorily this question! It is, however, a serious question, one well worth delving into and deepening.—May you be so kind, therefore, as to suspend your reprobation and the anathema of which you seem to think deserving both my person and my theories. Be so kind as to follow along with me for a few moments more, for I am going further: I believe, along with Mr. James de Laurence, if need be, in the necessity of a liberty without rules or limits, a liberty as extensive as possible, based on mystery, which I am making the foundation of the new morality, even if it might drive us into the helter-skelter that seems to you vulgar and disgusting.

Today man and woman are often thrown into each other's arms without loving each other, without knowing each other, by the wish of despotic and absolutist parents to satisfy some motive of convenience or calculation of interest or fortune.—Thence so many ill-matched couples, so many unhappy lives condemned to endless tears, to a hatred so eternally revived, so eternally reborn, so increasingly inflamed and exalted over time, that as it drags on for long years through ruse and deceit, it more than once succeeds, after atrocious suffering, in at last demanding relief with poison or the liberating dagger.

I do not speak of a few very rare marriages which, motivated by a reciprocal passion and contracted in spite of all the laws of convenience in our old society, sometimes join the hand of a poor, simple, naive, trusting young girl to the hand of an idle, rich, powerful, envied nobleman!—These unions, so common and classic in the sublimated and spiritualized world of our novels, are very rare indeed in our totally cold, unsentimental, and calculating real world. I have personally witnessed very few take form. And a few months of free contact and complete pleasure have always sufficed to demolish these great passions, so much so that by the end of the honeymoon, the marriage of love and inclination, founded on attractions almost always poorly examined, resembles to the most discerning eye a marriage of convenience, founded on the imperious law of personal gain or fortune. For both kinds of marriage one can predict in all certainty the same phases of disgust and repentance! . . . Such are the unions of the old society that you repudiate; such are the consequences of the Christian law that you are breaking.

The union of the sexes in the future must therefore be the result of attachments as expansive and as well examined as possible from every conceivable point of view, without the intervention of any outside desire, without the assistance of any determining circumstance other than free will, engendered most often by the boiling of blood inflamed with the exaltation of the senses.

I have the misfortune, Mesdames, I confess it to my shame as a sentimental woman; I have, I say, the misfortune of not believing in these sudden passions, so poetic to be sure, which from the simultaneous meeting of two individuals flare into an ardent, impetuous, irresistible love, like a living spark from the collision of two stones.—I have the misfortune of not believing in the spontaneity of feeling, in the irresistible law of the attraction between souls. I do not think that a first encounter or a single conversation can result in the certainty that between two people the awareness of a thought or sensation is always the same and identical in every respect. Only after long and mature analysis and serious reflection can we be permitted to admit to ourselves that we have at last met our *other soul, our complement,* who will be able to *live of our life, think of our thoughts, feel of our feelings,* fuse with us, a soul with whom we can give and receive mutual strength, power, joy, and happiness!

Therefore, then as now, it will be up to time and study to reveal the existence of a more or less expansive, more or less strong, more or less complete attraction, the foundation of all love!—Therefore, we will have to know each other, establish relationships, study each other, and try each other out for a more or less long period of time, lest we wander from disappointment to disappointment in illusory dreams or pursue a vain phantom, child of a delirious imagination, an elusive form endowed with illusory colors by a deceptive prism, lest we embrace, instead of a reality, a mere fugitive shadow that dissolves and vanishes at the touch and disappears in the light of day.

And how many times, alas, will it be quite necessary after all to admit that one has made a mistake, that one has been the toy of some sham, some deceiving appearance! . . . I appeal finally, Mesdames, to your *experience as women.*

But I want the existence of these intimate, secret, and mysterious relationships between two souls to be recognized. I want this unity of feeling, thought, and desire to become conscious. I am assuming the most expansive affection possible.

All that, Mesdames, would, in my opinion, probably lead to no happy result. All that would still, in my opinion, probably come to grief against a last decisive, but necessary and indispensable, trial!

Let me explain:

By what is without a doubt the providential necessity of a constant and invariable law of progress, life forms itself endlessly throughout the entire universe, under the double aspect of conception and execution, in the form of spirit and matter.

Compare and analyze every fact, every event, every accident; devise and compose every way you can each human being, each portion of the universe, each fragment of the great whole; and you will always come back to two principles: spirit and matter.

A spirit that conceives and orders, a matter that executes and realizes:—There you will find the only possible and understandable reason for each work, for conception would be eternally unproductive without execution, and I could not conceive an execution possible without a previous conception.

Spirit and matter!—That is the great formula, the final reason behind all that is the *way* of *God*—*God* who creates without end, because without end He conceives and executes, *God* who is the supreme conception and the supreme execution.

And it is in the complete equilibrium and perfect harmony of these two equally necessary principles, as they coexist equally for all eternity, that we must seek and place the future law of our happiness and the future of our emancipation and satisfaction. And it is for this reason that today we feel and demand the rehabilitation of stigmatized flesh, tortured for so many centuries under the Christian law that consecrated the unjust predominance of one principle over the other.

And the time has come when the *flesh* must be *rehabilitated*, when *matter* will be the *equal*, not the *slave*, of the *spirit*, when one principle will no longer develop to the detriment of the other, but each will realize its potential in all its strength, in all its energy, and in all its holiness. Life will resume its uniform, majestic course and will achieve in every way its fertile work!!—Only then will man finally be the image of *God*.

These abstract considerations were indispensable for an understanding of what I have left to say.—I arrive at last at the solution to the great problem that concerns us:

From love, the union of the sexes, as from all other causes, there must definitively result a work, a necessary creation. Here as everywhere else, the two principles, spirit and matter, must develop their simultaneous action; here too must there be rehabilitation:—Take note that I am not in any way complaining that until now this necessity of materialization has not been felt, understood, or satisfied. On the contrary, even under the most absolute dominance of Christian law, the most spiritual men have by and large taken the road of reproduction and life. From time immemorial they have practiced materialization—much materialization—and never, in this respect, has humanity ever had to fear that its development would be arrested!—I would only wish that we had the frankness to recognize and boldly proclaim this necessity, without lowering *disingenuous eyelids*, and without blushing with a *mystical* modesty that I do not understand!

Let us be a bit consistent with ourselves, all of us who proclaim the rehabilitation of matter, the sanctification of the flesh, and take into account the *material* principle. Let us give satisfaction to the *flesh*.

I repeat: the union of the sexes in the future must be the result of the most extensive affections, as well studied as possible from every point of view. And then even if we did recognize the existence of intimate, secret, and mysterious relationships between two souls, and even if we were conscious of a perfect unity of feelings, thoughts, and wants, all that could still come to grief against a decisive, but necessary and indispensable, trial:

The TRIAL of MATTER by MATTER; the TRIAL of FLESH by FLESH!!! . . .

I have thus finally pronounced the great word before which so many innovators have silenced themselves, frightened by the cries, commotion, and odious accusations that the resounding echoes of their audacious and incisive word would incite against them.

And I too, a weak, worried, and alarmed woman, had to weigh at length on the one hand the storm about to heave my woman's name into the agitation of the popular tide and hurl forever into the tempest of publicity the repose of my solitary, obscure life, and on the other hand the need to say what I understood and the duty to create the work that I felt it my mission to carry out.

My choice is made: I speak.—The strength to stand behind my word will doubtless not betray me.

Let slander now come; let him bring his entourage of stinging jibes, bitter words, and perfidious insinuations.—I am ready.—My completely cloistered life does not drift along in the voluptuously mysterious half-light behind the silk curtains of a boudoir! And no matter the time that anyone knocks at my door, it will always open for the visitor.

Let anathema and persecution come; once more, I am ready.

Does the surgeon, allowing himself to be overcome by the cries, tears, and insults of a patient, cast away from himself the iron that penetrates the flesh, the fire that cauterizes it?

And I think it well and good that she who would dare to plead the cause of material love would be very Christian and spiritualist in her actions.

I have spoken of the necessity for a *totally physical trial of the flesh by the flesh*.

It often happens that, on the threshold of the bedroom, a devouring flame *dies*. For more than one great passion, the perfumed bed sheets have become a *death shroud*. Perhaps more than one woman who will read these lines came to the marriage-bed *throbbing with feeling and desire*, only to wake up in the morning *frigid and icy*.

I myself, *the woman who is speaking*, could *voluntarily* lie in the arms of a man for only one hour and find that *this one hour* had raised a barrier of satiety between him and me, that this hour, the only possible one for him, was long enough to merge him back into the monotonous, indistinguishable crowd as far as I was concerned, and that he had become for me one of those elements that leave no other trace in our lives but an ordinary, indifferent, and banal memory, as worthless as it is pleasureless, leaving no regrets.

And I do not mean to speak here of the disappointments that on the one hand can result from the strange and enormous sacrifice through which more than one young child, under the burning skies of Italy, has risked the chance of becoming a famous opera singer,* or that on the other hand have their causes in the disproportionate liberalities that a cruel nature can mockingly lavish upon a person.—I am not making any allusions.—A thousand different causes can lead to the same result.

I know that the odious expertise of those matrons who used to be called upon when the testimony of two spouses contradicted each other has now been banned for a long time. But after all, has not the *Gazette des tribunaux* just recently filled long columns with details of an equally scandalous case, where the judges, at a complete loss to formulate a sentence, would have needed, to clarify the conviction, some of those experiences used to spice up the stories of a Boccaccio, a Lafontaine, or a Grécourt.

Once the necessity of a trial is admitted, what happens, I beg you, to the law of publicity?—Will it then also be necessary to intrude upon the privacy of these more or less lengthy trial periods, whether they lead to anything or not?—I do not think so.—But then, at what exact point must *mystery* come to an end? Who will mark the precise moment when *publicity* begins? . . . We are necessarily obliged on this point to leave it up to the free will of the concerned parties. We must allow complete latitude to every individual, so that those who want to remain in mystery may do so. Otherwise I no longer know what is supposed to be meant by liberty, by satisfaction given to every nature because every nature is good. . . .

Where does the trial period end?—Where does the marriage phase begin?—That is the whole question.—Or rather, is not marriage a continued and prolonged series of trials, which must sooner or later, at least for mobile, inconstant natures, end up in a cooling-down and a separation?

And this is the place to examine and discuss the law of constancy and inconstancy, mobility and immobility, around which the partisans of the Saint-Simonian doctrine hang the whole moral structure of the future.

Let us first of all pay our debt of thanks and tribute to the courageous man who, the first to struggle against universal censure, forcefully protested against the ancient Christian law of constancy, and who has come as a new messiah to redeem the mobile nature from eternal damnation!!! Honor to ENFANTIN! Honor to those men of faith, apostles of the new gospel, who have sacrificed and abandoned everything in order to follow him!! Praise be to Barrault!! . . . Glory to you all, companions of the Woman, knights of the pacific crusade; glory to you all who are going to darken your faces in the burning rays of the Oriental sun, who are going throughout France hardening, bleeding, and tearing your hands in prole-

---

*Until the eighteenth century, Roman opera engaged in the practice of castrating talented young boy singers in the hopes of making them into great sopranos in adult feminine roles. For a story of such a "disappointment," see Honoré de Balzac's *Sarrasine*.

tarian toil! Glory, eternal glory to you all!*—Others will perhaps finish your work and attach their names to it, forgetting yours: to you alone will go the honor of having laid the cornerstone of the edifice we must erect.—Such is the law of the world.—Saint-Simon pursues a new idea throughout his whole life, and on his deathbed, in the depths of his agony, he bequeaths to humanity a new future, a heritage accepted by a few cherished and faithful disciples. Soon these disciples themselves will continue the master's ever-growing work, and from their exhausted hands others will, in their turn, come to receive the sublime legacy and transmit it in a more developed form to those who will come, ever stronger and more numerous, to replace them.**

But in the end their word is a living, progressive word, which will expand as life does. Yet those who formulated so expansively the great law of progress are invariably subject to it, and it is one of the necessary consequences of their faith that the symbol they adopted to lead humanity along a new, more spacious, beautiful, and favorable path will be broken by humanity and thrown away like an arid shell, when, infertile and sucked dry by generations of men, it no longer provides their burning, parched lips with nourishing and refreshing sustenance. But they themselves, having thrown their new dogma in the face of the world, have called upon woman to fertilize their word which remains eternally sterile without her collaboration and, confessing their powerlessness and weakness, have withdrawn into the silence and repose of the wait.***

So be it then! I, a woman, called upon like and with all the others, make my point of departure the limit at which they have stopped, and under penalty of INCONSISTENCY, *DECEIT*, and *CHARLATANISM*, *they will be forced to acknowledge my action*, or at the very least to suspend *all judgment and censure*.

I repeat, it was an act of strength and courage to recognize and proclaim the existence of a mobile nature, to rehabilitate inconstancy, and to declare it holy and divine, because it *is*, and all that *is* comes from *God*, is *godly*, is *God*.—At that point came a boundary [*une borne*] whose sudden, unforeseen, and hasty overthrow would have been very imprudent

---

*Reference to Saint-Simonian missions in search of "the Woman." Barrault led a group, who called themselves "Compagnons de la femme," to the Middle East. His thought was that since the male messiah had been Jewish and was born in the East, so would the female messiah. In Constantinople, the "Compagnons" refused to bow as required when the Sultan passed by in the streets, but did bow to the women of the Sultan's harem who passed by next. Historians have repeated this story more frequently than any other example of Saint-Simonian feminism, obviously to ridicule.

**According to Olinde Rodrigues, who remained with Saint-Simon while he lay dying, the philosophe's final words were "l'homme et la femme, voilà l'individu social" ("man and woman constitute the social individual"). Saint-Simonians traced their feminism to this legacy, but took credit for its development.

***For the Enfantinian concept of "the Wait" for "the Woman," see chapter 2 and chapter 3.

without a cry of *caution*. Without therefore being willing or even able to deny the existence of another nature, they at least remained content with reciprocal guarantees between the two natures. And they did organize a few groupings that would permit the new principle to develop its consequences without too much constraint or difficulty, while still respecting the existence of the other principle, if indeed there is another principle, while still leaving room for the constant, immobile nature, if indeed there can be in nature two opposed ways of being, two dissimilar modes of *action*.—The result is a kind of transitory charter to consecrate new rights while still respecting established forms (podium style or journalism style)—a middle term before which, these days, we have very often been stopped—a softened slope that permits the chariot of civilization to arrive by an ever-accelerated, uninterrupted course upon a new path, without an unbalanced, overly hasty speed taking it off course and hurling it, as it flies from bump to bump, in a shattered wreck at the bottom of some abyss!! . . .

But the day finally dawns when the child is strong enough to disengage his limbs from the swaddling clothes of the cradle, when he breaks the ties and binds that restrained his first trembling and uncertain steps!—And so it is that today human reason can walk without support and guidance, using its own strength and free will; so it is that the world advances with an energetic and confident step to greet a new future and more expansive destinies! . . . Let this giant pass then, let him pass, lest in your vain resistance his broad foot pound you to the ground, lest he crush you like a grain of sand and mix you like powder with the dust of the road that he raises in clouds before him!! . . .

Of two *opposed* principles, is one the complete negation of the other? Must one kill the other?—If one is true, must the other necessarily be found false, absurd, inadmissable?

Yes, none but a stupid and inept man could have cried out in one breath the words monarchy and republic, the royalty of all and the royalty of one! To our century, in itself ultimately nothing but a long paradox, should it be reserved to hear, listen to, and applaud this strange paradox: the best republic is a king. Only to the men of today could have come the thought of an embrace between the revolution and Louis-Philippe; only they could think of anointing as with holy oil his forehead of royal origin with the blood of the July martyrs!!!*

And thus we see, after barely three years, what becomes of these het-

---

*Reference to the July Revolution of 1830 which toppled the restored rule of the Bourbons (Charles X). Republicans were instrumental in making this Revolution, but agreed to settle for a constitutional monarchy that recognized that the king (Louis-Philippe) ruled not by divine right but rather by the will of the people. The disappointments of the popular classes led to a series of workers' revolts and street riots (behind "barricades") in Paris and Lyon in the early 1830s and also contributed to the popularity of the Saint-Simonians.

erogenous mixtures, these anomalous alliances, and these monstrous theories:

A fetus of a government, ephemeral abortion that it is, drags itself, without pulse or breath, with great misery and effort, through the booing and hissing, toward the tomb and oblivion that reclaim it!! . . . Poor frail creature, brought up and nourished under the banner of despotism, in the shadow of palaces, who can breathe only the miasmas of the court and feels smothered in the ardent and reinvigorating air of liberty, who falls ill at the popular odor of the tricolor and wanders from his palace in the Tuileries to his farm in Neuilly, pursued by the eternal nightmare of paving stones and barricades!

Misery and pity!

Pity the weak reed that claims to stop the flow of the foaming, rushing torrent!! Pity the microscopic insect whose imperceptible stinger tries to strike the heart of the ferocious lion through his broad loins.

The torrent rushes on toward the ocean, the lion toward his prey, the principle toward its ultimate final consequence: but what becomes, pray tell, of the stream, the insect and the barriers, the charters and the futile transactions?

As for me, I never could and I never can understand these classifications, these subtle and metaphysical distinctions, by means of which one tries to divide humanity into a series of orders, classes, and genres. I mistrust categories, and *for good reason*.

There are, you say, constant, immobile men, and others who are on the contrary mobile and inconstant?—Then show me the point of *separation* between *constancy* and *inconstancy*, between *mobility* and *immobility*, the point where *one ends* and the *other begins*. In truth, my weak and myopic eyes could not distinguish it.

You proclaim two natures! All right, but tomorrow, depending on which side the majority chooses, you will give a more or less greater share to one than to the other; you will, perhaps involuntarily, make one predominate over the other; you will proclaim it better than the other; and soon we will have a good and bad nature, an original sin; and soon we will once again fall back upon a paradise and a hell. You will fasten to the forehead of the former a saint's halo and plunge the other into the avenging flames of the damned. You will be godly and I satanic.

You believe in the progress of the universe and all its parts. But what then is progress, if not an eternal movement of spirit and matter, a continual passage from one idea to another, from one feeling to another, from one way of being to a different way of being?

Contradiction!

You speak of immobility! Look around you: you were here only yesterday, and now you see that everything around you has changed, everything has clothed itself in new forms. The timid and weak child has become an ardent and impetuous young man; the young man who went about expending all his strength and energy in pleasures, disorders, and rowdiness has wrapped himself in calm, silence, and gravity; the cold and practical calculations of ambition and self-interest contract his once-laughing mouth, hollow his pink cheeks, wrinkle his pure brow, whiten and remove his black, scented, and graceful locks. What have become of so many stars that whirled toward power, around thrones and powerful monarchs? Where are the thrones and monarchs themselves? How many new species of being have taken the place of other species lost forever? And where are the traces of so many generations?—Of your friendships, loves, fears, hopes, and everything that made your heart beat just a few hours ago, what still survives? . . . —A weak and confused memory perhaps . . . which will itself soon be irretrievably erased.

You speak of immobility! Consult then your academicians and experts; interrogate the Cuviers, the Geoffrey Saint-Hilaires, the Brogniards, those audacious necrologists of eradicated races and destroyed species, those historians of shattered worlds and submerged planets.

Yes, inside and outside ourselves, everything changes, everything renews itself. And we can pronounce without laughing the word immobility! What! The things we loved yesterday, we detest today; the things we adored and exalted, we scorn and dash in the mud! Indeed our joy has been turned into grief, our pleasures into pain, our laughter into tears, our happiness into suffering and disease, and we have been wont to speak of constancy!

Immobility, constancy!—But where can I find you?—I'm getting carried away.—Must I therefore seek and find you only in the relationships between man and woman? Has a capricious, supernatural power, stronger than the immutable will of GOD, thus placed you as the sole foundation for the union of the sexes, for an end and purpose that I cannot fathom? Would Providence then have wanted to show herself inconsistent and bizarre in this case?

All right, let us keep digging; let us sink the scalpel deeper into this rotten mass, and let us see!!! . . .

If I were to ask society "what is love?" the millions of mingled voices in society would instantly buzz with a multiple response, from which I would have to choose at will some definition or other, and to which I would have to accommodate myself among a thousand others! For in what forms of nature has this poor love not clothed himself one after the other?—In what grove has he not nestled? In what flowers has he not made his nest? From the noblest hotel of the Faubourg Saint-Germain, the richest house of the Chaussée d'Antin, to the darkest, dirtiest, most dilapidated hovel in the old city, from the cellar to the attic, what room, what nook has he not inhabited? In what author's study, in what painter's studio has he not posed? What book has he not adorned with his insipid clichés and witty banter? What gallery has he not decorated with his portrait?—And have I not also met him in the latest salon, poor bloated and toothless child, with his oversized blond wig, his slack, moldy bow, his wooden arrows tarnished, his quiver of cardboard full of holes? Have I not met him near his eternal grandmama Venus? And so, of all these definitions that have fattened so many fat volumes, only one seems to me beautified by truth, concision, and energy, that of Madame de Staël, the woman who through her writings has best supported the strength of our sex, has best protested against our dependency and inferiority.—Madame de Staël, who while she wrote her proverbial sentences, enlightened by her own disappointments and her lived experience, perhaps dimly envisioned a ray of the future and raised up a corner of the mysterious envelope that conceals our destinies to come! . . .

Yes, strange woman, illustrious writer, you spoke truly: yes, up to this day, love has been nothing but a shared egotism! Man has loved only himself in woman; woman has sought only her own satisfaction with man; and despite the vows of eternal fidelity that each has made only for the right to demand it in turn from the other, both have reciprocally deceived, lied to, and betrayed each other; both of them have been unfaithful to each other with more or less frequency and duration.

May the women who read me put aside all their vain *pride* and displaced, *forced* prudishness. For one hour, once in their lives, may they forget their counterfeit blushing; may they refrain from hiding their faces behind the folds of a deceptive fan or hatbrim, and with their hand on their hearts, may they answer this: Tell me, ladies, is there a single one among you who, joined in the union of the most fertile in happiness and joy, has never for even the briefest moment turned her gaze away from her husband or lover to cast it obligingly and pleasurably on some other man and, unconsciously establishing a comparison entirely in favor of the latter, desired that the lover or spouse were like him?

Yes, if among *all* of you there can be found a single such woman, may she arise, condemn me, and cast a stone at me; for then I would have spoken an imprudent and slanderous word for which I must bear the painful consequences: I am resigned to it!

But I believe that if the duration of my life depended upon this condition, I should run the risk of immortality.

I already seem to see some punctilious polemicist go digging around in the debris of ancient Rome, to revive the inanimate ashes of Lucretia! Oh! do not disturb her in her unknown tomb, for her silence is no doubt more fortunate for you than her voice could ever be! Oh! Let her sleep; out of pity for her memory, let her sleep! For perhaps she would not have had to impose her name on all of human language, were it not for the repulsive face or the too precipitate haste of her impetuous swain. Perhaps at the moment he came upon her, his eye smoldering with lust, his mouth uttering threats, our poor Lucretia was dreaming of a very tender, mysterious love with some fashionable Roman, whose pale and tormented face topped a slender body; perhaps she recoiled only before the impetuosity of a love too tempestuous and energetic! . . . Why, thoughtless young man, do you thus without warning, and without even being announced, barge into the bedroom of the woman you love? It is your ardor that has destroyed you; a pair of gloves, a vial of melaino-come oil, and a few days of waiting . . . could perhaps have conquered this model of virtue! What then does the happiness of a man, the existence of a monarchy, the destinies of a world count on?

But what use is it to stir up the cold dust of a poor woman and all this fusty history of Rome, which could shed no light whatsoever upon the discussion?

From the moment you looked at a man with pleasure or satisfaction, and he seemed to you more handsome and witty than your lover or spouse; from the time you found him superior to one or the other, from whatever point of view, in whatever respect to spirit or matter, prostitution has, I must say, taken place, adultery has been committed, at least in intent.—Only prejudice, fear, or some other unknown secret motive held you back, and you added to adultery ruse and deception.

Adultery, ruse, and deception: that is where we end up again and again with the *law of constancy* propped up by *publicity*!

And so we must confess that the purest, most faithful woman has been guilty (I speak according to the ancient moral assumptions of the old society!), guilty at least in her desires and unfaithful in her wants. . . . If the act did not follow the thought, what does it matter? It is a painful necessity which will often make her groan. And when she comes along flaunting and boasting about her constancy, take it for certain, men, that in her heart she despises and pities herself; for her supposed constancy is nothing but lies and deceit, for her as well as for others.

After the pompous theatrical virtue of Lucretia, someone might evoke the furors of Othello, in order to conclude against me that jealousy is at the heart of constancy.

But what else is jealousy, pray tell, than the highest and best-articulated expression of this egotism that relates everything to oneself and which, exempting itself from all obligations, obstacles, and personal abnegation, would try to enchain forever the body, spirit, thoughts, will, and feeling of everyone it loves, to bend them to its law, its pleasure, and its whim?—What else is jealousy but the antisocial feeling of property that makes you say: my castle, my estate, my house; that makes you encircle the castle with a vast moat, the house with a strong wall, the fields with an impenetrable living hedge!

You speak of Othello: why do you not also evoke the matrons, eunuchs, and mutes of the harem! . . . Why do you not also speak of rings and chastity belts? Sublime inventions of Italy that ensure constancy and guarantee fidelity and permit the husband, doddering old man, to travel, assured of his young wife's virtue, whose key he carries in the folds of his valise!—It is true that, in this hiatus of the hymen, love also knows how to put a false key in the hands of the happy lover and make amends to the languishing, deserted young wife . . . a touching and sweet reciprocity of openness and trust! . . .

Finally, if I dared to cite myself as an example, and I can, I think, be *permitted* to do so after the above, I would make my confession with all the naive candor and kindly frankness of that poor donkey in the fable, who had grazed in a prairie upon grass as wide as his tongue, and whom tigers and lions decimated piously in a holocaust to the irritated gods! . . .

I would say that because I used to be jealous, and very jealous, I believed myself for a long time to be constant; and that later, arriving at a better understanding and analysis of the problem of my individuality, I understood that had I been assured of silence and privacy, I do not really know in truth what would have happened to my fidelity!—Among all men, there is one that I most assuredly loved above the others, toward whom my affection always led me out of preference; but in the end I met others who more or less pleased me and with whom I could willingly forget the first man from time to time, since I was sure of preserving all of his tenderness, thanks to his ignorance.—And this story of mine is still that of many women: I say it at the expense of my ego; honni soit qui mal y pense.

To sum up:

Jealousy is only an odious sentiment of egotism and selfishness that presumes nothing in favor of constancy. On the contrary. . . .

Fidelity has almost always depended on nothing but fear or the powerlessness to do better or otherwise.

And this is only the rigorous consequence of the fact and truth that there exist only mobile, inconstant natures.—For mobility is the condition of progress, and I could not conceive of any other immobility or constancy than that of GOD, alone eternally and necessarily immutable, because GOD is all that IS, is *progress* and *life*.

It is by proclaiming the *law of inconstancy* that woman will be liberated, and only that way.

The union of the sexes must depend on the most expansive and best-established affections, and, as life is constantly formed under the two aspects of *spirit* and *matter*, there will have to be sympathy of *spirit with spirit*, and *matter with matter, a trial more or less long for each by each*, with a more or less prolonged cohabitation.

When the terms are thus posited, does not mystery become necessary? Is it not an indispensable safeguard of woman's liberty?

What then becomes of the sad condition of this publicity, which today more than ever weighs heavily upon the world of morality?

Therefore, Mesdames, even though this system might lead us to a gross and disgusting helter-skelter, we must conclude, contrary to your opinion, that association will one day be based on a liberty without limits, surrounded by mystery.

Let us repeat with Mr. James de Laurence:

"May woman keep to herself the secrets of her heart; may she confess to God alone. Then will the serpent raise his head without doing evil to God's children; then will paradise be reestablished."

I must add a few observations.

The law of constancy, as it succeeded in opening the gynaeceums of Greece and Rome, where women had been languishing by the hundreds for the pleasure and service of a single man, and as it proclaimed that one man could not join in a religious bond with more than one woman and vice versa, was, like all laws whose time has come, good and useful; for it was the expression of a progress and a broader path of emancipation for woman.—Now that it has become sterile, in repudiating and breaking it like a useless instrument, we will be erecting a statue to it much as the grateful nation does to its great deceased men.

I have said that there can exist only a mobile, inconstant nature; but we must nevertheless be aware that since the diverse makeup of different individuals is more or less developed and perfected, they will be more or less mobile according to an infinite scale of variations, in such a way that, if we succeed in juxtaposing the most-developed and the least-developed individuals, we will find them in a relationship opposing constancy and inconstancy with respect to each other. But this soon disappears when we climb all the intermediate steps of the scale, filling in all the nuances and successive points of progress.

Finally there is a given but extremely rare circumstance, one almost impossible to encounter, where two individuals could remain in a situation of constancy and immobility with respect to each other: namely one where both of them, progressing at the same rate, would remain without interruption in an ever-identical and uniform relationship to each other.

It seems to me that I should stop here, having treated under all its principal aspects the question of woman's emancipation.—But my task does not end [se borner] here.—For this question raises another very serious one to which it is intimately bound, and on which it depends: that of filiation and generation.

I will be as brief as possible.

There still exists a monstrous power, a kind of divine right, which rises up amidst the smoking ruins of so many destroyed powers, a commandment upon its lips, imposing and severe on its ancient pedestal, against which the centuries have been smashing their waves without bringing it down:—a power under which all of us have groaned for many long years, a harsh and fatal exploitation of man by man, to which we have all been subjected.

Paternal power, consecrated by all peoples and all civil or religious law, armed with the imaginary thunderbolts of its maledictions, is like a holy ark that paralyzes and withers every incautious hand that approaches it. I do not know what cold and mysterious horror clings to the footsteps of those who dare to attack the *giant* and struggle against him. . . . Every man holds a bit of hatred and scorn for these people. Society erects around them an impenetrable barrier of reprobation and casts them out of its bosom like filthy things!

And I, who want to take my turn in protesting against the legitimacy and holiness of this paternal power, will perhaps succeed in breaking myself against it and see my name proscribed, my person insulted, and my memory shamed!

Yet behold that time, stronger and more powerful than a woman's words, has created this authority, the very time that endlessly destroys all authority.—See how he has shattered one by one the loveliest rosettes in the crown of this other royalty, he who needs no paving stones to crush royalty.

Abraham, fanatic and furious illuminated man, sets up a pyre, prepares the sacrificial fire, and *God* smiles upon the infanticide and heaps benedictions upon his head!

Jephte in his triumph slits his daughter's throat, and Jephte is a man according to *God*!

And the holy writ inscribes in the Pantheon of Jews the names of Abraham and Jephte, eternalizes their memory, and twenty peoples pillage at will this legend, translate it into every language, and surround it with their faith and admiration.

Brutus, the ferocious republican, forgetting his lengthy stupidity, chases the tyrants from his adored Rome, and without trembling slaughters his children!—And history, in its most marvelous pages, consecrates such deeds . . . and for thirty centuries we have been putting our children to sleep to tales of these horrors!

Roman law puts the sword in the hands of every father, and whether he sells or assassinates his sons, asks for no accounting from him.

Abraham, Jephte, Brutus, old Roman soldiers, sleep your sleep of death, for the times have truly changed. And if, thrown back to life from the bowels of the Earth, you were to offer to our eyes the sight of your still bloodied hands, some police officers would come to arrest you; and the king's prosecutor, his indictment in hand, would demand justice against you for the pure and innocent blood you so unjustly spilled.

How the stinginess of our laws would make you laugh with pity, sublime executioners!—Our paltry laws that grant that the harshest and most despotic father may put his son in prison for only a few months, and that with great difficulty!*

---

*An *ancien régime* law (*lettres de cachet*) permitted fathers to have their children (and husbands their wives) incarcerated.

The change is certainly remarkable, the progress immense. In times past any father could kill his children at will, and now he can barely imprison them for a few days! . . .

Time will continue its immutable, eternal, fertilizing course, will kick away this last phantom, and will blow away this final servitude.

Indeed, take a look at the foundation on which paternal authority is raised.

Man and woman, obeying the pressing desires of the senses, are driven toward each other by this need for pleasure to which an eternally good and clairvoyant God attached the preservation of our race. Throwing themselves in each other's arms, they merge their life in a long embrace, forgetting the natural and probable consequences that must spring from this union through a divine, impenetrable mystery.

The laws of nature, however, are vindicated, and the woman conceives.

How often you curse this natural issue of your pleasures, which comes unexpectedly to upset your egotistical and ambitious calculations and interrupt your pursuit of pleasure.

But then you are finally forced to submit to the decrees of a will more powerful than your own, against whose acts struggle is impossible.— And nine months later, you receive in your arms this weak creature, weighed down by your hatred and unjust anger from the moment of conception in its mother's womb, when it had not even asked to exist!

Soon this new social individual, still frail and powerless in your hands, is transformed at your whim into a toy whose movements you regulate according to the clock. You encourage with your laughter and caresses the slightest inanity of this flexible imagination whose every action molds itself to the look on your face or the frown on your brow. You are ecstatic, you faint with joy and contentment, you exclaim at every supposed civility that escapes from the *child.*—The child never stops growing and developing his body and spirit; he continues the games that you encourage with your caresses and approved. But the prism is broken, and your soul is satiated; disgust and weariness follow enthusiasm and replace admiration. . . . Then one day, whip in hand, you inculcate upon his bruised limbs the first lesson in injustice and good breeding, one that you will often renew.

From this day on, he will no longer know rest or joy. You have assigned him a square on the vast chessboard of the world, without worrying if the development of his character will permit him to fill it.—You mold him until he bruises, or you stretch him until he is mutilated, depending on what suits your plans. And after many long years, you require gratitude from the hideous monster who escapes from your hands for the gifts you have given him. You still pursue him with your insatiable demands; you force him to render unto you a cult of love and veneration. When, finally, at the moment of your death, he can catch his breath and seek to straighten his deformed limbs and bent head, he tries in vain: his limbs and head will retain the bend, and his rickety nature will carry forever a seed of destruction.

And so, with my argument supported by an immense pile of parricidal daggers, I stand in the midst of groans rising from so many breasts at the mere mention of mother and father and venture to raise my voice for the law of freedom and emancipation against the law of blood and generation!

No more slavery, no more exploitation, no more tutelage! Emancipation for all: slaves, proletarians, and minors from birth on.

But let us be careful; the power of paternity against which I am protesting would at least have to be able to clothe itself in the appearance of reason and legitimacy, and this right would have to be based on something.

And so we see that all certitude and presumption of paternity meets its doom against my theory of trial and mystery—for certitude is an equally doubtful presumption today.

Mr. James de Laurence, who recognizes as infallible only the line of generation from mother to daughter and who derives his whole system from this, has grasped this fact very well and has developed it with concision and clarity.

Powerless to say it better or differently from him, I let him speak:

"This title of father can be truly attributed only to *God*; for although everyone knows he has a father, no one can know with exactitude who his father was.

"What couple can say: *We are going to make a baby*. What couple can say: *We have just made a baby*. The success of their operation must remain uncertain for some time. A mother who has several lovers can suspect, but cannot demonstrate, who is the father of her child; nevertheless she cannot prove it.

"If a couple has several encounters, can the mother herself know from which one her child comes? A child is not made like a statue upon which the artist carves here a hand, there a foot.

"Since no one makes a child at will, their conception can be attributed by *skeptics* to chance, and by *believers* to providence.

"It is more logical to claim that all children are made by *God* than to say that all spouses are joined by *God*.

"Let us hope that cloistered young women no longer consider themselves the wives of the Lord, but that we honor pregnant women as God's favorites! For at the moment they conceive, God is present in them, as in the host consecrated by the priest: and this blessed mystery must safeguard the independence of women against the claims of men.

"Until now we have called marriage sacred, we shall now call conception divine: she who is pregnant is filled with the sacred spirit. . . .

"All that is, is miraculous. . . . The conception of all mothers is a mystery. . . . The conception of all mothers is immaculate. . . . What stain can be attached to the operations of nature? To maintain the contrary would be blasphemous, to call Jesus the unique son of God is to disinherit the whole human race. . . . "

We must stop, what could we add to this? I see but one further serious objection to combat, one which could be raised by the numerous partisans of property, who will come to reproach me for wanting to break the ancient law of inheritance, the immutable order of succession from father to son, perpetrated from generation to generation right up to our time.

Mr. James de Laurence proposes to substitute for this old mode of heredity the heredity from mother to daughter, in other words umbilical succession.

For those of us who believe and proclaim with so many others that property will cease to exist and that inheritance will disappear, because property and inheritance are a privilege of birth, and all privileges of birth must be abolished without exception . . .

For those of us who demand classification according to ability, and ability according to works . . .

For those of us who see everywhere and in everyone only officials who are succeeded or replaced, but whose positions are not inherited . . .

For us the objection falls of itself and remains without value.

To those who would claim that to abolish inheritance is to destroy society, I would reply that society has for centuries been exhausting itself in its unflagging devotion to this work of destruction; that it has pursued inheritance from battleground to battleground, little by little taking away all its prerogatives. Today, property, reduced to its simplest expression, vainly takes refuge behind the mighty ranks of the national guard, sheltered from the rampart of laws and ordinances. Decomposition has already set in; the word progressive tax resounds already with a funereal knell upon the ears of the idle and trembling property owner.

Man was once the slave, property, or thing of another man, transferable by way of heredity.—What has become of slavery, this great form of property? Destroyed, annihilated . . . and yet society survives ever more beautiful, grand, and perfect.

What has become of the heredity of the fief covered with vassals, burdened with tithes and dues?—Has society indeed buried itself under this ruin of the Middle Ages?

What has become even of the heredity of the title that conferred rights and privileges?—Did the Earth tremble on its poles when two or three privileged aristocrats came as the first to burn their parchments and charters upon the altar of the nation in the middle of the National Assembly.*

I know that a revolution does not happen abruptly and unexpectedly in one day; I understand that precautions are necessary to bring about

*In a legislative session of the National Assembly, the night of August 4, 1789, the French nobility relinquished its ancient feudal rights.

these changes and that society will be transformed only gradually, through an imperceptible and controlled transition.

The task of indicating what are or will be those precautions and transitions is not at all my work or mission:—at least not here.

And so:

No more paternity, always doubtful and impossible to prove.

No more property, no more inheritance.

Classification according to ability, compensation according to work.

Consequently:

No more maternity, no more law of blood.

I say no more maternity:

Indeed, once woman is delivered and emancipated from the yoke of tutelage and protection of man, once she no longer receives from man her food or wages, once man no longer pays her the price of her body, then woman's existence and social position will derive only from her own ability and her own works.

For that to happen, the woman must create a work and fulfill a function.—And how could she, if she is always condemned to spend a more or less long period of her life attending to the upbringing of one or more children? Either the work will be neglected and poorly done or the child will be badly brought up and deprived of the care his weakness and lengthy period of development demand.

You want to liberate *woman*! Well then, bring the newborn from the bosom of the *blood mother* to the arms of the *social mother*, the *professional nurse*, and the child will be better raised; for he will be raised by the woman who has the ability to raise, develop, and understand childhood; and every woman will be able to classify herself according to her *ability* and receive compensation for her works.

Then and only then will man, woman, and child all be liberated from the law of blood and from exploitation of humanity by humanity!

Then each and every woman and each and every man will be the daughters and sons of their works and only of their works.

VI

FLORA TRISTAN,
PEREGRINATIONS OF A PARIAH

[Excerpts from: *Flore Céléstine Thérèse Henriette Tristan y Moscozo (Flora Tristan)*, Pérégrinations d'une paria (1833–1834): Dieu, franchise, liberté. *Paris: Arthur Bertrand, 1838.*

Flora Tristan (1803–44) never joined the Saint-Simonians, but was imbued with the thought of all the utopian socialists in her words and acts as a socialist feminist. She lived a tempestuous life before becoming a theorist, an organizer, and the writer now considered second in importance only to George Sand among French women writers of the romantic period. Published here are the foreword and preface (omitted from both the modern French edition and the English translation) to her first major work, Peregrinations of a Pariah. *A memoir of her voyage to Peru in 1833–34, its publication in 1838 marks her entry into social activism and literary prominence. The foreword expresses her ideas on autobiography, and the preface recounts the early years of her life up to her departure for Peru.]*

Foreword

God has done nothing in vain; even the wicked figure in the order of his providence: everything is harmonized and progresses toward a goal. Men are necessary to the earth they inhabit, live its life, and, as if participating in this whole, has each a mission to which Providence has called him. We experience useless yearnings, are besieged by powerless desires for having failed to recognize this mission, and find our lives tormented until we are at last taken from it. Similarly, in the physical realm, diseases arise from the organism's false understanding of what it needs to satisfy its demands. We will therefore discover the rules we can follow to achieve the greatest happiness in this world by studying our moral and physical being, our soul and the organization of the body it was called upon to govern. We do not lack lessons for the study of either. Suffering, that harsh schoolmistress, endlessly lavishes them upon us; but man has been granted the power to progress only at a slow pace. However, if we would compare the ills to which savage peoples are prey to those which still exist among the most advanced peoples of civilization, and the pleasures of the former to those of the latter, we would be astonished by the immense distance that separates these two extreme phases of human society. But to verify progress, it is not necessary to seek a comparison between two conditions of social life so distant from each other. It is easy to verify the gradual progress from century to century by consulting historical documents that represent the social condition of peoples in times past. To deny this, one would have to close one's eyes, and only the atheist has reason to do this in order to be consistent with himself.

We all contribute, even if unknowingly, to the progressive development of our species. But, in every century, in every phase of social intercourse, we see men who stand out from the crowd and go forth as guides to light the way for their contemporaries. Special agents of Providence, they stake out the road which humanity will pursue after them. These men are greater or lesser in number and exert on their contemporaries a greater or lesser influence in proportion to the degree of civilization which the society has attained. The highest stage of civilization will be that in which each is aware of his intellectual faculties and will consciously develop them in the interest of his fellow creatures, which he will not see as different from his own.

If self-knowledge is the necessary condition for the development of our intellectual faculties, and if individual progress is proportionate to the development and application that these faculties receive, it is irrefutable that the writings most useful to men are those that help them study themselves, by showing them the individual in the various positions of social existence. Facts alone do not give us sufficient knowledge of man. If the degree of his intellectual advancement is not represented, and the passions that have driven him are not shown, then facts can only reach us as so many enigmas which philosophy tries to solve with more or less success.

Most authors of revealing memoirs have not wanted to publish them until the grave could shelter them from accountability for their acts and words, either because they were held back by egotistical sensitivity in speaking of themselves and the fear of making enemies in speaking of others, or else because they feared recriminations or denials. In so doing, they weakened their testimony, since we can trust it only when other authors of the period confirm it. Nor can one assume that progress toward perfection has been the major object of their thought. One sees that they wanted to be talked about by supplying food for curiosity, to appear in the eyes of posterity as other than they appeared in the eyes of their contemporaries, and that they wrote for a personal goal. Depositions inherited by a generation no longer directly involved in its events can of course offer the portrait of their ancestor's mores, but could have only a weak influence on their own. In fact, it is generally the opinion of our contemporaries that serves to curb us, rather than what posterity might think of us. Only elite souls aspire to this approval; the masses are indifferent to it.

These days, our leaders arrange to have their testamentary revelations published immediately after their death. That is the moment they choose to have their shadow bravely rip the mask off those who preceded them to the grave and those few survivors whom old age has pushed off stage. So did the Rousseaus, the Fouchés, the Grégoires, the Lafayettes, etc. . . . ; so, too, will the Talleyrands, the Chateaubriands, the Bérangers, etc. . . . The publication of memoirs, if it occurs at the same time as the death notice or the funeral oration, doubtless offers more interest than if they do not surface until a century after the author's death, like those of the Duc de Saint-Simon, but they have almost no repressive action. They are branches of a felled tree; fruit will not follow the perfume of their flowers; the soil will no longer make them bloom.

The interest inspired by great events generally leads writers to represent men in the midst of these events and to neglect showing their innermost self. Authors of memoirs are not always innocent of this fault, although they do reveal to us the persons about whom they are writing and the mores of their times much better than historians properly speaking. But most of these writers have taken the powerful men of a social order as the subject of their writing and have rarely portrayed the men of all the diverse professions that compose human societies. The Duc de Saint-Simon makes us see quite well the courtiers and their intrigues; but as for the mores of the bourgeoisie in Paris or elsewhere in France, the thought does not even enter his mind. The moral character of a man of the people represented no interest whatsoever to the eyes of a great lord of that time. However, the value of an individual lies not in the importance of the functions assigned to him, the rank he holds, or the wealth he possesses. His value, in the eyes of God, is proportionate to his degree of utility in his relationships with the whole human race, and this is the scale on which morality will henceforth have to measure his praise or blame. In the days of the Duc de Saint-Simon, people were still very far from knowing this measure of human actions. It is the man who has struggled against adversity, who has, in the midst of misfortune, come to grips with the power of rank or wealth, whose memoirs, if a religious belief could set him beyond all fear, would reveal men as they really are and appraise them according to their real value. He who sees in every human being his fellow, who suffers his pains and rejoices in his joys, must write his memoirs when he has found himself in a position to gather together observations, and these memoirs will make it possible for us to know men without consideration for rank, just as their time and place present them.

If it were merely a question of reporting facts, we would need only eyes to see them. But to appraise the intelligence and passions of man, information alone does not suffice. It is also necessary to have suffered and suffered greatly, for only misfortune can teach us to know exactly what both we ourselves and others are worth. It is necessary, moreover, to have seen much, so that, stripped of all prejudice, we can consider humanity from a point of view other than that of our own village bell tower. It is, finally, necessary to have the faith of a martyr in one's heart. If the expression of one's thoughts is stilled by concern for the opinion of others, if the voice of one's conscience is stifled by the fear of making enemies or by other personal considerations, one fails at one's mission and repudiates God.

You will perhaps ask if it is always useful to publish the deeds of men at the moment they have just been performed. Yes, I will answer, for all those that do harm, that come from an abuse of power, whether of strength or authority, whether of knowledge or position, or that hurt another in the independence that God has given without distinction to all creatures, strong or weak. But if slavery exists in society, if there be helots in its midst, if laws are not equal for all, if religious or other prejudices recognize a class of PARIAHS, oh! then, the same devotion that leads us to denounce the oppressor with loathing must make us cast a veil over the conduct of the oppressed who is seeking to escape the yoke. Does there exist a more odious action than that of those men who, in the forests of America, go hunting fugitive negroes in order to put them back under the whip of the master! Servitude has been abolished, you will say, in civilized Europe. True, we no longer hold slave markets in the public square; but among the most advanced countries, there is not one in which many classes of individuals do not have to suffer from legal oppression. The peasants in Russia, the Jews in Rome, the sailors in England, women everywhere: yes, everywhere that the mutual consent necessary to the formation of marriage cannot be broken simply by ending it, woman is in servitude. Divorce obtained at the express will of one of the parties can alone completely free her and put her on the same level as man, at least in the matter of civil rights. And so, so long as the weaker sex, subjugated to the stronger, is restrained in the least restrainable affections of our nature, so long as there is no reciprocity between the two sexes, to publish a woman's loves is to expose her to oppression. On the part of a man, it is an act of cowardice because, in this respect, he enjoys full independence.

It has been observed that the degree of civilization attained by diverse human societies has always been proportionate to the degree of independence enjoyed by its women.* Writers in the path of progress, convinced

---

*This idea had been popularized in the 1830s by the followers of Charles Fourier, who had written: "As a general thesis: Social progress and changes from one era to the next are brought about in proportion to the progress of women toward freedom." (*Théories des quatre mouvements et des destinées générales*, 147.)

of the civilizing influence of woman and seeing her everywhere restricted
by special laws, have tried to reveal to society the effects of this state of
affairs. To this end they have, for almost ten years, made various calls to
women to encourage them to publicize their sufferings and their needs,
the ills resulting from their subjugation, and the results we could hope
would come from the equality between the sexes.* Not one woman, as
far as I know, has responded to these calls. The prejudices that rule over
society seem to have frozen their courage; and while our courtrooms
reverberate with petitions drawn up by women to obtain from their husbands either support or legal separation, not one woman dares to raise
her voice against a social order that leaves them without professions and
keeps them in dependency even as it forges their chains through the
indissolubility of marriage. I am mistaken: one writer who has become
famous from her first writings, for her elevated thought, dignity, and
purity of style, has used the form of the novel to put into relief the
misery arising from the situation into which our laws have placed
woman. But she has put so much truth into her portrayal that her own
misfortunes were divined by the reader. But this writer, who is a
woman, not content with the veil behind which she has hidden herself
in her writings, has signed them with the name of a man.** What reverberations can there be from protests enveloped in fictions? What influence could they exert when the facts that prompt them are stripped of
their reality? Fictions amuse and occupy the mind for a moment but are
never the driving force behind men's actions. Our imagination is jaded,
our disappointments have made it mistrust itself, and we can no longer
act upon opinion except with palpable truths and irrefutable facts. Let
the women whose lives have been tormented by great misfortunes speak
of their sufferings; let them lay bare the misery they have experienced as
a result of the situation created for them by the laws and prejudices that
enchain them; but above all let them name. . . . Who better than they
would be in a position to unveil the iniquities that hide in the shadow
from public scorn? . . . Indeed, may every individual who has seen and
suffered, who has had to struggle with people and things, make it a duty
to recount in all their truth the events in which he has been an actor or
witness and name those whom he has to blame or praise; for, I repeat,
reform can only take place and there will only be probity and openness
in social relationships as a result of such revelations.

In the course of my narration, I often speak of myself. I portray myself
in my sufferings, thoughts, and feelings, all of which result from the
disposition that God has given me, the upbringing I received, and the
position that laws and prejudices have made for me. No two things re-

---

*Reference to Saint-Simonians and their "call" to women.
**George Sand.

semble each other completely, and there are doubtless differences between all the creatures of a single sex or species. But there are also physical and moral resemblances among people, so that custom and laws act similarly and produce analogous effects upon them. Many women live in de facto separations from their husbands in countries from which Roman Catholicism has driven away divorce. (The relevant statistics in France place the number of women separated from their husbands at three hundred thousand.) It is thus not *to myself personally* that I wanted to attract attention, but rather to all the women who are in the same situation and whose numbers are increasing daily. They suffer trials and tribulations of the same nature as mine, are preoccupied by the same sorts of ideas, and feel the same emotions.

Both sexes are equally concerned with the necessities of life, but they are not both affected to the same degree by love. In the childhood of societies, concern for defense absorbs the attention of man, and in a more advanced period of civilization, he is concerned about his fortune; but in all social stages, love is, for the woman, the central passion of all her thoughts and the driving force of all her deeds. Let no one, therefore, be astonished by the place I give it in this book. I speak of it according to my own impressions and observations. In another work, treating the question more fully, I will present the tableau of evils that result from its enslavement and the influence it would acquire once liberated.*

Every writer must be true, and if he does not feel the courage to be so, he must renounce the priestly position he has assumed to instruct his fellow creatures. The usefulness of his writings will result from the truths they contain, and, leaving the discovery of general truths to the meditations of philosophy, I intend to speak here only of what is true in the narrations of human action. This truth is accessible to all, and if knowledge of the human heart and study of one's own self requires knowledge of men's actions at different levels of intellectual achievement, and in all those innumerable life circumstances which call them to action, then publicity given to the actions of living men is the best curb one could impose on wickedness and the most wonderful reward to offer virtue. We would strangely underestimate the moral utility of publicity should we desire to limit it to the acts of state officials. Since morality exerts a constant influence on social organization, it is obvious that the aim of publicity would be lost if private actions were exempt from it. There is not a single act whose immunity would be useful, nor one that is indifferent to it; they all accelerate or retard the progressive movement of society. If we reflect on the great number of iniquities that are committed every day and how untouchable they are by laws, we will be convinced of the immense improvement to morality that would result from

*Reference to her novel, *Méphis* (1838).

the publicity given to private actions. Hypocrisy would no longer be possible, and disloyalty, perfidy, and betrayal would not endlessly usurp the rewards of virtue through misleading appearance. Truth would enter our customs, and frankness would become the norm.

But where will we encounter it? Will we be led to ask people of faith and intelligence, whose intrepid devotion consents to stand up against recriminations, hatred, and vengeance, to expose to the light of day both hidden wickedness and the names of its authors? In order to publicize actions in which one would not have a personal interest, committed by living people, inhabiting the same country or city, will we be able to find people who, renouncing all worldly interest, embrace the life of a martyr? I will answer with the faith I have in my heart that we will find such people every day. The religion of progress will have its martyrs, as all others have had theirs, and men will not fail the work of God. Yes, I repeat, I know that there will be people religious enough to understand the thought which guides me, and I am also conscious that my example will have imitators. The reign of God has arrived, and we are entering an era of truth. Nothing that obstructs progress could survive. Both customs and public morals will come into harmony with it. Opinion, that queen of the world, has produced immense improvements. And since she has means of enlightenment which increase daily, she will produce even greater improvements still. Once she has renewed the social structure, she will renew the moral state of the people.

By entering the new route that I have just traced, I am fulfilling the mission that was given to me and obeying my conscience. Hatred may rise up against me; but, *as I am a person of faith* before anything else, no consideration whatsoever can prevent me from telling the truth about people and things. I am going to recount two years of my life: I will have the courage to tell everything I have suffered. I will name the individuals belonging to diverse classes of society with whom circumstances have put me in contact. All of them are still living, and I will make them known by their words and actions.

Preface

Before beginning the narration of my journey, I must make known to my readers my situation at the moment I undertook it and the motives that determined me, and place readers within my point of view in order to associate them with my thoughts and impressions.

My mother is French; during the Emigration she married a Peruvian in Spain. Given the obstacles that opposed their union, they married in secret, and it was a French émigré priest who performed the marriage ceremony in the house where my mother was living. I was four years old when I lost my father in Paris. He died suddenly, without having had his marriage registered and without having thought to compensate for this with testamentary arrangements. My mother had only meager resources to live on and raise my younger brother and myself, and so she withdrew to the countryside, where I lived until the age of fifteen. My brother having died, we returned to Paris, where my mother *obliged me* to marry a man whom I could neither love nor respect. To this union I owe all my misfortune; but, as my mother has since made constant efforts to show me how keenly she regrets this, I have forgiven her, and, in the course of this narration, I will abstain from speaking of her. I was twenty when I separated from this man. By 1833, the separation had lasted for six years, and for four years at the time I entered into correspondence with my Peruvian family.

During these six years of isolation, I learned everything that a woman is condemned to suffer when she is separated from her husband in the midst of a society that, by the most absurd contradictions, has conserved the old prejudices against women placed in this position, while having abolished divorce and made legal separation almost impossible. Incompatibility and a thousand other serious causes the law does not recognize often necessitate the separation of spouses, but the perversity that does not credit the motives a woman might claim pursues her with vile slander. Except for a small number of friends, no one believes what she says, and, placed by malevolence outside of everything, she is, in this society that prides itself on its civilization, nothing but a miserable *Pariah*, to whom people believe they are showing kindness when they are not actually insulting her.

In separating from my husband, I had abandoned his name and taken back that of my father. Well received everywhere as a widow or *unmarried lady*, I was always shunned when the truth came to be discovered. Young, pretty, and seeming to enjoy a trace of independence, I gave people sufficient cause to poison their conversation and have me excluded from a society that groans under the weight of the chains it has forged for itself and does not forgive any of its members for seeking to be unfettered.

The presence of my children prevented me from passing myself off as an unmarried woman, and I almost always presented myself as a widow; but since I was residing in the same town as my husband and my former acquaintances, it was rather difficult for me to sustain a role that a host of circumstances could force me to drop. This role often put me in false positions, cast upon my person a veil of ambiguity, and constantly brought upon me the most alarming difficulties. My life was a torture at every moment. Sensitive and proud to excess, I was continually bruised in my feelings, wounded and disturbed in the dignity of my being. Were it not for the love I bore my children, and especially my daughter, whose future fate as a woman aroused too intensely my solicitude not to stay by her side, in order to protect her and come to her aid—without this sacred duty with which my heart was deeply imbued (may God forgive me! and may those who govern our country tremble!), I would have killed myself. . . . I see, at this confession, the smile of selfish indifference that idiotically fails to feel the correlation existing among all individuals of a single coherent whole, as if the health of a social body in which many members are driven to suicide by despair offered no cause for concern. In 1829, I had written to my family in Peru, with the half-formed plan of finding refuge with them, and the answer I received would have induced me to realize this plan immediately had I not been held back by the despairing thought that they too would shun a fugitive slave, because, however miserable the burden of her existence, it was her duty to die suffering rather than shatter the iron shackles forged by the law.

The persecutions of [my husband] Monsieur Chazal had forced me to flee Paris many times. When my son had reached his eighth year, his father insisted on having him and offered me peace on this condition. Weary of such a prolonged struggle and no longer able to sustain it, I consented to give up my son, shedding tears over the future of this child. But hardly had a few months passed in this arrangement when that man again began to torment me and tried to take my daughter from me as well, because he had perceived that I was happy to have her by my side. Under these circumstances, I was again obliged to go far away from Paris; and it was in order to escape from unending pursuits that I left for the sixth time the only city in the world that I have ever enjoyed. For more than ten months, hiding behind an assumed name, I wandered around with my little girl. At this time, the Duchesse de Berry was traveling through the Vendée, and I was arrested three times.* My eyes and long black hair, which made me fit the description of the duchess, served as my passport and saved me from all kinds of scorn. Poverty combined with weariness exhausted my strength. Upon arriving in Angoulême, I became dangerously ill.

God made me meet in this town an angel of virtue who gave me the possibility of carrying out the plan which I had been considering for two years, and which I had been prevented from realizing by my affection for my daughter. People had suggested the boarding home of Mademoiselle de Bourzac as the best place to send my child. At our first meeting this excellent person read in the sadness of my gaze the intensity of my pain. She took my daughter without asking any questions and said to me: "You can leave without worrying. During your absence I will be like a

---

*Caroline de Berry was the widow of a son of Charles X, the Bourbon king who had been overthrown in the Revolution of 1830. In 1832, she traveled through the Vendée—the section of western France that had remained royalist in the 1790s—attempting to foment a revolt in favor of restoring Bourbon rule once again. She was captured late that year and imprisoned.

mother to her, and if misfortune should will that she never see you again, she will always remain with us." Once I felt certain that someone would be taking my place at my daughter's side, I resolved to go to Peru to take refuge in the bosom of my paternal family, in the hopes of finding there a position that would help me go back into society.

Toward the end of January 1833, I went to Bordeaux and introduced myself to M. de Goyenèche, with whom I had been corresponding. M. de Goyenèche (Mariano) is my father's cousin, and since they had both been born in Arequipa, a childhood friendship had bound them intimately together. At the sight of me, M. de Goyenèche was struck by the extreme resemblance between my features and those of my father. They reminded him of his old friend, and this memory was associated for him with that of his youth, his family, and, in short, his country, which he never ceased to miss. He immediately transferred to me a part of the affection he had for his cousin, and this old man with his noble manners showered upon me attentions that showed how much he honored me; he introduced me to his whole circle as his niece and overwhelmed me with signs of goodwill. I similarly received a very kind welcome from M. Bertera (Philippe), a young Spaniard who lives with M. de Goyenèche and manages the affairs of my uncle Pio de Tristan. I announced to these gentlemen my determination to leave for Peru. I stayed two and a half months in Bordeaux, taking my meals at my relative's home and lodging next door with a lady who rented me a furnished apartment. I underwent delays before leaving, and a host of unpredictable circumstances succeeded in further complicating my situation. In 1829, when I had been staying in a lodging house in Paris, after returning from a journey, I had met a ship's captain on his way back from Lima. Surprised that my name was the same as that of the Tristan family he had known in Peru, the captain asked me if I were a relative of theirs. I answered no, as I was in the habit of doing. I had for ten years disavowed this family for reasons that I will later make known, and it was through the accident of this encounter that I was to enter into correspondence with my relatives in Peru, go on my journey, and experience all that followed from it. After a long conversation with M. Chabrié (that was the captain's name), I wrote my Uncle Pio a letter whose existence attests to the nobility of my sentiments and the loyalty of my character, but which destroyed me by revealing to him the irregularity of my father's marriage. I had been passing for a widow in the lodging house, and I had my daughter with me. It was in this situation that captain Chabrié had known me. He left; I left this house myself not long after meeting him there; and, since then, I had heard no more of him.

In February 1833, there were only three ships in Bordeaux leaving for Valparaiso: the *Charles-Adolphe*, whose room did not suit me, the *Flétès*, which I had to pass up because the captain refused to accept my uncle's credit as payment, and the *Mexican*, a pretty new sailing ship which

everyone spoke of in glowing terms. I had been presented to Monsieur
de Goyenèche and his whole circle as an unmarried woman; imagine
then the stunning blow I received upon hearing the name of the *Mexican's* captain when my relative told me he was called *Chabrié*. This was
the same captain I had met at the lodging house in Paris, in 1829.

I did everything I could to avoid sailing on the *Mexican*; but afraid that
my behavior would be considered bizarre in my relative's home, where
Monsieur Chabrié had been highly recommended by Captain Roux, a
longtime business associate of my family, I did not dare refuse to go visit
the ship.

I spent two days and two nights in an inescapable perplexity. I had
seen Monsieur Chabrié only two or three times, when we had taken
together the dinner provided by the lodging house. He had spoken of
nothing but Peru, and as I listened to him, I thought only of a family
whose abandonment had caused me much bitter grief, paying absolutely
no attention to the man who unknowingly spoke to me of my dearest
interests. I had completely forgotten him, and now I was straining to
make an effort to remember what sort of man I was going to be doing
business with. I was tormented by the most intense anxiety; I feared
missing my journey by deferring it, and the things I was continuously
hearing about ship captains were hardly calculated to assure me of the
degree of trust I could place in the captain of the *Mexican*. I could no
longer resist the entreaties of my relative, who was himself being pressured by Monsieur Chabrié to know my final decision, so that he could
dispose of the cabin he was holding for me in the event that I did not
leave on his ship. Whenever I have found myself in an awkward position, I have never sought counsel elsewhere but in my heart. I sent for
Monsieur Chabrié, who, the minute he entered, recognized me in surprise. I was deeply moved. As soon as we were alone, I held out my
hand to him: "Monsieur," I said, "I don't know you, yet I am going to
confide in you a secret of the utmost importance to me and ask of you
an exceptional service." "Whatever the nature of this secret," he answered, "I give you my word, *mademoiselle*, that your trust is not ill-
placed. As for the service you expect from me, I promise to perform it,
unless the matter is completely impossible." "Oh! thank you," I said,
vigorously shaking his hand. "God will reward you for the kindness you
are doing me." Monsieur Chabrié's expression and tone of truth had
convinced me that I could rely on him. "What I ask of you," I continued,
"is quite simply to forget that you have known me in Paris as a *married
lady* and *with a daughter*; I will explain the reason on board ship. In two
hours I am going to visit your ship; I shall choose my cabin, Monsieur
Bertera will settle its price with you, and, until we leave, speak to me as
if you have seen me only today for the first time." Monsieur Chabrié
understood me and shook my hand with cordiality. We were already

friends. "Take heart!" he said, "I am going to hasten our departure. I can imagine what you must be suffering in your position."

I can say that this first visit from Monsieur Chabrié is one of the happiest memories to have remained in my heart.

For the two and a half months I stayed in Bordeaux, I was painfully affected by the most worrisome apprehensions. I had lived in this city at two different times with my daughter before I had ever thought about my family in Peru; and I had known many people, with the result that every time I went out, I felt vulnerable to an encounter with one of these former acquaintances, who might come and ask for news of *my daughter* from me—from me, *Mademoiselle Flora Tristan*. I was in a continual state of anxiety. Imagine, therefore, my impatience as I waited for the day we were supposed to set sail.

I was longing to leave Monsieur de Goyenèche's house; yet I was treated with the greatest distinction, and above all with marks of affection that would have made me very happy if I had been in a true position. But I was too proud to take pleasure in the respectful attentions lavished upon a title which was not mine, and my heart, drenched with long suffering, could not open itself to the prestige of high society and its luxury. This social order, organized for grief, and in which love is an instrument of torture, had no attraction for me; its pleasures held no illusion for me. I saw in them emptiness and the reality of the happiness people had sacrificed to them. My existence had been shattered, and I no longer aspired to anything but a tranquil life. A state of rest was the constant dream of my imagination, the object of all my desires. I resolved to make my journey to Peru only with great regret. I felt, as if by instinct, that it was going to bring down new misfortunes upon my head. To leave my country which I loved in preference to all others, to leave my daughter who had no one but me to lean on, to expose my life, my life which was a heavy burden to me because I was suffering and could enjoy it only furtively, but which would have seemed beautiful and radiant had I been *free*, and finally to make all these sacrifices, to confront all these dangers because I was bound to a person who claimed me as if I were his *slave*! Oh! These reflections made my heart leap with indignation; I cursed this social organization which substitutes the chains of slavery for the bonds of love and divides society into *bondswomen* and *masters*. These involuntary thoughts of despair were succeeded by the feeling of my weakness. As tears flowed from my eyes, I fell to my knees and fervently implored God to help me bear up under my oppression. It was in the silence of the night, as I was besieged by these reflections, that the irritating picture of my past misfortunes unfolded before my mind's eye. Sleep escaped me, or softened my suffering only for brief moments. I exhausted myself with vain plans and sought to penetrate the character of my relative Monsieur de Goyenèche. He is so religious, I told myself, that he does not fail to go to mass a single day, so punctual in fulfilling all the duties that religion imposes. God, whom he constantly intersperses in his conversation, must be in his thoughts. He is rich. Could he, close relative that he is, refuse to take my daughter and myself under his protection? Oh, no, I thought, he would not spurn me. He is childless, and I am the woman God has sent him. Today, this very morning, I will confide in him all my troubles, recount to him the martyrdom of my life, and entreat him to keep my poor little daughter and me with him. Would this, alas, be a burden we would be imposing on him as an old bachelor, without a family, overflowing with every abundance, living alone in an immense house (the Schicler mansion) where his shadow loses him and where our friendly voices would ceaselessly resound with tones of gratitude? . . . But that morning, when I arrived at the old man's house, my heart palpitating with emotion, I was struck from the very first words he spoke by the dry and egotistical expression typical of old bachelors, rich and miserly men who think only of themselves, make themselves the center of the universe, and are always amassing wealth for a future they will never reach. This expression of dryness froze me. I remained silent, recommended my daughter to God, and ardently desired to be far away at sea. I thus never made that attempt, and there is no doubt that in spite of my relative's devotion, it would not have succeeded. I have had proof of that since my return. Roman Catholicism leaves us with all of our propensities and gives that of egotism the greatest intensity. It detaches us from the world but only to concentrate all of our reflections on the Church. There people profess to love God, and it is through the observation of religious practices imposed by the Church that people believe they prove to Him their love. Far from believing themselves obliged to come to the aid of their relatives, their allies, their friends, their fellows in a word, they almost always find religious excuses, taken from the behavior of the person who requested help, to refuse it. It is through generous gifts to the Church or through granting a few alms that people usually imagine they are satisfying the charity preached by Jesus Christ.

Monsieur Bertera, although a Spaniard and a good Catholic, had come to France, where he had been raised, at too young an age to be imbued with the same religious prejudices as Monsieur de Goyenèche. Yet I did not take him into my confidence. I bore him a disinterested friendship and did not want to implicate him in the lie I was telling my family. Ever since I have known this young man, he has never stopped lavishing upon me marks of affection. I believed in the sincerity of the attachment he demonstrated, and I took pleasure in showing him my gratitude. The pleasure I felt in doing this helped to alleviate the countless tribulations that assailed me during my stay in Bordeaux. Until then, most people with whom circumstances had connected me had only born me ill, but Monsieur Bertera experienced satisfaction in being useful to me. He confided in me his sorrowful regrets and troubles. He had seen his whole family, to whom he was tenderly devoted, die of the same disease. The sole survivor, he lived in loneliness in the midst of high society with its cold egotism. Misery loves company, however its causes may differ. From our first conversation, our souls established between them a melancholy intimacy, which, pious in its aspirations, did not touch the earth at any point. I loved this young man with that tender and fond affection that sensitive people in misfortune feel for each other. His companionship provided a gentle balm for my soul. Near him I breathed more freely, and the horrible nightmare that continually oppressed me weighed less heavily upon my bosom. I enjoyed going out with him, and almost every evening we would go on long walks while my old relative took his nap. For his part, Monsieur Bertera eagerly sought every occasion to make himself agreeable; his affection for me was manifest in the smallest details.

I have never in my life hesitated to sacrifice a personal enjoyment to what is for me the more intense pleasure of helping to increase the happiness and decrease the sorrow of the people I have really loved. The sincerity of Monsieur Bertera's affection gave me the conviction that he would have shared my sorrow if I had confided in him the secret of my cruel position, and the impossibility of changing it would have increased his pain. And then the false position in which I had been placed by the lie that the prejudices of society imposed on me was too painful for me to consent to burden a man I loved, and to whom I had so many obligations, with a portion, however small, of the consequences that could result from this lie. I kept my secret to myself, and I had the courage to remain silent when I was sure of meeting in the heart of this young man an intense sympathy for my misfortunes. I made this sacrifice to the friendship that I have pledged to him, and from God alone I await my reward.

I left, recommending my daughter to Mademoiselle de Bourzac and to the only friend I had. Both promised to love her as their own child, and I took away with me the sweet and pure satisfaction of not leaving any painful memory behind me.

VII

LETTERS

[Included in the Saint-Simonian archives—the Fonds Enfantin—is the voluminous correspondence of the inner circle of Saint-Simonians. The letters we present here were written by Claire Bazard, Cécile Fournel, Clorinde Rogé, Claire Démar, Pauline Roland, and Suzanne Voilquin. They were saved for the archival collection either because they were written by a member of the original hierarchy (Bazard and Fournel) or because they were addressed to someone of that inner group—to Prosper Enfantin, Charles Lambert, or Aglaé Saint-Hilaire, who was in charge of the indoctrination of new women recruits—as were the letters of Rogé, Démar, Roland, and Voilquin. The letters were collected, oftentimes recopied, and prepared for the official archives of the Saint-Simonian "religion." Following Enfantin's death in 1864, they were donated to the Bibliothèque de l'Arsenal. A reading of them offers a glimpse into the complicated personal relationships between Saint-Simonian women and men, among women of the same class, and between women of different classes.

The central importance of Prosper Enfantin as an object of complex emotional attachment is most striking in these letters. From the first moment, he had a magnetic effect on his followers—the men as well as the women. After he was sent to prison for his views on women's emancipation and sexuality, his attraction increased; he was then a martyr for their cause. For some of these women, the affection was, consciously or unconsciously, sexual, and for others it was mixed with considerable resentment. Although there were rumors of a relationship between him and Claire Bazard in 1831, and although there are ambiguous references in these letters that suggest some kind of intimate relationship between him and Clorinde Rogé, and him and Suzanne Voilquin in Egypt, one sees that "fantasy" and "fact" are equally important in these letters as in the many Saint-Simonian diaries and memoirs.

The male Saint-Simonian leaders intended that Claire Bazard would similarly have a magnetic effect on women adherents, but she lacked the personal charisma for this role. In late 1831, after Claire Bazard and Cécile Fournel resigned from the movement, Aglaé Saint-Hilaire was appointed the leading female figure of the inner circle. She had a powerful

*effect on Pauline Roland, who was far away in the provinces, but not
on the Saint-Simonian women in Paris to whom she was present. The
class and personal divisions among the women and their unwillingness
to bow to the authority of a female member of their group emerges in
these letters.*

*It would be interesting to compare the interpersonal relations among
the writers of these letters to the relations among the proletarian women
suggested by the writings in the* Tribune des femmes. *Is there more or
less divisiveness, more or less harmony, or divisiveness and harmony of
different sorts? To what extent is the divisiveness in these letters exacer-
bated by class differences? Also, to what extent is Enfantin (and for that
matter Saint-Hilaire) an imaginary recipient of the confidences and out-
pourings of these letter writers? Is their importance to these women exaggerated in these letters? However revealing these letters are of personal
matters, they are a special collection—the letters saved by the official
caretakers of the Saint-Simonian archives, intended to be read by a curious public of the future; in our readings, we should take note that their
authors understood the public nature of the letters they were writing.]*

Letters of Claire Bazard

*[Claire Bazard was the most prominent woman in the Saint-Simonian
inner circle from the earliest years until November 1831 when she and
her husband, Saint-Amand Bazard, left the movement in protest over
Enfantin's position on sexual morality. She was appointed by the male
leaders as the first "mother" to the daughters of Saint-Simon and was
the first woman integrated into the hierarchy—clearly on her demand.
At the time of the writing of these particular letters, the Saint-Simonian
movement had just organized itself on a religious model. Enfantin and
Saint-Amand Bazard formed a dual papacy, the "fathers Enfantin-
Bazard" or even "our father Enfantin-Bazard."]*

[Claire Bazard to Fathers Enfantin and Bazard, October 6, 1830, Fonds
Enfantin 7644, "Archives," 2: 309–10.]

My Fathers,

Completely astonished, completely confused even, to be for the first
time in opposition against you, persuaded that I would never dare express to you out loud everything that I feel and that is going on in my
mind, I have taken it upon myself to write you. I beg you to be willing
to hear me out and consider that the objections I am about to submit to

you are above all the simple expression of the feelings of a woman in her own cause.

Yesterday, when you talked about the seating arrangement for the college in the new hall,* I could not conclude, as you did, that the true and best place for me was the one you had assigned.** I do not and cannot believe, in effect, that I could be elsewhere than among the brothers whom you have given me. Is it not there, especially since you proclaim the liberation of woman, that you should be able to offer me to the incredulous eyes of men as proof of the truth of your words, and through my presence in your midst have the women become used to seeing me thus, in order to make them desire to join me up there soon?

In vain will you place me on a throne above all the other women, and proclaim me the first among them. They would see in me not their own elevation, but my personal elevation which they would envy or perhaps disdain. But—and please be willing to reflect upon this, dear Fathers— simply assign me to the least place in the midst of my brothers, and then say if you do not believe that the goal of the doctrine will be better fulfilled, and if you will not demonstrate much better, through this fraternal association before the world, what woman can become, since she is already almost the equal of man.

Ah! enough, my Fathers, enough of these temporary elevations from which we always fall back so painfully; enough of these illusory distinctions that have never brought us closer to you and have always distanced us further from our sisters. Yes, my Fathers, enough of these isolated thrones, which make the being who sits on them a being without a place among other beings, a sad and unfortunate symbol of those poor people who could not go forward except by escaping from their sex and being rejected by men who did not yet want to understand them. Ah! You too, do not push me far away from you and set up between my brothers and me this cruel distinction! Indeed! I would see them all gathered together, all at your side, and I would be alone, alone in the midst of this society, as if you did not dare acknowledge me, except in the secret of the family.

But, in this decision you have made, you no doubt pitied my weakness and thought I would be afraid to be the only one of my sex facing criticism and the ridicule of the old society. But, my Fathers, that could never make me shrink back or run away. When you spoke to me in the name of God and the sorrows of women, I conquered, at least to a great degree, the excessive shyness that neither society nor my age could have made me overcome. I have shattered all my old prejudices and the childish fears to which, much more than anyone else, I was subjected, but

---

*A large hall (Salle Taitbout) had just been rented for the highly ritualized "exposition of the doctrine" each Sunday.
**Enfantin and Bazard had intended a separate hierarchy for the women.

what I should fear and beg you to destroy in me is the depression into which I can still so quickly fall and the fright I feel when I see the apathy, lack of intelligence, and absence of activity in most of the women I approach. My fathers, give me faith, a strong faith in our rehabilitation, and truly admit, through me, all the women among you.

God has been willing to abandon to your efforts alone the task of placing the first woman under the new law, but it is through the efforts of this first woman, united with yours, that He can now lead all women to this law.

Therefore, listen to my voice, and believe that the feeling I have revealed to you will find a more or less deep echo in the hearts of all the poor creatures who today can raise themselves up only with me. My Fathers, you have announced great things to them, but do you think they could understand them and believe you, if you yourself were to thrust far away from you the woman you have ordered them to follow? I beg you, my Fathers, do not separate any longer what you have proclaimed to be forever united.

My Fathers, I remain yours truly in the most tender and respectful affection.

[Claire Bazard to Father Enfantin-Bazard, n.d. (likely early to mid-1831), Fonds Enfantin 7645, "Archives," 3: 114–15 verso.]

My Father,

You want to know how I have acquitted myself thus far of the task you have confided in me, and if my daughters have advanced on the road of progress along which you have charged me to lead them. Your request to me relieves me of a great weight, since I needed to unburden myself upon your bosom, so hear and judge me.

You have raised me to the first rank among your daughters and deemed me worthy of being their mother. I should therefore be strong and sustain the weak; but still weak myself, I have only been complaining to you, when all you should hear from me are actions of grace. But believe this at least, this is the last time I will ask you to turn your eyes away from the larger picture they embrace to lower them for a moment to the lowest rungs of the hierarchical ladder. It is the last time that I, who should constantly be between the lowest rungs and you, will beg you to let your own so highly respected words be heard by those who cannot credit mine or understand that they come from you and are sanctified by you.

My Father, I am terribly sorry, and this fault will already be large enough in your eyes, but although I am not discouraged by the obstacles I encounter, I had believed that in [illegible] of our new situation, I would not, among us at least, encounter any. No, I am not discouraged, I cannot be, for everything constantly reminds me that *you* who were able to raise me up from such a low level will still be able to raise me up to the level I must reach. But here I am imploring you for both the pardon for a presumptuous trust and the means to fulfill honorably the task you have imposed upon me.

The two reproaches that were addressed to me by one of my brothers have not been without fruit, and I bless him for having made them, because I deserved them, and for having set me on the path of reproaching myself even more severely. [. . .]

You have given me daughters, and until now I have not been their mother. They were ignorant of the doctrine, and I could not enlighten them, for my guilty humility made me treat them as equals, even though you had told me I was their superior. They were weak, and my weakness made me cry and moan over their sorrows, instead of endlessly seeking the way to make them strong. They were involved in personal issues and my personality recoiled in fear at the thought that exhortations, however maternal, would, by reminding them of their inferiority, make them withdraw from me.

Therefore, I have not yet done anything, nor fulfilled any of your hopes, my Father. The women whose love you commanded me to develop, whose spirit I was to enlighten, and whose efforts I was to direct, are still what they were when you put them into my hands. And yet many noble qualities distinguish these girls of your choice. If, furthermore, they have not advanced as much as I would have wanted, it's myself whom I must accuse, for it is up to *the superior to raise the inferior*.

Hierarchy is a vain word for us, it bears no fruit, and our meetings go on in turmoil and disorder. In this chaos it would be impossible to tell the inferiors from the superiors, for the mother has no idea how to impose respect upon the children, and the children do not know how to submit to the mother. Just like slaves who cannot recognize different ranks among them, we know neither how to command nor obey. We cannot recognize dignity and power except in the master, nor feel obedience and respect except for the master, and for us the master is man.

Until now, our meetings have been almost nothing but parodies of what we see you do. They have no definite meaning, and we follow you only for the purpose of following you. Weak echoes of glorious songs, we repeat them, not because they are the holy pact that must bind together all men, but because they flatter us, and you are the ones who compose them.

In our works, which have no rules but our caprice, we have no concern either for God or humanity. We have not yet been able to raise ourselves to a general level of sympathy, for our conversion is not yet complete. It is always about ourselves that we are concerned. It is always to our sex that we refer. Faced with all our brothers who suffer, we can only talk about our own sorrows, and your sublime thoughts on the happiness of all people are reduced with us into the narrow circle of our personal happiness, a happiness whose source and end we cannot seek except in ourselves. Lastly, our joys and sufferings are not the joys and sufferings of our brothers. In a word, we have not yet taken on that elevated social personality to which Saint-Simon calls us. [. . .]

My Father, you who can do everything, help me, and give me the strength I lack. And if you find that the voice of a woman is insufficient to call and to direct your daughters who have not yet recognized any other authority but that of man, my Father, extend your hand toward us, draw us toward you, if we cannot yet raise ourselves to your level. But in the name of God who calls us, and the future he promises us, do not, my Father, give up. Force us to be worthy at last to become your wives, mothers, and sisters. As imperfect as we still are, you cannot fulfill or accomplish your sublime plans without us. The hymn of grace you have dreamt can be sung only by a man and a woman, husband and wife in power, intelligence, and love. My Father, I dare to repeat it once more, raise us up, raise yourself up, raise up the whole of humanity which is watching us and waiting.

Help me, my Father: a daughter full of love and respect entreats you.

Letters of Cécile Fournel

[Cécile Fournel was the best-liked of the bourgeois women of the inner circle. Although both she and her husband Henri (sometimes spelled Henry) left the movement with the Bazards in November 1831, Henri rejoined Enfantin and the other male apostles at their celibate retreat at Ménilmontant the next spring. Cécile returned to the Saint-Simonian residence at rue Monsigny that summer but continued to hold firmly to her disapproval of Enfantin's views on sex. In 1833, she and Henri left for Egypt even before Enfantin's release from prison permitted him to join the Saint-Simonians there. (Henri, an engineer and the former director of the French Le Creusot works, was to head the project to build a dam at Aswan on the Nile.) When Enfantin finally arrived in Egypt, he ended his vow of celibacy. Cécile's chagrin over Enfantin's sexual adventures was enormous, although the final break between them may have been inevitable. Not only were there disagreements over sexual morals, but there were hurt feelings when Enfantin disparaged her attempts to take a more active role within the movement by publishing the Livre des actes, an official movement publication that would carry news of the various "missions" of the Saint-Simonian apostles.]

[Cécile Fournel to Aglaé Saint-Hilaire, June 8, 1832, Fonds Enfantin 7727, no. 24.]

Belleville, June 8, 1832

My dear Aglaé,

The first act on the road to freedom we are about to take should be for us to get used to a frankness between ourselves which would seem brutal and awkward in society, but would be for us a sign of liberty and at the same time unity.

Therefore, I will go straight to a fact that struck me sharply, I mean the way you passed yourself off as F[ather] Enfantin's sister. I think you meant the old fraternity, the kind he himself talked about when he gave you the name of sister and announced that his old father was going to come to you,* but I am convinced that you were not understood by everyone and that your words seemed in effect to apply to the religious, hierarchical fraternity. As for that, I must admit, F[ather] Enfantin could not accept it unless he stopped being the *leader*, for in that position he neither can nor should find *a brother* among the men *or a sister* among us. His equal, in my opinion, will be the woman who *feels* and whom *he recognizes as half of himself*. She will be the one who, by completing him, will finally succeed in constituting the couple, the power of the future.

On the road we wish to take, we doubtless cannot accept the paternity of any man. We are not *named* by them; they cannot be named by us. But then, dear Aglaé, it seems to me that our womanly dignity forbids us from taking toward them any titles that they would have the right to deny us. In my opinion, only the great priestess of the future, taking her place at the side of the great priest, will have the power to end this painful state of absolute separation which must be felt in all our relations with the men we love and with whom we are mystically united in the most holy of all communions. [. . .]

Yes, dear Aglaé, I firmly believe that if we do what we must, women will understand us and approach us; but in order for us not to expect this in vain, we must start upon this road where everything will be *true* and the position of each of us will be felt by all the others. We must, after all, perhaps in a different form, work to unite with each other as closely as these men from whom we are separated are united among themselves. The weaker we are at the beginning, the more glory we can hope for, and the more happiness we can expect in the future. We will not be *the first*, but we will be the cherished daughters of this woman prophet who will come to lay down the foundation of the new morality. She will name each of us according to our love and our works, and then

---

*Aglaé Saint-Hilaire was a close family friend of Enfantin's.

we will have *a father, a mother, brothers*, and *sons*. Until then we can have only *sisters* and *daughters*. At that time, dear Aglaé, the new family will be truly established, and our lives will become as harmonious and pleasant as they are now bitter and cruel.

Dear sister, let us quickly set to work. You would have seen me already if I had not been suffering so much; but Wednesday* was more than my strength could take, and therefore yesterday I was like a dead woman all day long, and I am still very weary and depressed.

Adieu, I kiss you with the tenderness of a sister.

Cécile Fournel

[Cécile Fournel to Elisa Lemonier, June 15, 1832, Fonds Enfantin 7727, no. 9.]

Belleville, June 15, 1832

My dear Elisa,

You who have suffered so much, and whom I have left so long without a sign of affection to let you know how sincerely I sympathized with your pain, pardon me, I beg you, for I too have truly been sick and suffering.** The letter I sent you in November could give you some idea, by the cruel exasperation that had dictated it, of the sad state I fell into shortly thereafter; a loving heart uselessly tears itself to pieces when it gives into the torment of hating and feeding upon spleen. Therefore, the sickness I came down with at that time did not lose its fatal nature until the day more pleasant feelings began to emerge and let me breath more freely. Let me assure you that this is in no way a metaphor, but I felt smothered by all those thoughts of anger that absorbed me, and I was really on the brink of dying from it. My God, how relieved I am to have been too sick to possibly hold a pen! I would have given you such sorrow that I cannot even imagine, and it is really the kindness of providence to have put me in such a state that I could no longer be depended upon to act. Since then I have often thanked and blessed it.

Your good Charles, whom I saw once more with extreme pleasure, has probably told you about my return to the Saint-Simonian family. He has probably told you, dear Elisa, what decided me, the hope I had for these

---

*On Wednesdays, the Saint-Simonians gathered outside the Ménilmontant retreat for rituals and ceremonies.

**The Lemoniers' situation in 1831–32 paralleled the Fournels' in interesting ways. Both Elisa and Charles left the Saint-Simonians in November in protest over the new morality; and, like Henri Fournel, Charles alone soon rejoined the movement. Cécile clearly felt close to Elisa—like her, bourgeoise, separated from a beloved husband, and soon to be a new mother (Cécile had a young daughter).

poor women who had been so offended and undermined for the past few months! . . . I feel that we really have difficulties to conquer and a lot of suffering to overcome. At stake is nothing less than truly beginning the emancipation of woman, which until now has been the expression of a desire among us rather than a reality. . . . Alas! perhaps as long as our action remained united to that of the men we could only follow in their wake without spontaneity or an inspiration of our own characteristically womanly feelings. Perhaps this separation that tore us apart was inevitable. . . . How useful you would be to us, kind Elisa! How happy I should be if I could persuade you to unite with us, and how much your elevated feelings would make you worthy to be associated with our efforts in this time of crisis, when we know in advance that we have to accept all sorrows without exception. I say without exception, and yet it gives me joy to think that there will be one for you, and that at least when you suffer, you will have a tender heart to lay your head upon and pour out your sorrows to. My dear Elisa, your presence here would be very pleasant, you would understand me so well, and you would know so well what words to say to me when I am suffering! But that is just one of a thousand good things that you would have to do. We have a great task to carry out to instill in the few women around us the religious feeling they've lost in our torment. That will come, but we must above all call upon other women not touched by this storm; and then we need to work *materially*, for several of us whose husbands have donned the apostolic habit are without resources, and the happiness of providing for the existence of the other women and their children is reserved to those of us who have the most courage and energy. This act will be a noble sign of our liberation, it will truly be our first step toward independence and freedom. And then, dear Elisa, shall I confess to you? This desire for emancipation has been combined with another feeling of indefinable charm. These men who give themselves to the apostolate and sacrifice themselves to their work with such absolute self-abnegation are just like other men in society because they also have sacrificed us—their wives— we whose lives rested on their love. In order to follow their path they walked over us without hesitating and trampled us under their feet like obstacles they had to overcome at any price. . . . Who can impose silence on the society that crushes them if not us? Won't this be a great lesson for *him* to see us thus accepting abandonment, poverty, and sorrow in all its forms, and won't he be brought to feel that God is there where such acts are performed and the victims love and justify those who have tortured them? Ah! my dear Elisa, I cannot help but believe that the influence of women on the situation of these men who are great in their perseverance and devotion will be enormous, and that this influence will be exactly what it should be, completely soft and tender, of a softness and tenderness that will not exclude energy, for we need it, a lot of it.

So come, dear daughter (I still like to give you this name because it is the most affectionate of all), come, unless that dear child who will soon be one more link between Charles and yourself holds you back, and with everything that I know is in you, you will, I am sure, provide us some very powerful help.

In the meantime, count on the good and tender affection of

Cécile Fournel

[Cécile Fournel to the FATHER (Prosper Enfantin), n.d. (likely June 1833), Fonds Enfantin 7647, "Archives," 5: 351–52.]

It is certainly a very cruel thing, FATHER, not to be able to tell you that your desires have been fulfilled, even exceeded, and that your daughters are at work, teaching the world what your beloved sons are doing for us and in your name. . . . * Ah yes, it is a cruel thing! And I myself, who wanted to be a messenger of hope and happiness for my FATHER, who never wanted to address him otherwise than with good, kind words, how sad and unhappy I feel at this time! . . . And yet, would my silence prevent our inertia from reaching him? Wouldn't it be better to tell him: *We desired* but we did not desire *strongly enough* to *be capable*, than to let him think we did not desire at all? . . . FATHER, the last time I allowed myself to interrupt your solitude, that out of respect I had stopped disturbing, was to transfer to your soul the soothing feelings that filled my own. Pardon me if today I tell you my sorrows and pour out to you the regret I feel because of our impotence. It will be temporary, I dare believe, for it hasn't curtailed our burning and complete faith which makes me tell you: We are marching onward. . . . Ah! if only we could have by our side her whom we call upon with all our heart and soul.** How easy everything would be then! How persuasive and alluring we would become! We would all be *united* then, and would all love each other for the good that God has put into each of us, whereas today each of us is isolated and feels the imperfection of the others' characters, and that is all. There is no feeling for the good, and when our goal is shared, our efforts to achieve it are no less divided. FATHER, I don't know where GOD has given birth to this other half of you, this

---

*Enfantin, who was then serving a prison term, wanted to launch a new publication, *Livre des actes*, that would report on the work of the Saint-Simonians on missions abroad or in the provinces. Cécile Fournel wanted the bourgeois women to take charge of it, but Enfantin distrusted their capacity to do this. It seems, however, that Fournel's depressions and insecurity slowed the realization of this work as much as Enfantin's hesitation to support her in her endeavors.

**Reference to the "Woman Messiah."

MOTHER of humanity; it does not matter, but she will come. Something moves my heart and tells me I must not die without receiving her tender blessing joined with yours. . . . If you only knew how much I would love her! First of all, I would love her for the sick and dying world, which she will revitalize with her immense love; I would love her for those women who can receive only from Her the sacred emancipation and the sweet equality you have promised them; I would love her for HERSELF, for being so strong, intelligent, and loving. And finally, FATHER, I would love her so much for you, for the love she will give you, and for that ineffable tenderness by which she will compensate each of our sufferings *in the name of all of us*, that in fact it seems to me that I would love her more than *you*. You know, however, how much I love you! . . . Oh! may she not be long in coming! May the love which awaits her smile upon her now, even if this be at the ends of the earth. She will soon be here.

I wanted to send you only a few words, and in spite of myself, I got carried away. Goodnight, FATHER. Accept the expression of my love and allow your daughter to tenderly kiss your hand. You are willing, aren't you! You know if anyone is more tenderly devoted than

Cécile

[Cécile Fournel to the FATHER (Prosper Enfantin), June 24, 1833, Fonds Enfantin 7647, "Archives," 5: 352.]

[. . .] Father, here is the copy of a note I have just sent to Béranger; it will show you what stage we are at:

My dear Béranger,

I understand that you are involved in publishing a text whose goal would be to make known the acts of the apostles; and I am writing, as a *woman*, to ask you to yield to us this work which is beautiful and glorious *for you*, but more beautiful and glorious *for us*. For *women alone* are unimpeachably entitled to tell the story of the danger and suffering endured *for them*; *women alone* are entitled to bless aloud the men who have exercised saintly devotion to *their* cause and to the cause of the people.

My dear Béranger, please send me a word or two in reply.*

---

*Eventually, Fournel has her way and she and Marie Talon become coeditors of the *Livre des actes*.

[Cécile Fournel to the FATHER (Prosper Enfantin), July 23, 1833, Fonds Enfantin 7647, "Archives," 5: 352–53.]

Bodrig-Rochette
July 23, 1833

God does not want you to breathe the stultifying prison air any longer; he has put into the heart of a man the idea of making the doors fall open for you, and that man is *king*.*

Certainly this manifestation of divine will foretells a great event for us, but until the assigned day, FATHER, until that happy day, when each of the sons you love, gathered around you, comes forth to press your hand and say: "FATHER, what do you want of me?" until that day, wouldn't it be nice [*doux*] for you to spend some time surrounded by our cares and love?

Your daughters dream of taking care of you and serving you. . . . That is how society will learn who you are. This proof of our love will have the power to enlighten and move it. . . . Oh may this dream of *women* not oppress your *man's* freedom, may it smile upon your tenderness as it does upon ours!

What would you say, FATHER, to a retreat chosen and embellished by us, where we would be your guardian angels? . . . According to your orders, we would permit or refuse entry to others. . . . Again according to your orders, we would be there, near you, or else at a distance out of respect for your solitary meditations, and we would keep away from you anything that could disturb you. . . . Ah, FATHER, it would be so sweet for us to embellish your life, while we wait for that life of fame and glory that GOD is preparing for you! . . . Do not refuse us; put yourself in our care, and soon everything will be ready. We are just waiting for your acknowledgment.

I am almost trembling as I write you, FATHER. For such a long time you have seemed unhappy with me and I am so sorry to have changed the tenderness you used to show me! But I must not mix sorrowful thoughts with the pleasant hope of seeing you again. So I'll be silent.

Goodnight, FATHER. Let me tenderly kiss your hand, and count more than ever on the love of your daughter.

Cécile F.

---

*The Saint-Simonians had just gotten word that Louis-Philippe would soon pardon Enfantin. He was released from prison on August 1, after serving seven months of his one-year sentence.

[The FATHER (Prosper Enfantin) to Cécile Fournel]*

To answer the request you make of me, my dear friend, I would need more enlightenment than you give me. Your heart, full of love for me, has been moved by a piece of good news. And you rushed to write to me, leaving in your letter a mystery that I cannot penetrate.

[Cécile Fournel to Aglaé Saint-Hilaire, September 1833, Fonds Enfantin 7727, no. 38.]

From Cairo, September 31 [sic], 1833

My dear Aglaé

[. . . .]

As for other matters, I will say right now only what I feel, for Clorinde** seeks in all this something quite different from me. She must have more noise and brilliance, and I am limiting myself to praying a thousand prayers that she is not going to break herself there where she seeks fame and glory (this is strictly between us, except for Marie alone). [. . .]

[Cécile Fournel to Prosper Enfantin, February 2, 1834, Fonds Enfantin 7727, no. 5.]

In Cairo, February 2, 1834

FATHER, when your daughter who is separated from you does not write to you, it's not because of coldness or fear, for she loves you and does not fear you. She is sure of your kindness above all else.

Ah! if I have not sought through you that strength which you assume I lack and which I have so often been happy to draw from your paternal affection, it is because for me there was no hope at all and because, in spite of myself, the efforts of my tenderness for you and my confidence in you, each word from your mouth since I have arrived in Egypt, even the readings from your letters to Henry and Lambert, in a word everything has conspired to make me feel the sad impossibility of receiving from you a faith that cannot be mine, which my intuition as well as the most intimate beliefs of my being totally refuse. . . . You have faith, FA-

---

*Enfantin responds as a matter of course to letters from the bourgeois women, but rarely from the proletarian women. One could conclude that this was simply because the bourgeois women were his close friends and the proletarians—except for Voilquin—were strangers, but Voilquin clearly felt he kept a greater than necessary distance from her and does suggest that this may have resulted from class prejudice.

**Clorinde Rogé.

THER, in the swift realization of your plans. In your mind, industry, morality, one might say everything is about to leap from theory to practice, and the times of sacrifice will soon be transformed into times of pleasure. . . . Do excuse me, but I no longer believe in these deceptive hopes which every one of our steps has just contradicted. I am deeply convinced, FATHER, that society will have all the more difficulty embodying the faith you bring it, the more it sees you trying to realize it while it is still *incomplete*, having neither the sanction of the *woman* who is great among all women, as you *yourself* are great among all men, nor the sanction *of a people of women* coming to proclaim the future and to say what will be the *bonds* of love, *marriage, the family*, and the NEW ORDER.

And do not tell me: "we must put out a call to this people of women." My FATHER, they would not be able to come; the *Past* and *Present* both confirm my deep intuition about this, and even if the modesty and exquisite delicacy that GOD has placed in the heart of woman does not oppose [this realization] as I believe they do, I would still say to you: "this people will not come," and the proof I offer is the impotence you now experience, *you* who came to Egypt to strike women with a brilliant work, and touch their hearts by a great act in *practice*. I need as proof, I say, only this impotence of yours to do anything other that act in the shadows, secretly and so inconspicuously that even most of your children do not have a clear awareness of your influence here. . . . Ah, it is not, FATHER, that I want to disavow this influence; no, I would like to believe in it, even when I do not see it, as a symbol or seed to be fertilized in time and space. Your action on society could not be in doubt for me. But if in the midst of what is now going on I want to seek something else, and if, preoccupied with your desires and my own, I try to see a realization coming to life in what is presently being accomplished, then I suffer and no longer feel that greatness I need to find in everything that emanates from you, *you* the FATHER and SAVIOR OF WOMEN.

FATHER, my voice is not agreeable, and I am really distressed about that. Alas! silence is possible for me but never lies, and to keep silent from you what I feel when you call upon me could not even enter my mind.

Intimately linked to everything I have just said is Henry's personal situation.* We suffer from it together because we share everything between us, and I would not have come to Egypt except to help this good and tender friend bear those aspects of this country that are false and out of harmony with the need for action and clarity which he has to such a high degree; and I am delighted to be here. But FATHER, if I feel in myself the tenderness which supports and consoles, I am far from being able right now, I confess, to be *a cause of strength and hope* in the sense

---

*Henri had turned over his personal fortune to the Saint-Simonians and resigned his position as director of the Creusot ironworks when he joined the Saint-Simonians. Now his lack of fortune and employment was complicating his decision to leave the movement.

you would wish. . . . My faith *in you* and *your coming* is still the same, I repeat, but its terms have changed. Time recedes before me, and I no longer say as I did in my days of illusion: the time has come. I say on the contrary: the time has passed; it grows more distant even as I think I am coming nearer, as I did in the period of my audacity when I wanted to mark the time and fix the day when GOD's will would be done. [. . .]

Ah! FATHER, you ask about my dreams. Right now they all lead me along this path. I am not at all absorbed or *framed* by the work of industry. On the contrary, your conception of it seems to me right now an obstacle to the pressing desire I feel to join with this general movement of women, which, in my opinion, should operate within the very bosom of society, and take the mysterious form [illegible] and I talked about. The role my dreams give to woman today does not consist in defying the world, throwing herself outside its conventions, rebelling against its feelings, or provoking its prejudices. No, her role is to make it love what she loves, to convert it without *preaching* to it, and also without ostentatiously displaying the irreligious scorn of her opinion *through acts* that repel it. Her role is to embrace it softly, so softly that it feels attracted, happy to be led by this impulse full of tenderness that knows how to make it love. Her role, FATHER, is to take back as quickly as possible the soft character she deviated from, however little, among us; for that softness is her greatest charm, her truest strength, and her only elevated power, and I don't see her equality or her saintly emancipation anywhere but there. GOD did not create her soft *in form* and tender *in heart* for nothing. Ah yes! This is the role, the sacred role of woman. As long as people see us abandoning our children* and breaking openly with the family, we will not create any proselytes, but as soon as we become examples for all women and show ourselves to be the best mothers, the most devoted sisters and daughters, people will easily convert to this faith that we have made frightening for all women who have the heart of a mother, wife, or sister, and they will plainly see that GOD is really with us. When we heal the wounds we have opened, we will spread happiness around us, instead of continuing to sow sorrow in the steps of those who love us.

You see, FATHER, why your daughter was silent, and why her voice could not go find you in the desert, even as she tried to force open that prison. . . . Do not hold it against her, and be assured that whatever the pain of her new situation, her respect and love will follow you wherever you are; promise her to tenderly press your hand.

Cécile F.

*The Fournels themselves had left their daughter behind in France.

[Cécile Fournel to Aglaé Saint-Hilaire, n.d. (Summer 1834), Fonds Enfantin 7727, no. 40.]

Tuesday morning

My good sister,

We are back home, and yet I cannot satisfy my impatience to go visit you. I am in a frightful mess. If you have a little time tomorrow and if the weather isn't as horrible as today. . . . [but] do not count on me.

What I heard about Pauline really gave me grief,* both for her and for those poor women she thinks she is working to liberate and whose chains she is helping to tighten. . . . May God help us, good sister! That is not the future, not what my heart had dreamt, and therefore I am throwing myself back into this old, doubtless quite imperfect world, but still in any case less repulsive than these so-called novelties that are in fact only a pale copy of society seen from its sad side.

Try to visit me; you are sure to find me at home unless a splendidly raging toothache sends me to the dentist.

Friendship from both of us and from [illegible] who sends you a kiss

Your devoted Cécile

Letters of Clorinde Rogé

[Clorinde Rogé was one of the most daring and independent-spirited of the Saint-Simoniennes. *She was introduced to Saint-Simonianism shortly after her marriage to Dominique Tajan Rogé, whose role in organizing the musical events and rituals for the Saint-Simonians was central to the movement's propaganda and "missionary" work. In late 1832, the couple were on mission to Lyon; in the summer of 1833, they departed for Egypt, where Tajan Rogé was to organize music for the workers who would construct the dam.]*

[Clorinde Rogé to Aglaé Saint-Hilaire, February 15, 1833, Fonds Enfantin 7624, no. 42.]

Lyon, February 15, 1833

Your letter, good Madame Saint Hilaire, gave me a great deal of pleasure. I feel an ever-greater need to converse with the person I love. Since

---

*Reference to Pauline Roland, who had left Adolphe Guéroult, by whom she was pregnant, and begun an affair with Jean-François Aicard.

I'm far away from you,* I find it a great compensation to receive your letters. Think, therefore, that in writing to me you perform a good work and also make me happy, for sadness often takes hold of me, and at those times I feel more keenly the need to have faith in a future life. I am reading Eugène Rodrigues's letters, and from them I draw a strong belief in *God*. Yes, I do have that belief, and if I happen to let myself get depressed, I immediately pick myself up and find ever more courage to work for women's independence. Madame Fournel has probably shown you the letter I wrote her, in which I discuss my plan to organize a group of women. I am still persisting in this, but I cannot give you any details since we have not yet been able to meet in a general assembly. Our only meeting took place three days ago when a worker gathered about twenty of us at her home. At this meeting, some women raised objections which I answered, and the next day the person at whose home we had gathered came to me on behalf of all the women to ask me to lead them, and brought me a small collection to rent a room. But it is really difficult to get a room, because when you say that it is for meetings, they don't want to rent. We will, however, find one, and I hope that my next letter will announce some news. I really have hope that soon women will be on the march and for that we must labor at our work. Women must speak and act to stimulate all the others whose complete lethargy makes them neither man nor woman. They are in a manner of speaking bastard women. It is up to us to make them act for all women and for the people.

You tell me that you also have meetings every Thursday, and I earnestly ask to be kept abreast of everything you do. On my end I will let you know what happens in my assembly. [. . .]

Thank you for giving me details about the *Father's* health. Because he launched the cry for the freedom of *woman*, the men have put him in prison, but the *woman*** will make up for the suffering he is now undergoing. He awaits her with so much love. When, therefore, will she come? I read today the letter from the Father to Barrault*** and from Barrault to the *Father*. I cannot decide upon these two letters. Poor women of the West! We are still treated like children, and the beret which should only fall in the presence of women still stays on their head when they speak to Western women. Ever since Barrault has been

---

*She is with a Saint-Simonian mission in Lyon.
**Reference to the "Woman Messiah."
***Emile Barrault established the Order of the Compagnons de la Femme and, in 1833—the year he proclaimed "the Year of the Woman"—set out in search of the "Woman," whom he reconceptualized into a "Woman Messiah." The Compagnons traveled East (the birthplace, after all, of the male messiah)—to Turkey, Palestine, and finally to Egypt, where Enfantin joined them. Typical of Europeans of that period, Saint-Simonians used the word "Orient" to refer to what we today would call the Near and Middle East. The men's writings on this "Orient" exemplified the sense of "otherness," which Edward Said has termed "Orientalism."

breathing the wind of the Orient some of the men can no longer stand still. They cry out for the Orient with the same excitement as sailors lost at sea who cry out: "land! land!!!" They'll soon be singing: "There all our ills will be forgotten. Cheers for the Orient!!!" Barrault wants to present his lion head to his *Mother*. As for me, I don't think she needs a lion head. I'm even convinced that this is not what will charm her the most about Barrault's person. He also wants to prepare satellites for her. Why is he doing this? She won't need support, and I really hope that she will march alone, without the help of brute strength. I cannot define what I feel now, but when I see that they are still only concerned about themselves, and that woman is still so subordinate, I get extremely annoyed. [. . .] Our efforts to spread the faith are going well in Lyon, and the songs have created a great effect. Even the most pious clamored for them. After the singing, Barrault talked about his departure for the Orient. His speech was very beautiful; tears fell from my eyes in front of everyone, and I could not stop. I don't know if anyone noticed. There was at least one lady next to me who saw it and took my hand, offering me words of sympathy, but she was not in my heart and could not know the reason for my tears! Yes, I cried because I did not see any women and I would have liked to see in place of Barrault a woman who could also let us hear her inspiring words. But I was alone, I'm sure, for probably none of the other women felt as I did the need to see themselves become greater, for their faces did not show any enthusiasm for the woman of the future. Most were cold and simpering. It doesn't matter; I love them not for what is bad about them, but for their future. I repeat, women do not have their nature, there is only the work of men, and we really cannot pay them any compliments about it. Let us hope that the sun will shine for us after all! How long I've waited to warm myself in its rays. Hope!!!

As for me, I am living with Madame Durval the bookseller. She is a very lovely lady, and above all very kind; she really loves the doctrine. I am well, but that does not prevent moments of sorrow. Right now I'm engraving one new piece for the *Father's* prison: we are going to take up a collection to publish all the music that Monsieur David* has composed. I think it will sell very well. If we had engraved music, we could make a lot of money, because people ask for it every day. [. . .]

Give me as well some news about the brilliant Mother Fournel. I've been told that she was sick, and that grieves me very much. I fear that she is sicker than we thought because I have not had any reply to my letter. My God! My God! Let her be. She may still have some time left for us. Let me have some news of her as soon as you can.**

Adieu, good mother. I send you a tender kiss and my love, as well as

---

*Félicien David was the most accomplished of the Saint-Simonian composers.
**Cécile Fournel was sick throughout the period from December 1832 to spring 1833.

a thousand friendly greetings to all our good friends. Give me as well
Paulette's address. Adieu again.

Many loving things from

Clorinde Rogé

[Clorinde Rogé to Aglaé Saint-Hilaire, May 26, 1833, Fonds Enfantin
7624, no. 43.]

Lyon, May 26, 1833

[. . . .]

I will also tell you that women, bourgeois as well as proletarian, are
putting me through a rough apprenticeship in the matter of woman in
the old society. They are so quarrelsome that they would create conflict
with no cause at all among the best of friends. [. . .]

Several women have ambitions to take the title I've been given and
want also to be leaders. The women are dividing up into several camps;
so much the better if that contributes to their progress. As for me, I've
put them at ease, for I'm giving them a month to think about this. I
don't want to influence them, for if I were not religious, I would not, I
assure you, mix with this any more. But I feel, nevertheless, that they
need a woman who is better than them. [. . .]

Adieu, a heartfelt kiss

Clorinde Rogé

[Clorinde Rogé to Prosper Enfantin, June 20, 1845, Fonds Enfantin 7776,
no. 52.]

Paris, June 20, 1845

Enfantin,

I feel the need to write to you in order to analyze with you in its
entirety the relationship that existed between us in a past whose picture
I would like to draw today with utmost frankness. You never really
understood it, as I was in a position to notice more than once, and so we
need to go all the way back to its source.

If I want to go back to this past, it is not just for a narrow purpose, but
also to establish a counterpart to that time when I rendered justice to the
devotion of the man to whom I had given, in my naive gratitude, the
name of father. The time came when I took this name away from you,
and yet I did not let you know in a written form that could be juxtaposed
with the letters in which my thoughts situated you as the best among

men. It is because, not yet trusting myself, I wanted to wait and be really sure that I was not committing an injustice. Eleven years have come and gone during which I could follow each of the acts by which you confirmed my judgment of that time. I could not write you from St. Petersburg,* for very good reason, about things that were of great importance to me. When I first came back to Paris, I was still suffering a lot. Today no obstacle holds me back, and I will tell you everything that is on my mind, but shorn of tenderness, because your pride might still lead you to mistake its intent. May God will, however, that this letter find in you the religious man who did not believe he was infallible, and who consequently sought to do better. God's will be done.

You saw in me, at the rue Monsigny, at what we then called the doctrine, a young woman who was like a little girl, dreamy, affectionate, married for only a few months to Rogé, whom I loved with that first, exclusive love in which my life was lovingly cradled, and in which I lived quite unconcerned with you gentlemen and your doctrine. In the goodness of his heart and soul, Rogé could not hear the words with which you then proclaimed the liberation of women and of the people without being converted. You asked for his heart and life, and he gave it all to you. After many struggles, he said to me one day: "My child, do not fret, do not cry like this because I am one of these men. They are good men and want the happiness of all people. Should not those of us who understand them help them and work for the liberation of women and the people?" With a sigh I told him: "Go where your conscience calls you!" You would have to be a woman to understand the sorrow which tore at my heart. In spite of the fact that I suffered a great deal, I am not sorry, because I think I did the right thing.

Enfantin, I did not understand why there were fortunate and unfortunate people. In my heart I prayed to God for those who were suffering. My childhood was spent with a father and mother who gave me from their soul every good and beautiful thing that God could put into privileged people. The tender care of my brothers protected me from contact with anything impure; for them, I was an idol that nothing profane could sully. How could I have been bad with such good people? My heart, as you see, was well prepared to receive from Rogé all the teachings of a new faith. I loved him and followed him without asking any questions. Later the little girl became a woman. She then understood what had made her so dreamy, and a mysterious instinct pushed her to the work of freedom for women.

On the day you shut yourself in at Ménilmontant, Rogé said to me:

---

*The Rogés were in Saint-Petersburg, Russia, in the late 1830s and early 1840s at the same time as Suzanne Voilquin; Dominique Tajan Rogé played the cello in the imperial orchestra.

"Have a little more patience, my dear Clorinde. The Father tells us that in six months we will once again be reunited, and we will never have to be separated again."* I raised my head to him and answered: "Enfantin does not and cannot know what will happen. He is putting you in God's hands and who knows what God wants from all of us. Whatever happens," I told him, "even while foreseeing great sorrows, I too will give Marie to God, I will labor at the work of women even as I feel bound with you, for I still love you in spite of the freedom you have given me." A few days later Rogé also shut himself in at Ménilmontant. Then came the trial. At Rogé's side, I followed you to the courthouse. Then too came the time for [. . .] Rogé's departure for Lyon, which made me decide to leave Paris too. Until then, I hadn't really noticed you in my milieu. I saw in you only the man a lot of women were running after, but to whom I was quite indifferent. I loved Rogé too much to think about you. [. . .] But later I saw you in prison, and from the moment I saw this act of faith and devotion for women, my feelings changed. My eyes rested upon you, you seemed to me the best of men, and from then on I gave you in gratitude the name of father.

At about the same period I joined Rogé in Lyon. I formed a women's club and stayed at the head of it for six months. There Rogé and I, still united in heart and mind, vowed to consecrate our lives to the new faith. I asked him for my complete freedom so that I could act without lies or remorse. Strengthened by my awareness of my love and my faith in God, I threw myself onto this new path of the woman apostle without placing any barrier before my heart or my acts. I left behind me all the prejudices I had respected until then and proudly set forth. God knows! Never did woman carry [illegible] to her work a purer heart or a more ardent faith. Never did woman seek with so much zeal the secret of the freedom of women! . . .

You came to Lyon, and I rejoiced, for I was still under the spell of the prestige and aura that prison had placed upon our first meeting. When I gave you the kiss of welcome, your symbolic necklace fell broken to the ground. I would not have noticed, if you hadn't called my attention to it. You were kind, but there was, nevertheless, in your manner something that struck me. The next day was the same and you still acted with the same lack of tact. All these little things began to open my eyes to the man to whom I had attributed such nobility. I did not dwell, however, on such little deeds, but they did make me easily suspect what the Father was lacking. Women were an enigma for him, and the realization of this brought me, one day, to give him, on behalf of the women under my direction, a silver half-circle inscribed with the words: *To the Father from*

*The Rogés, like the Fournels and the Lemoniers, were separated by the men's retreat at Ménilmontant.

the women of the Mother. It was the complement to the half-circle made only of copper, which had been on the necklace that broke during our first meeting. If you had not been so proud, you would have understood the true thought behind this symbol (women will be for you, as love is for the heart, the complement of your life), and you would not have said, as you did one day in showing it to me: "It is only made of silver and I must have one of diamonds," to which I answered: "Yours is only copper." Your ambition will make you end up having none at all and you will remain alone. (I was not mistaken, for you are probably reading this letter alone.) Your pride made me think that you would be an obstacle for women instead of the support they needed to break the bonds that had held them for so long in slavery to prejudice and society. I understood that there had to be a power beyond you that could support them *materially and morally.* Therefore, I later created the Order of the Knights of Women. God did not let me develop it to the point of being workable. I shall wait upon his will and always try to understand it. I felt that if I ever came upon you along my way, I should give you, as a woman, the love you lacked, but also set you aside as an obstacle. I did both. Your pride made love slide off your heart like water off oilcloth, and also hurt you when I deemed it appropriate to set you aside.

Let us return *to the facts.* Rogé and I decided that I would go to the Orient. My thought was of the harem. In fact, after a long struggle, I obtained from the viceroy of Egypt, and from his son Sutrain Baiha, what no other woman before me had ever tried: permission to establish a vast house of education, in the form of a harem, for slaves of all races and classes. The most absolute devotion caused me to ignore my personal needs, and I thank God today for the insurmountable obstacles he put in my path at that time in order to have me give myself for a while to a work that took away all my freedom of action.

I saw you again in Egypt right after I arrived. I still found in you the same man, and to convince you of this, I will remind you of the following fact: You visited me for the first time in Old Cairo on the day I arrived, December 29, 1833. As you entered my room, your beret *on your head* as your passed through the doorway, this same beret fell, not out of your hand, where it should have been, but off your head, where you had arrogantly left it. Seeing it on the floor, you did not want to lower yourself to pick it up. Petit, your assistant, spared you the trouble. He put it back in your hand, in which place you thenceforth understood you should leave it. How did it fall? I don't know; I am no more learned about this than about the iron chain broken before me in Lyon. I felt you had to be treated a little abruptly. I did so, and you came to me more properly. [. . .]

Later, during my first trip to Alexandria, where I had gone on business, I saw you at the dam. Still more annoyance from you, and, exasperated, I sent you on your way. I saw you come back sweet, kind, and friendly in order to make me forget your haughty airs of the morning. In fact, I had so perfectly forgotten them that I was sorry to see you mistreated. One really has to be a woman to have had such remorse. I ended up by blaming myself for being too standoffish, and, silencing all mistrust, I wrote to you from Alexandria with all the tenderness that lies in the heart of a woman. When I came back to Old Cairo, I saw you once more, and you took it upon yourself to talk to me about David,* and one more time, I had to ask you to mind your own business. It must be said to your credit that you agreed you were very clumsy. [. . .] I'm very sure you're impatient for this to be over, for you are in all certainty not convinced that I'm right. However, since you have committed wrongs, you really should have the patience to hear them out to the end.

Do you remember another conversation we had in the harem of Monsieur Lessiau? I told you in one of those moments of naive confidentiality, when one thinks she can with complete sincerity say whatever enters her head: "It's strange that I read perfectly clearly into the souls of those around me, that I can foresee events, and that nevertheless, with respect to my own situation, I lack confidence and am still feeling my way. There is however no doubt that I feel I won't accomplish anything definitive until I have arrived at a very clear consciousness of myself. I ask God everyday to give me what I lack, for I feel I can become better and grow." I told you that in all simplicity as if, under the beautiful moonlight, leaning alone against a tree, I could, raising my soul toward God, think out loud. What was my astonishment when your answer made me feel that you had not understood anything from my completely intimate talk.** You posed as always as the Father protector, and therefore very strong with himself since he had said one day: "I don't acknowledge our right to judge or guide the women in their work," but that did not prevent you from saying to me: "But just look at this a bit: you see—look around you—each woman making a place for herself. Madame Linan makes a pleasant home for her husband. You, for example, let's suppose that you were by my side. Wouldn't you feel that you had a work to accomplish, that of creating a Court for me?" You [illegible] a little sarcastically, I [illegible] your thoughts . . . of love! "And why not," you said. "There's only one difficulty in that, which is that I don't [illegible] feel it right now," I told you. "First, I'm not asking you to search for what I want, and second, it's very strange for you to talk to me this way, knowing full well that Rogé and I love each other, that we are perfectly happy, that if the two of us had taken a different path than that already laid out by society, it was not at all to seek our individual happiness now, but instead to labor for a work of regeneration." [. . .]

---

*Félicien David, the composer.
**At this point the manuscript becomes incoherent and the writing illegible.

Tired finally of not being able to exchange a thought with you, without the Father always coming to intervene between us, and feeling that you were not mine and that you hadn't given me anything in the way of religious thoughts or love, it would have been difficult. I wanted to put a stop to it, for your air of protection toward all women was irritating. As for me, without being a Christian saint, I understood my value well enough to want to make this bothersome shadow of a Father disappear from my path, so I would no longer run into a man who could speak only to men. I was therefore very consistent in telling you that I would no longer let you *tutoyer* me as you did with those you regarded as your inferiors, for in my own situation as a woman who knows how to love, I considered myself your equal, and I therefore told you that, from then on, you would be only Enfantin for me. I added that if you were looking for a companion, you would not find her by persisting in this haughty [illegible].

Thus I told you good-bye. Just when Rogé was about to arrive, I saw him from the dam, and my heart trembled with joy. He saw you as well and was not happy with you. You had hurt him by your words and manner, and, later, he was convinced that you had not acted properly with him. This is, however, between you and him.* Since I was not detached from Rogé, I neither could nor would separate his cause from mine. Therefore, I did not see you again after the dam, except for one or two times at my house with Rogé present. We took leave of each other very coldly.

And so it was that toward the end of 1834 I saw you for the last time, and at the beginning of 1836 I left Old Cairo, Egypt, without saying good-bye to you. I could not give my regards to the Father; he did not exist for me. And I would not give them to Enfantin, since through him the man I loved had suffered and had not seen fit to pardon him. I gave regards to the two women (former members of the order of the women of the mother) who lived in the same house under the same roof as you.** On a beautiful sunlit day, Rogé and I left Old Cairo; we went away from the banks of this Nile which had witnessed my first acts of faith and so much love and suffering. And yet, Oh God! you know it, I bade them good-bye with respect, gratitude, and love, tears in my eyes and faith in my heart. Thus, at my departure, under the bright sun of the Orient, God permitted my faith to grow and the poetry of my soul to take a perceptible form in me and, finally, permitted this perfumed land to become the vast field where my thoughts could begin to become reality and my heart could open up to all the impulses that its faith had

*It may be that Tajan Rogé sensed what had occurred between Enfantin and Clorinde; but there were also tensions because Enfantin seemed no longer to value his work as musical director. See Ralph P. Locke, *Music, Musicians, and the Saint-Simonians*, 190–95.
**Judith Grégoire and Caroline Carbonel.

inspired. This beautiful Nile carried us proudly, while lovingly murmuring words of farewell. The sky was calm and pure, and it seemed as if God had given us all of his light to better illuminate this imposing spectacle of nature and engrave in our hearts the memory of all this faith and hope. In thanking God, I said good-bye to the humble house and the palace tent. I asked God to make the chalice that was reserved for you less bitter. The winds carried to you your part of the memory. I prayed for the poor people, the unfortunate women, and the beautiful land of Egypt. I mingled my tears with the waters of its Nile. May God grant through this marriage of tears that its silt be fertile. May he bring forth abundance, wealth, and happiness. Adieu beautiful land. I take away with me memories that will never die. Adieu beautiful Egypt, adieu you who were great and who will be reborn from your radiant dust, adieu! Send me by the evening breezes your perfumed caresses to refresh my soul. Alas! who will still cry: Adieu, au revoir! . . .

Such were the good-byes that ended [illegible] only one of whose parts in which you were involved I have just unfolded for you. If I remind you of it today, it is because I think it necessary to awaken in you a question which has been kept entirely asleep, that of women. You say, Enfantin, *that the question of women will emerge completely armed from the industrial movement going on today.* But how? I don't understand this too well. This seems to me a game of logic. If that were so, it seems to me, then it would still be you gentlemen who would regulate our future. But in the things that concern us, you are not just. The reason is simple: since the world has been the world, you have been used to dominating us, and therefore you have developed in relation to us a nature completely made of pride. Accordingly, I would truly fear, gentlemen, that the question of women that would emerge from this very movement all armed with masculine arguments would mitigate our situation without offering any radical remedy. What then, gentlemen, would be our place with respect to you? To enrich your life? This would doubtless be very fine! Certainly one day this will be the goal of our lives with respect to each other. But in the meantime you alone will be so happy, and to redress the balance I don't believe that you alone are capable and can judge. Your concern today simply with getting rich* seems to me insufficient for regulating right now the relations between man and woman. Poor women, you are so used to saying amen to everything that the men do. [. . .] Fortunately God will awaken you and will no longer permit your indolence to let society engage in an endless struggle between two sides, *man* and *woman.* The protector and the protected will replace the master and the

---

*After his return from Egypt, Enfantin—and many of the other Saint-Simonian men— obtained important positions in industry and banking; to them it was the practical application of Saint-Simonianism.

slave. Well do I know that to this beautifully reasoned argument can be added *love* which will always provide influence to woman. I remain in agreement with this, and I also recognize that the goodness of the two sexes along with these two powerful motors of life have made the situation of women tolerable. But I repeat that these are only partial facts and not rights acquired before God and men. I tell you that we need all of our freedom so that the defects inherent in our situation will disappear, leaving us worthy in society to say what we *feel* and *want* in order to regulate our relation with you. [. . .]

What I have to tell you now could, if necessary, be put in a postscript, but since everything is related to everything, as would say an innovator of a very particular kind, I don't see why I shouldn't make it follow everything I've just said.

I was pained as a woman by one of your acts toward two women who in Egypt had given you love and tenderness.* You were alone, often sad, and the two of them came to live in your house. Both were good to you. They loved you very much and had absolute trust in you. They left for France soon before you were to return. And in fact you came to Paris where they were waiting for you with the greatest impatience. They waited for a long time, but you did not visit them! The poor daughters of the people had perhaps aspired to the honor of being at your side; and perhaps you were terrified of this! Who knows if this were not on your mind! Be that as it may, if you did not want to continue your life of the Orient, you could at least have shaken the hand of these two women who would have accepted any behavior from you, and neither of whom, as a result of this religious act, would have suffered from the appearance of an ungrateful abandonment. As I know about the wrong, I am bringing it to your attention.

In truth, gentlemen, one could say that your main duty right now is to redress the wrongs that you did to public morality.

What I have written you about these two ladies is quite simply the expression of my feeling. They are completely ignorant of the fact that I

---

*A careful reading of Enfantin's and Suzanne Voilquin's unpublished letters from Egypt and Charles Lambert's private and unpublished journals provides some information on the relationship between Enfantin and Judith Grégoire and Caroline Carbonel, but leaves many questions unanswered. Enfantin and Charles Lambert shared a residence in the section of Cairo called Old Cairo. Grégoire, a young, unmarried, "femme prolétaire," and Carbonel, who was married but separated from a Saint-Simonian apostle, moved in with them in late 1835. It is clear from the sources that Enfantin was involved in a sexual relationship with Carbonel and that Lambert and Grégoire shared quarters. It is not clear, however, if the intimate relationships were more complicated than that—if for example, Enfantin also had a sexual relationship with Grégoire. Grégoire became pregnant, and no one doubted that Lambert was the father. He described his unwillingness to marry Grégoire and his unwillingness even to recognize the child legally. A compromise was worked out which had Lambert recognize his paternity privately and provide 1,500 francs per annum support to Grégoire for the rest of her life.

have said anything to you. I saw them recently, and the subject did not even come up among us.

Adieu Enfantin. May God enlighten you. May *He* spare you sorrow.

Clorinde Rogé

108 rue St. Honoré, Paris

Will you be good enough to render me a service? As you see, I am trying to come to terms with the past, and I am lacking the letters I wrote you. You would give me great pleasure if you would have the kindness to lend them to me so I could make copies of them. As soon as I am done, I promise to return them to you if you so desire. My intention is not to take back from you what I have freely given.

In addition, I beg you also to kindly put this letter at the end of the ones I wrote you from Lyon and the Orient.

This is a womanly idea, and I have enough faith in you to be sure that you will have regard for it.

Letters of Claire Démar

[Claire Démar joined the Saint-Simonians in 1832. The loneliness she expressed in these letters suggests that it was difficult for a newcomer to be accepted among the close-knit Paris "family." Her daring views may have also contributed to her isolation. Several of these letters have been signed Emilie d'Eymard. Valentin Pelosse, who carefully compared the penmanship, spellings, and style of these letters to letters signed Claire Démar, has established that the authors are the same. (See Claire Démar, Textes sur l'affranchissement des femmes, followed by an explanation of Saint-Simonian symbolism and ideology by Valentin Pelosse.)]

[Emilie d'Eymard (Claire Démar) to Father Enfantin, December 16, (1832), Fonds Enfantin 7647, "Archives," 5: 517 verso–518 verso.]

Sunday evening, December 16

To the Father,

It is already late at night. Outside, all is calm; around me, everything is quiet and dead. Only my thoughts are alive here, my thoughts which follow you into the depths of your retreat.*

---

*Enfantin began serving his prison term on December 15.

Yesterday morning, after your last good-bye, I returned to Ménilmontant,* my heart filled with emotion. Seated at your place, I paid my debt to a suffering which was more than I could bear: I cried. That same evening, and again at dinner at the Porte d'Italie when I heard the voice of your son Barrault, feelings of weakness overwhelmed me again. It was impossible for me to control myself; I would have suffocated. In the future, however, I will guard myself against this tendency to let myself go. I honestly do not know what came over me. Before, I did not even know how to cry. But tonight at the Porte des Amandiers, I made such a disgraceful spectacle of myself, crying in front of Legallois, that I regretted it. It seems that his wife had told him about my emotional outburst last evening, and with a certain pleasure he told me to my face that my emotions were nothing but an affectation. I became very angry and we got into a heated argument in front of the entire crowd. [But] just when I was telling him that his behavior did not suit a Saint-Simonian, I remembered that my own behavior under the given circumstances was no better. I remembered all the insults you yourself had to put up with and I became quiet. Two strangers who witnessed this scene were offended by it. One of them is a republican with a noble soul, who seems to me to have great potential. The other seems to be a selfish man, a proper type who loves women, gives into them out of self-interest, but does not believe in anything. These two men are both atheists. They do not want to know anything about religion,** but I will bring them around, I am sure of it. If it becomes necessary for our political discussions, I will ask your son Lambert for help.

It was my first religious act that made an impression on these two men. I justified the behavior of Legallois at my own expense. I was very eloquent; your memory inspired me, Father. You have planted the seed of religious feeling in me. And it has already germinated. It will grow.

Father, you touched an open wound in talking to me about the causes that trouble my sleep. Yes, without a doubt, one must be at peace in one's heart in order to sleep restfully. Until now, everything has been a big disappointment for me. My life has consisted of a series of cruel sufferings. All my relatives were immoral. By the age of fourteen, I loathed and despised the world, and yet this same world exploited me, for I had a great need to love. I was always looking for something or someone to complete myself. I searched in vain. I had dreamed that love was other than what I encountered. I have very strong feelings, but all my emotions go to my heart from my imagination; and the pleasures that men seek from women are not in the least necessary for my happiness. So I was forced to feign what I wasn't feeling. In sum, love itself

---

*Where the Saint-Simonian men were then living in celibate retreat.
**Reference to the Saint-Simonian "religion."

was false for me, since I found it stripped of the poetic magic that my imagination had vested in it. Thus, I finished with it.

But now, my heart is filled with great feeling; this will be sufficient for me. I begin a new life. I have a *Father*, a Father whom I love and *in whom I have faith*. And now, I will search for *my Mother*. To find her, I will use any human means available to me. I will look for her among women and also among men. Because those whom I hope to convert will be able to bring her to me.

At the Court of Appeals, I remained in the audience during your entire sentencing. And there, though I was very tired, I did manage to annoy some of your enemies.

I have been resting my pen for a quarter of an hour, and during this time a bold idea flashed through my mind. [. . .] There is a woman in France who is a *prisoner* like you.* And in that prison, she has great courage. Perhaps, one day, she also will study your call. Father, this idea comes from a woman, and that woman has sometimes predicted correctly.

I will think more about it. . . .

Good-bye, Father.

[Emilie d'Eymard (Claire Démar) to Prosper Enfantin, December 29, 1832, Fonds Enfantin 7647, "Archives," 5: 518 verso–520.]

December 29, 1832

To Father,

Since you have gone into prison, I have chosen a rather serious mission for myself. I'm trying to bring the republicans to us. I'm having a really hard time, Father. There is one whom you doubtless know, Adolphe Rion, whose writings are published under the name of *Father André*. Next Thursday, he will come back here to spend the evening with me; and during the week he is supposed to visit your son Lambert. This man will belong to you within a month. I see others who belong to the society of the Friends of the People. There is one who makes me lose my mind. I would give up on him, if he were not the head of the party and, as such, very important to win. He has great hostility on the religious issue. He is named Louis Le Maistre and lives at 101 Faubourg Poissonière.

---

*Reference to Caroline de Berry, imprisoned after having attempted to provoke a rebellion against the rule of Louis-Philippe. Démar was sympathetic to the person of Caroline de Berry, if not the politics—perhaps because of the scandal the prisoner caused when it became obvious that she was pregnant. (She claimed to have been married secretly to an Italian nobleman, although it was not clear that this was the case.)

There is another man who makes me suffer even more. He is named *Franque*. He is the editor for the review of journals at the *Messenger*. It would be a good thing if a few enlightened men of the Doctrine would try to reach him. He is a cold, egotistical person, who believes in nothing, and calls everything said and done by *you yourself as well as your most devoted sons* charlatanism. He is violently carried away when anyone wants to prove to him that he judges that which he knows nothing about; and it's true, for he has not studied the Doctrine. You will see for yourself by a question he asked me. He asked: "How could one succeed in preventing marriages of convenience?" I answered that they would be destroyed by the practice of classing people according to their ability and remunerating them according to their works. This man is so deeply wicked that he makes me feel a great disgust for the society you are sacrificing yourself to. What ingrates! what insults! in return for your devotion. My word is nothing to him. I desire for him to hear a stronger one by your order.

I doubt that anyone can bring him to understand and practice your *work*. It is too beautiful *for his personality*, but he is dangerous. His caustic and nasty wit harms us. Your *own* behavior, Father, and the devotion of your sons had made an impression on quite an important man, the brother of Alphonse Rabbe, the author of *Several Summaries of History and That of Alexander, Emperor of Russia*. This man is full of courage and pretty well connected in society. He can be persuaded to understand that which is noble and great. But this accursed Franque near him worries me very much. Oh! I often, very often, feel a mortal disgust when I cross paths with people so deeply corrupted.

My God! Father, if you could multiply yourself, we would go faster, much faster. Your word and presence would convert the strongest disbelievers. You give us the proof of that by your stay in prison. As for me, I am not surprised by your success; for right in the courtroom itself I announced in advance that prisoners and jailers alike would all soon be subjugated by your word.

I now come to the women; we don't love each other yet. We are, however, beginning to form small groups; and we are feeling in general the need to unite with each other. Some of us see each other very often. Do you know why, Father. Because they love you, and their devotion can stand up to any test. They therefore try to discover each other and seek each other out. You know them; they are the young lady with the bouquet of violets and her mother, Madame Vincent, the ladies Bérenger, Bazin, Froligère, and *me*. Of course, all the women who follow the Doctrine love you; but they are more or less denuded of individuality; and the six I've named belong to you without reserve. The others often make me suffer. There are petty ambitions. Poor women! What disappointments when the *Mother* classes everyone.

I visited a lady of the privileged class. This lady is involved in a lawsuit for a legal separation from her husband whom she left two years ago. She is about twenty-nine or thirty years old and quite pretty. Her name is Fournier, and she lives at 11 (bis) rue Montholon. I am going back on Friday to arrange a day when I can send your son Lambert* to her. I would rather put her into his hands than keep her to myself alone; for in general the hypocrisy of women bores me, and I have very little patience when I hear them lie.

We really need some strong women to come among us; it would be time, it seems to me, to throw some writings out into society. As for myself, I am forced to give up on this for three reasons: my pen exudes too many effects of the bitterness of my thoughts; second, I am never satisfied the next day with what I have written the night before. As for the third reason, the real source of all my sorrow is the lack of money. This pain is all the greater in that I cannot even put my name next to that of someone else at those moments when one is concerned with mitigating your fate. Imagine my torment!

There is also a fourth reason: women still understand my ideas very little. Perhaps you, Father, would not approve them more. I speak, however, according to my heart and conscience. In the future, woman will most certainly be the head of the family; and the children will be raised by the Fathers working at the expense of the state. I truly have faith that the Saint-Simonian Religion will have power only when these two points are accepted by the Family.

As for marriage, I haven't explained myself yet. I will submit to you one day my ideas on the relation between man and woman.

I often have very lively discussions concerning this point; and there is one thing worthy of note: the new proselytes understand my thoughts more easily than the old members. However, I should tell you, Father, that I have quite a reputation in the family. In general, the men like me all right; the women not much, but they are coming closer to me and listen to me attentively. They all have the same opinion in my case; they say that I'm exalted and pure Enfantinian, and that the boldness of my ideas comes from my attachment for you. They rarely approve of me; but all is not lost. They modify my thoughts and throw them out into society in detached fragments as if they had made them up themselves. I do not appear to pay attention; but all these petty miseries make me suffer.

You have no doubt learned that Madame Martin and the two mad women who were supposed to go with her to Lyon have given up this journey. I was the first to dare disapprove of this project, and this disapproval has stirred up against me a storm which I bore bravely. I had a lot of trouble persuading Madame Martin, who did not give in until she saw

---

*Charles Lambert.

that the two other travelers were breaking their word. I think she bore a little grudge against me; but since she is a kind enough person, we will make it up again. I am not telling you, Father, about the party on Sunday; your son Alexis Petit should have given you a report.

It remains for me to tell you that I go to Vendel's every week to take up the opposition. For I myself do not feel like joining the houses of association or the love courts of Madame Voilquin.* The women's meetings are temporarily at a halt. This lady claims that they are almost useless, but I, on the other hand, am angry about that, for something tells me that the *journal* is run by men. Anyway, I don't really know what will happen to it; we'll have to wait.

Voilquin is setting up a meeting of men and women every Friday. I'll go see what they say. Reine and Désirée are completely Fourierist.

My letter is long, careless, and even boring. But how can one escape from this disadvantage, when you have to go into a lot of details, and I'm only telling a simple story where the imagination has no role to play at all.

[Claire Démar to Prosper Enfantin (January 1833), Fonds Enfantin 7647, "Archives," 5: 521.]

Father,

I found out too late that the republicans were staging a protest. Every time the republicans of Sainte-Pélagie** are planning something that concerns you, please let me know of it as quickly as possible.

I am sending you two letters from Adolphe R. to let you know where I stand with him. I am suffering, Father, because my life at present is still full of falsehood.

I do not share the republican's [Adolphe's] love, and I must be very shrewd to prevent him from declaring himself for me. I will see him tonight, and tomorrow I will see another republican in a higher position than he. If I hear something important, I will let you know.

Father, I refrain from giving you an account of the Paris Family;*** the news would only distress you.

The women behave like corpses and it is impossible to move them to do anything! The men understand, in theory, the call you have made to

*Suzanne Voilquin's proposal for "love courts" was published in the *Tribune des femmes* and is reprinted here.
**Where Enfantin was imprisoned.
***Reference to the Saint-Simonians who remained in Paris after the "apostles" retired to Ménilmontant.

us [women], but in practice they rebel against it. Thursday evening, I spent six hours in conversation at Voilquin's home. There were about fifty people present, men and women. I felt opposition from all sides. All the women rejected my opinions, and the men's reaction was about the same. *Only Mercier** understands the work that women have to accomplish. He defended my position.

Father, I suffer physically as well as morally. I don't really know what to do with all these people; nothing; especially without having money, because I have been unable, so far, to start work. I borrowed money, and I am going to sell my last two pieces of furniture in order to pay my debts. And afterwards, Father, well frankly, this world is killing me. Each time I close my eyes, I always see a pistol, and already I can feel the bullet entering my head. This will be my end; yes, I am sure of it.

Father, please return to me the letters from M . . . and try to understand mine, if you can. I am sick, my hand can no longer guide my pen, and my thoughts are no longer clear and are difficult to understand. You will have to guess them.

[Claire Démar to Louise Crouzat, (late May-June 1833), Fonds Enfantin 7624, no. 50.]

To Madame Louise Crouzat, née Du Parc, in Lyon,

No, madame, your approach did not surprise me. It pleases me to learn that there are perhaps some women I could call by the sweet name of sister. Up to now, I have never called anyone that. Please do not be surprised, therefore, if even for you, I use the ordinary formulas of banal and ceremonious etiquette.

Like you, I feel that *isolation* is killing us, that we need to unite and to communicate our ideas to each other. Like you, and like every woman and man, I still have to improve in many areas, and the advice you seem to expect from me, I will give without reservation and ulterior motives. I will speak to you frankly and perhaps even bluntly, because I am incapable of framing my thoughts in flowery words or sweetening my expressions. I will give you my advice in return for the right to ask for your advice when I need it.

I understand very well your position with regard to Madame Rogé and several other Saint-Simonian women in Lyon.** I agree with you and

---

*Jules Mercier was a musician who wrote songs for the Saint-Simonians. He committed suicide in 1834.
**Clorinde Rogé had accompanied a mission to Lyon, where she tried to organize the Lyon *Saint-Simoniennes* hierarchically, with herself as head.

those women who, like you and with you, have understood that today, and until the day when the Mother comes, no hierarchy among women is possible. However, there is one thing that surprised me in your letter: you tell me that *Lyon, like Paris,* is divided into two factions. If your count is correct, praise be to Lyon, city of agreement and harmony, because Paris is divided not into *two* or *three* factions, but rather into almost as many factions as there are individuals! . . . Unfortunately, our epoch has such an aversion to any sense of association and religious bonding that surely you must have miscounted.

I like the text of your sermon. You have feelings, you understand the apostolate, and if it is not a bed of roses, I clearly see that you are prepared to walk on thorns without stopping. You are the first and only woman, not only in Lyon, but also in Paris, who has preached to *men*!!

Thus, for the first time since I've become involved with Saint-Simonianism, I have found in your letter a woman who is able to, who wants to, and who *dares* to march forward. I see a woman who has enough strength to renounce the protection, help, or support (whatever name we give to our subordination) of a man or men in general. I never thought or believed that Barrault's missionary activities in the Orient* would result in anything more than spreading the word of liberation and the future and disseminating Saint-Simonian doctrines. At the same time I have to admit, and I admit with joy, that I never went so far in my thinking as to realize it is up to women to call the Mother, to discover her. All the honor and glory for this revelation belongs to you, and I would like to thank you for it. I accept it as a new road to progress. For a long time, I too looked toward this young America, a country that I always called the land of liberty and which I, from today on, will call the land of the Mother. To me, it is a rather surprising, providential coincidence that your thinking would agree so much with the historical studies I pursued all my life and that are now being confirmed by your own thoughts which give a new impetus to my own.

Without a doubt, this must sound rather obscure to you. In order for you to better understand what I am saying, I would have to develop an entire historical system, which would be quite a lot of work and would divert me from the topic of my letter.

Paris, as much as Lyon, lacks the two elements that are absolutely necessary for carrying out your generous and great undertaking: women and money.

Among all the Saint-Simonian women I know in Paris, I don't believe there is another one besides me who, with or without me, would want to join you in your work. Even I have always, up to this moment, walked

---

*Barrault had left on his search for the "Woman Messiah."

alone in my strength and independence and would rather feel the power to command than the duty to obey!

O well! Yes, I, who cannot remember an instance in my life that was not a sacrifice; I, who made the biggest and most complete self-sacrifice by renouncing my individuality at the time I joined Saint-Simonianism, something I have never had the occasion to recant since that time; I will follow you, and I probably will be the only one to follow you!

I will follow you, but only if you, like me, joyfully and emphatically sacrifice your individuality to the common good, and only if all of your acts are guided by love for humanity!

I would also have to believe and be convinced that our souls share the same ideas and feelings concerning all other matters! And, as you see yourself, in order for this to happen, it is absolutely necessary that we see each other, understand each other, and find out more about each other. Please find out whether your work permits you to come to Paris without compromising your financial situation. Because, as I have tried to convey to you, our financial resources are minimal, if not to say non-existent.

Here is an example for you to judge me by: I had violently broken my ties to the Old World in order to join the Saint-Simonians, renouncing by this act of free will a life of luxury and idleness in order to regenerate myself in a life of work and industry.

Since I felt that it was my mission to perform a work, I was in need of money. To get money, I organized a ball: but all the Saint-Simonians, men as well as women (with the exception of a small number of the most advanced who understood what I was trying to do), abandoned me. The proceeds of this event were too little to even cover the costs of the ball, and I was left with the burden of a rather big deficit.

I therefore have to repeat: you may not be able to count very much on financial help, and even less on cooperation from strong and educated women.

I had to tell you the truth, as disillusioning as it may be. But let me now add the following:

I understand your work, and I wish to be able to associate myself to it in some way. But let me repeat: we must be able to talk to each other. Therefore, please see to it that you can overcome the obstacles which hinder your trip, or, if this is not possible, let me know what prevents you from coming so that I can, if at all possible, help to clear your way.

In letting the Paris family, and particularly the women, know about your letter, I obviously cannot express my own opinion. Because the only way in which I could let my opinion be known would be to declare openly that I will leave with you, follow you—which, for me, is still uncertain.

It would, perhaps, be a good idea to print your letter, thus giving it some publicity. My initial reaction was to send it to the *Tribune des femmes*. But after giving this some more thought, I decided to wait for your permission before I go any further.

As far as the necklace is concerned,* I have little to say about it: it is a material symbol of the history of Saint-Simonianism, made by men for men, and in which women are not represented nor were they meant to be represented. Try to find out—you women who do not want in any way whatsoever to feel the influence of men's dominating actions on women, you who dread this influence even when it concerns the Mother—try to find out whether it would suit you, women, to ask for or to accept a sign that specifically symbolizes the works of men and is always given to us by a man, in the name of a man—no matter whose hand is involved in this transaction. I myself believe that we also must have our own symbolic necklace, and if we are still lacking names and acts, it is up to all of us, madame, to fill this lack. It is up to each one of us and our noble ambition to forge one of the rings, and it is particularly up to you to forge one of the most beautiful rings—you who formulate so eloquently the act, the apostolate of women, you who point out a new phase in our life of the doctrine.

In this matter too I will wait until I hear from you before placing an order with Holstein who, according to the decision of the Father, is in charge of the distribution of the necklaces.

You are perhaps aware of a brochure which I published recently.** Please let me know if you could place about a hundred copies of it in Lyon. I would send you several dozen, postage paid.

It is very likely that I will send you a short story which has not yet been published and which, on certain points, will give you more information about who I am and whether it is possible for us to work together. I say *whether it is possible* because, in spite of my strong desire to work with you, I am afraid to completely surrender myself: I have not yet found the woman who could fully and completely understand me. And—how I have looked for her—Heaven knows, I have not rejected the few who came to me! . . .

Will the future bring more luck?

It is in your hands to either fulfill or destroy a hope that came to life with your first letter.

Claire Démar

---

*Saint-Simonian male apostles wore a special costume which included a necklace made from rings representing many of the male leaders of the movement. Crouzat had asked Démar to place an order for these necklaces for some of the Lyonnaise women.

**She is referring to her *Appel d'une femme au peuple*, originally published in March 1833. Following her death, Suzanne Voilquin republished it, along with *Ma Loi d'avenir* (Paris: Au Bureau de la *Tribune des femmes*, 1834).

[Claire Démar to Charles Lambert, August 3, 1833, Fonds Enfantin 7714, no. 8; reprinted by Suzanne Voilquin in her preface to Démar's *Ma loi d'avenir*, published posthumously.]

Lambert, there is something that is stronger than the will of the individual or personal promises! We cannot lie to or fail this will which is stronger than ours. . . .

I wanted to keep the last promises I made to you; the last words which I said to you were sincere . . . who then has changed all of this? Oh, it is neither a word nor a will of man! No!

And yet, I am not leaving alone. . . . With whom? Need I tell you?

But if it wasn't his voice that lured me away, and if it wasn't he who invited me to this last celebration—at least it wasn't me who hastened his journey: he had been ready for a long time.

We met at the entrance to the same road and we offered each other a helping hand. That is all.

Once before we believed that the last hour had come, for one as well as for the other.

We were wrong, and the sorrow which tormented each of us proved that to us. We were like demons, each for the other, who fought at the edge of an abyss into which neither wanted to hurl himself without dragging the other along!

We were covered with sweat, grinding our teeth. . . . Today, we are like good and honest friends. Today, the journey is light for each of us.

Lambert, I pledge my word that we are calm, very calm! I did not believe that anyone could be so peaceful.

The last time you saw me, I was feverish. You witnessed only one phase of this strange crisis; the other is much less frightening.

In order to live up to my word, as much as I was able to, I went to Ménilmontant: I asked for you.

Désessards [*sic*]* was with me. Since we were unable to meet with anyone, we left a note with Madame Bazin.

Lambert! Good-bye. No matter from what point of view you consider this act, do not grieve over it; do not say it was bad.

For a religious man, this is the moment to submit to providence, with all its mystery.

Claire Démar
August 3

---

*Little is known about Perret Désessarts, Démar's friend and accomplice in this act of suicide. Valentin Pelosse (in *Textes*, 145–46) presents convincing evidence that he is not the same Désessart who was among the "apostles" at the retreat at Ménilmontant and who authored *Pensées politiques et religieuses du Saint-Simonien* (1833).

Letters of Pauline Roland

[Pauline Roland was born in 1805 in Falaise, Normandy. She was introduced to Saint-Simonianism by her tutor, M. Desprez, whom she had come to love. In late 1831, she began this correspondence with Aglaé Saint-Hilaire, who was charged with the indoctrination of women adherents to the Saint-Simonian doctrine. In late 1832, Roland moved to Paris, but the correspondence continued until January 1836, when her growing independence—perhaps in response to Saint-Hilaire's disapproval of her pregnancy—cooled their relationship. Roland wrote for the Tribune des femmes (book and theater reviews), although she was not part of the group calling themselves "femmes nouvelles." During the Revolution of 1848, she joined with many of these same women—this time, however, taking a position of greater leadership among them. For her activities, she was imprisoned first in Paris, then in Algeria. Her case became somewhat of a cause célèbre, and Victor Hugo wrote a poem about her. She died in December 1852, during her trip back from Algeria, her sentence commuted but her health ruined.]

[Pauline Roland to Aglaé Saint-Hilaire, January 31, 1832, Fonds Enfantin 7777, no. 1.]

It's to my mother that I want to write today, it's to her I want to reveal my atrocious sorrows, it's her whom I ask to soothe them, because I know she won't abandon her daughter to despair, and that she'll do everything she can to prevent a terrible calamity. But before I open our relation by asking an immense service, and show you a poor heart broken by sorrow, I want to thank you for the good your letter did me and let you know the deep impression it made on me and the consolation it brought me in the midst of a suffering to which I did not see any possible consolation before receiving it. Oh, mademoiselle! be happy for the good that you have done me in making me feel I could obtain the affection of a superior woman and an artistic soul, an affection I can return and whose price I can consequently feel. In baring your soul to me, you have felt that far from frightening me by the faithful portrait of your energetic personality you would give me confidence in you and in myself by showing me that our souls understand each other. May grace be rendered unto you! Angel descended from the sky to save me from my sorrow.

I won't reply to your letter today; my poor head is too upset by unhappiness for that: a single subject touches me right now, and I feel I cannot speak to you except about this. May the exalted mark of trust I am giving you not make me lose anything in your esteem and affection. I'm not afraid of that, for, let me repeat, our souls understand each other.

To ask the service I expect from you, I must first make a painful confession; the hope and trust I have in you gives me the strength to do it. For four and a half years, M. Desprez has been my *ami*.* Our first relationship together was as master to pupil; I was twenty-two and he twenty-nine. My mother left us** alone with him because he was a married man. Imagine if you can, mademoiselle, two young souls, ardent and unhappy, finding themselves constantly in contact with each other, studying literature, philosophy, and science, reading Shakespeare and Byron, and ask yourself if the sparks ceaselessly flying would not eventually devour us. What had to happen happened: unhappy in an imprudent marriage contracted four years before, and which had tied him to a woman with a sweet personality but no soul or spirit, my poor friend recognized, or thought he recognized, in her whom you will name your daughter, the woman created for him. My heart answered his, and, without admitting it to each other, we guessed our mutual affection, and this feeling made us happy. Strong in our innocence, for we couldn't consider guilty an affection totally of the soul, we saw each other every day, and every day increased our affection. But for goodness sake, mademoiselle, believe in the truth of what I am telling you. It has always been pure, pure as the sky. One time only, my friend seized and kissed my hand, and this silent cold kiss was given and received in the despair of the moment of eternal separation pronounced five days ago by the caprice of my mother, who without any motive but that of the Saint-Simonian religion adopted by Monsieur Desprez and by us, decided that he would no longer come to her home. That, let me repeat, was her only motive. She is far from being able to suspect our affection, for her soul could not know how that could happen.

Here now is what I want from you: my poor friend,*** for whom our liaison was life itself, is, as I was told by a mutual friend, reduced to the most atrocious despair. He is perhaps going to die, and society would lose a noble creature, for whose brilliant attributes it could certainly find good use. There remains only one way to snatch him from discouragement. That is to show him that his life can be useful to a religion to which he is as devoted as generous souls know how to be, in a word to call him to Paris by giving him a job that can support him and the wife and child he is taking with him. [. . .]

I have made a confession to you that my sister and my friend have never received from my lips. I ask you once again as a favor, my mother,

---

*In French, the ambiguous word "ami" has the meanings of "friend" and "lover."
**Pauline and her sister Irma.
***Desprez.

save two unhappy people in despair; for if my friend dies, I feel that I will not survive him. Oh my mother, my mother, have pity on us, save us!

The disorder of this letter will indicate to you the state I was in when I wrote it; I am giving you an enormous proof of my trust. I appeal to you as to God; you are my only hope. A moment ago, I received news of my poor friend. I am told he is in a deplorable state. My God! my God, how horrible it is to cause the unhappiness of a person one loves. [. . .]

Adieu my mother, my true mother, receive the tender kisses of your daughter, love her and pity her, she is worthy of your love and your pity. [. . .] When you write to me, do not speak of this unhappy passion; my sister will see your letter and has never heard this confession from me. Poor flower, I was afraid of breaking her; she is, unlike your Pauline, one of those souls little made for the storm of passions and which a little too much sun can whither. Adieu.

Here is how I want my letters addressed, first to me and sealed, then put in another envelope with this address: Mademoiselle Pauline de Beaurepaire, rue du Camp Ferme, Falaise. This way they will certainly get to me without awakening my mother's suspicions, Mademoiselle de Beaurepaire being her friend.

[Pauline Roland to Aglaé Saint-Hilaire, April 1, 1832, Fonds Enfantin 7777, no. 4.]

[. . .] [In your letter] you also speak about the influence of the couple-priest, and that influence, such as you describe it, certainly seems to me excellent and moral, but this same influence, exercised by the means indicated by Monsieur Bazard and which he says belongs to the moral thought of F[ather] Enfantin, seems to me monstrous. It seems to me that even if this truly adulterous intimacy of the priest or priestess with an inferior could be justified, there would still be exploitation, not as Monsieur Bazard says because the future of the inferior is dependant on the superior, and therefore the former could not freely grant or refuse without fear of compromising this future, but because of this involuntary seduction! (seduction is there for want of a better word) exercised by the person whose superiority one is forced to recognize. Then I would still ask: would the inferior, after knowing the love of the priest or priestess, happily return to his equal? Wouldn't the comparison he made between the two people and their two loves make for a continuous disenchantment? After all, mother, wouldn't he feel what Shakespeare expressed so successfully in one of his plays where one of the characters says to another: "You seem terribly misanthropic and disgusted." "Ah!" replies the other: "I have seen perfect beauty; tell me, haven't you often felt that it was a misfortune to have seen or dreamt perfect beauty." To go on, explain to me very clearly how you understand this moralization of the flesh in the future. You are admirably equipped to make me understand and adopt the ideas most distant from my own; *I love you.* I see in you what I would like to become: your noble independence and *saintly audacity* move me and sweep me along, so do not be afraid to frighten me away by anything that you have to tell me. I have, I dare say, too much true virtue to scream and blush from a new moral theory, as bold as it may be. [. . .]

Your last sentence invites me to continue a letter which is already very long: I heartily invite you, you say, to write me so that I may know what is going on in your life, which I would love to know about. And I who would love to live under your eyes, who feel the need in my rare joys and especially in my sorrows to call out to you, who sometimes when I have committed a fault according to the old society feel the desire to talk about it in order to know from you if it is good or bad—for right now good and evil are not clearly visible to me—I want to tell you what in my life is not habit, platitude, or boredom.

First, I will tell you that *my friend* has returned to the house, since my mother had no reasonable motive to allege and so was obliged to let him come back when he asked in a letter the reasons for his banishment. [. . .]

I am still in doubt [about Father Enfantin's moral theories]. That is one way of saying, madame, that while Father Bazard responds to the idea I myself had developed about the future, he could not uproot the ideas inculcated in me by Father Enfantin. I wanted with all my heart for Monsieur Bazard to be right, but I am not convinced, and while deploring the road that the former is following, I recognize in him and in those who have followed him that iron will, power of attraction, and deep love which seem to me the attributes of founders. Father Bazard seems to me to lack warmth, and I find him more philosophical than religious. He seems to be a man of conviction and his judicious doctrines can be adopted by everyone. But he does not have either the enthusiasm which sweeps one away or the boldness which subjugates. In conclusion, madame, although I accept without restrictions the moral doctrines of Father Bazard, and *today* reject those of Father Enfantin, I have *faith* in the latter and not in the former. [. . .]

[Pauline Roland to Aglaé Saint-Hilaire, May 13, 1832, Fonds Enfantin 7777, no. 6.]

May 13, 1832

I had to muster up all my courage to write to you today, mother. Your last letter distressed me. I did not find in it your love, which I had gotten used to and need so much. Throughout the letter, and perhaps unbeknownst to you, you seem to have been dissatisfied with me. Perhaps I deserve it because I have overburdened you with the details of my unhappy life. But, dear mother, I have suffered so much. Tell me, to whom else can I turn? [. . .]

You soothed my feelings of uselessness somewhat, and you showed me clearly that if God lets me live in a situation where I feel bored and where I get tired, in an unproductive way, it is most likely because this unfortunate situation forces me to progress. Then God will perhaps deem me worthy of taking on the life of an apostle* for which I yearn so much. You know the bonds which tie me down. Think of how difficult they are to break. Well, in spite of them, I am telling you today that I AM READY. And when your voice or the voice of the *supreme father*** calls me, I shall leave without raising any objections. Mother, this word was difficult to write, but I have enough faith in our father to know that if I put myself totally in his hands, I will not be a victim of whim or thoughtlessness. I would like to convince you that what I am writing to you now is the result of serious reflection on my part, of deep conviction. Yes, it is one of those resolutions of mine that nothing can ever change.

One thing that astonishes me is the way you detect my secret feelings, often even before I myself am aware of them. Thus, I recognize how right you are in saying that my feelings of love, my unhappy love, take away from me the courage to admit my inclination for the doctrine of our father. To this I would like to add that the fear of giving in to self-interest, believing as I do that the sacrifice of oneself and one's happiness is a worthwhile matter, naturally made me reject with horror a doctrine which could bring me happiness or which at least would justify those feelings that up to now I have considered sinful. But, mother, now that I have become more calm, having fully accepted that I will *never* belong to the one I love because this would destroy the happiness of *his wife* who, as a young woman, put all her trust in him and who, deprived of his protection, would remain alone, without friends and without strength in a world where her life would be filled with agony and torment; now, as I was saying, that I am able to put aside self-interest and examine the important questions raised by *our father*, I have become *firmly convinced* that his voice is that of God. I accept everything; intervention by the woman*** is only necessary to confirm what he has said.

I also have perfectly understood the necessity and the holiness of the couple priest's intervention. Again, it was through deep reflection that I

---

*Reference to a life committed to Saint-Simonian work.
**Enfantin.
***The "Woman Messiah."

understood its necessity. Perhaps if the world were organized according to Saint-Simonian principles, it would have been easy to pull out of the profound misery into which I was thrown by a hopeless love, a love against which I feel weak because it still preoccupies my thoughts and I can't find anything worthwhile in me. Well, dear mother, are you satisfied with your daughter? She has finally come around, and the slowness of her conversion must be a sure sign of her sincerity. [. . .]

There still remain a lot of things in your letter, answers to my earlier arguments, for instance, to which I would like to respond. But in explaining to you above where I now stand, I can see that everything you tell me is true. And although your letter was very crucial to my progress, it was not the only factor which helped me to be where I am today. Something happened which frequently happens: namely that during the time between my objections and your convincing response my own reflections and most of all the *Globe** already had destroyed my objections. I always give into my initial feelings and I have often written to you under the influence of these first reactions. Afterward, I like to come back to my thoughts, and the words "*I was wrong*" or "*I made a mistake*" always come easy for me, because when I do make a mistake, it is always in good faith. [. . .]

[Pauline Roland to Aglaé Saint-Hilaire, June 16, 1832, Fonds Enfantin 7777, no. 7.]

[. . .] mother, I was, as you know, at first intensely repulsed by the moral ideas of our father. I equivocated long enough to become persuaded that they were false, and now, looking around me with attention, I have come to this point. And yet a horrible hypocrisy eats away at our provincial societies even more than those of Paris, everyone *keeps a happy household* in appearance, and last year we saw a twenty-year-old woman keeping *a happy household* take two ounces of arsenic to escape the boredom of a situation made for her at the age of sixteen. This woman might have been saved by divorce or adultery. [. . .]

[Pauline Roland to Aglaé Saint-Hilaire, August 9, 1832, Fonds Enfantin 7777, no. 10.]

My kind and tender mother,

It is my poor friend who will hand you this letter. You will find him still very depressed, a little better, however, reassured, I hope, since

*The official Saint-Simonian newspaper.

yesterday he received from me the promise that never will another possess the woman who could not give herself to him. This promise was very sweet and easy to make. When one has once been loved as I was, one could not stand an ordinary love, and I do not fear that another could love me as he did. Would you believe, mother, that he thanked me as if I had only just committed a generous action; he kissed my hands and hair. He was really happy, I think. Our Irma showed herself an angel of affection and devotion for the two of us. The poor child suffers from my situation. She does not suspect that the joys of such a moment compensate for the most cruel ills. [. . .]

[Pauline Roland to Aglaé Saint-Hilaire, August 23–24, 1832, Fonds Enfantin 7777, no. 11.]

[. . .] Now I want to explain what you call a *slave's promise*, the promise that your daughter did not make without reflection, and of which she does not repent even after your letter. I love, as you know, Monsieur Desprez, and yet I can still understand that I might love another as much. But it is certain that I would not consent to marry any man in a society where I could not have my perfect equality recognized with the man to whom I would *unite myself*, or rather *sell myself*. It is not domination by ruse that I want to exercise, but perfect freedom and equality. I want to be able to say: I don't love you any more; and in leaving: I am leaving; and I don't want to prostitute myself to [illegible] that I would receive only with disgust. If society were organized in such a way that I could make this declaration to the priest before everyone and see a divorce decreed, well then, I would go forward with love and maternity, which has been my most enchanting hope for a long time! Maternity, whose name alone moves me to the bottom of my soul! Maternity, the need for which makes me embrace the state that I want to take up and through which I will create an artificial maternity, to which will be lacking conception, childbirth, and nursing, perhaps the three strongest bonds which bond the mother to the child by the memories of happiness and sorrow connected to them. You see, therefore, mother, that in this simple negative promise there is no great sacrifice. On this very day I want to disabuse my friend in this respect, show him that I have not been as generous as he thinks, since I only promised not to form a bond in which I could not find happiness. I was happy to make this promise since it makes him happy. I saw myself loved by him as few women have been. I feel that I could no longer satisfy myself with a weaker love, and that deprived of youth and beauty I can no longer inspire one like it. What then can I fear? the impossibility of contracting a *marriage of reason*? But in truth I would love to put myself in this impossibility, even if the circumstances that accompanied my promises had not been what they were. Mother, I have known happiness; I have been held in his arms, and although the pressure was light when I called for a violent embrace, I have known, I believe, what is best in love. My life is fulfilled in this respect and now I am going to turn toward a greater and more useful goal. You will be satisfied with your daughter. But this promise was necessary; it was necessary for the fate of your daughter to be irrevocably fixed, and for her to see tranquility once more in the features of the man she loved. Isn't it true, mother, that I did well? [. . .]

[Pauline Roland to Aglaé Saint-Hilaire, October 24, 1832, Fonds Enfantin 7777, no. 16.]

[. . .] Furthermore, I don't think I will have to suffer like the other women who find themselves in the same situation.* The experience of my whole life has taught me that I naturally exercise a great influence on everyone around me; I have not found a single person on whom I haven't done so after knowing them for a few days. Everyone has loved, respected, and listened to me. Would this be different in the future? Furthermore, I am not very sensitive, no one can humiliate me, because my loftiness increases considerably my consciousness of my value. The exterior world can do very little to me. Usually meditative, I mix with it very little and can be made unhappy only by myself or by those who are a part of me. Other people as *individuals* are as if they did not exist; as members of the humanity I adore, it is another thing. You see here a frankness that is perhaps a little bit conceited; but I don't care, the letter will be sent to you as it is. [. . .]

[. . .] [M]y mother wrote to the editor of a journal published by the women of the doctrine.** She received a reply which I unsealed, thinking I recognized the handwriting of Pauline,*** and that the address was wrong. Fortunately she did not notice. This letter, signed Suzanne Vulpion [*sic*], I think, disconcerted her a bit; it was sweet and simple. These ladies seem to have been totally deceived by my mother; at the sight of her first letter, they solicited her objections. She has nothing but hatred for our holy faith, and the most odious and brutal hatred, she is one of those people on whom nothing normal can have any affect; she does not think, she loves nothing. Hate! That's her whole life. What good can be done with such a person? I ask you? We have therefore abandoned her for a long time. [. . .]

---

*Pauline is seeking to leave Falaise and find a position as a teacher in a girls' boarding school. For a picture of the difficulties of women in such a position in that period, see Charlotte Brontë's novel *Villette*.

**The *Tribune des femmes*.

***Pauline Chevalier was one of the bourgeois ladies of the former Saint-Simonian hierarchy.

[Pauline Roland to Aglaé Saint-Hilaire, January 6, 1833, Fonds Enfantin 7777, no. 20.]*

[. . .] My mother writes and tells me among other idiocies that she is sure I am writing in *La Femme nouvelle*. I replied to this imputation as I should. Oh that wicked woman! that wicked woman! When my poor Irma is rescued from her claws, we will not long thereafter remain friends, *I hope*. [. . .]

[Pauline Roland to Aglaé Saint-Hilaire, June 18, 1833, Fonds Enfantin 7777, no. 23.]

June 18, 1833

Mother,

It has been only two days since you left me and I am already writing to you; but for several days, several weeks in fact, I have been feeling the need to write to you. Mother, there are many things that I do not dare tell you and my love for you is one of them. I am overtaken by a sort of modest repulsion from talking about it face to face with you, and yet I want you to know it, mother. I want you to accept it.

Mother, for some time now, you have been telling me things that have broken my heart and made me cry in front of you, cry like a baby, but they have made me cry even more when I am alone. Yet they were blows of a club that stunned me without knocking me down, and without killing me. A few hours after the fall, I was again standing stronger and more courageous than before. Mother, do you remember the two times you expressed the desire for me to give you another name than that of mother? Do you remember what I answered? Have you well understood what your Pauline, she whom you once named your beloved daughter, felt? Mother, do you accept it?

Think about it, mother, I want to be *your daughter*. It's up to me to take care of you and make you happy. It's up to me to *nourish* you if one day you lack bread. But also, Mother, it's up to you never to hide from your daughter the place of your retreat; you should never be separated from her except by death, and even then, Mother, it's to her that you will bequeath your thoughts. It is she whom you will charge with the duties that death might prevent you from carrying out to completion. Mother, do you count enough on your daugher to want all this?

Mother, I don't need an answer, what good would it do! Won't I see this answer in the way you kiss me when you come back; won't I sense

*Pauline has now left Falaise and is living in Paris.

it in the way you pronounce the words *my child*. And now don't you believe that this word moves me right to the bottom of my soul? And when I say *Mother*, you will also understand me? And the two of us alone together will understand each other, and yet one day our bond will be known by all men and women. One day you will solemnly adopt me and say aloud: Behold my daughter. But on this day you must be proud of her. Mother, this day will come. You know the nature of my faith and will. You know my enthusiasm. You will see, Mother, you will see that it does not march alone and that there is also reason and reflection in your daughter. [. . .]

You no longer count on me any more than on the rest of the women. Mother, I am not complaining, but I feel that there is more to me than the others. I especially feel that God leads me by the hand more than the others. His protection is palpable and should be striking to everyone. Mother, he wants something from me, I feel it and insistently ask him to tell me. [. . .]

Mother, perhaps you don't notice that your daughter is making great progress. Mother, I am worth much more than when I was near you, when my pride was perhaps wounded without my revolting. I do recognize superiors. I don't have any more individual love, or at least it no longer dominates me; for that which I feel for you or for the FATHER is social and hierarchical, so to speak. I am becoming calm without losing my warmth; I am no longer seeking the love of others with the sort of fever that used to make me do so before. I can wait for everything, even for your adoption and affection. I can wait, and wait with ardent desire, but with patience. Thank you, Mother. It's you who have given me all that. [. . .]

Mother, I spoke to you of a retreat. It is because I believe that your retreat is near if the FATHER is hiding from everyone. You will discover him, and you will take care of him in spite of himself and without seeing him. Your daughter would do it if she were you. Your daughter would leave with joy the society where she is one of the fortunate ones to share with you this sacred function. But you must allow her to do it, and you won't. And to you alone belongs this glory; you have paid for it dearly enough. But your daughter will remain the only bond between you and society; and maybe once a year you will permit her to see you and to kiss your hand. The rest of the time you will authorize her to consecrate her life and work to you and the Father. Mother! Mother! Yes, in this retreat, it is your daughter, your daughter who is also the daughter of the FATHER, who will nourish both of you. Mother, this is not a mad enthusiasm which makes me talk like this. I will do what I say. Mother, you alone will remain close to the FATHER, I *alone* close to you.

Adieu, Mother. I had a lot to tell you and don't recall any of it. Mother, I will see you soon, and you will find out then the things which I omit today; but I did not want only to say those things, but also write them, also engrave them in bronze. Mother, keep this letter; it was written in a single impulse and I don't have a rough draft. Think of it as a contract between us; I'm making you its trustee. Adieu again, *Mother*.

[Pauline Roland to Aglaé Saint-Hilaire, March 21, 1834, Fonds Enfantin 7777, no. 28.]

[. . .] You are uneasy about my new situation with respect to Monsieur Guéroult, and I can easily see why. His past offers little certainty about his future, and you are afraid to see me fall back into sorrow. I hear your voice and advice, and I can tell you all my thoughts about this.

A woman who approached love only for personal happiness would certainly retreat, but I see something else here. I have already told you I think that the era of abstinence and celibacy is over, and there is nothing more to be done with them, because that would be to hang onto the past. I don't believe this means that every Saint-Simonian woman should throw herself into the arms of the first man who comes along. But each woman, like each man, should seek the other half of him- or herself, seek it in risking sorrow or their life, for man without woman and woman without man are impotent. This is what I think with respect to everyone, and now I will tell you what I think about myself: I have interrogated myself pitilessly; I had come here for that and I think I know myself now.

I am a woman of love, but not of mystical love, love of the flesh as well as the heart, complete love in sum. The celibacy I kept for so long, and which I reentered more than two months ago, has been painful for me. It was sometimes worse than that. Listen and don't hate me; it was vicious. You understand, and you condemn no doubt, but I have really suffered, you see. I have suffered physically and morally atrocious pains, and even since I've been here, desire has so raged within me that I have rolled around in my bed screaming. That is my nature, not beautiful to you, no doubt, but I don't prettify myself; women really must tell the truth today.

Today, it is M. Guéroult whom I love. Among all the others who surround me, there is not another I could imagine loving. He lives in a different world from the men whom I would feel worthy of saving through my love. But to those men I would *give myself*, while with him I *am happy*: I receive as much as I give. Yet, I do not feel as if he were my *husband*, and I do not believe this love will last *forever*, neither on his part nor on mine. I love him because I can talk to him like I talk to you, without fear of hurting him. I love him because I do not know any man who is more honest and more faithful, and, though consumed by desire, he would not buy me with a lie or a promise. I love him because we are both free, as free as we were a year ago. I have been carefully thinking about this since September, and I have taken enough risks already, which is why I do want to be cautious. Occasionally, he has been irresponsible, because he is young and is still trying to find himself. But he has always been honest, sometimes to the point of being rude. No, I do not want to be a victim just for the pleasure of being one. But neither do I want to be the victim of what remains of Christianity, no more than I want to be the victim of a man. Thank you, thank you a million times, for your fears. But I would appreciate if you would explain yourself more clearly. What are you afraid of? That I will be abandoned? I am prepared for that, and this possibility was part of our contract, which is not to say that I would not suffer if it happened. [. . .]

I am tired of bearing my life alone, and I am waiting for the man and woman who will be willing to say: there is your road, for as I say, I'm still groping somewhat, but I would rather grope than stay seated. Oh, you whom I have called *mother!* why don't you have enough trust in yourself to take me by the hand and say: follow me. You would relieve me of a heavy burden, that of making my life myself. Last night I dreamt about you; you were suffering and tears were streaming from your eyes; you called me to you, and without knowing it prevented me from keeping a meeting with Adolphe. What does this mean? I really love you, you know, and the sorrow in which I see you really hurts me. [. . .]

[Pauline Roland to Aglaé Saint-Hilaire, November 1834, Fonds Enfantin 7777, no. 30.]

Anniversary of the dissolution of the women's hierarchy.

My dear *mother,*

[. . .] *Paris to the women;* the FATHER had said,* and I had repeated: *Paris to the women.* And I, a woman, had felt my part in the great legacy left to us by the *son* of GOD; and when to all appearances I was supposed to leave for the Orient,** I was being swept away by my affection for *our friends* and not by the conviction that my place was near them. I felt I had two things to do there: one was to present myself to the FATHER, holding the hand of one of his sons and asking him to bless a union which might last for only a few days; the other idea was to establish in the service of the FATHER in his state of celibacy a corps of vestals, specifically charged to serve his person. To these two works was

---

*These words were first uttered by Emile Barrault in January 1833, when he left for the East with the Compagnons de la Femme.

**Roland considered joining the Saint-Simonians in Egypt and wrote constantly about her indecision throughout 1834; she finally decided against going.

connected a political work. There was, I think, something in this, but if I did not leave, it is because that was not the work that providence destined me for.

Today *mother*, listen to what I want. [. . .]

Abstinence, always abstinence; is this living? Is this going forward? So why would I continue to spend in celibacy a life in which the twelve most beautiful years were consecrated to this ferocious Moloch of the Christian. Is this my desire? And isn't every desire holy to HIM who *put* these in our hearts! But in leaving celibacy, I should not, I feel, become either the wife or the mistress of a man. I want to give myself to him, as I feel like it, with the title that suits me and only as long as *I* would like, and such as *my* woman's will is today when I feel *my husband near me*, to give myself above all for the good I can do to the man I shall give myself to. This will is still that society know everything except the name of the man I shall give myself to. I shall allow it the suspicion, but I don't want it to arrive at certainty. And he alone who can understand and submit to this woman's will, he shall renounce the right to *protect* me, and not even believe that he has *this right* with respect to me. That man will be strong enough that I won't think I am demeaning myself in giving myself to him; for he will have been carried away by me, voluntarily abdicated his masculine role, and acknowledged not only the equality between man and woman but the superiority of a woman over him as a man.

Another question that has also been resolved for me is that of motherhood.* I desire to be a mother—a *mother*, but with a mysterious paternity; I have questioned myself pitilessly on this subject. I asked myself whether in the state of sickness that pregnancy always brings I would be strong enough not to ask a man to give a name to the child in the eyes of society to whom he would be the father before GOD. I also asked myself whether I had the right to give life to a being who would be rejected by society because of his birth. I resolved both questions in the affirmative. I will be proud of my maternity, and my child will be proud of his birth, and his mother will be great and saintly in his eyes. [. . .]

[Pauline Roland to Aglaé Saint-Hilaire, June 24 (1834), Fonds Enfantin 7777, no. 31.]

June 24, at 3 o'clock

Since Friday, I have had a strong desire to see you, mother. An *important revolution* took place in me and I did not want to keep it from you.

---

*Roland is already pregnant.

But it happened so suddenly that I needed time to think about it in order to explain it to myself. Was it a mistake? Was it a further step in the direction toward God? I did not know. I needed to learn by suffering and from the suffering of others. If it was a mistake, I would admit it to you and we would seek to learn from it. If it was good, I would thank God for it.

Friday, I gave myself voluntarily to Monsieur Aicard. He is a strong and noble man, but skeptical and in great distress. I hope to save him by making him happy, and already, through me, he has come to believe in love and the sincerity of a woman. His life, which I already know to a certain extent, is far from being as pure as Adolphe's. There is unhappiness and there are faults, all caused by pride and atheism.* Three hours after I had given myself to him, I received a letter announcing that Adolphe was coming to see me, and I feared that he would feel a deep sorrow. Immediately, I had a note sent to him in which I explained what had happened, and he came to my house as soon as possible. Our meeting, which lasted three hours, was sweet and good for both of us. Adolphe proved a noble and deeply religious man. He cried about losing me but felt that I was a great and strong woman. Perhaps by ceasing to be my lover now, he will become my best friend forever. He has not forgotten that the child I am carrying came out of his happiness. But today he understands fully what I myself have always felt, that I *alone* was the *family* of this child. He will love the child but will feel no rights to it. [. . .]

Good-bye, *Mother*. I love you and embrace you. I have told no one what I have just told you. I don't know what I will do later on. For the moment, it seems to me that hardly anyone is capable of bearing the whole truth. At noon, both will be at my house. They love each other dearly, and I hope that their conversation won't be painful.

Pauline
7:00 a.m. on Tuesday, June 24, 1834

[Pauline Roland to Aglaé Saint-Hilaire, October 9, 1834, Fonds Enfantin 7777, no. 34.]

It has been ages since I last wrote to you, dear mother, but you should not think that I have forgotten you. I was very busy, and I was sick again. That is why I could not write to you. As I told you, I recuperated for two days after my trip to Paris. And I felt so well that I hardly let a day pass before I started to work again, and with a sense of fury that usually takes hold of me when I live alone. For several days, I worked

---

*Adolphe Guéroult (who was still Roland's lover when she began the relationship with Aicard) was a Saint-Simonian; Aicard was not.

twelve to fourteen hours, hardly taking time out to eat. As a result, I fell ill again and it is only since yesterday that I feel better. Aside from being physically ill, I also felt morally distressed again. But finally that passed, and what remains are only headaches and the kinds of aches that are typical of my condition. I hope to return once more to Paris before the delivery. This will be my last trip and I will spend my time shopping for the baby. Irma still does not know about my condition, and this state of dishonesty between us is very distressing to me. But I fear an outburst of sorrow would be fatal to me in my condition. It's not only myself that I must take care of now, but also the little angel that I carry under my bosom and whom I already love dearly.

For several serious reasons, and in particular due to the necessity of a strong will to continue working, I have decided not to breastfeed my baby. This was an enormous sacrifice to reason on my part. I have a very nice wet nurse who lives only twenty minutes walking distance from my house. I therefore will see the baby every day since I have made up my mind to stay in the countryside.

Please forgive me for mentioning these insignificant domestic details. But I feel as though what is important to me cannot be boring to you, and that these four months of almost complete separation did not turn me into a stranger or make you indifferent to me.

When I go to Paris, it will be very obvious that I am six months pregnant. Would it be unpleasant for you, because of your dear father, to receive me at your home in the state I am in? Tell me frankly and without fear of hurting me. It would sadden me if you yourself did not want to see me, but if it is only because of him, it would hurt me less than a pinprick. There are not too many people to whom I grant the right to judge me, and those I respect sufficiently so as not to fear them.

I am often alone, and the absence of M. Aicard, which will have to last for another six weeks, is hard for me to accept. Sometimes I wonder about my peculiar and bizarre fate: born to have a family, to be with loved ones all the time, to give and take care continuously, in other words, not to live alone—I always find myself separated from those people whom I love the most. I don't think that this is a coincidence, and although I accept these circumstances, I keep looking for signs of God's will in them. At this moment, I don't feel up to any great act. I do not even know for sure whether this will ever be my lot. But I am ready and when my day comes, I will not fail to recognize the call of God.

Today, a man is suffering on my behalf. But his suffering will make him grow, and it will serve as an example to him and to me. Whether for good or ill, it will not be for naught. Another man, rather sick, is sometimes happy and at other times victim of horrible tortures because he fears losing me and needs to have me forever near him. One of these days, he will completely recover from it; and the hate he currently feels toward the FATHER will change to love. At that point, he will be a strong arm to help build God's work. I am not sure whether I am mistaken, but I feel that he will be the one with whom I will accomplish great things. At the moment, his entire life seems to be limited to his *adoration* for one woman. But, already, he is vaguely tormented by the desire to do something for her and through her, and he knows that this woman will not mistake abject things for great deeds: she can wait, for him as well as for herself, but she cannot be mistaken. [. . .]

[Pauline Roland to Aglaé Saint-Hilaire, December 3, 1834, Fonds Enfantin 7777, no. 35.]

December 3, 1834

I was unable to visit you, either because I had sharp pains or because extreme fatigue stopped me at the moment I had set aside for this. Most of the time I am detained by my work, and, in spite of my condition, I am forced to spend some of my time in libraries or reading rooms, preparing my work for the newspapers in advance so as not to lose my position during the time I will be ill. I decided to write to you, not because I wish to announce my return [to Paris] or to give you my address, something the men should have done, but to tell you how really pleased I would be to see you or to receive from you some sign of your affection for me.

One thing I should not forget to mention is that I was informed of M. Enfantin's* return, which has made me ask myself whether my presence at your house, given that my condition is quite apparent now, would not cause you some unpleasant scene.

I have not quite made myself at home here and do not dare to ask you to come and see me. I fear that I would make you waste your time, since I am at home *for certain* only in the evening. But in the evening, I would love to see those who, even though few in numbers, come to let me know that they have not forgotten me. I therefore would like to ask you to give my address to those who express a sincere desire to see me and to tell them that they are sure to find me at home after 7 p.m.

I am perfectly satisfied with my work. I have more than I can handle, even though I do work a great deal. My historical study will be published this month. Unfortunately, I always have to wait to be paid and the move into my new and quite nice home has cost me a lot of money. Even though I am far from having paid for everything, I hope eventually to be able to pay for it all.

I embrace you and love you.

P. R.
10, rue Jacob

*The father of Prosper Enfantin.

[Pauline Roland to Aglaé Saint-Hilaire, January 7, 1835, Fonds Enfantin 7777, no. 37.]

January 7, 1835

Do you by any chance know of a maid or a housekeeper who could stay for the entire day? Who could perhaps even sleep at my place until the end of my confinement? I am very dissatisfied with the one I brought back from the country. She is terribly filthy and does not know how to cook. I am extremely busy with my work and need someone I can count on and whom I do not have to supervise constantly. Cleanliness is extremely important to me, and it is also of great importance that she have the talent, if not the skill, for cooking. [. . .]

I am in rather good health. For the last two weeks I feared that this would change for the worse, due to an increased workload forced upon me by the articles which I foolishly agreed to do for the *Encylopédie pittoresque*. On several occasions, this extra work kept me up until two o'clock in the morning. Thank God I was able to finish the most urgent one, and now I can spend two or three days taking care of the necessary preparations for the arrival of my child. In the six weeks since I have been in Paris, I have been able to write no less than sixty columns for the encyclopedia. This was an enormous amount of work. Unfortunately, the encyclopedia pays less than it used to. Nevertheless, I am happy to have a guaranteed and regular job. [. . .]

Pauline
10, rue Jacob

[Pauline Roland to Aglaé Saint-Hilaire, September 17, 1835, Fonds Enfantin 7777, no. 41.]

Madame,

For a long time I have been noticing on your part a coldness that I did not know how to account for. I have loved you very much, you know it, and there is no woman whose friendship I desired as ardently as yours. For a long time I thought I had attained this end, and when I saw in you an affection so dear to me fade away, I wondered in vain what I had done to deserve it. I found nothing. Nothing is as antipathetic to me as false situations, and so I desire to know where I stand with you. I demand an explanation that I think I can expect from your frankness. For a long time I have had the desire to ask you for this explanation. I was hoping that the cloud would blow over. I was counting on trying once more to see you, but I haven't had the courage to confront you in a conversation like the one I had with you about six months ago. [. . .]

Adieu, madame, whatever your answer, I will always preserve a grateful memory of your past kindness, and if you disavow me today, I will wait for better times and trust in God for the future. From a friend who does not fail

Pauline Roland

Letters of Suzanne Voilquin

[Voilquin's letters to Enfantin are from the years following the Egyptian adventure. Earlier, her relationship to the inner circle of Saint-Simonians had been ambiguous; she was both insider and outsider—insider because she and her husband worked for the movement, supervising the communal meals at one of the maisons de famille; *outsider because she was never part of the hierarchy. In Egypt, however, where class distinctions among the Saint-Simonians seemed to have mattered less than in Paris, she became closer to Enfantin and to the other bourgeois Saint-Simonians (especially Charles Lambert and the Rogés). These letters suggest the distance that Enfantin had chosen to put between them again when they returned to Paris.]*

[Suzanne Voilquin to Prosper Enfantin, January 6, 1838, Fonds Enfantin 7627, no. 60.]

My heart is full of love and anger for you. I must relieve it today of all the bad feelings to keep in it only the love for you that I vowed for eternity.

You were unjust and hard toward me when I told you in confidence just before leaving Cairo how much I suffered from having to owe anything to Delong.* You did not fear to leave me captive to this martyrdom, even as you counted on me to be useful to those ladies during their voyage back home.** You were very concerned with providing them the

---

*Voilquin never writes about her relationship with Delong; the information for piecing the story together comes from Charles Lambert's Egyptian journals (Fonds Enfantin 7744, 7745). Voilquin had had a sexual relationship, and a child, with Delong in Egypt. Much to Voilquin's sorrow, the child died after only two weeks. After she had become pregnant, Delong urged her to marry him, which she considered; but after their child died she decided against this. Her desire not to take money from Delong for the return voyage seems motivated by a desire to be sensitive to his feelings of rejection rather than any anger on her part at him. Both Lydia Elhadad, in her introduction to a recent French edition of Voilquin's *Souvenirs d'une fille du peuple*, and Valentin Pelosse, in his commentary to Démar's *Textes*, state that Lambert was the father of Voilquin's child. Although the archival sources are clear that this was not so, it is possible that Lambert and Voilquin did have a sexual relationship after she broke off with Delong, but before their child was born. Lambert's diaries are ambiguous here and a lot of information has been crossed out.

**Reference to Caroline Carbonel and Judith Grégoire. Voilquin, who had been trained as a midwife in Egypt, delivered Grégoire's baby on the return voyage.

means to make that voyage, and yet you let me leave, me your daughter and friend for six years, without offering me the least mark of interest. You had, however, been apprised of my financial situation, for, not daring to tell you about it myself, I resorted to a rather crass ruse in order to leave you without the slightest doubt about it. But no. Caroline came back, and your silence was the only answer she brought me. This was the very thing that forced me a few days later to accept the 800 piasters that Delong offered me.

Later, at the time we boarded the boat, I wanted to tell you one more word of farewell although I was very sick. But it, like the letter written to Lambert, also remained without a reply. My heart was broken by this injustice, but I kept this in the mystery of my inner self, for those ladies were not its cause. And so they found in me, in spite of my secret sorrow, a devoted and spirited companion.

In the eighteen months that have just passed, I have often thought about the way you acted toward me, and I confess that it has seemed to me even more harsh and inexplicable since I have come back to France. There were three of us who left Cairo, and all three of us arrived together in Paris. I was received because you had written ahead to recommend the ladies, and all three of us were welcomed with affection by the proletarians. [. . .] Your first letters, so impatiently expected, finally arrived. You asked about the two travelers Judith and Caroline, and that was all. This act of seeming to disown me before these brave souls [. . .] at a time when the loss of my child still weighed so heavily upon my heart was neither just nor politic; it was cruel. My sorrows and lamentations were laid nowhere but on the bosom of God. I did not hate you in the least. I would not have known, and I still don't know, what name to give you when talking to you, but before society and those who called you father, you were always the first among men, whom I constantly sought to make both better known and better loved. With this huge weight upon my heart I had to reject your pity, for the money you sent without writing a word took that form in my eyes, and never will pity be to my measure. [. . .]

Listen, five years ago, I wrote you in prison, "I want to try to form a family of proletarians for you, and we will involve ourselves with a few women of religious but above all moral feeling. The further we advance, the vaster the horizon we will embrace. Do you want to help me with your influence upon the men?" At that time you had no confidence in me and sacrificed me to Cécile.* Cécile in turn disavowed you and has since descended into limbo. And I, a poor proletarian, have always remained straight and firm under the divine thought! . . . What are you

---

*Suzanne had solicited the assistance of the Saint-Simonian leadership for the *Tribune des femmes*, but received none. Cécile Fournel's *Livre des actes*, however, was fully supported by the movement.

today? Will you answer me as you did then, "I am dead"? I come to you with the same thought and feeling. You know me better now than then, and so in this letter I won't give you a program or detailed plan. I'll just tell you that I am filled with love for my sex, with faith in God and in the future. From another point of view, do you know what obstacles are for me? If you doubt my strength, look at the year which has just passed. Although I have often had nothing to eat but bread watered by my tears, I have received a diploma, and I am ready to send to the printer a bound edition of my letters on Egypt with many additions.

In this letter I put an end to thoughts which are painful to keep in a loving heart. I am outlining for you the direction of my ideas on the future along with my present situation and resources. It is almost complete. Until your reply, I must end here and wait.

Suzanne

P.S. It is not at all without purpose that I spoke to you about the little volume I intend to bring out soon. Are you willing to let me dedicate it to you, with or without your acknowledgment as you deem fit?

[Suzanne Voilquin to Prosper Enfantin, January 29, 1838, Fonds Enfantin 7627, no. 61.]

Amnesty already! Even though you replied to only a few parts of my letter, and even then very incompletely. Amnesty even for "rebel," a term that I do not accept. If, in this life, *God* should one day put us face to face with each other, I will be able to prove you were wrong, in the event however that the happiness of seeing you again does not completely absorb my being.

No, you know neither *how much* nor *how* I love you if you thought that I wanted to compromise you by the desire to link you to just any activity no matter what. If you knew how much I make you *great* and *beautiful* in my thoughts, you would *never* fear anything from me that could debase you. But just like you, I also say at this time, let us leave the past behind and talk about the present.

I did not seek to obtain a diploma in midwifery except to use it as a *means*. I said to myself let us heal the *flesh*, and the *spirit* will be with us, and the *heart* will love us. With this thought in mind, I would want to use this means for women, and especially unwed mothers, only free of charge. I had at first thought about writing a few newspaper articles to subsidize the expenses of my home, but that work would take too much of my time and also detract from my project and the studies in homeopathy connected to it. Therefore, I have to give it up, especially since I'm taking my old father in to live with me, and make of this noble task a *trade*, but in any event the least often possible. In spite of this, I intend through my position and my free and independent situation to establish a center of influence important enough to produce at a later time an enormous good. This good will extend not only to maternity but also to all the feelings that make up life, for I do not in the least wish to see grouped around me a bunch of pale copies of the Sister of Charity. It is rather woman that I wish to see rising up in all the beauty of her nature.

After your birthday celebration, I intend to plan some meetings for women. I have been involved for a long time in making them desire this, as well as in making them feel the need to give it its own individuality with regard to the men. I hope that love and a real desire for association will emerge here among the members of this little family of proletarians. My great old friend Vinçard, who has an influence on the male members that I feel to be good but too incomplete, is ready to support me in everything I undertake. As for me, I want the women to know you and to know what you have said and done for our sex. Many of them love you already, and later we will increase their number. Right now I strongly feel that God did not take away from me my dear little angel and save me from the plague so that I could spend the years he still gave me doing nothing. Yes, I will certainly fulfill my family duties. My old father and my sister can count on me, but this narrow life alone is not enough for me; it would soon smother me.

Now that you have told me again that you love me and will always love me, I accept your help in the only way you can possibly give it. The first money from such a pure source will be sanctified once again as I use it to procure a homeopathic pharmacy, which I have not yet been able to buy, and which will gain, through the confidence of the proletarian women, a general utility. Perhaps you know that since I've come back, I have been studying this science. Doctor Simon was willing to admit me to his courses for eight months, and since August I have continued this study in another clinic operated by a man named Laffitte, a proletarian whose reputation was ruined, even among us, and who in the past three years has redeemed himself completely, and has regained the general respect.

When we have our women's meetings, you will sometimes have to let me tell you the results of them, but you will continue to abstain from making any judgment with regard to the acts or thoughts of the women. You will also, from time to time, have to let me gladden your heart with some tales of good deeds and the name of those among your good proletarians who accomplished them. Your last reply is full enough of refusals, and I in no way intend for you to make any more of them about all this. From the depths of your solitude you will in this way be present at the development of those who love you. This will be the balm that soothes the tears you have caused to flow and which should have landed in your heart. [. . .]

I want you to understand that I need a reply other than the last one.
[. . .]
Adieu, friend, lover, father, adieu to you!

[Suzanne Voilquin to Prosper Enfantin, February 5, 1839, Fonds Enfantin 7627, no. 62.]

Good father and friend,

It is still doubtless the future which has the task of justifying this phrase: "What woman wants, God wants." For it is the same with this consoling thought as it is with the theory of the liberation of woman: all divine promises, and that's all for now. As for me, I want a number of things that God is in no hurry at all to realize, let me assure you.

Above all, I would like to know that you are happy and that your beautiful life does not go on in such obscurity. In other words, I would like to see events speed up so that you can come out of your noble solitude without risk and take up again in the world of deeds a position worthy of you.

In my moments of moral lethargy, when I feel as discouraged as I was in Old Cairo after a night spent crying over my child, I would like to feel your lips pressed against my forehead; or if I think of the distance that separates us, I want a few words from you. . . . Other times, in my moments of religious exaltation, I would like to be able to spread my wings and be transported as swift as lightning to your side, lay my head upon your shoulder, and murmur heavenly thoughts in your ear. But alas! silence and distance still! It's sad, but let's change the subject since I want neither to feel sorry for myself nor to pain you.

I see it as a step forward for us that your birthday will be celebrated this year. Yes, us—women and workers joined together. The invitations have all been signed by the hands of Suzanne and Vinçard. We have been notified by Réboul, who has just written to Sophie Lambert on behalf of Charles, that this celebration will find us in communion with our brothers in Egypt. [. . .]

I have finally carried out the project of association that I told you about in my previous letters. Our first meeting already took place eight months ago. It happened on June 1, 1838. You see, dear father, that it has some strong prospects of lasting and that I must be permitted to speak to you about it. We have established ourselves as the "Maternal Society Founded in Favor of Unwed Mothers." The principles that guide it will be the subject of another letter, however little you wish to know them. In order to meet our expenses, each associate contributes a small sum every month. I put in the savings bank what is left over from the expenses incurred in the course of each month. Our savings have already risen to

280 francs. In order to have a right to our services and financial aid, one has only to be in poverty and outside of legality. The poorest and most abandoned have all the more right to our services and help; in these cases I deliver their babies for free. Next June first, on the anniversary of our founding, we will establish a festival of *maternity*, which along with your birthday and Saint-Simon's birthday will make three festivals sacred to the proletarians.

Let me now add to these details about an association I consider important the names of the ladies who belong, and I am of course the directress:

Mme Julie Vinçard	Mlle Joséphine Milizet
Mlle Adeline, niece	Judith Grégoire
Mme Ménouillard de Vinçard	Mme Louise Lebourg
Two dames de Fremont	Mlle Sophie Lambert
Mme Ducatel	Mme Laffitte
Mme Léonie Serat	Mme Telle
Mlle Aglaé Ducatel	Mme Pauline Baïsas
Mlle Daix	Mme Delphine Yvon
Mlle Cécile Dufour	Mme Sophie Oudet
Mme Claire Martinrose	Mme Marie Delmare
Mme Caroline Carbonel	Mlle Baret
Mme Froligère	Mme Gauthier
	Mlles Peret

Twenty-eight ladies in all, plus a half-dozen of those gentlemen who also want to contribute each month, compose at this point the entire numerical strength of our association.

In order to obtain a little publicity for our association, I wrote two articles about it which were published a few months ago in a monthly magazine called *Providence*. The editor is a friend of ours and will take anything I care to give him. It's just vexing that I don't have more time to myself. [. . .]

Three weeks ago I received some letters from New Orleans. I don't know if it's a good thing for me to tell you all my personal affairs, dear father, but why not? I so need affection, and I believe in it so much that I want to keep on deserving it by remaining in your benevolent gaze exactly as I am, with my little band of affections as well as the sorrows and disappointments they carry in their wake.

One of these letters from abroad is from my dear [sister] Adrienne. [. . .] She is devoting herself to education, has just set up a class for girls, and does not seem inclined to come back here. I am going to write to her soon.

The second letter is from a lawyer in New Orleans appointed by the court to defend me before the court and the parish, and he informs me that M. Voilquin has filed a complaint against me which accuses me of having left the conjugal home, as a result of which I am forced to appear in court within six months under penalty of being convicted by default. He also tells me that attached to this complaint is a request for a legal separation, followed by a request for a divorce. In order to help me understand this set of legal actions, he informs me that my ex-husband has been naturalized as an English citizen, and that as an advantage of the English laws whose protection he now enjoys, he will be free after a fixed period to enter a new marriage. I was certainly far from expecting such a maneuver from Voilquin, after the way things happened between us and the letters he had written during the first year of our separation.

Wanting nothing to do with such an ugly business and well satisfied with what I did six years ago, I have consulted through the mediation of Messieurs Froussari and Genevois a famous lawyer named M. Boinvillier, so that I won't get caught in the tortuous twists and turns of the legal system. From these consultations I have learned that a woman, following the condition of her husband, loses her nationality if he desires to change his. Therefore, since Monsieur Voilquin has turned himself into an Englishman, I have quite naturally also become English, and in six months I will be very legally divorced and eligible to enter a new legitimate union as soon as my divorce procedure is finalized. What arbitrary laws! Monsieur Boinvillier was amazed and outraged by the consequences of this law that hands over to caprice the dowry, the name, and the entire position of a woman.

I began this separation with Monsieur Voilquin in a religious spirit, and I want to end it the same way. I will not reply to the New Orleans lawyer, and in a few months I will be convicted as a criminal woman. I will not remind Voilquin of the promises and even the vows he made to give me a small annual pension and to help me, with his affection and funds, bear my isolation and complete the mission I had conceived for myself. I won't tell him that since I counted on him to be the first among our brothers and to carry out someday even a part of his promises, I accepted from a friend a fairly sizable loan to enable me to learn my profession and establish a clientele. Absolutely no. Let him be free, let him make his wife and child legitimate, let him reject as if she were an inconvenient burden to be kept as far away from him as possible an old friend of twelve years and the responsibility of a common name. I'll remain alone with my debt and my old father, but also with my courage and faith in God.

I could have put a stop to this whole affair by writing the lawyer that I was ready to accept the court order as soon as Monsieur Voilquin sent me the money I needed for the trip, but what good would that do? This tactic would have been dishonest, for I know in my conscience that I have absolutely no intention of going to find him. And so my mind is made up; let God's will be done. If he had only written to me!

[Illegible] and this other friend I loved so much, Lambert. I haven't had a single word from him. My dearly beloved friend, what then do we have to do to obtain the affection of a man's heart? I loved and cherished everything that he loved; I was present at the death of his mother and the birth of his child.* For the past two years I have taken care of his daughter and the mother of this child and even his sister Sophie with the devotion of a sister, and I have done all this to show him that a great and true affection is exempt from pettiness and base jealousy. And now? Nothing! not a word for me in his sister's letter.—How sad I am, dear father, at all this ingratitude of man. Without you I would think that your sex had no heart.

Adieu, adieu. It's two o'clock in the morning, and I am going to bed calmer today because I acted out the desire that had been tormenting me for the past two weeks.

A thousand kisses,

Suzanne

[Suzanne Voilquin to Prosper Enfantin, n.d. (early May 1839), Fonds Enfantin 7727, no. 63.]

Dear Father and Friend,

Here I am, as I was in Alexandria, ready to send you a good-bye that will last a long time and will doubtless remain without echo. On Sunday morning, May 5, I am leaving Paris for a few years. . . . I am going to move to St. Petersburg to practice my profession and gain an honorable independence based on the respect that society grants to perseverance and work.

I have been working on this plan for two months, and in that time circumstances seem to have converged for me so completely that they not only made me deem this journey indispensable but also eased all the difficulties for me. I asked for friendship, help, and support, and I was immediately understood. Money, letters of recommendation, and all kinds of information were obtained for me. And so I am leaving well endowed with elements of success.

I am leaving! May your affection go with me and be as soothing as a blessing from God! You owe me evidence of it for your influence played some role in my expatriation. Yes, for a brief time I lost my faith in you. I wrote you on the occasion of your birthday celebration at the beginning of February when I was in a painful situation. I thought I had the right to a few words of consolation. . . . By the first of March no sign or mark

---

*The child of Judith Grégoire and Lambert.

of interest had come from you to me. I thought I'd been abandoned by all that I loved, that I had loved! I therefore had to raise my energy to the level of the difficulties pressuring me, and I promised myself I would force you to respect me since I could not obtain your love. Therefore, when Holstein, notified by Genevois of my approaching journey, came to bring me a mark of remembrance from you and him, it did my heart good but did nothing to change my resolution. It was too late!

Farewell then to you for whom my love is so different from all other loves. May your fatherly blessing and friendly affection go with me to those far-off lands and renew for me through the power of thought the warm blue sky of *Old Cairo*.

                                                                    Suzanne

[Suzanne Voilquin to Prosper Enfantin, February 5, 1848,* Fonds Enfantin 7791, no. 138.]

                                                              Feb. 5, 1848

Dear great friend,

Every time a desire or a plan unfolds in my head, my thoughts naturally turn to you, as toward its North Star, and seem to say to you: "would you help me find my way again."

At this time I have two means of getting out of our precarious situation. I'll just sketch them out briefly for you here. But if you are willing to grant me fifteen minutes of conversation, I'll add some necessary background.

The first plan, the one that I am the most inclined to, would be to obtain through your intervention** a tobacco shop at the Paris station for the Lyon railroad. My associate would be the sister of my Suzette, a young woman of twenty-one, for whom I have great affection. I would provide management and direction for the business; Victorine, attraction and activity; and I think that with this the enterprise would be successful.

In the second plan, for which you could also be of great help, I wouldn't be on the front line, but I wouldn't care because it will permit me, as well as my two young women, to find a lucrative employment. Here it is: Monsieur Dian, who is doing well at a hotel dining room on the rue Neuve St. Augustin, seems to me very capable in his profession.

---

*This is just a few weeks before the outbreak of the Revolution of 1848.

**From 1848 to 1864 Enfantin held a high post in the Paris-to-Lyon railroad. Many other Saint-Simonian men also held high positions in French industry and banking after the 1840s; to them it seemed the practical application of Saint-Simonianism.

He would like to obtain the food concession at the Montereau railway station from the Compagnie du Midi, in order to run a restaurant, or even a cafeteria, depending on what the importance of this station will permit him to establish.

Monsieur Dian is forty-five years old, a good family man, and in perfect command of the profession he has practiced since childhood. He brings together in his person all the elements of success, and therefore the administration could have complete confidence in his ability to fulfill all responsibilities entrusted to him.

In such a well-equipped establishment, I will easily find work suitable to my abilities, either in the laundry or elsewhere, especially if through my intervention I could influence you to make your choice for Monsieur Dian. His gratitude, he says, would have him provide a very advantageous position for me as well as for my two nieces.

I wait for your reply with faith and hope.

To you, forever,

Suzanne

[Suzanne Voilquin to Prosper Enfantin, September 2, 1848, Fonds Enfantin 7791, no. 139.]

Adieu Enfantin, I am leaving France once again. Be happy there; this is my heart's most intense desire.

May *God the Mother*, in blessing you, forget the moral sorrows you have made the women of our age suffer.

Adieu Enfantin!

Suzanne
Paris, Sept. 2, 1848

VIII

TRIBUNE DES FEMMES

[In April 1832, Reine Guindorf and Désirée Veret, two young proletarian women, founded this journal, expressing the intent to publish articles "only by women." In September, Veret stepped down; Guindorf withdrew a few months later. Suzanne Voilquin, whose first article in the journal appeared in the second issue, was codirector or director from September 1832 to the journal's demise.

The first issue was titled La Femme libre *(The Free Woman). For the second issue, these words appeared in smaller type above a new title—*Apostolat des femmes *(Apostolate of Women). In using the Saint-Simonian religious terminology for their activity, the editors emphasized their connection to that movement. The third issue used the words "*La Femme de l'avenir*" ("Woman of the Future") and the fourth issue used "*La Femme nouvelle*" ("The New Woman")—the name a group of mostly proletarian Saint-Simonian women took for their women-only association—above* Apostolat des femmes. *Later issues used "*Femme nouvelle*" above* Affranchissement des femmes *and, in 1833–34, above* Tribune des femmes. *The title* Tribune des femmes *is used for all citations herein.*

Most issues are undated. The first four issues are paginated individually; after that, issues are paginated consecutively. The Bibliothèque Nationale has a complete collection (in two volumes of 280 and 184 pages) of all thirty-one issues. The Fonds Enfantin collection at the Bibliothèque de l'Arsenal is incomplete.]

[*La Femme libre (Tribune des femmes* 1, no. 1), 1–3.]

Call to Women*

When the people everywhere take up action in the name of *liberty*, and the proletarian demands his freedom, shall we women remain passive

---

*Reference to the Saint-Simonian "call" (*appel*) to women to speak.

before this great movement for social emancipation going on under our very eyes?

Is our fate so happy that we have nothing of our own to demand? Up to now, woman has been exploited and tyrannized. This tyranny and exploitation must end. We are born as free as man, and one half of humanity cannot be enslaved to the other without injustice.

Let us understand our rights; let us understand our power. We have the power of attraction, the irresistible weapon of our potent charms; let us know how to use it.

Let us refuse as husband any man not generous enough to agree to share his power. We no longer accept this dictum: *Woman, submit to your husband!*

We want marriage with equality. . . . Better celibacy than slavery!

We are free and equal to man; a just and powerful man has proclaimed this, and he is understood by many followers.*

Honor to these generous men! A halo of glory awaits them in the future. Let us raise up our voices, and take our place in the public forum, in the new temple which recognizes rights for woman equal to the rights of man.

The age of universal association is beginning. There will be nothing between nations but industrial, scientific, and moral relations. The future will be peaceful. No more war, no more national antagonism, love for all. The reign of peace and harmony is being forged over all the earth, and the moment has come for woman to have her place within it.

Freedom, equality . . . that means a free and equal opportunity to develop our faculties. That is the goal we have to conquer, and we can achieve this only if we all unite in one group. Let us no longer form two camps: one of women of the popular classes, and another of women of the privileged classes. Let our common interest bind us together. To reach this goal, let jealousy disappear from our midst. Let merit and ability be honored regardless of social position.

Women of the privileged class: you who are young, rich, and beautiful believe you are happy when you breathe in your salons the incense of flattery lavished upon you by your entourage. You reign, but your reign is of short duration and ends with the ball. Back in your own home, you become slaves again; you return to a master who makes you feel his power, and you forget the pleasures you have tasted.

Women of all classes, you have a great power to exercise; you are called upon to spread the sentiment of order and harmony everywhere. Turn into a force for the good of society the irresistible charm of your beauty and your soft, alluring words, which must make men march together toward a common goal.

---

*Reference to Prosper Enfantin and the Saint-Simonians.

Come inspire the people with a holy enthusiasm for the immense task that awaits us.

Come calm the warlike ardor of our young men. Grandeur and glory are in their hearts, but men recognize greatness and glory only with a helmet on its head and a sword in its hand. We shall tell them it is no longer a question of destroying but of building.

The ladies of Rome bestowed crowns to warriors; we shall weave flowers to encircle the heads of the peaceful and moral men who will lead the march of humanity to a social goal and enrich the globe through science and industry.

Jeanne-Victoire [Jeanne Deroin]

[*La Femme libre* (*Tribune des femmes* 1, no. 1), 3–6.]

Until now, women have been submissive slaves or rebellious slaves, but never free.

The first group, bent to the conventions which form the base of our upbringing, are slaves to social prejudice but find protection from individual despotism by submitting to this very prejudice.

The second group, on the other hand, unfettered from general opinion, cannot evoke the aegis of this opinion they have disdained and fall under the personal dependence of men who, not bound by a unified morality, have no other sanction to their isolated principles and judgments than their own caprice or pleasure.

Although we understand the nature of women who prefer abnegation to unsanctioned pleasure, and also the spirit of order and noble pride that makes them faithful to duty, we also understand the nature of those who have not been able to submit to a law now deprived of that gentle religiosity which fills the heart and softens duty.

Their revolt was sanctified and legitimized from the moment that men violated the very law they had themselves formulated, and retained no memory of its sublime purity except to exact it of us, and to impose upon us the yoke of an austerity from which they excused themselves.

From that moment on, religion ceased to exist, and women were forced to use subterfuge in order to struggle against the egotism of men. Prejudice replaced healthy morality and kept only its mask, while the debauchery of private life increased with the dry rigidity of public life.

The first link of our chain was broken, and our freedom unfolded in the midst of a license which dragged into it women who had no consciousness of their insubordination, but also no rule to guide them wisely in the flood of dissolution that swept them away and was the ultimate negation of a morality too exclusive to remain in harmony with the enlightenment of our age. If there was once some use to our being subjected to a law which made us the subordinates of men, but at least assured protection for our weakness against the force that was also useful for the ordering and progress of humanity, it is now well known that brute strength is disappearing and being replaced by moral strength, and therefore it is useful for us to take by right the place we hold in fact. The protection of men is nothing more than an empty word. For a long time our protectors have taken advantage of the power they obtain from this title only to seduce, judge, and condemn us. Reduced to our own strength, in order to resist their immorality, we do not drag them into vice except after being dragged there ourselves by them. . . .

Glory to the women who, crushing their nature and subjecting it to the requirements of Christian law, have sacrificed to a noble pride the beating of a heart that our society could not understand since it can only play at real virtue, which it forces into the mold of a flaccid uniformity. They have preserved that dignity which results from a conscience satisfied with the sense of duty accomplished. These women have an ascendancy over men that commands respect, and makes men recognize without knowing it our moral superiority.

But glory as well to the women who have followed the instinct for freedom within themselves, thus smoothing the road of our emancipation. Wherever disorder and weakness may have dragged them, even if they be plunged in the mire, their name will one day be blessed. Branded by opinion, they have been seen only from the perspective of degradation; it is up to us to *rehabilitate* them and sound the depths of these abysses of corruption that engulf so many existences, so many brilliant hopes. . . . May the men who read and see us abstain from judging us if they do not understand the high morality that makes us act, and the religious faith that gives us the strength to conquer the reserve in which our upbringing has swaddled us, so that we may boldly reveal the profound mysteries of woman's heart, which produces a fertile source of sublime virtues or a bottomless pit of vice and dissimulation, according to whether it is developed or repressed. . . .

Without any bias, we will go back to the source of this horrible depravity that makes part of society into a true hell. There, all the resources of wit, cunning, and beauty are used to attract those not yet ensnared by this depravity or those who are as yet only on the edge of the abyss, a horrible lair where power can only demoralize and reproduce itself in a million different forms—by fraud, theft, murder, suicide, prostitution. . . . O! pity, pity for the wretches swept away by the flood. And although we ourselves may have had the strength to resist or have even been kept away by circumstances other than our will, far from placing the unhappy victims under a curse too heavy for them to lift, we will raise up our voices for them and protect them with our love and the esteem we have the right to require for ourselves, because our life has been pure of stain according to Christian law.

Whatever the past of women who file under our banner, they, like us, have a right to respect, for our banner is religious,* and more than one woman, with our support, would, if she unveiled her sorrows, make the mud fall back on her accusers even as they try in vain to cover her with it.

As the women who raise this banner, we declare ourselves free, not to violate in our own private life the ancient moral law, which we will practice until a new and less exclusive law replaces it, but free of all external forms imposed by propriety.

Practicing Christian morality as rigorously as those very people who judge everything by it, we will be bound to them by our acts and our love of duty and order. But we will also be bound to those who repudiate it, by our ability to appreciate their nature, by our abandon, and by our desire to bring them to the law that will rehabilitate them and so end the ills and disorders of which they are often the authors.

Thus, placed between two such opposed camps, one of which is as exclusive in its regularity as the other in its disorder, we will use all of our conciliatory power to end the antagonism between them and to make them appreciate each others' virtues and valor, until their mutual progress allows them, not to form a single and identical camp, but to be seated together in the new temple and be united by the same love, desire, and harmonization of personal interest in the social interest. Then the new law will come into being to give satisfaction and regularity to each of them, and our apostolate will be over. By her works woman will have elevated her nature to the height of man's, she will be his equal, and their union will bring about the reign of God on earth.

Jeanne-Désirée [Désirée Veret]

[*La Femme libre* (*Tribune des femmes* 1, no. 1), 6–8.]

This publication is not a commercial venture; it is an apostolic work for the freedom and association of women. Because we have deeply felt the slavery and nullity that weighs upon our sex, we are raising up our voices to call upon women to come with us and demand the place we should hold in the temple,** the state, and the family.

Our goal is association. Since until now women have had no organization that allows them to give themselves to something great, they have only been able to concern themselves with petty individual matters that have left them in isolation.

---

*Reference to Saint-Simonianism, which was conceptualized not simply as a social movement but as a "religion." See chapter 2 and chapter 3.
**Reference to the Saint-Simonian "religion."

In offering for their activity a social work* to accomplish, and a goal to reach, we have faith that many women will rally to us, and that others will imitate us by forming their own groups, each acting according to the ideas of the women who form them, until the time when their own work is achieved, and they reunite to form only one single association.

This publication is therefore only a means to arrive at the end we are proposing. That is why we call to all women, whatever their status, religion, or views, as long as they feel the sorrows of woman and the people, to come and join us, associate with our work, and share our labors.

We are *Saint-Simoniennes*, and precisely for this reason we do not have that exclusive spirit which rejects everything not identical to itself. Our new religion makes us see in everything that which is good and great about it, and makes us seek and take the progressive element everywhere it is to be found.

In our involvement with the work of regeneration, we are not claiming to impose upon ourselves a task beyond our forces. We will take account of the position in which women are placed by their upbringing, for we know that in general it can give them only narrow and incoherent ideas.

Nevertheless, some do escape the common law; others go easily from a very profound idea to a very superficial one. That is why we who understand what is good in these natures and feel the necessity to satisfy them all adopt an irregular form which is the distinctive sign of woman's character in our time.

We will talk about morality, politics, industry, literature, and fashion, not according to received opinion or convention, but according to our heart. We will hold less to science and the elegance of style than to frankness of thought. For what we want above all is for women to shake off the state of restraint and discomfort in which society holds them, and to dare to say from the complete sincerity of their heart what they foresee and want for the future.

Marie-Reine [Reine Guindorf]

P.S. We will publish articles only by women. We invite those who want to write in this journal to address themselves to Marie-Reine, editor, 17 rue du Caire, from noon to 4:00, everyday except Sunday.

We will also accept personal letters *relating to questions which will be discussed in our publications. (Postage required)*

Jeanne-Désirée [Désirée Veret], Founder
Marie-Reine [Reine Guindorf], Editor

---

*The French—*une oeuvre sociale*—emphasizes the creative quality of "work" and the socialist meaning of "social" (broader, more transformative, than either "public" or "political").

[*Apostolat des femmes (Tribune des femmes* 1, no. 4), 2–4.]

On Prostitution

People generally understand in the word "prostitution" only those women, about 35,000 of them, who, under the shelter of a police permit, offer to every passerby their degraded charms, stigmatized by impure caresses and accompanied by rudeness and insults—those women who are rejected by society and by men who, after having heaped their shameful caresses on them, turn their eyes away in disgust.

But prostitution is also found elsewhere. It exists in sumptuous palaces and elegant hotels, as well as in the dirty hovels of alleyways. Yes, prostitution is everywhere. It lodges with the young girl of the people who, misguided by her innocence, adds to the number of victims who contribute to the revolting glory of a clever seducer only to be abandoned by him afterward to even more unworthy hands. It is with that unhappy young woman who fights against misery by obstinately holding down a job that does not, however, pay enough to relieve her from the hunger which devours her, until she sells herself to the vulture—who watches for her moment of distress—for a piece of bread that the girl, sobbing, brings home to her old, sick mother. It is with that young, beautiful woman who has high ambitions for fine attire and the pleasures of life, but whose family is too poor, lacking a prestigious name, to satisfy her desires for splendor and glory.

Prostitution exists with you, young girl of the privileged class. With you, who was surrounded by so much care in your childhood, so many compliments in your youth. With you whose delicate feelings were finely developed through maternal education—you too will be sold. Your father will give you away as a wife, not to the one most worthy of you, but to the one who will bring you the most money, who will be capable of handsomely buying your person and your dowry. Poor girl! You too are condemned to bestow your caresses upon a stranger whom you don't know and who does not know you and who, perhaps, will never be able to really understand you. You are ten times lucky if your eyes and your heart were not set on another object of affection whom you will have to renounce. And you, noble daughter of the king, whose beautiful brow is adorned by a crown. Is your brow exempt from the seal of prostitution which marks the brow of your sisters? It is true that you were given the most beautiful guarantee that can seal the union of two people, and it is a fine thing to devote oneself to the happiness of others. But tell me, did they truly allow you the glory of sacrifice? Did they allow you the will to choose from among the rulers the one with whom you can best accord in order to educate and direct the masses whose happiness you so desire?

No, you are the slave of some diplomats who have given you away without taking into consideration either your tastes or your personal will. You have been *prostituted*. Thus, prostitution is everywhere. It is flagrant in our midst. And yet, the very men who practice prostitution so openly dare to accuse and judge other men, because the latter have the courage to protest against their immorality.* With a fearful voice they proclaim the word "scandal" . . . A historian once said that only corruption blushes when it finds itself depicted.

Such disorder should not be allowed to continue. It is up to us, women, to stop it. It is up to us to pursue, with our inquisitorial justice, every man who uses against us the right of exploitation which is given to him by old laws and current prejudices, and who would like to confine us within the limits of Christian morality as he has formulated it—a morality that he does not want and cannot accept for himself. It is up to us now to become their accusers and judges and to continually strip away the mask of hypocrisy behind which they are hiding. It is up to us to make them finally recognize our rights to a well-deserved equality, which is, in fact, necessary under the new social order which reveals other needs than those of the past.

Christine-Sophie [surname unknown]

[*Tribune des femmes* 1: 36–39.]

Improvement of the Destiny of Women
and the People through a New Household Organization

As young women of the people with no other science than that of our religion** and no financial resources except from the labor of our needles,*** we have begun a project still small and obscure, but which will assume rapid growth and raise major political questions. Relegated to the domestic hearth, the proletarian woman knows better than man what to expect from the ideal of domestic privacy and the sovereignty of the people. Illusions of political freedom make her feel more brutally the pressures of need or poverty in the family home. That is where ancient slavery has found refuge! That is where marriage is a heavy chain and motherhood a surplus to her woes and afflictions!

Only by emancipating woman will we emancipate the worker. Their

---

*Reference to the trial of the Saint-Simonian leadership.
**Reference to Saint-Simonianism.
***Désirée Veret and Reine Guindorf worked as seamstresses in the garment trades.

interests are connected, and the security of all classes depends upon their freedom. This is the problem that the zealous friends of the people have been unable to solve. They have relied on the increasing enlightenment and the new needs of the masses to destroy the antiquated privileges of nobility. They have forgotten that our sex has also advanced along with this progress and should participate in the general emancipation. We shall tell the politicians: God did not permit you to overthrow unjust prerogatives in order to stop midway and use for your sole profit the arms he entrusted to you for the profit of everyone. You will have plenty of difficulty and absolutely no success if you continue to subordinate her will to your own. If you preserve this old belief that woman's sole purpose is to bear children, clean man's house, and give him pleasure; if you do not associate woman and the people, each according to their talents, in all branches of the social order; and if you do not give flight to genius in whatever sex or class it is found, you will not be following the path of God, who wants a place and happiness for everyone, and you will always fail. You will be able to satisfy your love of property, enjoy it in tranquility, or increase its value only by changing the commercial system and associating industry with the household. Otherwise it will slip from your grasp in every way: through business problems, bankruptcy, competition, the lack of order and ability in women who are not all born good housekeepers, and the high cost of consumer goods, which results from the fragmentation of interests and inefficient distribution. These questions indeed closely affect women. They are often for women a cause of quarrels which increase social unease and will stop only when women join in solidarity together with the desire to make a name for themselves and the dream of organizing themselves and having their own laws for the social functions which belong most especially to them.

Our first step in moral freedom will therefore be used to make women understand through our teachings and writings the benefits of such an organization, so that, freed from the errors and prejudices of habit, their voices will rise up in unison to demand a new order of things and win over the thoughts and efforts of persons of goodwill for industry and household reform, as an indispensable condition for the peace and happiness of the people.

Our first steps in moral freedom will also be to glorify and make others love as we ourselves do the man who is great among all men, for the holy call to freedom he has offered women.* His words have found an echo in their hearts. We answer the call by smoothing the ways toward the WOMAN chosen by God among all women to announce to the world the new law that must govern new family relations. The moment has not

---

*Reference to Enfantin and to his "call" to women to speak out on the moral question.

yet *come* for HER;* the world is not prepared, and everything will be done in its own time; God's CHOSEN WOMAN will not remain silent. We must now concern ourselves with immediate matters. All nuances of religious opinion must fuse into a single thought, that of our emancipation. The banner of women is universal, for as sister Suzanne has said, are they not all united by the same bond of MOTHERHOOD? Among the men who understood at the same time as Saint-Simon that the time for the emancipation of woman had come, there is one whose hair has turned white in obscurity, but who nevertheless brings the key of immense labors to society. This man is Monsieur Fourier. His theories of association are the most complete of any that have yet appeared on this subject. By making industry attractive, he employs individuals just as they are with all their passions, but which become a powerful means to embellish the globe and enrich the human race in the new societary order.** Men whose devotion equals their knowledge are now engaged in preparing its realization. We are happy to count among them men who have shared our faith. We are marching toward the same goal and are not as far from it as they would like to believe. [. . .]

                                                            Jeanne-Désirée [Veret]

[*Tribune des femmes* 1: 45–47.]

                                              Women alone will say
                                              what freedom they want

Advice, counsel, and opinions come to us from all sides with a striking diversity. Each person represents himself as the liberator of women and wants to make us free in his own way. Be that as it may, I am following the goal I have set for myself, without deviating to one side or the other. Let no one believe that I am under the influence of any system. Whoever else may desire our freedom, I want it, and that is the essential point. I wanted it before encountering the Saint-Simonians or Monsieur Fourier. I want it in spite of those who oppose it, and I am perhaps working for it separately from many people who want it. But I am free. Men have advised, directed, and dominated us long enough. It is now up to us to advance along the path of progress without tutelage. It is up to us to work for our liberty by ourselves; it is up to us to work for it without the help of our masters. Let no one go about accusing me of contradiction here. The men I listen to on the matter of our freedom are not our masters. They are only our predecessors, for the customs of society have done everything for them and nothing for us. But they want neither to

---

*Reference to the "wait" (*attente*) for the "Woman Messiah." See chapter 2.
**Fourierist term for the transition stage to "harmony."

govern nor to advise us; they want our freedom, and they are fair enough to recognize that their happiness depends upon it. They do not clothe themselves in the title of liberator to keep in their hands a while longer the scepter of despotism that is escaping them. What am I saying? They reject it and do not want a happiness that will not be shared by women with complete equality. They are working as we are, but in proportion to their more developed abilities, for this great social work [oeuvre sociale], the emancipation of women and the people. But they are not our liberators; they have a right to this noble title only by halves with us, and not exclusively for themselves alone. And although the long slavery to which we have been subjected puts obstacles across our path, we are advancing toward our goal, and very quickly. You see us united—true, in small numbers but we are all working body and soul for the most beautiful of all causes that a woman could embrace, once she finds herself in this society where there is only slavery or contempt for her. And, however different are the dispositions of our character and feeling, we are all dedicated to the same goal. There are no more cliques among us, no more petty interests, and, I shall almost dare to say, no more artifice. Love of freedom illuminates the depth of our hearts like a divine torch with a thousand rays, and we can see in them a clear place for the great feelings that such a beautiful work [oeuvre] demands. Oh, women, may our example move you; may no obstacles stop you. In vain would you resist, for soon the torrent of progress would drag you along this ground which you fear to approach, and you would not have had the glory of flying there. Mothers who dread slavery for your daughters: unite under the pacifist banner. And you daughters who are broken by sorrow in your sweetest affections and feel the love of great things smothered within you by the narrow circle of prejudices that enclose you: raise your voices to demand the free exercise of so many beautiful qualities that remain in darkness. You will find an echo in all generous hearts when you make these words resound throughout society: Emancipation for the people; emancipation for woman. You will be welcomed everywhere, for we are in an era of progress, which will grow slowly but surely, and we judge its brilliance by seeing its dawn. Disregard the clamor that resounds in your ears. The fools! They mock the good path that they cannot follow themselves. Greater ideas will turn you away from all this disapproval, and once you have taken these ideas of freedom to heart, you will have in your sight the future which readies itself for posterity, and contempt would wish to arise before you in vain. You will not perceive it. You will no longer know the disgust now inseparable from the chains you bear, and your heart will no longer be dulled by the paltry pleasures your protectors now offer you. Your happiness will grow as quickly as your chains fall.

Joséphine-Félicité [Milizet]

[*Tribune des femmes* 1: 62–66.]

Excerpt of Regulations Which Unite the *Femmes nouvelles**

The goal toward which we all strive is our triple liberation: moral, intellectual, and material. But we are still far from achieving freedom thus conceived and toward which we have gravitated for such a long time. The Saint-Simonian religion, which declares woman to be free and equal to man without imposing any conditions or limitations, has left us, through its sublime confidence in our sex, with the equally great task of proving to men (still our tutors) that we are worthy of this confidence and can completely regenerate our social condition without going through a period of disorder and anarchy. We, the editors and founders of the *Femme nouvelle*, invite those of our sisters who are close to us and want to march under our banner, to reflect seriously on the terms of the apostolate which we are establishing. We call on all women to participate. In our hearts, we exclude no one and no one will be rejected. It does not matter if there are amongst us women whose lives are filled with one sole passion, or if there are others whose lively imaginations elicit the need for change. At this point, we do not have to worry about justifying or satisfying these different natures.** If we are to act as one and obtain positive results from our common efforts, it is more important to feel that our apostolate is only a preparation for the moral law which will rule the future.

The interest of our cause gives all women the duty to remain faithful to Christian morality—no matter how inconvenient it may seem in certain ways—and to recognize that it is more consistent and more religious for each one of us to attribute to our acts a general goal, rather than to act on the basis of individual feelings or the desire for the immediate practice of freedom without rules or limitations. According to us, this would only result in disorder, because who—in the absence of the law of the future—would sanctify new bonds? Let us thus acknowledge that whatever our secret desires may be, in whatever way we dream about our future life, we must remain subject to the law of the world until the day when there will be over us a couple who are superior in every respect and to whom we will grant the right to unite and separate us.

But, while still conforming our acts to Christian rules, let us learn how to merit the title of *femme nouvelle* through our devotion to the cause of

---

Femme nouvelle or *New Woman* was the title of the journal at this moment in its publication history. In the plural ("femmes nouvelles" or "new women"), it was also the name the editors gave to themselves and the group they were organizing.
**Reference to "constant" and "mobile" natures—those who desire a monogamous sexual relationship and those who desire more variety.

our sex and through our thoughts on the future expressed with strength and truthfulness. Thus, as we continue our apostolate, let us have faith that a truly great woman, as good as she is wise, will come to epitomize us all, and through her will joined to that of the head of our religion* will grant the force of law to the feelings and wishes which we have expressed.

But let us repeat: no nature will be rejected by us and we beg all women to adopt a common motto in order to form a general bond with our longed-for sister. I believe that the motto "Union and Truth" could fulfill this goal. And then, let a different color ribbon indicate how each one of us understands her freedom. For example, we *femmes nouvelles* have adopted, as a symbol of our devotion and waiting, the [deep violet] color of the Dahlia. Those who wear this sign will remain subject to Christian rules as we have outlined above. Other women, full of force and candor, plan to choose another color: respect and silence also for these women, if the free love conceived by the charm of their delirious imagination benefits social happiness. The *femme nouvelle* does not make herself into a judge of her companions; it is not for us to praise or blame. Aren't we all in the process of renouncing our present condition—be it on moral or political grounds? Let the grand council of women be established: only then can the limits of good and evil be discussed.

Suzanne [Voilquin]

No, I am not Christian, ladies; you have heard that, but have you understood? It is up to me to tell you why I am not Christian, for I aspire to your approval and would not want to see you recoil from my approach. May ideas of disorder, vice, and deception disappear; may prostitution and adultery disappear from the mind of society when I pronounce these words: I am not Christian. No, I have never known the yoke of the morality of Christ, nor have his austere duties ever enslaved me. Free of this belief from my earliest years, my feelings took flight as I grew, and when I was led to the baptismal fountain at the age of ten and clothed with the sacred sign, my young heart disavowed it, for I had already said I was not Christian. Surrounded by my young companions and as innocent as they, I perceived their saintly emotion at the sight of the God they were about to receive, and I was calm. I admired them, but that was all I could do; and this fair day of my first communion, when I was surrounded by so much pious prestige and love for the God of the Christians, found me a pagan even at the foot of the altar, in spite of the priest's holy attire and the majesty of the sanctuary. My twelve-year-old [*sic*] imagination was not in the least dazzled.

*The "Woman Messiah," for whom Saint-Simonians were waiting, would direct the Saint-Simonian religion alongside Enfantin.

It is therefore a sentiment reinforced by familiarity with the Christian religion which I have presented to your observations in telling you I was not of this religion. And what could it have offered as consolation to a person as exalted as I? What could it have offered that a person as passionate as myself could have accepted? It said that passion is the domain of Satan. To me who wants to love, it has said: do not love; to me who wants pleasure, it has commanded suffering; to me who values matter as much as form, the body as much as the spirit, it anathematized the former and exalted the latter. And its anathemas made me tremble, but a moment later I saw them break against that which they wanted to crush as they had broken against my desires. And I soon saw their impotence with regard to society, with regard to the very people who had cast these anathemas, as I had seen, with regard to me. And I saw women first accept this morality and then reject it, slipping far . . . very far . . . into the abyss! The unfortunate women had a first step to take, a yoke to break, and a whole religion to disown. And I myself escaped disorder, prostitution, and adultery, for I never knew the yoke; renunciation had never been a duty for me; I had nothing to break; and it never took any extraordinary event to lead me to love outside of marriage.

Like you, I know the happiness of an affection that fills your whole life. Like you, fidelity in love is the object of all my desires, and I never envision the passage from one affection to another without some loss of happiness. I too love the duties of a wife, and yet I do not want to bear the name, because I am not Christian. Any oath I swore would be illusory, for it would be sworn before a God I did not believe in. Sworn before the civil officer, it would still be illusory; for since I don't have any wealth to regulate, it would be nothing but a contract of sale. Besides, an oath is something absurd to me. I will not, therefore, have the respect of society or the glory of adorning myself with the title of wife, but in return I will have love and happiness, and without being contemptible.

It is in the name of these feelings I boldly profess that I call upon women today, women who love the joy of the ball and the pleasure of parties, women who find the courage to defy opinion and have not had the strength to resist those who speak to them of love, women who feel in themselves the love of great things and want love and pleasure, but who also want duties and respect—I call all of them to the freedom they already have and to the freedom that still remains for us to win for the present and especially for the future. I call them to concern themselves with the destiny of that freedom flung by the iron yoke of Christian morality far into the inevitable morass that the present social order offers them. And I present to them as pledge and sign of the communion of ideas between us this flaming red ribbon. For to this color is connected those ideas completely in harmony with our characters.

Joséphine-Félicité [Milizet]

[*Tribune des femmes* 1: 69–70.]

By My Works You Shall Know My Name

During the last meeting of the ladies, when I said I did not want the name "Saint-Simonienne," it was not because I deny the good the Saint-Simonians have done, or that I doubt the good they will do. I think that they have foreseen humanity's future better than anyone and are the most advanced men of our era. If I wanted to place myself under a name, I would certainly choose theirs.

But I feel a different work to carry out. For me, all social questions depend on the freedom of women; it will determine them all. It is therefore toward this goal that all my efforts are directed, and to the banner of the *femmes nouvelles** that I will relate everything I am doing for our emancipation. The cause of women is universal and not exclusively Saint-Simonian, for we also draw strength elsewhere. Other men understood at the same time as Saint-Simon that the freedom of women was linked to that of the people. We have already cited two of them, and it is probable that we are still unaware of others. Other men have since propagated these ideas, and they will be found to support us and to unite with us in the same thought, even though they are baptized with another name than that of Saint-Simon.

Leave to men these distinctions among names and opinions, for they are useful to them. Their minds, more systematic than ours, need to attach the progress they make to a name or an individual to act with order. But we, as people of feeling and inspiration, leap over these rules and traditions that men deviate from only with great difficulty. We should see in the human race only the children of a single family, for whom our constitution makes us the natural mothers and educators. All men are brothers and sisters united with each other through our motherhood. Men give birth to doctrines and systems and baptize them in their name, but we, on the other hand, give birth to men. We should give them our names, and take our own only from our mothers and God. This is the law that nature dictates to us. If we continue to take the names of men and doctrines, we will be slaves without knowing it of the principles they have engendered and upon which they exercise a kind of paternity to which we will have to submit in order to be consistent with ourselves. We will thus have fathers; their authority will be milder and more loving than in the past, but we will never be the equals and mothers of men.

*Reference to the autonomous women's group "femmes nouvelles."

There you have, in general terms, the motives that have made me act. I am connected to you and maintain the same motto—"Union and Truth"—but in order for union and truth to last between us, I want to be independent from everyone.

Jeanne-Désirée [Veret]
November 4, 1832

[*Tribune des femmes* 1: 92–97.]

Ladies,

We have arrived at a stage where the need for association, a religious bond that unites all individuals, is urgently felt. Only yesterday a meeting of the Saint-Simonian men took place. During this meeting, ways were proposed that would seem the best to reach this great goal, namely to link the men in such a way that they might support one another and create among themselves association and religion.*

Today, we women who have declared ourselves free and capable of taking part in this great work [*oeuvre*], i.e., that of progress and liberation, need to labor toward this goal with courage and without giving up.

If until now women have been completely subjugated and enslaved, it is because they have not been united, because they have not had an association, a religious bond among themselves. The main occupation and care in their lives to date have been limited to trivial rivalries and hatred without cause or reason. This lack of union and harmony exposes them every day to the pitfalls and brutalities of men.

Ladies, these painful reflections are based on a recent event which has just now come to my attention. A young, nice girl, a practicing Christian who nevertheless had adopted our ideas of liberty and emancipation, fell victim to a man. She was an orphan and lived by the labor of her hands, alone in a wretched hovel. Below her lived a man, a tall, strong man. She was pretty and had awakened his desire. One day, he came up to her room under some pretext and took her by force. . . . What could the poor girl do? She was sixteen, and the Court of Justice grants the right to file a complaint only up to the age of fifteen.** The law offers her no recourse. Now her tormentor refuses to rehabilitate her in the eyes of the world; he does not want to marry her, yet continues day and night to knock at her door to renew his vile attempts.

---

*Reference to the Saint-Simonian religion.
**In the French law, "seduction" of young girls under age fifteen was a crime, but rape or seduction of older girls and women was not.

This is the event which I wanted to bring to your attention.

Well, ladies, in today's society this crime bears consequences, and this girl bears the marks of the violence done to her; she will be dishonored forever and stigmatized. It will do her no good to cry out to the public: "I did not want this to happen; I defended myself, but I was not strong enough!" The public will scoff at her and reject her; men will laugh at her when she walks by; women will call out to her to be gone. In fact, it would be ridiculous nowadays to believe in the chastity of a woman. And this nice, innocent girl will suffer shame and infamy because a man was stronger and more robust than she.

These events happen everyday in our society. If we wanted to seek out and take note of all that is immoral in men's behavior toward women, we would discover that there is not one day, not one hour, when similar crimes of exploitation do not occur.

And in fact—be it rape or seduction—it is very rare that poor daughters of the people, who find themselves alone in this world, do not fail at what we call honor and virtue. Poor children, abandoned by everyone, without parents or friends to console them through the storm, to brace their spirits, and to lend them a helping hand. They are thrown into the midst of this society which offers them only danger, or whose cold indifference does not deign to bother with these hearts so much in need of love and which encounter only contempt and hurt.

Now, without support, without anyone to defend them, and without even an avenger—how can they escape men's brutality? And then, when they are sad and tearful in their isolation and turn their eyes toward those around them, they see faces frozen with selfishness, hearts that cannot respond to the beating of their hearts nor understand what they want.

Poor girls! If a man approaches one of them during those moments of suffering and whispers in her ears the magic word of love, if he promises to love her, this naive, trusting young girl, totally given over to the happiness of loving and being loved for the first time, lets herself go, follows the guide who seduces her, and falls.

Then it is that we have the splendid sight of men laughing at her downfall, laughing with contempt; women calling her names and condemning—society women who are born to happiness and love—for they can have love, yes love as they want it, as much as they want, because of their dowry and their wealth.

Privileged women, who live only for their own happiness, puffed up with self-importance, do not understand the cries of distress of their suffering companions. They know not at all how to extend a helping hand. And yet, a stock market reversal, a fire, a bankruptcy—one of those strokes of fate which reoccur so frequently—could throw these women rudely off their silken sofas, out onto the streets or into a miserable garret, and force them to share the hard life of poor girls of the popular classes.

What will they do then, when they see how their rich friends withdraw and flee from them? Because this world even associates shame with poverty and makes people feel they have to apologize for being poor. What will become of them, I ask, when they are so deprived? What will they do? How would they behave? Which direction would they choose? How awful their lot would be, abandoned by everyone. I would like the wives and daughters of the wealthy to imagine themselves for a moment in such a predicament. To see themselves, for a moment, poverty-stricken and reduced to living by the labor of their own hands. I would like them to think about it, giving it careful, serious consideration.

Well then, wouldn't it be good, for them as well as for the daughters of the poor, if we had houses founded on religious thought and love, houses of artists' and workers' association where young girls, united by a common mind, would find safe asylum from poverty, hunger, men's brutality and seductions, or the lure of gold that commands such power over those who suffer from cold, thirst, and hunger.

Yes, let us repeat it, association is the only means to emancipate at the same time women and men: women, because their means of existence will no longer depend on their fathers or their husbands; men, because they will be able to devote themselves more freely to their vocation, knowing that their daughters and wives will no longer depend on them for food.

Association between women is therefore essential; it is association that we must achieve, and to achieve this goal, this is what we propose to you. We request that:

Under the name of *Artists' and Workers' Saint-Simonian Assembly*, an association be formed of young girls who are "in waiting"* and of widows whose husbands have died or are absent and who, through their experience, can counsel and guide their younger *sisters*.

This home will be open to all young girls, no matter what their position in today's world, provided they are and want to continue to live *in waiting*, and provided that through their work, no matter what kind, they can cooperate in a useful way in the material existence and well-being of the community.

Before presenting herself as a future member of the association, each person must understand the need for socialization, unity, and love among all members of the community. In our artists' and workers' house, individual efforts must serve the general well-being of the group. This need for focusing on the general good is particularly important in the beginning stages.

---

*Reference both to "the wait" for the "Woman Messiah" and to those new women (*femmes nouvelles*) who pledged themselves to obey coventional morality while "waiting" for a new order.

Those whose work is more lucrative than others' shall seek their individual satisfaction in the esteem and love of their sisters, particularly in the beginning stages.

There will, however, exist a register where the contributions and products of the labor of each woman will be recorded, in order to take them into consideration at the time of her departure, should she want to leave the community. However, she will not leave without taking precautions and making sure that her departure does not unduly harm the general well-being of the community.

Not only must material products be shared in the community, but religious sentiment, which stimulates and guides all its members, will encourage each member to mutually share all the treasures of scientific, artistic, or industrial knowledge that they may individually possess. Certain hours of the day, especially on Sundays, shall be dedicated to religious singing.

Ladies, these are the basic principles of the association which we want to propose to you.[. . .]

Angélique [surname unknown]
Sophie Caroline [surname unknown]

[*Tribune des femmes* 1: 98–102.]

Speech Addressed to the Family of Paris, Meeting of the General Assembly, December 2

Gentlemen,

All acts of a religious society which, like our own, feels the mission to regenerate the fate of humanity must, I say, be serious. Therefore, I present myself before you with the trust that we can decide among ourselves and you upon a form of organization that can serve us at least temporarily.

Last Sunday, within these very walls, you all heard this remarkable phrase in the farewell address of our beloved preacher Barrault: "We leave Paris to the women."*

Yes, gentlemen, we accept this legacy. There is already a beginning of union and association among us, as women have gathered around the banner of the *Femme nouvelle*. In the newspaper of this name, edited

---

*Barrault was about to leave with a group of Saint-Simonians on a mission through France and then to the Middle East in search of the "Woman Messiah."

entirely by women, all of us have already been able to express our feelings and desires for the future, each in her own way, and to perform at last an act of our own free will. In the preparatory meetings we have felt that at first our work must be very distinct from yours, so that we could later take our place by your side, *as your equals*, in every walk of life, once we have understood our strength and value. But do not think, gentlemen, that this is a wild independence I wish to see befall my sex. No, no, nothing could be farther from my mind than this antireligious thought. The proposition that I have come to offer you is, on the contrary, to coordinate and unite our efforts to yours, so that we may sooner reach the result that we *all* desire, which is to obtain through pacifist means a universal association and the emancipation of women and the people.

Since all the feelings I am expressing have been drawn from the love I bear my sex, I do not fear being refuted by my sisters when I ask you, in the name of them all, to create *a place, love, and respect* for us everywhere you go. You must feel, gentlemen, that in compensating for the contempt and slander the outside world showers upon us, you could not give us too much consideration among you.

It is therefore as women who have already shown ourselves worthy of freedom that we ask of your justice that no more general assemblies be called without admitting us.* Imitate the supreme father, and above all envision the future of Saint-Simonianism within the solution to the women's question. It will be beautiful and great, gentlemen, if the family of Paris can present itself to society as an example to soften our customs and to awaken and exalt the chivalrous feelings of the Middle Ages in the souls of workers. Share as much as possible your solemn ceremonies for taking the habit,** whether during a festival for the family or when a new brother called to our communion declares, as his only profession of faith, that he rejects all exploitation of individuals as backward and barbarous. And then let the father and his delegate offer him the belt, and the brothers the cap, but may the women alone confer and arrange the scarf. The new brother will regard himself from then on as the knight of women and the people, and will feel the necessity of letting himself be stripped immediately of his diverse symbols if he ever fails in his work.

Gentlemen, to sum up in a few words, we demand that different groups of women which may form themselves under Saint-Simonian in-

---

*After the dissolution of the female hierarchy, in November 1831, Enfantin had declared Saint-Simonianism a movement of men. Thus women were excluded when, in the fall of 1832, the men who remained in Paris (most of the leaders were on retreat at Ménilmontant; Enfantin was in prison) held a general assembly to reorganize the movement.

**Saint-Simonian male adherents, called "apostles" after November 1831, wore a special costume which they called their "religious habit."

spiration be admitted to take part in your assemblies and be able to deliberate like you on the general questions at hand. But, moreover, the more we endeavor to bring the two sexes together, the more the need for a completely moral justice will make itself felt. In accordance with this thought, we ask that a family council be formed, presided over by women and men, to redress the wrongs of anyone who might act culpably toward individuals or the collectivity.

Let the name of this family tribunal vary according to the cases it will be called upon to judge. For example, it will be constituted under the name *court of justice* if the delinquent is culpable toward the father, his brothers, or the people. But in all cases that specifically concern our sex or a wrong committed against a woman, we want the assembly to convene under the name *court of love*, so that all acts of woman may be absolutely distinct from yours and preserve the imprint of her character.

It is not necessary to specify here the type of wrongs to be judged or the nature of punishments fit to be applied. These are, it seems to me, extraneous details which can be settled upon later, at the time of the infraction, as a decision made among ourselves, when you have as I do the strong inner feeling that women must take an active part in everything that is decided within the family in order to advance our work.

I have presented to you, gentlemen, these thoughts of women in a doubtless very formless manner. I leave to your own reflections the effort to examine how applicable they are to present circumstances. However, I want you to feel as strongly as I do that publicity, this moralizing principle that influences all individuals, could be an *active* and *living* force in the education of women, who until now have been relegated to the privacy of their immediate family, and so do not have enough feeling for what is excellent and progressive in social life.

Saint-Simonians, in order to make our freedom more than a vain revolt, desire it with all the sincerity of your souls; the better you understand these words, the more woman will act.

                                                        Suzanne [Voilquin]

[*Tribune des femmes* 1: 105–107.]

Since the imprisonment of Father Enfantin, several ladies of the provinces have expressed to us the fear of seeing the Saint-Simonian family without a bond in the leader's absence. We think that a few simple and true details about the interior life of the family will respond to their kind concern.

Oh no! no! my sisters, Saint-Simonianism has not been annihilated in Paris. Rest assured, and have faith in us; it is more alive than ever, since it is beginning to be embodied in women and the people. The phase of the doctors* is over; all the theories have been made. Let the phase of sentiment, of women, in a word, arrive, and give birth to the new Genesis.[. . .]

In the sketches I will draw for you, you will see in turn the influence of the *male* family of Paris and the influence of the *Femme nouvelle*, acting upon and mutually inspiring each other. To make myself understood, I must tell you in a few words about the respective positions of the *Saint-Simonienne* [sic] men and women. Generally, the women among us, here as elsewhere, understand very little the freedom which is offered us. Almost all of them are still under the influence or will of men. They do not have confidence in themselves. Still under the charm of the brilliant theories that these gentlemen have made for us, they dare not make their weak and timid voices heard. Lastly, they do not yet feel that all questions address themselves to our hearts, detached from all individual sentiment. Our hearts alone are called upon to resolve them; in a religion that is completely about *love*, the most *loving* becomes the most *capable*. And perhaps too the women are not *listened to very well*.

From the time when the *man of genius*, who has guided the Saint-Simonians and continually inspired them in our favor, has been *expiating* in prison the wrong of having wanted to confer upon this egotistical society *life* and *happiness* by putting us on the level of the equality due us; from that time, I say, our brothers, completely astonished by the revolution that has taken place in them under the inspiration of the *father* and by the immense leap he has let us take, have taken notice of us, listened to us, and, I would say, are almost intimidated by us. Because authority has always been arbitrary and despotic, they do not yet in their turn understand what place we can occupy without harming their rights. They think they see a tendency toward usurpation on our part when we dare to demonstrate our *will*. In general, men, even somewhat those in the [Saint-Simonian] family, act toward women the way governments act toward the people; they fear us and do not yet *love* us. They talk about disorders, but, my God! what would we gain by that? Disorder! But what about the brutalization and exploitation of our sex! Oh, may they rest assured: the freedom we envision will be *beautiful* and *pure* when relations between the sexes are based on the *true* feeling of *love*. Then *exploitation* and *fraud* will be unnecessary or impossible. May women let their hearts speak. Yes, I sense that a single and identical cry will rush forth: "Away, away, flighty caprice that plays at forming a thousand ephemeral liaisons! You drag in your wake disgust and weariness. No, no, you are not happiness. Away, mad, vagrant imagination whose delirium is like

---

*"Intellectuals"—designated by Saint-Simon to direct the new order—are meant here.

that of love, but who is neither love nor happiness!" Women, women, listen to your hearts and speak out.[. . .]

Suzanne [Voilquin]

[*Tribune des femmes* 1: 116–18.]

The Two Mothers

Since hours spent in observation are not always lost hours, and since, moreover, Paris is so beautiful at the beginning of each year, so adorned with all those pretty *nothings* that make so little profit for the ingenious worker who invents them, that the desire takes me to try out the profession of an idler today, and walk without *purpose*. . . . Let us stop in front of this store. This place will no doubt provide me with some useful observations. But you, poor woman huddled in that corner, what are you doing with your three poor little children by that door? You are not there out of curiosity. Oh no, no, in your lusterless eye, your pale face, and the rags that cover you, I see the reason. It is need, the cruel need to exist, that keeps you there. Let us see if I cannot perceive on all these rich faces that pass before me a compassionate movement that would indicate a soul. But it is not in evidence. This cold and disdainful expression is definitely theirs. Oh, rich people! since your souls are too narrow to understand association, then at least practice philanthropy. That is today's virtue. You, poor woman, do not lose heart. Here is an elegant young lady getting out of her carriage. She is also rich, that is true, but a woman's heart guesses so many things that, without having suffered, she may understand your grief. How brilliant her attire, what extravagant horses and carriage! Oh! with what servility her servants care for her! I believe I notice that this is not affection which gives nor the heart which grants, but rather wealth which is paying cupidity its wage. And would the honest merchant not feel himself obliged to bow reverentially to a woman who alights from a carriage to go into his shop! Certainly, in seeing his hurried manner, one can be assured that he is far from wishing to leave Fortune waiting at the door. [. . .] Fortune! the sole divinity of the day. It seems, when we observe how she surrounds her favorites with attention, that they epitomize in their persons all the merit and happiness in life, and that to attain the favor of this capricious goddess, one must sacrifice everything, everything including one's human dignity. But why are you waiting, poor woman; don't you see by the servile but impertinent tone of her valets that their mistress's selfish and unfeeling heart is about to spurn your lament. What expressive looks you give this brilliant carriage and the tattered clothes that barely cover you; and then, raising your eyes to heaven, you seem to question the justice in the mystery of this inequality! Nevertheless, there is still hope. Like you, this woman is a mother. She must sympathize with your misery. Oh! oh! good merchant, your beaming air shows that your excessive civilities are not for naught. What trifles are brought from your shop to the wealthy carriage! Poor woman, hasten to present your mother's request. The elegant young lady is herself ready to get in with her children. Now insinuate yourself amongst them. Quickly. . . . Alas! only an outburst of anger answers your touching prayer, and she informs the servants and the merchant himself that they must hasten to push away the troublesome solicitor. . . . And I, watching this carriage roll off and flee with a wringing heart, need to think of eternal justice in order to breath more freely. *To each according to their works.**

Yes, rich woman, your life will go on like that of the poor woman! You, mother, have not deigned to help end the sorrows of a mother. May God help you achieve progress and soften your soul by making you suffer through your children all the anguish of hunger, cold, and poverty that you have not prevented. Let me remind you, rich woman: *To each according to their works!*

Suzanne [Voilquin]

[*Tribune des femmes* 1: 121–27.]

The Justice of Men

Some time ago my interest in a case concerning a member of the popular class drew me to the criminal court. [. . .] By giving you the details of another case that was also being tried that day, I hope you will feel as I do how little we are protected by men, even *those* of the law.

A young woman first appeared before the court. She moved me by her pallor, her moral suffering, and a poverty she did not deserve. Before these cold, severe men's faces, this poor young woman recounted simply but truthfully how her husband, after promising her support and protection before all of *society* (*represented* in the person of *Monsieur the Mayor*), then sold everything they owned, so that the only material resources left to her were their common debts. And afterward he spent all this money with an immoral, degraded girl. Poor little *legitimate* wife! . . . You who religiously bent your head under the yoke of their laws. What consolation do these men bring to your broken heart when one of them destroyed

---

*A Saint-Simonian slogan, indicating their position against inherited wealth.

your existence by abandonment, contempt, and poverty? [. . .] In spite of the all too just grievances this woman had against her husband, she appeared pained at the obligation to enter into all these details. It was not against him that she complained, but against the unfortunate girl who, not content to bring disorder into her marriage, had brutally hit her one day, so as not to endure from the poor abandoned wife a few all too just and deserved reproaches. There were proofs, medical certificates, and another court had already sentenced her to six months of imprisonment and a fine. But vice of this magnitude is audacious; this girl had appealed, and the court had appointed her a counsel. Oh! How can I explain to you the indignation I felt when I heard this lawyer playing on the emotions of the court and audience with his despicable argument: "You see, gentlemen, the plaintiff's jealousy prompted her to these insults, and my client retorted a little vigorously. Gentlemen, you will overturn the sentence for lack of cause, for, you see, this is *only a woman's quarrel.*" (The accused was not completely pardoned, but her penalty was cut in half.) If a woman had been presiding beside the judge, such an important question as the relations between the sexes would not have been resolved so lightly as a *woman's quarrel*! What indecency for a lawyer to express himself that way! Where then is morality? Where then is the protection that one owes to the weak and unfortunate, if they do not find it in the sanctuary of justice? In this society with no *bonding*, there is only hurt for us, whether we follow or discard your laws. [. . .]

To prove to you, dear readers, that this [. . .] is not exaggerated [. . .], I will go back to the root cause, that is to say I will examine civilization's masterpiece, the code of laws that men impose upon us.

Whoever says "code of laws" speaks of the social regulations made in *everyone's* interest and approved and consented to by *everyone*; but who in truth are *we*? Humanity is not composed only of men. Legislators of all ages, tell me, if we are half of *everyone*, have you ever at any time admitted women among yourselves to uphold the rights of their sex? And if we have never had representatives to *discuss* and *prevent* the oppressive laws that you have drawn up against us, explain by what right you would have us remain forever submissive to these laws? Men! be therefore no longer surprised by the disorder that reigns in your society. It is an energetic protest against what you have done *alone*.

Frail woman that I am, I feel the strength and need today to *protest* boldly against what is arbitrary and depraved in your social system, as it is summed up in several articles of the law that I attack as the forced consequence of a bad principle. For example, how can we in the nineteenth century listen with composure to a delegate under your authority who says in all seriousness to us: "The wife must obey her husband" (Art. 213). I have already asked *why* in another article, and my gauntlet remained on the ground. No one picked it up. Only *La Revue des Deux Mondes* joked about it, but *joking* does not *prove* anything. (Art. 214):

"The wife is *obligated*" (emphasis in the text) "to live with the husband, and to follow him wherever he judges it appropriate to live." Does not the spirit of his laws establish our slavery, so that we cannot be ourselves?[. . .]

The spirit of your law is even more malevolent for the *mother* than for the *wife*. Against the wife there is the arbitrary despotism from which she escapes through a constant silent struggle. But it is the mother's heart that you wound and break by the mistrust and injustice which are palpable in the following articles. (Art. 373): "The *father* alone exercises authority over his children during the marriage." (Art. 374): "The child cannot leave the *paternal* home without the father's approval." What then is the mother in the family? *Everything*; her influence is immense. And her rights? *None*. Oh, justice of men! . . . (Art. 389): "During the marriage, the father is the administrator of the personal belongings of his children in their minority." More than once while reading this article I asked myself: But does the father alone then have innate knowledge? Does infallibility then find refuge in the little conjugal fortress? Probably so in the mind of the legislator. For if woman in her maternal love finds the strength to control her husband's acts, the *law of man* is there ready to tell her: *back*! usurper, this is a right that you have appropriated and do not possess. (Art. 390): "After the death of one of the spouses, the guardianship of minors belongs to the survivor." This article appears to establish too much equality between spouses; what follows serves as a corrective. (Art. 391): "Nevertheless the father will be able to appoint a special advisor to the surviving mother and guardian, without whose advice she will not be able execute any action over her ward." Since it is generally known that maternal love is the strongest and deepest of all feelings, why this mistrust? [. . .] Who more than the mother is in a position to supervise her children's happiness? Who more than she knows with certainty that they are definitely a part *of her*, definitely *her own*? If the law wants to prevent presumed misconduct by one of the spouses, then why does the mother not have the same right to consideration? Why not allow her tranquillity after death, by letting her consolidate *her* children's future. Cannot everything that can be prejudged about the subsequent conduct of women once widowed be applied in the same case to men? They do not have as we do a feeling for the intimate family; and besides, if a new love were to bring the woman new children, would they not *all* be drawn from the same *life* source that is common to them all? Does she not unite them all in her mind and maternal heart? And if, forced by this law of inheritance (which is impious since it is against nature)* to divide in an unequal manner the property among *all*, she at least does not disinherit them from any of her care or love. It is not the

---

*An attack on inheritance was central to Saint-Simonianism.

same for the man. The children from a first bed are almost always driven away from the father's house by the maternal selfishness of the second wife, and meanwhile the father *alone* has the right in dying to appoint a guardian-counsel. Oh, justice of men! . . .

Young mothers, chase such dark thoughts away from your mind, so that the love of your children may prepare you for years of happiness if marriage is only a long disappointment for you. Find refuge in your children's future, so that your imagination may embellish their existence with those things of which you have been deprived; for these children are assuredly yours, young mothers. Find joy in your daughter; watch how her charms unfold in adolescence, how her face blushes and grows pensive when she feels her heart pound for the first time. Oh yes, tender mothers, become her confidante, for you know well the needs of a woman's heart. Prepare her from her earliest years for her first love, for it is often a woman's whole destiny. You know that the sentence your society hurls against you will still be the irrevocable sentence against us for a long time. Therefore, kind mother, do not mistakenly think that your child's heart *alone* will be consulted. (Art. 148): "To form a marriage the father's consent is sufficient." (Art. 150): "If the father and mother are dead and there is a disagreement between the grandfather and grandmother, the grandfather's consent is sufficient."

Oh, justice of men! truly the time is near when you will be declared impious. Soon the mother will no longer be martyred in her spirit or her flesh. *God* entrusts the *certitude* of the family to the mother *alone*. In the young girl's bosom lies the *living bond* that links forever the generations to come with those that pass away. A mystery that realizes itself in *God's* bosom under the great name of *humanity*! . . .

Suzanne [Voilquin]

[*Tribune des femmes* 1: 127–29.]

To the Men*

You are appalled by our ideas of freedom, gentlemen—you, who spend your entire lives working to have us break the ties which constrain us, if your personal interests as brothers, husbands, or fathers are not hurt by it. When our freedom brings you pleasure and a kind of pride which, at best, I would call immoral, then you want us to be free—free from obeying our parents, free from the duties imposed on us by religion

---

*Referring specifically to Saint-Simonian men.

and society's opinion. But you still want us to remain slaves to your desires. This very freedom, which you so adamantly want us to espouse, you now ascribe to us as a criminal offense. When we want to break away from the slavery imposed on us by the world, and particularly by you—which is even worse because our enslavement to you is intimately linked to our happiness—we must be more than simply courageous. You invoke immorality. You say that we are lost, that we have lost our morals and our feelings. Is it because we are opposed to your exploitation that you say we are lost? Quite the contrary, I believe that we are saved, provided we have the necessary courage to brace ourselves against your condemnations. If we are modest and reserved; if we devote ourselves to the care of the household; if we prefer a quiet life to the bustle of worldly pleasures, we live this kind of life not because you, as masters, would have imposed it on us as a duty. We live such a life because our temperament apparently agrees with it. If we openly assert the virtues of steadfast and lasting love, it is not for fear of being rejected and defiled by you—you who would not hesitate to incriminate us if we dared be something other than what you want us to be. Rather, it is because it is in our nature to love in this way. And would you not prefer those noble and generous feelings, which must exist between equals, to those mercenary feelings which a slave has for his master? You surely must be either foolish or blind. Whatever the case may be, you will never again hear us pronounce the word of the Virgin Mary, "thy will be done," while smiling at your despotic power. The woman we are waiting for, the New Mary, has been summoned to do God's work, but to act in concert with man and not as man's submissive slave. She too will save the world and crush the serpent's head.* But the redeemer,** who will save the world together with her, shall not say to her in an authoritarian voice: "Woman, what do we have in common?" He calls her to his side, in order to share authority with her, so that she may bring to the work, which he began so nobly and which he undertakes so courageously, her luminous, graceful, modest, and wise attributes, no matter what our critics say. And if she rejects old customs in matters of taste and appearance as well as in matters of feelings, she will be guided by a sense of decency, modesty, and grace. And contrary to what you gentlemen—purists in questions of morality and appearances—take pleasure in believing, she will not bring us new customs whose novelty would cause resistance, no matter how small the discomfort this novelty might cause, without much careful consideration. Therefore, refrain from criticism until this moment comes. If you make your judgments now, you will

---

*Claire Démar, in *My Law of the Future*, reprinted here, also represents this image. See p. 182.
**Reference to Enfantin.

only be thrown into confusion, because the future is approaching, and it will come on azure blue clouds, on purple and golden clouds, to replace your foggy and storm-filled past.

Joséphine-Félicité [Milizet]

[*Tribune des femmes* 1: 169–71.]

Several ladies have refused to write in this newspaper because the title *Apostolate* it bore signified a solidarity that they could not accept.* And since we have never wanted to hinder the development of social ideas, we have decided that in the future this little paper will be entitled *Tribune des femmes*.

A *free* place will be accorded to each opinion and each woman's thought. With us, no censorship. Under this new format we call upon women capable of understanding their century. What in truth can go on around us that is so great and lofty as to intimidate us and about which we cannot speak? Could it be that we should not meddle in the shadowy politics of protocol and deceit? I think there is cause for women to speak about *everything*, because *everything* influences their happiness. They are connected to *everything*.

And don't women have something to say about morality? Will they always content themselves to protest in secret, and then appease their conscience by adding aloud: "Morality is divine; we have contented ourselves with it for centuries. It is the ark of the Lord. Keep us from raising a sacrilegious hand against it." But it truly does not take a profound logician to grasp this simple reasoning: GOD gave all his children a general law to guide them and lead them to progress. If it is complete and men have translated and explained it well, it should suit *everyone*, and *everyone* must follow it equally with love.

Let the *facts* speak for themselves. What then is the source of this violent, energetic, and unruly protest that has gone through the centuries alongside this same moral law which is much too strict and absolute to satisfy all individuals, a protest voiced not only by men, who themselves violate the law they have made everyday, but also by a huge number of women? It is thus in the name of a *single* GOD, of whom we are all children, that I beseech women to concern themselves with these grave questions. May the foundations of morality and the relations between the sexes command our primary interest. We shall not content

---

*The title "Apostolate" signified that they were Saint-Simonians. In her "Notice Historique" to Claire Démar's *My Law of the Future*, Voilquin suggests that the title "Apostolate" had an even narrower meaning, referring to membership in the autonomous women's group, the "femmes nouvelles."

ourselves, like superficial people, to state the effects. We will go back to the root causes to remedy the source of this evil. Our spirit is too enlightened to think any longer about categories.* There should no longer be outcasts among us.

Suzanne [Voilquin]

[*Tribune des femmes* 1: 185–95.]

Thoughts on the Religious Ideas of the Century

For those of us who seek and find *life* in the *faith* we have in GOD, even if our hope and trust in the new religious era we proclaim were not so intense, it would still be very comforting for us to see how much this century is inclined to make everyone concerned with religious feelings. The entire society seeks a new poetry in this great thought of GOD, under whose inspiration it could once again traverse many centuries.

But before we arrive at universal association and attain religious *unity*, what chaos must be cleared up and reorganized! [. . .]

In this nomenclature of men *calling themselves religious*, explicating and commenting upon the Gospel of Jesus, let us not forget to mention the *Neo-Christians*, men of movement, but nevertheless remaining pure spiritualists. [. . .] At least these men may arrive, for they are going forward. [. . .] They say that since Jesus said nothing against equality between men and women, there is no reason that, in our era when intelligence has been developed as rapidly in one sex as in the other, this equality should not be boldly recognized. Certainly, from our point of view, these are very remarkable men. [. . .]

There is yet another man in this world who *also* interprets Christianity, but in a manner even more favorable to our sex. He is Monsieur *Jamme de Laurence [sic]*, author of a booklet entitled: *Children of God or the Religions of Jesus.*** The huge difference between him and the court of Rome consists in the *moral freedom* without rules or limits that he wants to give us, which, along with the mystery that he permits and with our being accountable for our acts only to a mystical God, would drive us straight to a gross and disgusting helter-skelter. Besides, this is not the way to create association, this is not the way to reconstruct a society that is crumbling on every side.

---

*In Saint-Simonian parlance, this refers to categories of sexual tendencies, i.e., "constants" and "mobiles."

**For more information on James de Laurance, see chapter 2 and Claire Démar's *My Law of the Future*, reprinted here.

[. . .] This complete freedom in love, however, would certainly bring about great results. According to him, the family should be based on *maternity*. Justifying his system, he says that *paternity* is a *belief*, and *maternity alone* is a *certainty*.

Since the author is not Saint-Simonian, but on the contrary seems rather feudal, he does not recognize the reign of capacity or the abolition of hereditary rights of birth,* and so in order to be consistent he makes heredity descend matrilineally. This system, although incomplete, is assuredly quite advantageous to us. I have faith that a portion of his ideas will enter into the new morality and will be highly esteemed in the future religion, and that the principle of maternity will become one of the fundamental laws of the state. The society of the future will not rest upon mystery but upon confidence, for mystery still prolongs the exploitation of our sex; publicity and confidence will form the foundations of the new morality.**

[. . .] In the midst of our religious anarchy, need for a new faith, and society so lacking in conviction, a sublime madman (as our Béranger calls him), SAINT-SIMON, came to give the world this great principle as a foundation for future law:

"Woman and man form the social individual." A simple formula! Therefore the world was not moved by it. "The Count de *Saint-Simon* is galant," it said lightly, and dismissed him. But since then devoted disciples and a hierarchy of *capable* men have succeeded the prophet and *misunderstood* philosopher. They acknowledge a religious head,*** who, the *first* among *everyone*, has attached his life to the development of this seed fertile in results and has declared that the highest manifestation of GOD upon the earth *is* man and woman, that *His* will resides within *them*, and that everything must therefore be resolved by *them*. [. . .] The Father's theories of the *call* were anathematized without examination. Society punished him for [. . .] saying boldly to men: "Woman is your equal; you do not have the right to judge her; it is up to her alone to tell me if I have sounded the depths of humanity's wounds. [. . .]

It is for women, their emancipation and their future happiness, that FATHER ENFANTIN endures injuries, poverty, and prison. It behooves women who understand him to rehabilitate and glorify him. For the moment, the best way to act upon this world too biased to be just is to make him known and to repeat and popularize his ideas.

[. . .] The new religious conception is entirely consigned to writing in

---

*Saint-Simonians advocated a "ranking by capacity" or individual merit and the abolition of inheritance.
**For the differences of opinion over "publicity" and "mystery," see Démar's *My Law of the Future*, reprinted here.
***Reference to Enfantin.

the words pronounced by the FATHER last April 8 in the criminal court, of which I will here report a few fragments:

"I have said: GOD the father and mother of *everyone* and *everything*, because this simple word sums up our *religious faith*. [. . .]

"Therefore I ask you: When the sacred name of GOD is pronounced before you, what *qualities* does he recall to your mind? What virtues does he awaken in your soul? Are they not the *qualities* of *man* and *male virtues* only that your men's hearts divine always and everywhere?

"Now, I beg you to reflect—for I would like to be very well understood here—upon the huge difference that exists between the *man* who sees in his GOD only those *qualities* and *virtues* of a DEIFIED *man*, and the man who also senses the graces and *virtues of woman*, poetically elevated to an INFINITE strength.

"Oh! it is certainly through a miraculous *conception* of the *spirit*, but *man's spirit*, that WOMAN already occupies in MARY such a beautiful place in the Christian *faith*, which adores GOD the Father, GOD the Son, and GOD the Holy Ghost.

"But don't you see that all of that is always *male* and dismal like *solitude*, heavy and cold like the marble of a tomb, and harsh like a cross?

"Now, we, on the other hand, say GOD the Father and Mother, and I assure you that anyone among you who communes in spirit and love with our GOD, who is not only *good* like a FATHER, but also *tender* like a MOTHER, will commune, I declare, with HIM and HER, and will by that alone clothe himself in a *new life*. [. . .]

"Yes, certainly we have a *political* goal, for we have a *religious faith* that tells us what God wants from human *society*, and so we are forming a POLITICAL and RELIGIOUS association. [. . .]

"We have *faith* that GOD will bring an end to the political *hatred* which rips all of you apart, the *poverty* and *ignorance* which provoke the *workers* and push them to riot, the *laziness* which eats away at the *rich* and *enlightened* classes and brings them boredom, disgust, and fear, and finally *atheism* and egotism—this double leper which covers the world with hopeless sorrow and remorseless immorality. We have faith that GOD will bring an end to all this, but only through WOMEN."

                                                    Suzanne [Voilquin]

[*Tribune des femmes* 1: 201–205.]

To Women

In one of my articles, responding to those who accuse us of not knowing what we want when we speak of *freedom and equality*, I formulated, though in very brief terms, what I meant for myself when I spoke of freedom. I say "for myself," for each woman who exposes her ideas here cannot accept responsibility for the ideas of the others and therefore can speak only for herself. But I have not said through what means I thought myself able to gain this freedom. It is above all here that women find the greatest obstacle, for everyone wants freedom, but few understand by what means they will be able to gain it. Only in stating it well can we answer those who accuse us of preaching disorder and causing trouble to society when we speak about changing its moral relations. First, I want to establish a fact here, which is that this mobility that you claim to banish exists everywhere, for it is flagrant in your streets and public squares. To express the desire that it be exercised religiously is not to augment it, but to avoid as much as possible the sorrows which accompany it today, and to replace the disorderly way in which we see it carried out.

But first I want to present to you some thoughts on the position of women in relation to Christian morality. Before a woman would call us to freedom, there were women who felt just how oppressive Christian law was for them. Some revolted openly, trampling under their feet all the bonds intended to enchain them, and abandoned themselves to all the delirium of a constitution that through its very repression had acquired more force. These unfortunate girls did not think at all about what was dragging them along the path they followed. They were happy and thought themselves loved because men came everyday to flatter them with *deceitful incense*. They did not think that those men who had flattered them the most, with the motive of *making them serve their pleasure*, were the very men who would most crush them with *scorn* when they had *passed the age of pleasure*. Most of them ended up dying on *straw pallets* or in the *poorhouse*, victims of a law that could only *repress* but in no way *guide*. Other women, also feeling how oppressive it was to live under the law, but feeling as well how much pain they would experience if they went outside of the law, submitted. For them, life as a whole was a *continual battle* and a *perpetual renunciation*. And they forced those men who blamed all women to recognize that there are some women who understand what they owe to themselves and how to make themselves respected. And it is in the face of all these sorrows that we have been accused of immorality even as we talk of the necessity of changing this oppressive law, which *drives out of the society* it is called upon to rule most of its members, because it is not *strong* enough to *guide* them.

Oh, it is because I have so well understood all about these women's sorrow that I raise my voice to demand a complete change in our position. But I must explain the difference that exists between us and the women who have already protested. When we raise our voice to demand our rights, after the former have already done so, one imagines that we too are going to end up increasing the disorder that was already so great.

But rest assured, it is in regard to a social reform that we speak of free-dom. Therefore we are not *practicing* but simply *demanding* a *new moral law*. We would not be able practice it anyway, since it has not yet been formulated and could not be so, since a *woman powerful* enough to make it accepted by others has not yet arisen. If we did do so, we would deserve the reproach that we are acting in our own personal interest, for we owe it to ourselves to remain within the limits of a law which is certainly oppressive for many of us, but which we must respect until the new law is formulated. Those who go outside of it must truly understand that they expose themselves to the reproach of bringing about disorder, since instead of acting in regard to a social idea, they will only be satis-fying themselves, without *serving in any way the cause of women or the people*, and will only be continuing a protest that has been going on for a long time. I am writing these lines for people who say that all the women who have spoken or will speak of freedom want disorder. As I am far from wanting that, I want to express my understanding of the question.

Up to this point I have spoken only of moral freedom, because that is the question which today most preoccupies a great number of women; but in my opinion they are mistaken. The best way for women to gain moral freedom is to proselytize for *hastening the realization* of a new social order in which *association* would replace isolation, all jobs would be or-ganized so that there would be a place for us in all those we could per-form, and, lastly, we would be able to own property, for as long as we cannot, we will always be the slaves of men. As long as a man provides us our material needs, he can also demand that in exchange we submit to whatever he desires, and it is very difficult to speak freely when a woman does not have the means to live independently.

This brings us to the complete reform of society: A new educational system for children. They are a part of ourselves, and we must think of improving their position as well as our own. The new social order should be organized so that the mobility of affections* can be satisfied without harming in any way children's interests and nurturance, or in other words that there will be a *social provision for them*. A new organiza-tion of housework, based on association rather than fragmentation. Today the majority of women are absorbed by household cares, which are an enslavement for them, since they prevent them from devoting themselves to all the careers for which they might have talent. When household organization has *association* as its *foundation*, it will employ no more than a small minority of women, only those with a taste for it. Then the other women will be able to develop themselves in any direc-

---

*Reference to Enfantin's theory of the two sexual natures, the "mobile" and the "con-stant."

tion that suits them. This they would not be able to do today without causing disorder in their household. [. . .] Next, and not to be forgotten, our destiny is tied to that of the people, and our emancipation cannot occur except together with theirs. If we were to demand our moral freedom and not also concern ourselves with a new social order, would we not be acting only in our own interest, leaving it still misunderstood, for it would not change in any way the lot of the people? If we respond to women who plead for a remedy to their sufferings and those of children, for women often suffer more for their children than for themselves, by saying to them: "demand your moral freedom," do we not resemble those who tell the people when they are hungry: "demand your political rights," as if those rights could satisfy them and reorganize their work? I am certainly far from believing that *material emancipation* is *everything* that *the people and women need*. I know that they also need *social emancipation*, but, I repeat, one cannot be established without the other, for they are essentially connected and cannot be separated.

Marie-Reine [Reine Guindorf]

[*Tribune des femmes* 1: 249–54.]

Suicide
of Claire Démar and Perret Désessarts

With my soul seized by the lugubrious drama which has just occurred under our very eyes, I can do nothing today but mourn the loss of these two victims of the social and religious anarchy of this century and speak of the thoughts this sad event has engendered in me. But I must seek above all to destroy a slander that all the newspapers were happy to repeat. They all have made it known, in their cold recounting of this event, that Claire and Désessarts were involved in an intimate relationship. To anyone who has plumbed the depths of the human heart, this would seem very unlikely. If they had loved, or if love, this creative fire, had animated their souls, they would have had faith in themselves and would still be among us. For if love is grasped in its most noble, elevated, and expansive expression, is it not a belief, a religion, or even life itself! On the contrary, it is because they no longer loved and because gentle and lively feelings no longer flowed through their hearts, which were petrified by strife and doubt, that they became discouraged by this cold and colorless existence, and used the remainder of their energy to join in an association of the tomb. . . .

It was on the night of August 3–4 that they executed this fatal resolution. This double suicide demonstrates a pair of personalities marked by extraordinary composure and force of energy. Perret Désesserts, twenty-three years of age, had recently left his birthplace in Grenoble. Already haunted by the thought of suicide, he came to Paris toward the beginning of the year. It was also at this time that he met *Claire Démar* for the first time. This woman, still young and attractive, with a soul of iron, had the courage to accept poverty and cast away from herself a life of ease, but ambiguous and without respectability. *Glory to her!* Through this act she had climbed to the ranks of *woman,** for her decision was free and spontaneous. It was at this time that she met Désessarts. They loved each other and sought renown. They understood each other. The similarity of their natures made them friends. As such, they thereafter saw each other often and associated their efforts of propagation. The extremely interesting letters they wrote, like their last farewell (which will probably be made public),** affirmed that this was only a simple relationship. Let no doubt therefore be raised against the affirmation of the coffin!

In order to accept life as it was, and not see it as one great irresolvable absurdity, these poor victims of skepticism needed poetry and religion to come and revive their souls. As they looked around them, *everything* in this great wreck of Christianity—*morality, religion, dogma*—seemed to them *dull and dead.* Our society of the nineteenth century, cold and selfish as it is, threw only icy mockery and disdain upon their enthusiasm.

With their intelligence obscured by doubt, they then came to demand of the new religion a guiding thread through life, that of *truth.* But bruised and exhausted from the struggle they had to sustain with the world, they regarded with fear the innumerable obstacles that egotism, this deep evil that consumes all of society, would bring to their efforts. Despairing at the thought of relieving so many sorrows, they fell into the most absolute discouragement, doubting themselves and disavowing their mission. It was then that they [. . .] demanded [. . .] from death the poetry of a beautiful departure. Hand in hand, they fell together, finding a kind of horrible voluptuousness in this fraternity of the tomb. A few moments before his death, the young man wrote to one of his friends: "I wish that you, my friend, in your quest for a calm and happy death, may find, as I have, a loved one who will accompany you right to the place where doubt is no longer possible."

To die for want of *one's place* in life! . . . What an energetic protest against what *is.* To die exhausted from the struggle! . . . What deep despair this is which proves itself through death! Unfortunate *Claire!* Poor Désessarts! May they be reborn in a more harmonious time, when the great and beautiful religion we foretell, and which is now still only a faint point of light on the horizon, has grown strong enough to shine

*That is, a woman inspired by the "Woman Messiah."
**Reprinted here.

brightly upon the sight of everyone and serve as a torch for humanity in
its entirety! Oh, then the cold poison of skepticism will no longer freeze
your young hearts from childhood on. You will believe in *God*, for you
will sense harmony. *Your place*, which you could not now find, will be
reserved for you, for there will then be a *social* and *material* providence to
watch over your individual development.

Journalists, society wags: a woman and man who have died for lack of
belief in the prime of life are not such pallid individuals that it is permitted to speak lightly of them. Respect, therefore, for these two coffins!

For those of us who must not restrict ourselves merely to affirming this
fatal event, but see in it the indication of how much progress remains to
be made, this misfortune will bring us closer together. We will feel the
need to support each other, unite more and more with each other
through the bond of religious fraternity, and make sure that women who
would break with the old society, in order to adopt more completely the
new faith, are not driven by isolation and the meager support they would
find among us to discouragement and death.

You may well believe that for this to happen it is not enough to call
women *to freedom*, and then to leave them to struggle *alone* with this
egotistical world, which has as its only regulator and sole God *money*, this
cold and mocking world that smiles in pity upon any enthusiasm. For
aside from the religious feeling that the *new faith* seeks to establish in
people's spirit, to what anchor of salvation can women who foresee the
future attach themselves? Is it to the *freedom* that is so misunderstood by
everyone who wants it? What about even this magic word which makes
so many hearts vibrate? We have the right to pronounce it in this French
society, the most advanced of all societies, only under men's patronage
and for their sake. The most intelligent republicans have not yet arrived
at understanding *woman* and that *justice, right*, and *God* are equally on
our side.

Turning our gaze upon ourselves, I wonder: Is there in our beautiful
France a woman whose position gives her the ability to lend support to
all others? Who is the woman who can represent the unity of our rights?
From the most elevated in dignity to the lowest on the social ladder,
what can they do? What are they? *Legally* speaking, *nothing*? All of them
are sheltered behind a *name, place*, or social position that they receive
passively from the good graces of another. Alas! the French people have
a queen, but women have no mother!

With their minds oppressed by ideas of the future, ideas as vast as the
world since they tend to enclose it, what means of propagation are left to
women in their attempt to develop or to bring closer this future? Whatever their strength may be, how can they do it alone? Wearing themselves out on powerless attempts and then . . . , think of poor *Claire
Démar*. . . .

Our hope for emancipation thus rests entirely on this family of men, scattered almost entirely across the earth, preaching *our rights and equality*.* But it is above all when the propagation of these ideas can be united and carried out in *groups*, through *the whole family*, that they will gain power and activity. I am not venturing to give advice, and I even believe that it would be too soon to attempt this effort. But this thought and desire which has been dominating my mind for some time and which I naively express today may have stirred other hearts as well. It is good to reflect upon it. . . . But, before this bond could form, you men of the *new belief*, all of you who call yourselves *the apostles* and *companions* of *woman*,** must think of the duties to which your faith engages you. Through the privileges attached to your sex, you are still in possession of an immense power to direct *opinion*. May the moral support that comes from it be extended to *all women* and primarily to those who have the courage to enter the arena and take an active part in the action. [. . .]

Oh! it is no doubt *useful* and just to call attention to men's devotion, and I applaud with all my heart any work whose goal would have this result; but before society adores and recognizes in the divinity the attributes of a *male* and *female* GOD [DIEU *bon et bonne*], *father* and *mother* of the human family, and reclasses *its members* according to this divine thought, it is still *more just* and *useful* to regard temporarily the action of man as secondary to that of woman. Thus to participate with ardor in facilitating any work that would exalt only man would, in my opinion, be to take the detail for the whole, to place the accessory in the center and the centerpiece in the shadow. Take heart, therefore. The most beautiful crown is reserved for the one who reaches the goal.

Suzanne [Voilquin]
August 11, 1833

[*Tribune des femmes* 1: 263–64.]

To propagate her individual feeling on women's freedom, *Claire Démar* published a small pamphlet, which is especially remarkable for the energy of its style and thought, with the title: *A Woman's Call to the People on the Emancipation of Woman*. She had just finished a second one entitled *My Law of the Future* when she made the fatal decision to put an end to her existence. If women are determined to consign this last piece of writing to print, as a final homage rendered to the tomb, since the author is no longer here to defend the opinions included therein, I will abstain from giving my own opinion.

*Reference to Saint-Simonian "missionaries."
**The name taken by Barrault's group that was on a "mission" to the Middle East.

[*Tribune des femmes* 2: 153–55.]

A Woman's Voice

London, January 10, 1834

For some time to come, the *femmes nouvelles* will have great things to do, things completely different from those accomplished by men.

Men have called the *Mother* and *Wife*.

Women will reveal this *Mother* and *Wife*.

Today a single word of woman makes itself heard, but it will not be isolated for long.

The *Mother* and *Wife* is not one woman; she is all women.

She is the *feminine* sex: *Mother*, *Lover*, *Wife*, and *Friend* of the *masculine* sex.

We must take care not to fall into the trap that has ensnared men and which they lay for us in turn.—NO!—They will not find the ideal they seek so long as their narrow view does not expand to see it in all women.—YES!—These sublime blind men will suffer as long as they look for this ideal only among brilliant women in burning climates, who flatter their pride and enflame their senses.*

These women and climates are the poetry of the past, and the tomb is their apostolate.

Woman as the poetry of the future is still covered by a dark veil. She is not yet attractive— although SHE bears in her bosom the seeds of attraction!—for SHE is still swathed in the dirty rags of poverty and prostitution. Her face is pale, her eyes are hollow, and her hands are gaunt. Every evening, she makes herself up and speculates on the sensuality of the masters of society. She holds her child in her arms and her features contract to assemble the elements of a smile that she lavishes upon him! She supports him with one hand while she invokes her daily bread with the other.

Poetry and brilliant theories cannot touch her—*she is hungry*—*she is degraded*! Words of *hope* and *consolation* from devoted women who call themselves her liberators are for her bitter *irony* and *alms* that tear her apart and debase her.—Do these women not have the soul of a *mother*? Do they not have a sisterly heart, since they abandon their children and their sisters to follow a *husband* and an *ideal* into misfortune?**

---

*Reference to the quest of Barrault and the "Compagnons de la femme" to find the "Woman Messiah" in the Middle East.

**This is an allusion, perhaps, to the bourgeois Saint-Simonian women who, like Cécile Fournel and Clorinde Rogé, followed their husbands to Egypt; the Fournels left their daughter behind in France.

Ah! women have the virtue and poetry of the past.—The virtue of sacrifices!—The poetry of trumpery!—One single voice of woman says so today, but the time is near when the MOTHER, with her thousand voices, will answer the man who calls himself the FATHER.

—MAN, who are your children? By what right do you call yourself the *father* of mine?

—What have you done for the children that woman has been giving you for centuries?

—You have sacrificed them to the only children you have the right to call your *own*: your *systems*, your *ideals*!

—Your pride has torn them apart through war!

—Your egotistical pleasure has swallowed them up through prostitution!

And now, MAN, that all your mistakes have created the countless sufferings all around you as well as within you, you call upon woman to cure them.—You understand that woman is the wife and not the slave of man.—You seek her, this FREE *woman*, but your pride and egotism seek her in an *individual wife*, whom you call the *mother of your children*, and you abandon the civilized daughters of the West, because your civilization has disfigured them.

Ah! There you have him, MAN THE FATHER!

Be off, MAN!—and with you the principle of paternity! Go, follow your ideal! . . . The Orient is the tomb of your reign. WOMAN! You will be born in the Occident, and the Orient will be your throne! But, before you have a throne, you need *an independent living*. Think about that.

—Free yourself from the false prejudices of men's laws. Teach your sons to see their MOTHER in all women, for all of them will give him life, happiness, and the law of love.

—Say to MAN: "You have used your authority too poorly; you will no longer be the *only head*.

—You have been the *master* and not the *father* of the children I have given you.—I will no longer call you FATHER.

—My children will have no other FATHER but GOD.

—You have divided up the *earth* among a few individuals. Instead of uniting yourselves to distribute to everyone the gifts you had in your hands, you set yourselves the task and challenge of competing for the greatest number of slaves!—And then you established *national barriers* to enclose them.—And you deified WOMAN and fertility, because she created subjects for you!—You took your *slave wife* out of the domestic prison and led her to the public square, enchained by flowers, adorned with jewelry, surrounded by homages, and you said to her: Be the *spiritual* lover of warriors; use the gifts you have received from heaven to arouse knightly ardor.—I need it in order to destroy the slaves of my rivals or make my principles triumph.

—Oh! *proud and egotistical* MAN! You have put a thick blindfold of *ignorance* over your wife's eyes, in order to make her the instrument of her children's punishment, and so that the sight of your barbarity would not weaken her love for you and the pleasures that you procure from her!—And when your power—the power of force—was weakened, all of your authority was brought to bear on the home.—Then you said to your wife: "your *universe* is the *family.*—I no longer need your inspiration for the warriors.—War is in decline, and besides the perfecting of my machines of destruction will replace you.

—WOMAN, BE MODEST!—Use all of your talents and activities to provide me with the most pleasant life possible in my domestic realm.

—WOMAN, BE ECONOMICAL!—When my head has been spinning from politics and my body exhausted by debauchery or from working for *ten hours,* ah, WOMAN, I need to relax in your arms or draw life and freshness from the naive charms of your little children.

—WOMAN, BE DEVOTED TO ME!—May a smile be always on your lips, for you are *sympathetic!* and besides the laws that I have made forbid you the *fatigue of debauchery!*—WOMAN *of the people,* you often work *sixteen hours or more* a day, but you are *courageous!* and besides, *your work is not harsh!* —You suffer for me and your children.—But you are *patient!* and besides, you aren't tormented by *great ideas!* Your knowledge is limited to knowing how to raise small children.—Oh, WOMAN! make them *peaceful* and *obedient,* for their noisy activity disturbs me and their unruliness irritates me.—If I am rich, give me your son. Your tenderness would not be able to tame his *nature.* I have strict rules for him in boarding schools, and there I will make him into a man and teach him *my knowledge.* As for your daughter, raise her on the principles I have given you; extinguish her ardor and repress her love, so that cold rationalism dominates her feelings. In short, I have had an *individual wife!*—For myself, I had pretty daughters of the people to satisfy and satiate the passion of my earliest youth. I *pay* them so that they will invent pleasures for me—without danger of increasing the population!—for I am truly afraid of all these starving slaves. Almshouses, prisons, and penal colonies are not enough, and the cannons no longer destroy them since *war has become civilized!*—Oh, WOMAN, your fertility is a scourge! WOMAN, *be cautious!"*

WOMAN, WOMAN! Will you never blush from the role you play? Will you always be duped by the *false knowledge* of MAN? Do you not see him now, forced as he is by circumstances to call you to equality, donning the cloak of pride and egotism and seeking it in an *individual wife.*

Oh, MAN! the voice of the individual wife will be weak.—Her kisses will be cold!—Her glory will be your glory, and, chained to each other, you will either be useless to society or else despots in a new form.

Women! give thanks to God, the *only* FATHER of the COLLECTIVE *husband and wife.* Render thanks unto him for using the cause of our slavery, *the pride of men,* to call us to your freedom.

Our freedom has been formulated by several men, and in several works we will find the science of the future which we will have to put into practice. In renewing the mystery of creation a second time, GOD has formed a wife from the rib of a husband, and when he awakens, he will again be astonished by her beauty! GOD will give this collective couple the knowledge of good and evil, which our MOTHER Eve had unveiled before its time, and the reign of evil will be destroyed, for WOMAN will have crushed the serpent's head: *Individual pride.*

A *new* MOTHER,
Unita*

[*Tribune des femmes* 2: 169–79.]

A Divorce**

Dreaming of a perfection not of this earth, we believe that one day God will introduce us to a man worthy of all our love, who will himself love us for eternity.—This is the dream that poor mortals dream from the moment that their eyes sparkle and their hearts beat with the inexplicable charm of a sweet revery of love. We want to love only once, and isolate ourselves from all of nature to clothe the beloved object in the form created by our imagination. Then comes a day when the illusion ends. . . . This moment is frightful for anyone who does not know how to find a noble subject of compensation in a great thought.

Keep us from the errors of our imagination, heart, and senses if we do not feel in ourselves the power to rise above the *absurd prejudice* which insists that only a *first passion* or *bond* seal the destiny of *woman.* Or rather, since this completely divine precaution belongs only to GOD, let us fear to share society's disingenuous terror of *divorce.*

So long as *marriage* exists, *a law of divorce* will be the *necessary* complement—but not as it has just been voted in the legislative chamber. Resurrected from the eighteenth century, it can have only a negative value.*** [. . .] What is its spirit? Is it moral? Does it take account of antipathies—repulsions—the weariness of always having to live the same life as another? Does it make individuals happy?—Does it show them another way when they have taken the wrong path? Not in the least.—

---

*This anonymous author might be Désirée Veret; she had recently moved to London.
**A somewhat different version of this episode, recounted decades later, appears in Voilquin's autobiography *Memories of a Daughter of the People,* reprinted here.
***Between 1831 and 1834, several divorce bills were passed in the Chamber of Deputies but were never approved in the Chamber of Peers. Divorce was re-legalized only in 1884.

When, then, will it intervene? When falsehood, fraud, discord, and the scourges of intimacy are introduced into the household, and harmony has been banished?—It is then that *divorce*, as dry, cold, and insensitive as a written text, and the same for all situations, comes not to *disassociate* two individuals who no longer understand each other, but to *break* violently two existences and cast them far away from one another.

I too understand and want *divorce* in this transitory period. I request and demand it as a justice and the essential corollary for reaching our *moral freedom.*—But at the same time I do not want it to be as it was in the past, accompanied by *injustice, hatred, violence,* and *fraud.* In one issue of the *Tribune des femmes*, I have already discussed such matters by lightly touching upon this important question: "Who does not now understand, however little one has advanced in the knowledge of life, that it is absurd to contract a marriage without this corrective? Who can be sure that a few years will not bring about a complete transformation of our tastes, desires, and thoughts? It is unheard of that in this century of *guarantees*, one does not seek to be sure of what is most noble in us, *the independence of our will.* Why do we thus shackle ourselves, finite creatures that we are, with eternal chains? GOD alone has the *right* and *strength* to establish *eternal* laws." I announced that I was going to follow these words with an article which should complete my whole thought upon this important subject. I had at that time the intention I am going to fulfill today of practicing a living morality, that is to say of recounting a *fact*, an act carried out under the inspiration of a very elevated social feeling, in accordance with my very strong desire to emancipate women from the necessity of *falsehood, moral adultery, and legal prostitution in marriage* by my example. In order to provide an introduction to the public declaration of *my divorce* and a better understanding of the spirit in which this great act was decided and carried out, I put these words in the article already cited: "May the religion of the future be as beautiful and vast as infinite love, receiving to its bosom all kinds of individuals and natures. Oh, then the laws supported upon this foundation will no longer be repressive, but will prevent evil, soften separation, calm sorrows, and prevent the birth or propagation of hatred, etc., etc." If at the time of my separation from *Voilquin* (about fifteen months ago) I did not carry out this resolution, it was certainly not from any feeling of self-pity. I did not shrink before the consequences of my desire. I was ready to brave anything, for within me, in my conscience, was the affirmation that what I had done was *great*! But I had to stop myself, faced with the certainty of not then being understood by *women.*—My goal was to be useful to my sex through my example, and to instruct rather than demoralize it.—I waited . . . A few women understood me and loved me for my courage and devotion to the cause I was embracing.—Thank you, dear companions, the good that you have done me is a sacred debt in my heart. I will acquit myself of that debt by paying it back to other women.

Today society has come back to me, and *women* are ready to understand me.—I can teach *everyone* about the new route that I was the first to dare travel. Placing myself above the narrow, petty customs that men *alone* have transformed into law, raising my thought to a universal conception—the freedom of woman—I have rejected as antihuman a law which oppressed me. *The name of a man* seemed to my independent spirit too heavy a yoke to bear, and I put it down. . . . But I am stopping here, I must hasten to make known and appreciated the man to whom I was united for eight years through more detailed explanations. His *kind, loyal* character, his true enthusiasm for everything that is *generous and great*, his conduct in regard to me during those eight long years—everything has made it my duty not to allow *his name, character, or honor* to be darkened by an injurious doubt.

On *April 26, 1825*, I married *Voilquin*. This union was contracted *freely* but without *love* on my side. Alas! does one know the whys and wherefores of *love or indifference*? No. It is one of the impenetrable mysteries of life.

—In truth, despite my horror of lies and any *lack of faith*, I do not believe it right to attribute the entirely Christian behavior I observed during the eight years of our union to what society calls *virtue*.—My merit was entirely *negative*, to be found in my *indifference*, or rather in my *contempt* for all *men*.—In the morning of my life, one of them had so *vilely* deceived me . . . playing with that which is most sacred in the soul of a tender, exalted girl . . . and pledging his faith upon my *mother* and my GOD!—my two cherished beliefs—to make me believe him. From that moment on, the brilliant dreams of my imagination, the joyous illusions I had expected and demanded from life, and the expansive trust I felt in my soul for everyone who approached me *were all annihilated*.—At that time I lived a life of *anguish, doubt, and mistrust*.—From then on I expected no more from life . . . and yet I did not destroy myself.—I believed in the immortality of the soul!!

Two years later, too passionate not to have suffered cruelly from the emptiness of my soul, I resolved to become a mother.—These little angels have slipped out of GOD's bosom for such a short time, I thought . . . they are so *pure*! that one doubtless need only surround them with a great deal of love to keep them safe from the contagious breath of men and the vices of society. But I would have to give them my *love, a name*, and an *existence*. This thought convinced me to sacrifice my independence and *get married*.—*Voilquin* loved me; he had a sincere nature which was very likable in my eyes.—I married him, promising myself to make him happy and repay his devotion through constant and diligent care.—*Voilquin* has openly testified that I kept my word. I alone lived in renunciation and sacrifice for these eight years and, alas, without seeing my hope realized. . . .

Today I want to recount only the *act* which relates in a very special way to the work of emancipation that has henceforth been an integral part of my life. Too many details from before this time would therefore be superfluous, and I would not even have *mentioned my past* in regard to the present, were it not that a better understanding of my thoughts on *divorce* would establish the connection between the new ideas which had awakened my soul from its long lethargy and the moral frame of mind in which the two of us then found ourselves.

We came to know *Saint-Simonianism* in 1831. The political principles of this doctrine revived the hopes and illusions for the future of the *people* that the aftermath of the *July Revolution* had so quickly taken away from us.—Later, persuaded that *this* was the future, we resolved to dedicate ourselves wholly to the propagation of this new social science.—As soon as *Voilquin's* talents could find a place within *this family*, he left his architectural clientele, and we became participants—body and soul—in this *new world*.

A little later the FATHER gave the *theories* on the *liberty of women* to the *Saint-Simonian family* and the *world.—Voilquin*, as a man of faith and enthusiasm, was among the first to feel their lofty morality and adopted them completely.—He did not think then that he would be among the first called upon to justify his *faith* through *practice*.

Between the theory of a principle and its translation into practice, there is an abyss to fill even for the strongest men.—It was therefore up to me, for the tranquillity of my heart and conscience and also for the sake of the religion I had embraced, to prevent *Voilquin* from falling into it and becoming demoralized. And so, from the moment I decided to be no more than a *sister* for *him*—since the most intimate relations had demanded from me a constant dissimulation—I had to set my mind to a long and sustained preparation in order to avoid later, at the moment of this declaration, a shock too painful for him.—I had promised before the altar of the Christians to make the man I still call with pleasure *my good Eugène* happy. I could not, therefore, do things halfway if I were to fulfill this vow. *Voilquin* was only thirty-four years old and loved women passionately. He could never have stood being abandoned by the woman whom he had often taken pleasure in naming the cherished companion of his old age, if his imagination had not previously presented another *type* to him and if his heart had not fallen in love with another *woman*.

In the winter of 1832, I held some small gatherings at my home. A young woman named *Julie Parsy* came. She loved *Voilquin* first, with all the ardor of a deeply sensitive nature. I noticed this, did not encourage the feeling, but let it be born, persuaded that if I saw him divided I would have the strength within me to *sanctify* it, by ceding to *Julie* my function of *guardian angel* (as later I wrote to him) toward the man she loved, as well as all the rights society had vested in me.

What I had foreseen happened: *Voilquin* felt touched in spite of himself by such a true love, the love he was unable to arouse in me. . . . It was at this moment that I thought I must end the difficult and even painful situation restraining the three of us.—At the end of January 1833, I announced to *Voilquin* that even *marriage* seemed like *prostitution* to me, if *love* did not unite the two partners. I told him that since I felt for him only a tender affection, I wanted to restrict our intimate relations and limit them to a state of absolute fraternity.—He understood me and yielded to this desire.—I must confess, however, that this moment had an aura of sorrow and at the same time solemnity for both of us.

When we had given each other our word without any restriction, we agreed to inform the man we so tenderly loved of this divorce. We both wrote to the man we call the FATHER *in his prison*, and announced to him the *act* we had just carried out in such a religious manner.—Since we did not communicate our letters to each other, so that we could feel more free, I do not know the contents of *Voilquin's* letter.

In my own, I said among other things: "I am free!! I have deposed my rights on the altar of humanity! I have freed a man from a love that was not shared. *Voilquin* showed himself to be *great*; yes, I say that with pride. I have put a man into the world; I have given him to *everyone*, etc., etc."

Since then, *Julie Parsy* and *Voilquin*, whom I regard as truly united and legitimately belonging to each other, have left for *America* and have been in *New Orleans* for ten months, where I hope they will be able to regain a social position for themselves.

Despite the difficulty of my material situation after their departure, it must, however, be seen that the new ideas did not succeed in upsetting my destiny, but rather in bringing me to a superior existence by reviving in me the life I thought was extinguished. [. . .]

Since this separation, I have remained *alone* before the world.—My reconquered freedom has permitted me to work more effectively for the freedom of my sex.—Reassured of my friends' future in America, I feel happy about their love. As much as I can, I am propagating this maxim that I wish to see adopted by women as a foundation for the relations between the sexes.—Any intimate relation that does not have love for its foundation is a profanity of the flesh.

It is up to great and sublime women to say and show how far *social love* should go.

Suzanne

[*Tribune des femmes* 2: 180–84.]

The *Tribune des femmes* will no longer be published under my direction.* The *antireligious law* against *associations*, just promulgated by our blind governors, will soon drive many generous and enthusiastic hearts

---

*Suzanne has decided to join the Saint-Simonians in Egypt.

away from our beautiful France. It is time to think about the practical side of life, for soon the *Orient* will demand our active and powerful participation. Other women will continue this work of theory. They too will be strong and devoted women, but attached by their bonds and affections to our dear France.

For us, feeling an ardent desire in our soul to cooperate in every way with this gigantic work of regeneration, as prelude to universal association; for us, marked by GOD for this work, it is necessary to hasten our preparations, for the hour of departure, the impatiently awaited sublime hour will soon, for some of us, be sounded. Two of our sisters have already preceded us. Courageous women, GOD is just, and in the future your names will be repeated with love. *Cécile Fournel*, model of conjugal love, your past of complete devotion will be remembered. And you, young and beautiful *Clorinde* [Rogé], who, through devotion to your sex, felt in your soul the strength to leave the man who is for you at once *friend, lover,* and *husband,* our good *Roger* [sic], and go far away to blaze new paths for women, your name will henceforth recall the *new heroism,* the *woman* ready to sacrifice her most intimate and cherished feelings for *religious* and *social* ideas.

Yes, *Barault* [sic] was right when his thought, so to speak, stopped the *century* and created a *new era by feminizing the year 1833* and naming it the *year of the MOTHER.* It was in this year that the feeling for *woman* was deeply incarnated in the hearts of a host of men who had adopted the theory of equality between the sexes, but without being aware of the consequences of this principle. Glory to *Barault*! [sic] for fertilizing the thought of the FATHER, for the great enthusiasm he imprinted upon our spirits, for his new knighthood, for his voyage to the Orient and his audacious call to the MOTHER in the land of slavery, right where *woman* is most oppressed. He allowed women to penetrate into *the practice of the new life* through their *acts.* Yes, this *year* will remain the *year* of the MOTHER of WOMAN. Although still mystical, this will be more and more understood and will in the eyes of the future rehabilitate every act and work carried out in the present.

It was only toward the beginning of this year that the act which has had such an important place in my life, *my divorce,* could be realized.

Shortly thereafter occurred the union of two young people: *Angélique* [surname unknown] and *Javary,* both free to accept the laws of society, instead refused them and, inspired by the new life, placed their trust in each other's honor.

Then *Jeanne Désirée* [Veret]'s departure for England took place. This young woman of the people was not the first to think of creating a newspaper by *women,* but the first with the courage to execute it. It was she who founded our little paper under the title *Apostolat des femmes* without any material means for beginning this work, together with *Marie Reine*

[Guindorf] and myself, who did not join with these two young people until the second issue.

Désirée's wholly artistic way of thinking did not permit her to remain attached to a long-term work, and she withdrew a short time later, asking us to preserve her title *Journal Founder*. It was also she who had the energetic audacity to present to *Louis-Philippe* a powerfully conceived petition in favor of the people. . . . Now she is in England where she serves in any way she can the cause of *women* and *progress*.

Marie-Reine, my codirector for a long time, left this position only to satisfy more specifically her ardent compassion for the people in this *year of 1833*. She became a member of the Association for Popular Instruction, and since then her days have been dedicated to work and her evenings spent educating women and girls of the people.

In this same year, women in *Paris* and *Lyon*, impressed by the new life, became active in every possible way. In *Lyon*, proletarian women even sold their looms in order to devote themselves more completely to the propagation of their faith, and some are still on mission in southern France in order to share their hope with other women.

Later on, all these names and events, as well as others that cannot now be placed in this summary because they still belong to the women who accomplished them, will be written into the new history.

To you a remembrance, poor *Claire Démar*! who came to agonize and die in our midst—rejected by this society which could not understand the urgency of your passionate affections. Poor soul! Soon will come the time of justice for you. I will rehabilitate you by making your last thoughts known—you who practiced life to its limits without, however, being debased by it, since through your strength alone, you raised yourself to the conception of a social theory—you who knew moral pain, who felt it so profoundly that you *died* of it! Poor Claire! To grant you rest, I will make known in a short while to *everyone* your last piece of writing,* the remedy that you thought fit to apply to so many evils.

In times of moral revolution, as in times of political revolution: "One must dare." This maxim is true.—Therefore I highly affirm it for every woman who has the consciousness of her strength and the courage of her opinion. She must act and carry others along by her example. From the multiplicity of these acts, we will rise to the unity of their principle.—GOD is ONE and MANY at the same time, equally *great* and *sacred* in each of these two eternal aspects.

Until a sublime woman comes to epitomize her sex and receive from a burst of our heart the noble name of MOTHER, let us all act according

---

*It was Voilquin who published *My Law of the Future*. Its appearance is noted in a small announcement in this issue.

to our own conscience, but without reprobation or anathema for those who have the boldness to justify their theory of the future through daily practice. —Timid women, do not, therefore, allow yourselves to be frightened by the clamorings of society.—Has the man you lovingly call the FATHER hesitated to confer his word of the future upon society, in order to emancipate you from a decrepit moral law?—It is better to take the wrong road and have to retrace one's steps than to remain huddled at the edge of the path, freezing life through inaction. As for myself, I no longer ask women to come and raise argument against argument on such a delicate subject and remain inactive before the ideal thought of the MOTHER.

The future is before us.

Does not each of us have her heart to understand this future? And since the sun of our God, who is all-loving, illuminates all paths—let us advance! Only, oh women! have consciousness of your strength and find at the bottom of your heart this thought as motive for your acts: *In order to be religious and sublime, the influence of woman must join together with the social harmonization and progressive pacification of the globe.* May this compass guide and help us to travel new roads. Let us grow enough to deserve the recognition of the whole world. May the *century*, before leaving its name on the urn of time, see the *Pantheon of Women* erected in our honor. And may these words be engraved in gold letters in the center of its base:

TO WOMAN, FROM A GRATEFUL HUMANITY!

Suzanne [Voilquin]

NOTES

1. Introduction

1. See Claire G. Moses, "Saint-Simonian Men/Saint-Simonian Women: The Transformation of Feminist Thought in 1830s' France," *Journal of Modern History* 54 (June 1982): 240–67; and *French Feminism in the Nineteenth Century* (Albany: State University of New York Press, 1984). See also, Leslie Wahl Rabine, *The Other Side of the Ideal: Women Writers of Mid-Nineteenth Century France* (Ph.D. diss., Stanford University, 1973); and "George Sand and the Myth of Femininity," *Women and Literature* 4, no. 2 (Fall 1976): 2–17.

2. See Dominick LaCapra, "Between History and Criticism," and Stanley Fish, "Being Interdisciplinary Is So Very Hard to Do," in *Profession 89* (New York: Modern Language Association, 1989), 4–14.

3. Especially useful for the relationship between history and poststructuralism are Joan Scott's *Gender and the Politics of History* (New York: Columbia University Press, 1988), "Deconstructing Equality-versus-Difference: Or, the Uses of Poststructuralist Theory for Feminism," *Feminist Studies* 14 (Spring 1988): 33–50, and "The Evidence of Experience," *Critical Inquiry* 17 (Summer 1991): 773–97. See also Jeffrey Weeks, "Foucault for Historians," *History Workshop Journal*, no. 14 (Autumn 1982): 106–18; and a series of articles published in the *American Historical Review*: John E. Toews, "Intellectual History after the Turn: The Autonomy of Meaning and the Irreducibility of Experience," 92 (October 1987): 809–907; David Harlan, "Intellectual History and the Return of Literature," David A. Hollinger, "The Return of the Prodigal: The Persistence of Historical Knowing," and David Harlan, "Reply to David Hollinger," all in 94 (June 1989): 581–626; and Joyce Appleby, "One Good Turn Deserves Another: Moving beyond the Linguistic; A Response to David Harlan," 94 (December 1989): 1326–32.

4. This point is made by Ruth Roach Pierson, in a thought-provoking article—"Experience, Difference, Dominance and Voice in the Writing of Women's History"—published in *Writing Women's History*, ed. Karen Offen, Ruth Roach Pierson, and Jane Rendall (Bloomington: Indiana University Press, 1991), 79–106. She uses the example of Joan Kelly's article "Did Women Have a Renaissance?" (in *Becoming Visible: Women in European History*, ed. Renate Bridenthal and Claudia Koonz [Boston: Houghton Mifflin, 1977], 137–64; reprinted as chap. 2 of *Women, History, and Theory: The Essays of Joan Kelly* [Chicago: University of Chicago Press, 1984], 19–50) in discussing how feminist historians have privileged the concept of "women's experience" in their challenges of what Jean-François Lyotard has called the " 'grand narratives' of western history." In calling for a reconsideration of the Renaissance, Kelly based her argument on the claim that women did not "experience" this historical moment as men had. Pierson also cites a later article by Kelly, "Feminist Theory and the *Querelle des Femmes*, 1400–1789" (*Signs* 8 [Autumn 1982]: 4–28; reprinted as chap. 4 of *Women, History, and Theory*, 65–109) plus Virginia Woolf's *A Room of One's Own* to illustrate the importance that feminists attach to "experience" as the source of our knowledge of oppression. "The spark of feminism, or 'proto-feminism,' has been seen [by Kelly, Woolf, and most feminist historians] to be ignited in a woman's consciousness at that moment when she senses a discrepancy between the cultural definition of 'woman' and her own experience of herself or of other 'women' " (83).

5. See Pierson. Also see, however, "A Statistical Representation of Work: *La Statistique de l'Industrie à Paris, 1847–1848*" in Joan Scott's *Gender and the Politics of History*, 113–38, where she argues convincingly that even such seemingly neutral "facts" as government statistics are shaped by hegemonic discourses.

6. Roland Barthes, "To Write: An Intransitive Verb?" in *The Structuralist Controversy: The Languages of Criticism and the Sciences of Man*, ed. Richard Macksey and Eugenio Donato (Baltimore: The Johns Hopkins University Press, 1970); Emile Benveniste, *Problèmes de linguistique générale* (Paris: Gallimard, 1966); and Michel Foucault, "Qu'est-ce qu'un auteur," *Bulletin de la Société de Philosophie 63*, no. 3 (1969): 75–104.

7. See Ruth Milkman, "Women's History and the Sears Case," *Feminist Studies* 12 (Summer 1986); Carol Sternhell, "Life in the Mainstream: What Happens When Feminists Turn Up on Both Sides of the Courtroom?" *Ms.* 15 (July 1986): 48–51, 86–91; Jon Weiner, "The Sears Case: Women's History on Trial," *The Nation*, September 7, 1985, cover, 176–80; "Exchange," ibid., October 26, 1985, 394, 410–11; Samuel J. Freedman, "Of History and Politics: Bitter Feminist Debate," *New York Times*, June 6, 1986, B1, 4; "Misusing History," *Washington Post*, June 9, 1986, A20; Jonathan Yardley, "When Scholarship & the Cause Collide," ibid., June 16, 1986, C2; and Joan Scott, "Deconstructing Equality-versus-Difference."

8. See Sally Alexander, "Women, Class, and Sexual Difference in the 1830s and 1840s: Some Reflections on the Writing of a Feminist History," *History Workshop*, no. 17 (Spring 1984): 125–49. See also the most complete study of Owenite feminism, Barbara Taylor's *Eve and the New Jerusalem: Socialism and Feminism in the Nineteenth Century* (New York: Pantheon, 1983).

9. On the "women's culture" of white, middle-class women, see especially Nancy Cott, *The Bonds of Womanhood: "Woman's Sphere" in New England, 1780–1835* (New Haven: Yale University Press, 1977); and Carroll Smith-Rosenberg, "The Female World of Love and Ritual: Relations between Women in Nineteenth-Century America," *Signs*1 (Autumn 1975). On white, working-class "women's culture," see Alice Kessler-Harris's *Out to Work: A History of Wage-Earning Women in the United States* (New York: Oxford University Press, 1982), and "Problems of Coalition-Building: Women and Trade Unions in the 1920s," in *Women, Work, and Protest: A Century of U.S. Women's Labor History*, ed. Ruth Milkman (Boston: Routledge & Kegan Paul, 1985). On black women, see Jacqueline Jones, " 'My Mother Was Much of a Woman': Black Women, Work, and the Family from Slavery to the Present," *Feminist Studies* 8 (Summer 1982); and Deborah Gray White, *Ar'n't I a Woman? Female Slaves in the Plantation South* (New York: W. W. Norton, 1985).

10. Ellen DuBois, Mari Jo Buhle, Temma Kaplan, Gerda Lerner, and Carroll Smith-Rosenberg, "Politics and Culture in Women's History: A Symposium," *Feminist Studies* 6 (Spring 1980): 26–64.

11. Nancy F. Cott, *The Bonds of Womanhood*.

12. For the influence of religious beliefs and organizations on early American feminism, see Barbara J. Berg, *The Remembered Gate: Origins of American Feminism: The Woman and the City* (New York: Oxford University Press, 1978); Ellen Carol DuBois, *Feminism and Suffrage: The Emergence of an Independent Women's Movement in America, 1848–1869* (Ithaca: Cornell University Press, 1978); and Nancy Hewitt, *Women's Activism and Social Change: Rochester, New York, 1822–1872* (Ithaca: Cornell University Press, 1984). For the British experience, see Jane Rendall, *The Origins of Modern Feminism: Women in Britain, France, and the United States, 1780–1860* (London: Macmillan, 1985); Barbara Taylor; and Joan Scott, "Women in *The Making of the English Working Class*," in *Gender and the Politics of History*, 75–79.

13. See Rosi Braidotti, "The Politics of Ontological Difference," in *Between Fem-*

inism and Psychoanalysis, ed. Teresa Brennan (London: Routledge, 1989), 89–105, 89–95; and Leslie Rabine, "Ecriture féminine as Metaphor," *Cultural Critique*, no. 8 (Winter 1987–88): 19–44.

14. *Tribune des femmes* 1: 105; reprinted here.

15. Eléanor H. Kuykendall, "Questions for Julia Kristeva's Ethics of Linguistics," in *The Thinking Muse: Feminism and Modern French Philosophy*, ed. Jeffner Allen and Iris Marion Young (Bloomington: Indiana University Press, 1989), 181.

16. François-René de Chateaubriand, *René*, trans. Irving Putter (Berkeley: University of California Press, 1967); Honoré de Balzac, *The Lily in the Valley*, trans. Lucienne Hill (London: Elek Books, 1957); Stendhal, *The Red and the Black*, trans. C. K. Scott-Moncrieff (New York: The Modern Library, 1953); Gérard de Nerval, *Daughters of Fire: Sylvie-Emilie-Octavie*, trans. James Whitall (New York: N. L. Brown, 1922); Gustave Flaubert, *Sentimental Education*, trans. Perdita Burlingame (New York: New American Library, 1972). See Leslie Rabine, *Reading the Romantic Heroine: Text, History, Ideology* (Ann Arbor: University of Michigan Press, 1985). See also Peter Brooks, *Reading for the Plot: Design and Intention in Narrative* (New York: Knopf, 1984); and Naomi Segal, *Narcissus and Echo: Women in the French Récit* (Manchester: Manchester University Press, 1988).

17. For the classic formulations of this theory, see Claude Lévi-Strauss, *The Elementary Structures of Kinship* (Boston: Beacon Press, 1969); Luce Irigaray, *Ce Sexe qui n'en est pas un* (Paris: Minuit, 1977), 165–194; and Gayle Rubin, "The Traffic in Women: Notes on the 'Political Economy' of Sex," in *Toward an Anthropology of Women*, ed. Rayna R[app] Reiter (New York: Monthly Review Press, 1975), 157–210.

18. For the debate on essentialism in psychoanalytic and poststructuralist theory, see Teresa Brennan, ed., *Between Feminism and Psychoanalysis; The Essential Difference: Another Look at Essentialism*, a special issue of *Differences* 1 (Summer 1989); Judith Butler, *Gender Trouble: Feminism and the Subversion of Identity* (New York: Routledge, 1990); and Tania Modleski, *Feminism without Women: Culture and Criticism in a "Post-feminist Age"* (New York: Routledge, 1991). For this debate in historical theory, see Joan Scott, "Deconstructing Equality-versus-Difference"; Denise Riley, *"Am I That Name?" Feminism and the Category of "Women" in History* (Minneapolis: University of Minnesota Press, 1988); Nancy R. Cott, "Feminist Theory and Feminist Movements: The Past before Us," in *What Is Feminism: A Reexamination*, ed. Juliet Mitchell and Ann Oakley (New York: Pantheon, 1986), 49–62; and Claire G. Moses, " 'Equality' and 'Difference' in Historical Perspective: A Comparative Examination of the Feminisms of French Revolutionaries and Utopian Socialists," in *Rebel Daughters: Women and the French Revolution*, ed. Sara E. Melzer and Leslie W. Rabine (New York: Oxford University Press, 1992), 231–54.

19. Luce Irigaray, *Le Corps-à-corps avec la mère* (Ottawa: Editions de la pleine lune, 1981), quoted in Domna C. Stanton, "Difference on Trial: A Critique of the Maternal Metaphor in Cixous, Irigaray and Kristeva," in *The Poetics of Gender*, ed. Nancy K. Miller (New York: Columbia University Press, 1986), 157–82, 160.

20. Stanton, "Difference on Trial," 161. For analyses of the debate concerning Irigaray's essentialism, see Christine Holmlund, "The Lesbian, the Mother, the Heterosexual Lover: Irigaray's Recodings of Difference," *Feminist Studies* 17 (Summer 1991): 283–308; Naomi Schor, "This Essentialism Which Is Not One," *Differences* 1 (Summer 1989): 38–58; and Margaret Whitford, *Luce Irigaray: Philosophy in the Feminine* (London: Routledge, 1991).

21. *Tribune des femmes* 1: 38; reprinted here.

22. Leslie W. Rabine, "Essentialism and Its Contexts: Saint-Simonian and Post-Structuralist Feminists," *Differences* 1 (Summer 1989): 105–23.

23. Luce Irigaray, *Speculum de l'autre femme* (Paris: Minuit, 1974), 74.

24. Flora Tristan, *Pérégrinations d'une paria (1833–1834)* (Paris: François Maspero, 1979).

25. Flora Tristan, *Peregrinations of a Pariah*, trans. Jean Hawkes (London: Virago, 1986).

2. "Difference" in Historical Perspective

1. See Sylvia Ann Hewlett's *A Lesser Life: The Myth of Women's Liberation in America* (New York: William Morrow, 1986) for a demand for preferential treatment instead of "equality." Lenore Weitzman, *The Divorce Revolution: The Unexpected Social and Economic Consequences for Women and Children in America* (New York: Free Press, 1985) is the source most quoted against gender-neutral, no-fault divorce laws that have hurt homemakers and their children. *California Federal Savings & Loan v. Guerra*, the Supreme Court case involving preferential maternity benefits, found NOW in the uncomfortable position of arguing against California's law guaranteeing maternity leave to Lillian Garland. *EEOC v. Sears, Roebuck* found historians Rosalind Rosenberg and Alice Kessler-Harris on opposing sides (Rosenberg for Sears; Kessler-Harris for EEOC), basing their arguments on these divergent tendencies.

2. Shulamith Firestone, *The Dialectic of Sex: The Case for Feminist Revolution* (New York: Bantam Books, 1970); Kate Millet, *Sexual Politics* (New York: Avon Books, 1970); Elizabeth Janeway, *Man's World, Woman's Place: A Study in Social Mythology* (New York: Dell Publishing, 1971). Firestone went the furthest in the direction of "equality," envisioning that scientific advances in artificial reproduction would make possible the liberation of women even from childbearing—and that this was desirable.

3. Barbara Welter, "The Cult of True Womanhood, 1820–1860," *American Quarterly* 18 (Summer 1966): 131–75.

4. Adrienne Rich, *Of Woman Born: Motherhood as Experience and Institution* (New York: W. W. Norton, 1976); Mary Daly, *Gyn/Ecology: The Metaethics of Radical Feminism* (Boston: Beacon Press, 1978); Carol Gilligan, *In a Different Voice: Psychological Theory and Women's Development* (Cambridge, MA: Harvard University Press, 1982); Jean Bethke Elshtain, *Public Man, Private Woman: Women in Social and Political Thought* (Princeton: Princeton University Press, 1982).

5. Nancy Cott, *The Bonds of Womanhood: "Women's Sphere" in New England, 1780–1835* (New Haven: Yale University Press, 1977); and Carroll Smith-Rosenberg, "The Female World of Love and Ritual: Relations between Women in Nineteenth-Century America," *Signs* 1 (Autumn 1975).

6. On feminist political struggles in France, see Claire Duchen, *Feminism in France: From May '68 to Mitterrand* (London: Routledge & Kegan Paul, 1986), especially for information on the abortion rights movement and on the struggles of socialist women for representation in the Socialist party and in the Mitterrand government. See also Dorothy McBride Stetson, *Women's Rights in France* (New York: Greenwood Press, 1987), especially for information on reform legislation, including reproductive rights, married women's property rights, day care and maternity leave, equal pay, and affirmative action laws covering both the workplace and education.

7. See Hester Eisenstein and Alice Jardine, eds., *The Future of Difference* (Boston: G. K. Hall, 1980); Ellen DuBois, Mari Jo Buhle, Temma Kaplan, Gerda Lerner, Carroll Smith-Rosenberg, "Politics and Culture in Women's History: A Symposium," *Feminist Studies* 6 (Spring 1980): 26–64; and Linda K. Kerber, Catherine G. Greeno and Eleanor E. Maccoby, Zella Luria, Carol B. Stack, and Carol Gilligan, "On *In a Different Voice*: An Interdisciplinary Forum," *Signs* 11 (Winter 1986): 304–33.

8. See the *Tribune des femmes* 1: 197: "The French Revolution produced anarchy." And also, ibid. 1: 234: " . . . women who ask only for *rights* . . . will create only *republicanism* and not *religion*."

9. *Tribune des femmes* 1: 106. Subsequent references to this journal will be included in parentheses in the text and referred to simply as "Tribune."

10. Paule-Marie Duhet, *Les Femmes et la Révolution: 1789–1794* (Paris: Julliard, 1971), 155.

11. Translated and reproduced in Susan Groag Bell and Karen M. Offen, *Women, the Family, and Freedom: The Debate in Documents*, vol. 1, *1750–1880* (Stanford: Stanford University Press, 1983), 99–103. Subsequent references appear in parentheses in the text; they are all to this version.

12. I have translated these passages from the text that is reproduced in Hubertine Auclert, *La Vote des femmes* (Paris: V. Giard & E. Brière, 1908), 78–79. The entire text is translated and reproduced in Darlene Gay Levy, Harriet Branson Applewhite, and Mary Durham Johnson, *Women in Revolutionary Paris, 1789–1795* (Urbana: University of Illinois Press, 1979), 87–96. Subsequent references are to the Levy, Applewhite, and Johnson version and will be included in parentheses in the text.

13. In Levy, Applewhite, and Johnson, 75–77.

14. Ibid., 123.

15. Ibid., 77.

16. Londa Schiebinger, "Skeletons in the Closet: The First Illustrations of the Female Skeleton in Eighteenth-Century Anatomy," in *The Making of the Modern Body: Sexuality and Society in the Nineteenth Century*, ed. Catherine Gallagher and Thomas Laqueur (Berkeley: University of California Press, 1987), 48.

17. Thomas Laqueur, "Orgasm, Generation, and the Politics of Reproductive Biology," in *The Making of the Modern Body*, 4. Laqueur explores these theories through the works of the second-century medical writer Galen, who was still influential at this time.

18. Erna O. Hellerstein, "Women, Social Order, and the City: Rules for French Ladies, 1830–1870," (Ph.d. diss., University of California at Berkeley, 1981), 67.

19. Schiebinger, 46–47.

20. Laqueur, Schiebinger, and Hellerstein. Both Hellerstein and Schiebinger maintain that a medical, biological, or anatomical view of women that stressed their difference from men did not predominate until the nineteenth century. Laqueur gives more weight to earlier, mid-eighteenth-century views which already articulated the biology of "difference." He believes that biological views stressing difference grounded both the antifeminism of the Revolution and a new kind of feminism whose emergence he dates to the Revolution. I, however, note that Revolutionary feminists most often argue from "sameness" and locate the emergence of a feminism of "difference" in the 1830s.

21. Hellerstein, 67.

22. Ibid.

23. Phillipe-Joseph-Benjamin Buchez, letter to Enfantin [October 1829], "Archives," 1: 508–10, Fonds Enfantin 7643.

24. *Tribune des femmes* 1: 223. The author continues: "Mary has influence but no power, and no action, in the government of heaven; her prayer is all powerful upon her divine son, but she prays, she intercedes; by herself she does not act."

25. See Leslie Rabine, "Essentialism and Its Contexts: Saint-Simonian and Post-Structuralist Feminists," *Differences* 1 (Summer 1989): 105–23. See also, Alan Richardson, "Romanticism and the Colonization of the Feminine," in *Romanticism and Feminism*, ed. Anne K. Mellor (Bloomington: Indiana University Press, 1988), 13–25.

26. Joan Landes, *Women and the Public Sphere in the Age of the French Revolution* (Ithaca: Cornell University Press, 1988), 87.

27. Ibid., 40.

28. Ibid., 116. Although it is true that the kind of goals we associate with Revolutionary feminists—education, equal rights, etc.—were of less concern to *Saint-Simoniennes*, there were a few occasions when they wrote about these matters as well. When they did so, their depiction of women changed from positive to negative. For example, (Marie-)Reine Guindorf (see *Tribune des femmes* 1: 114), in calling for "equal opportunity . . . in education," explains that women should not be excluded from a career in science just because of their "flightiness," since they are "flighty" and (later) "frivolous" only because of their inferior education. Depicting women as flighty or frivolous is typical of Revolutionary rhetoric—one is reminded here of Mary Wollstonecraft—but rare among the *Saint-Simoniennes*. However, Guindorf could not express a "Revolutionary" goal (for education) without using the Revolution's discourse; it was as if it were a package deal.

29. Robert B. Carlisle, *The Proffered Crown: Saint-Simonianism and the Doctrine of Hope* (Baltimore: Johns Hopkins University Press, 1987), 22. Carlisle's full-length study of the Saint-Simonian men—the first in almost a century—was especially helpful in providing the kind of biographical detail that points to a relationship between the men's theory and their lives.

30. Carlisle (21) gives these interesting statistics to illustrate the aging of the group holding positions of power in Restoration France: Between 1818 and 1830, the percentage of prefects who were over fifty years old increased from 15 to 55. At the same time "France was becoming young. Those under forty years old constituted 67 percent of the population." He cites Bertier de Sauvigny: "The youth was, therefore, bulging with lawyers without cases, doctors without patients, sons of workers and peasants whose studies had incapacitated them for manual labor [and] . . . young bourgeois furious at having to mark time in waiting rooms or seeing themselves hopelessly relegated to subordinate administrative positions."

31. Carlisle, 21.

32. Gustave d'Eichthal, in Prosper Enfantin and Henri, comte de Saint-Simon, *Oeuvres de Saint-Simon et d'Enfantin* (Paris: E. Dentu, Ernest Leroux, 1865–78), 47: 405–27.

33. Saint-Simon, in *Oeuvres*, 1: 159.

34. Cited in Carlisle, 86.

35. This is a more pluralist conception of androgyny than is common today: rather than a unitary being that blends male and female personality characteristics into something different, the concept of androgyny in the 1830s supposed that male and female existed side by side inside a dual being.

36. Buchez, letter to Enfantin [October 1829], "Archives," 1: 509, Fonds Enfantin 7643.

37. Enfantin, response to Buchez [October 1829], "Archives," 1: 513 verso.

38. These words are Enfantin's, uttered at his trial and reprinted in the *Tribune des femmes* more than once (1: 193, 194, 222).

39. Carlisle, 152.

40. Enfantin, letter to his mother, August 18, 1831, in *Oeuvres*, 27: 194.

41. See above, p. 22.

42. According to Roderick Phillips, the 1792 divorce law "gave France one of the most liberal and permissive divorce policies that have ever been applied on a national basis in Western society; it is rivaled in these characteristics only by modern Swedish divorce law." See his *Putting Asunder: A History of Divorce in Western Society* (Cambridge: Cambridge University Press, 1988), 159.

43. Phillips (256–76) gives information and statistics on the frequency of divorce during the Revolutionary period that make clear that divorce was very acceptable, particularly in the cities and particularly in the first years of the new law (a pent-up demand may also have figured in the high incidence of divorce in

the first years). Among unilateral divorce actions, women petitioned for two-thirds to three-quarters of divorces. I found Phillips particularly useful for sorting out France's various laws on divorce, which changed repeatedly and rapidly during this period.

44. Cf. Rousseau: "Woman is made . . . to be in subjection to a man. . . . [The man] must have both the power and the will; . . . [the woman] . . . should offer little resistance." Rousseau, *Emile*, trans. Barbara Foxley (New York: Dutton, 1933), 322.

45. Louis de Bonald, cited in Raymond Deniel, *Une Image de la famille et de la société sous la Restauration* (Paris: Les Editions ouvrières, 1965), 103.

46. This is not to say that the discourse associating the late *ancien régime* with powerful women accurately reflected "reality"; the so-called power of women in the courts of Louis XV and Louis XVI was undoubtedly overrated. But deconstructing this discourse is a complex matter and certainly worthy of further attention.

47. Charles Fourier, *Manuscrits publiés par la Phalange*, 622, in Jonathan Beecher, *Charles Fourier: The Visionary and His World* (Berkeley: University of California Press, 1986), 305.

48. Beecher, 238–39. Fourier's notebooks were published only in 1967, by Simone Debout-Oleskiewicz. For this passage, see *Le Nouveau monde amoureux* (Paris: Editions Anthropos, 1967), 391.

49. See Beecher, 299–301; see also Mark Poster, *The Utopian Thought of Restif de la Bretonne* (New York: New York University Press, 1971), esp. chap. 3.

50. In other western European countries and in the United States, the decline in fertility rates was as precipitous as in France, but it did not begin until later in the century.

51. See Louis Henry, "The Population of France in the Eighteenth Century"; and Pierre Goubert, "Recent Theories and Research in French Population between 1500 and 1700"; both in D. V. Glass and D. E. C. Eversley, eds., *Population in History* (Chicago: Aldine, 1965).

52. Etienne Van de Walle, *The Female Population of France in the Nineteenth Century* (Princeton: Princeton University Press, 1974), 9, 136–44.

53. Philippe Ariès, "Interpretation pour une histoire des mentalités," in Hélène Bergues et al., *Prévention des naissances dans la famille* (Paris: Presses Universitaires de France, 1960), 314–23.

54. William Parish, Jr., and Moshe Schwartz, "Household Complexity in Nineteenth Century France," *American Sociological Review* 37 (April 1972): 154–73.

55. Roger Price, *The Economic Modernisation of France* (New York: John Wiley & Sons, 1975), 188–89.

56. Alfred Sauvy, "Essai d'une vue d'ensemble," in Bergues et al., 389–90.

57. Ariès, "Interprétation pour une histoire des mentalités," 316.

58. Caroline to Suzanne Voilquin, no date, Fonds Enfantin 7627.

59. Angus McLaren, "Abortion in France: Women and the Regulation of Family Size, 1800–1914," *French Historical Studies* 10 (Spring 1978): 461–85.

60. William H. Sewell, Jr., "Property, Labor, and the Emergence of Socialism in France, 1789–1848," in *Consciousness and Class Experience in Nineteenth-Century Europe*, ed. John M. Merriman (New York: Holmes & Meier, 1979), 45.

61. See Barrie Ratcliffe, "Saint-Simonism and Messianism: The Case of Gustave d'Eichthal," *French Historical Studies* 9 (Spring 1976): 497–99.

62. Carlisle, 157.

63. [Saint-Amand Bazard], *Religion Saint-Simonienne. Discussions morales, politiques et religieuses qui ont amenées la séparation qui s'est effectuée au mois de novembre, 1831, dans le sein da la société Saint-Simonienne* (Paris: Paulin, Delaunay, and Heideloff, 1832).

64. Duveyrier was able to arrange to serve his prison term in a clinic, but

Chevalier and Enfantin refused to do this, choosing instead the martyrdom of prison at Saint-Pélagie. Chevalier served five months of his sentence before arranging to be transferred to a clinic. Enfantin served seven months before being pardoned in a general amnesty in celebration of the king's birthday.

65. Carlisle, 189–90.

66. These words are Carol Gilligan's, from the title of her book *In a Different Voice: Psychological Theory and Women's Development*.

67. Enfantin, *Oeuvres*, 3: 21.

68. For the number of women, see Enfantin to Fournel, October 26, 1830, "Archives," 2: 33–34, Fonds Enfantin 7644. Sébastien Charléty (*Essai sur l'histoire du Saint-Simonisme* [Paris: Hachette, 1896], 115) estimates the total number of people in Saint-Simonian audiences at this time at 400–500.

69. Suzanne Voilquin, *Souvenirs d'une fille du people ou la Saint-Simonienne en Egypte* (Paris: E. Sauzet, 1866), 78. Subsequent references will be included in parentheses in the text and referred to simply as "Memories."

70. Marguerite Thibert, *Le Féminisme dans le socialisme français de 1830 à 1850* (Paris: M. Giard, 1926), 202–203n. 2.

71. Charléty (115–16) says that women comprised one-third of the total 330 adherents.

72. Louise Crouzat to Claire Démar, in Claire Démar, *Textes sur l'affranchissement des femmes*, followed by an explanation of Saint-Simonian symbolism and ideology by Valentin Pelosse (Paris: Payot, 1976), 136.

73. In the *Tribune des femmes* 1: 111, the editors declared that their periodical would first address "religious" and "moral" questions, although they were also willing to consider some articles on women's "material misfortunes."

74. Fournel: "[I] must declare before you that I reject the important-sounding theory that has been exposed here, no matter what you say. . . . I think that all the women who hear me, who know me, understand that to reject this theory . . . I must have felt something profoundly immoral in it, and I hope to share my fears and make the women, over whom I may still have some influence, aware of the danger they are running." The *compte rendu* of that meeting also records the outcry of "many women: Yes! Yes!" in response to Fournel's words. See Enfantin, *Réunion générale de la famille: Séances des 19 et 21 novembre* (Paris: Bureau de *Globe*, 1832), 36–37.

75. Fournel to Aglaé Saint-Hilaire, Fonds Enfantin 7727, no. 40. Although this letter is undated, it was likely written in June 1834.

76. See *Tribune des femmes* 1: 153–57, for the first of Gertrude's articles; for the editors' response, see 1: 157–61; for Gertrude's second article, see 1: 171–77; for the editors' second response, see 1: 195–98.

77. *Tribune des femmes* 1: 63. Compare the title of Claire Démar's publication, *My Law of the Future*.

78. Jeanne-Désirée [Veret], in *La Femme libre* (*Tribune des femmes* 1, no. 1), 2; Josephine-Félicité [Milizet], in *Apostolat des femmes* (*Tribune des femmes* 1, no. 2), 3; Marie-Reine [Guindorf], in *Tribune des femmes* 1: 202. See also Christine-Sophie, "On Prostitution," in *Apostolat des femmes* (*Tribune des femmes* 1, no. 4): 2–4.

79. "Réponse à Gertrude," in *Tribune des femmes* 1: 159. This article was signed "the new women," but I cannot tell which of the editors actually wrote it. A later response to Gertrude's second article was signed "A.I."—perhaps Angélique and Isabelle?

80. Jeanne-Désirée [Veret], in *La Femme libre* (*Tribune des femmes* 1, no. 1): 2; Suzanne [Voilquin], in *Tribune des femmes* 1: 170. Jeanne-Désirée [Veret], in *Apostolat des femmes* (*Tribune des femmes* 1, no. 2): 3; Christine-Sophy, in *Tribune des femmes* 1: 44. See also the second response to Gertrude, signed "A. I.," in ibid. 1: 198.

81. Clorinde Rogé to Prosper Enfantin, June 20, 1845, Fonds Enfantin 7776, no. 52.

82. Eugénie Soudet, "Une Parole de femme," Fonds Enfantin 7627, no. 57.

83. Carlisle, 175.

84. A selection of the letters to Saint-Hilaire are reprinted here.

85. Roland to Charles Lambert, January 1834, Fonds Enfantin 7777.

86. Claire Démar, *Ma Loi d'avenir* (Paris: Au Bureau de la *Tribune des femmes*, 1834). Démar's *Appel d'une femme au peuple sur l'affranchissement de la femme* is included in this edition. Both works were reprinted in 1976 by Valentin Pelosse in Claire Démar, *Textes sur l'affranchissement des femmes*. Subsequent references to *Ma Loi d'avenir* are included in parentheses in the text and referred to simply as "My Law."

87. Démar to Father Enfantin, December 16, 1832, "Archives," 5: 517 verso, Fonds Enfantin 7647.

88. Claire Démar to Louise Crouzat, late May-June 1833, "Archives," 5: no. 50, Fonds Enfantin 7624.

89. "Enseignement," December 1831, in *Oeuvres*, 16: 131.

90. Bazard had an affair with Margerin and "confessed" this to Enfantin who, in turn, used this information to gain the upper hand in his power struggle with her husband, Saint-Amand Bazard. Claire Bazard complained: "Among us, we are obliged to reveal all the secrets of the heart; . . . we lose, little by little, our spontaneity; we withdraw into ourselves . . . we write no more letters which had become like bulletins of the Grand Army." (Claire Bazard to Gustave d'Eichthal, March 1831, "Archives," 3: 124 verso, Fonds Enfantin 7645.) Both Aglaé Saint-Hilaire and Cécile Fournel expressed disapproval when Roland broke off with Guéroult, with whom she was expecting a child, to begin a relationship with Aicard. Saint-Hilaire commented: "She is probably looking for a third one who need only be passing through." (Quoted in Edith Thomas, *Pauline Roland: Socialisme et féminisme au XIXe siècle* [Paris: Marcel Rivière, 1956], 71.)

91. Démar to Enfantin, January 1833, "Archives," 5: 521, Fonds Enfantin 7647. Démar, who was then a recent "convert," may have found it hard to make friends among the Saint-Simonians. Roland also complained of their "cliquishness" when she first arrived in Paris.

92. Démar to Enfantin, January 1833, Fonds Enfantin 7647, "Archives," 5: 521 verso.

93. In 1837, Reine Guindorf-Flichy (the "Marie-Reine" who founded the *Tribune des femmes*) also committed suicide. She was married, to a man described in Eugénie Soudet's eulogy for her as jealous, and in love with another man. Soudet cried out: "Reformers, make it so that feelings which we cannot master no longer bring on blame." ("Une Parole de femme," Fonds Enfantin 7627, no. 57.)

94. "Journals de Ch. Lambert en Egypte," Fonds Enfantin 7744, 7745. Also, Voilquin to Enfantin, (undated, but likely February 1838), Fonds Enfantin 7627, no. 62.

95. Cécile Fournel to Aglaé Saint-Hilaire, September 31 [*sic*], 1833, Fonds Enfantin 7727, no. 38.

96. Démar to Father Enfantin, December 16, 1832, "Archives," 5: 518, Fonds Enfantin 7647.

97. See Martha Vicinus, " 'They Wonder to Which Sex I Belong': The Historical Roots of the Modern Lesbian Identity," *Feminist Studies* 18 (Fall 1992).

98. See Sara Maza, "The Diamond Necklace Affair Revisted (1785–1786): The Case of the Missing Queen"; and Lynn Hunt, "The Many Bodies of Marie Antoinette: Political Pornography and the Problem of the Feminine in the French Revolution"; both in *Eroticism and the Body Politic*, ed. Lynn Hunt (Baltimore: Johns Hopkins University Press, 1991).

99. Flora Tristan to Olympe Chodzko, London, August 1, 1839, reprinted in *Flora Tristan: Lettres*, ed. Stéphane Michaud (Paris: Seuil, 1980), 104–105.

100. Edward Shorter, "Illegitimacy, Sexual Revolution, and Social Change in Modern Europe," *Journal of Interdisciplinary History* 2 (Autumn 1971): 265–67.

101. Women of the working classes were in a legal double bind: to marry meant giving up legal rights to their earnings or even their right to work (without the husbands' authorization). To live in "free unions" meant that neither they nor their children had any claims on husbands' earnings or property.

102. See Louise Tilly, Joan Scott, and Miriam Cohen, "Women's Work and European Fertility Patterns," *Journal of Interdisciplinary History* 6 (Winter 1976): 447–76; and George D. Sussman, "The Wet-Nursing Business in Nineteenth-Century France," *French Historical Studies* 9 (Fall 1975): 304–28.

103. Roland to Aglaé Saint-Hilaire, June 24, 1834, Fonds Enfantin 7777, no. 29.

104. Roland to Aglaé Saint-Hilaire, November 1834, Fonds Enfantin 7777, no. 30.

105. Cf. Veret: "We . . . should give [men] our names and take our own only from our mothers and God." (*Tribune des femmes* 1: 70.)

106. Valentin Pelosse discusses this work and also suggests that his earlier utopian fiction, *Le Panorama des boudoirs ou l'Empire des Nairs, le vrai paradis de l'amour*, published in German in 1800 and in French in 1814, may have been a source for Fourier. (See Pelosse's commentary in Démar, *Textes*, 161–62.)

107. Démar to Enfantin, December 29, 1832, "Archives," 5: 518 verso–520, Fonds Enfantin 7647.

108. In her preface to Démar's *Ma Loi d'avenir*, Voilquin reacts: "But *maternity*! It is our most beautiful attribute. It encompasses all other feelings without excluding a one; it is woman in her full flowering. In the religion of the future it will no longer be a virginal madonna, as a feminine model, that we will present for the adoration of Believers, it will be the mother!" (Voilquin, "Notice Historique," in Démar, *Ma Loi d'avenir*, 19.)

109. See Joan Scott, *Gender and the Politics of History*, chap. 7. In France, perhaps because of its slower population growth, the nineteenth-century wage workforce included a larger percentage of married women than in other European countries; but, even in France, wage-workforce participation rates were highest among the young and single.

110. Démar to Enfantin, January 1833, "Archives," 5: 521, Fonds Enfantin 7647.

111. Voilquin to Enfantin, January 9, 1847, and February 5, 1848, both in Fonds Enfantin 7791.

112. Theresa McBride, *The Domestic Revolution: The Modernization of Household Service in England and France, 1820–1920* (New York: Holmes & Meier, 1976), 57–69.

113. Charles Fourier, *Traité de l'association domestique agricole* (1822; reprint, Paris: Edition Anthropos, 1966–67), 334.

114. Some attempts to create schools for girls were made after this, but only in 1850 was the creation of girls' primary schools finally ordered in every commune with a population of over 800—and even this law was not always implemented. Of nearly 50,000 public schools that existed in 1860, only about 12,000 were for girls. Real change occurred only after 1879, with a series of laws which reformed the primary school system (making it free, obligatory, and secular), and which established secondary schools for young women, schools to train teachers, and the Ecole Normale Supérieure for women at Fontenay-aux-Roses. Throughout the century, upper-middle-class and upper-class women were educated at private— usually Catholic—boarding schools. (See Moses, *French Feminism in the Nineteenth Century*, 32–33, 174–77, 209.)

115. It was Marx who characterized the Saint-Simonians as "utopian," suggesting that they were impractical visionaries. We should keep in mind, however,

that his opinion of them had more to do with later socialist power struggles than with providing some "objective" historical judgement.

116. Claire Bazard to the Fathers Enfantin and Bazard, October 6, 1830, "Archives," 2: 309 verso, Fonds Enfantin 7644.

117. Claire Bazard to Resseguier, September 2, 1830, in ibid., 2: 341.

118. Claire Démar to Louise Crouzat, late May-June 1833, Fonds Enfantin 7624, 50.

119. Enfantin, *Réunion générale de la famille: Séances des 19 et 21 novembre*, 55.

120. Ibid.

121. J. Désirée [Veret] to the Father, October 20, 1832, "Archives," 4: 388 verso, Fonds Enfantin 7646.

122. These words are Adrienne Rich's.

123. Crouzat to Démar, May 18, 1833, in Démar, *Textes*, 136–37.

124. Carlisle (144, 221) hypothesizes that it was the Saint-Simonians' activities—both their practical enterprises and their propaganda work—in the working-class neighborhoods of Lyon and Paris rather than their espousal of a new sexual morality that actually got them into trouble with the bourgeois government.

125. Saint-Simonians, borrowing from Saint-Simon, termed what later came to be called "class analysis" the "science of society."

126. Judith A. DeGroat, "Women's Work Identity: Female Labor in the Transitional Manufacturing Economy of July Monarchy Paris," paper presented at the 38th Annual Meeting of the Society for French Historical Studies, El Paso, Texas, March 1992. DeGroat provides these definitions: *brodeuses* pierce the tops and soles for sewing; *joineuses* close or stitch together the boot or shoe pieces; *cordeuses* bind the soles and heels.

127. Scott, *Gender and the Politics of History*, 107.

128. *Tribune des femmes* 1: 117–18. The Saint-Simonian slogan—"to each according to their work"—fit well their challenge to inherited wealth and "unproductive" property. Note its difference from the later, Marxian "to each according to his needs."

129. See Joan Scott, *Gender and the Politics of History*, 135–36, 142–43, who also makes this point. She notes that the term *"femmes isolés"* was used by the police to refer to "illegal" prostitutes, that is, those who did not register their trade; the same term was used in the 1848 survey, *Statistique de l'Industrie*, for young women workers who lived alone and earned their livelihood by doing outwork for the garment industry. "The fact that the term was the same was not coincidental" (142).

130. Notice the distancing that is evident even in their language: whereas poor women had been "we," prostitutes are not positioned in the parallel category; prostitutes are "they."

131. See Démar, *Ma Loi d'avenir*, 42–43. It is interesting to compare her reasoning to Bazard's. He also feared the instability of Enfantin's system of "constants" and "mobiles," but feared that the predominant category would be the "mobile" one: "[Given] the impossibility of the coexistence of several moral laws . . . [and that] the priest must act . . . *materially* as well as spiritually on mobiles as well as constants, it will follow . . . that everyone will be made *mobiles*." ([Saint-Amand Bazard], *Religion Saint-Simonienne*, [January 1832].)

132. Démar, "Appel d'une femme au peuple sur l'affranchissement de la femme," in *Ma Loi d'avenir*, 71.

133. Ibid., 1: 147. See also 1: 148—"our fate is tied to that of the people"; 1: 167—"the women's question is essentially tied to that of the workers"; 1: 205—"our destiny is tied to that of the people and our emancipation can take place only interdependently with theirs."

134. Démar, "Appel d'une femme," 65.

135. See Moses, *French Feminism in the Nineteenth Century*, 98–107, for a fuller account of this journal, its politics and particularly the various petitions it wrote or publicized, and also biographical information on Herbinot and Poutret.

136. See also Moses, "Debating the Present, Writing the Past: 'Feminism' in French History and Historiography," *Radical History Review*, no. 52 (Winter 1992): 79–94. In this article I argue that "Offen's individualist/relational dualism—a categorization that suggests the equality/difference dualism but is not exactly the same—does not adequately address the urgencies of present-day antisexist, antiracist, and antiheterosexist politics."

137. Aileen Kraditor, *The Ideas of the Woman Suffrage Movement, 1890–1920* (New York: Columbia University Press, 1964), 52; Denise Riley, *"Am I That Name?" Feminism and the Category of "Women" in History* (Minneapolis: University of Minnesota Press, 1988), chap. 4; Karen Offen, "Defining Feminism: A Comparative Historical Approach," *Signs* 14 (Autumn 1988): 119–57, esp. 121, 124.

138. Enfantin to Duveyrier, August 1829, *Oeuvres*, 26: 19.

139. "Prédication: Le Prolétaire et la femme," in ibid., 45: 359.

140. In the words of Désirée Veret, citing Suzanne Voilquin: "The banner of women is universal, for as sister Suzanne has said, are they not all united by the same bond, MOTHERHOOD?" (*Tribune des Femmes* 1: 38).

141. Elizabeth Fox-Genovese, "The Personal Is Not Political Enough," *Marxist Perspectives*, no. 8 (Winter 1979–80): 94–113.

142. Nancy R. Cott, "Feminist Theory and Feminist Movements: The Past before Us," in *What Is Feminism: A Reexamination*, ed. Juliet Mitchell and Ann Oakley (New York: Pantheon Books, 1986), 49.

3. Feminist Texts and Feminine Subjects

1. Marianne Hirsch, *The Mother/Daughter Plot: Narrative, Psychoanalysis, Feminism* (Bloomington: Indiana University Press, 1989), 48.

2. Pauline Roland, letter to Aglaé Saint-Hilaire, June 24, 1834, Fonds Enfantin 7777, no. 31. Reprinted here.

3. Margaret Homans, *Bearing the Word: Language and Female Experience in Nineteenth-Century Women's Writing* (Chicago: University of Chicago Press, 1986), xi.

4. Claire Démar, "Ma Loi d'avenir," in *Ma Loi d'avenir*, ouvrage posthume publié par Suzanne (Paris: Bureau de la *Tribune des femmes*, 1834), 21–59, 28, reprinted here. Further references to this text will appear in parentheses after the citation.

5. Suzanne Voilquin, in *Tribune des femmes* 1: 107, reprinted here. Further references to this journal will appear in parentheses after the citation.

6. Sidonie Smith, *A Poetics of Women's Autobiography: Marginality and the Fictions of Self-Representation* (Bloomington: Indiana University Press, 1987), 144.

7. Nancy K. Miller, *Subject to Change: Reading Feminist Writing* (New York: Columbia University Press, 1988), 11. Miller traces this double literary history through women's literature properly speaking. In her analysis of "the circulation throughout literary history of French feminist writing" (5), she reads "women's fiction" rather than "écriture féminine" (27). This study reads instead a certain kind of "écriture féminine" in writings that have been considered nonliterary. It thus situates itself within a critical endeavor that, as Jonathan Culler says, has "discovered an essential 'literariness' in non-literary phenomena." Jonathan Culler, "Criticism and Institutions: The American University," in *Post-structuralism and the Question of History*, ed. Derek Attridge, Geoff Bennington, and Robert Young (Cambridge: Cambridge University Press, 1987), 82–100, 88.

8. Robert B. Carlisle, *The Proffered Crown: Saint-Simonianism and the Doctrine of Hope* (Baltimore: Johns Hopkins University Press, 1987), 107; see also 155.

9. Marguerite Thibert, *Le Féminisme dans le socialisme français de 1830 à 1850* (Paris: M. Giard, 1926), 44. See also Claire Goldberg Moses, *French Feminism in the Nineteenth Century* (Albany: State University of New York Press, 1984), 46; and Christine Planté, "Les Féministes saint-simoniennes: Possibilités et limites d'un mouvement féministe en France au lendemain de 1830," in *Regards sur le Saint-Simonisme et les Saint-Simoniens*, ed. J. R. Derre (Lyon: Presses universitaires de Lyon, 1986), 87.

10. Prosper Enfantin, "Religion saint-simonienne. Réunion générale de la famille. Séances des 19 et 21 novembre 1831," excerpted and reprinted in Claire Démar, *Textes sur l'affranchissement des femmes (1832–33)*, ed. Valentin Pelosse, 115–21, 120. Further references to this text will appear in parentheses after the quotation.

11. For more on the structure of desire as the structure of romantic narrative, see Peter Brooks, *Reading for the Plot: Design and Intention in Narrative* (New York: Knopf, 1984), 56–59.

12. For the romantic fascination with the Orient, see Richard Terdiman, *Discourse/Counter-discourse: The Theory and Practice of Symbolic Resistance in Nineteenth-Century France* (Ithaca: Cornell University Press, 1985).

13. Speech of Prosper Enfantin, April 8, 1832, quoted in *Tribune des femmes* 1: 192.

14. Jacques Lacan, "God and the *Jouissance* of the Woman," in *Feminine Sexuality*, ed. Juliet Mitchell and Jacqueline Rose, trans. Jacqueline Rose (New York: Norton, 1983), 137–48, 144.

15. Luce Irigaray, *Ce Sexe qui n'en est pas un* (Paris: Minuit, 1977), 67. Further references to this text will appear in parentheses after the quotation.

16. Irigaray, ibid., 93; see also Hélène Cixous, "Castration or Decapitation," trans. Annette Kuhn, *Signs 7* (Autumn 1981): 42–55, 49.

17. For an argument that "the claim to deconstructive feminism . . . cannot be sustained in the name of 'woman,' " see Gayatri Chakravorty Spivak, "Feminism and Deconstruction, Again: Negotiating with Unacknowledged Masculinism," in *Between Feminism and Psychoanalysis*, ed. Teresa Brennan (London and New York: Routledge, 1989), 206–24, 218.

18. Claire Démar, letter to Enfantin, December 16, 1832, "Archives," 5: 518 verso, Fonds Enfantin 7645.

19. For feminist restatements and revisions of the Oedipal triangle, see: Elizabeth Grosz, *Jacques Lacan: A Feminist Introduction* (London: Routledge, 1990), 50–51; Homans, 7; and Julia Kristeva, *The Powers of Horror: An Essay on Abjection*, trans. Leon S. Roudiez (New York: Columbia University Press, 1982), 59.

20. See Nancy Chodorow, *The Reproduction of Mothering: Psychoanalysis and the Sociolgy of Gender* (Berkeley: University of California Press, 1978); Luce Irigaray, *Et l'Une ne bouge pas sans l'autre* (Paris: Minuit, 1979); and Ellie Ragland-Sullivan, "Seeking the Third Term: Desire, the Phallus, and the Materiality of Language," in *Feminism and Psychoanalysis*, ed. Richard Feldstein and Judith Roof (Ithaca: Cornell University Press, 1989), 40–64, 56.

21. For the history of the family in the eighteenth and nineteenth centuries, see: Philippe Ariès, *Centuries of Childhood: A Social History of Family Life* (New York: Vintage, 1962); Mark Poster, *Critical Theory of the Family* (New York: Seabury Press, 1978); and Lawrence Stone, *The Family, Sex, and Marriage in England, 1500–1800*, abridged edition (New York: Harper and Row, 1979). For this new ideal role of the mother, see Elisabeth Badinter, *Mother Love: Myth and Reality* (New York: Macmillan, 1981).

22. Pauline Roland to Aglaé Saint-Hilaire, January 31, 1832, Fonds Enfantin 7777, no. 16, reprinted here. Further references to the Roland-Saint-Hilaire

correspondence (all located in Fonds Enfantin 7777) will appear in parentheses after the citation.

23. Suzanne Voilquin, *Souvenirs d'une fille du peuple ou la Saint-simonienne en Egypte* (Paris: Chez E. Sauzet, 1866), 187. Further references to this text will appear in parentheses after the citation. Excerpts reprinted here.

24. For an analysis of the relation between writing, the maternal subject, and second person voice, see Barbara Johnson, "Apostrophe, Animation, and Abortion," in *Worlds of Difference* (Baltimore: Johns Hopkins University Press, 1987), 184–200.

25. Hélène Cixous, "Le Rire de la Méduse," *L'Arc*, no. 61 (1975): 40. (For the English version, see "The Laugh of the Medusa: Viewpoint," trans. Keith Cohen and Paula Cohen, *Signs* 1 (Summer 1976): 875–93.

26. Jacques Lacan, *Ecrits 2* (Paris: Seuil, 1971), 111.

27. Jessica Benjamin, "A Desire of One's Own: Psychoanalytic Feminism and Intersubjective Space," in *Feminist Studies/Critical Studies*, ed. Teresa de Lauretis (Bloomington: Indiana University Press, 1986), 78–101, 92. For an analysis of such an intersubjective process in the texts of twentieth-century French women writers, see Martha Noel Evans, *Masks of Tradition: Women and the Politics of Writing in Twentieth-Century France* (Ithaca: Cornell University Press, 1987), 28.

28. Luce Irigaray, "The Gesture in Psychoanalysis," in *Between Feminism and Psychoanalysis*, ed. Brennan, 127–38, 133.

29. See Suzanne Voilquin, *Mémoires d'une Saint-Simonienne en Russie* (Paris: Editions des femmes, 1977).

30. Margaret Talbot, "An Emancipated Voice: Flora Tristan and Utopian Allegory," *Feminist Studies* 17 (Summer 1991): 219–40; and Barbara Taylor, *Eve and the New Jerusalem: Socialism and Feminism in the Nineteenth Century* (New York: Pantheon, 1983), 264, 285.

31. Luce Irigaray, *Speculum de l'autre femme* (Paris: Minuit, 1974), 101.

32. Luce Irigaray, "Interview" in *Shifting Scenes: Interviews on Women, Writing, and Politics in Post-68 France*, ed. Alice A. Jardine and Anne M. Menke (New York: Columbia University Press, 1991), 101–102.

33. Elizabeth Grosz, *Sexual Subversions* (New York: Routledge, 1989), 123, quoted in Christine Holmlund, "The Lesbian, the Mother, the Heterosexual Lover: Irigaray's Recodings of Difference," *Feminist Studies* 17 (Summer 1991): 300.

34. Philippe Lejeune, *Le Pacte autobiographique* (Paris: Seuil, 1975). Further references to this text will appear in parentheses after the quotation.

35. Jean-Jacques Rousseau, *Les Confessions*, 2 vols. (Paris: Garnier-Flammarion, 1968); François-Auguste de Chateubriand, *Mémoires d'outre-tombe*, 3 vols. (Paris: Le Livre de poche, 1973). Further references to these texts will appear in parentheses after the quotation.

36. Nancy K. Miller, *Subject to Change*, 61. For other critiques of Lejeune's empiricism from a deconstructive point of view, see: E. S. Burt, "Poetic Conceit: The Self-Portrait and Mirrors of Ink," *Diacritics* 12, no. 4 (Winter 1982): 17–39, 25; and Paul de Man, "Autobiography as Defacement," in *The Rhetoric of Romanticism* (New York: Columbia University Press, 1984), 67–81, 70.

37. Domna Stanton, "Autogynography: Is the Subject Different?" in *The Female Autograph*, ed. Domna Stanton (New York: New York Literary Forum, 1984), 5–22, 9. Further references to this text will appear in parentheses after the citation.

38. For a poststructuralist analysis of women's autobiography, see Sidonie Smith. See also Leah D. Hewitt, *Autobiographical Tightropes* (Lincoln: University of Nebraska Press, 1990).

39. See Elizabeth Fox-Genovese, "My Statue, My Self: Autobiographical Writings of Afro-American Women," in *The Private Self: Theory and Practice of Women's Autobiographical Writings*, ed. Shari Benstock (Chapel Hill: University of North

Carolina Press, 1988), 63–89, 65, 67–68. On the other hand, an excellent post-structuralist analysis of autobiographical writing by Francophone women writers can be found in Françoise Lionnet, *Autobiographical Voices: Race, Gender, Self-portraiture* (Ithaca: Cornell University Press, 1989).

40. Shari Benstock, "Authorizing the Autobiographical," in *The Private Self*, ed. Benstock, 10–33; and Candace Lang, "Autobiography in the Aftermath of Romanticism," *Diacritics* 12, no. 4 (Winter 1982): 2–16.

41. Claude Lévi-Strauss, *Les Structures élementaires de la parenté* (Paris: Mouton, 1967), 29.

42. Gayle Rubin, "The Traffic in Women: Notes on the 'Political Economy' of Sex," in *Toward an Anthropology of Women*, ed. Rayna R[app] Reiter (New York: Monthly Review Press, 1975), 157–210. See also Lévi-Strauss, 549, 565, 568–69.

43. Jean Starobinski, *Jean-Jacques Rousseau: La Transparence et l'obstacle* (Paris: Plon, 1957), 213; and Philippe Lejeune, "Le Peigne cassé," *Poétique*, no. 25 (1976): 1–29, 4.

44. Paul de Man, *Allegories of Reading: Figural Language in Rousseau, Nietzsche, Rilke, and Proust* (New Haven: Yale University Press, 1979), 283. Further references to this text will appear in parentheses after the citation.

45. Barbara Johnson, "Rigorous Unreliability," in *Worlds of Difference*, 17–24, 23.

46. E. S. Burt suggests an escape from the role of the judge by reading the scene of the broken comb as a fiction wholly invented by Rousseau, in "Developments in Character: Reading and Interpretation in 'The Children's Punishment' and 'The Broken Comb,' " *Yale French Studies*, no. 69 (1985): 192–210. Starobinski also suggests that the episode is a fiction by saying that it is a "réponse inconsciente à la faute commise envers Marion" (213).

47. Sigmund Freud, *Totem and Taboo: Some Resemblances between the Psychic Lives of Savages and Neurotics* (New York: W. W. Norton, 1950).

48. René Girard develops the model of mimetic desire in *Deceit, Desire and the Novel: Self and Other in Literary Structure* (Baltimore: Johns Hopkins University Press, 1965), and opposes it to the Freudian Oedipal model of desire in *Violence and the Sacred* (Baltimore: Johns Hopkins University Press, 1977). Eve Kosofsky Sedgwick expands upon the Girardian model of desire as a model of the exchange of women between men in *Between Men: English Literature and Male Homosocial Desire* (New York: Columbia University Press, 1985).

49. For an analysis of Rousseau's treatment of the ever-absent mother, for whom language is the substitute, see Jacques Derrida, *De la Grammatologie* (Paris: Minuit, 1967), 210–21; and Lionel Gossman, "The Innocent Art of Confession and Reverie," *Daedalus* 107, no. 3 (Summer 1978): 59–78, 73.

50. See Louis Althusser, "Ideology and Ideological State Apparatuses," in *"Lenin and Philosophy" and Other Essays* (London: New Left Press, 1971), 123–73.

51. Margaret Waller analyzes Chateubriand's fictional hero René as a model for bourgeois male identity in the romantic period in "Being René, Buying Atala: Literary Production and Cultural Reproduction in Post-Revolutionary France," in *Rebel Daughters: Women and the French Revolution*, ed. Sara Melzer and Leslie W. Rabine (New York: Oxford University Press, 1992).

52. See the excellent introduction of Lydia Elhadad to the modern edition of Voilquin's *Souvenirs d'une fille du peuple* (Paris: Maspero, 1978), 5–48, 43. See also Maïté Albistur and Daniel Armogathe, Avant-propos to *Suzanne Voilquin, Mémoires d'une Saint-Simonienne en Russie*, 7–80. They criticize her "moralisme béat" (65).

53. Valentin Pelosse, "Symbolique groupale et idéologie féministe saint-simoniennes," in *Démar, Textes*, 203.

54. For most of her biographers, Tristan is, as Dominique Desanti, citing the Communard Benoît Malon, says: "le précurseur de L'Internationale ouvrière."

Dominique Desanti, *Flora Tristan: La Femme révoltée* (Paris: Hachette, 1972), 304. See also Jules Puech, *La Vie et l'oeuvre de Flora Tristan* (Paris: Marcel Rivière, 1925). For him, Tristan is "l'ancêtre du mouvement féministe et du socialisme ouvrier" (i). Pierre Leprohon says: "toute l'évolution sociale et même morale de notre temps, elle ne l'a pas seulement devinée, mais voulue." *Flora Tristan* (Antony, France: Editions Corymbe, 1979). Stéphane Michaud contrasts her favorably to the Saint-Simonian feminists, saying: "leur action se place dans le sillage saint-simonien. Mais la grande nouveauté de Flora consiste à dépasser le cadre de la Bourgeoisie." Introduction, in *Flora Tristan, Lettres*, ed. Stéphane Michaud (Paris: Seuil, 1980), 16. Tristan did have contacts with the Saint-Simonian feminists, most particularly with Pauline Roland, a visit with whom she describes in *Le Tour de France: Journal inédit, 1843–44* (Paris: Tête de feuilles, 1973), 21. In an otherwise perceptive article, Margaret Talbot incorrectly says that "Tristan's particular contribution, in her life and her writings, was to bridge the chasm between the spiritually charged precepts of utopian socialism and the organized workers' movement." Margaret Talbot, "An Emancipated Voice: Flora Tristan and Utopian Allegory," *Feminist Studies* 17, no. 2 (Summer 1991): 219–40, 221. Laura Strumingher is more accurate when she identifies Tristan's contribution as seeing the need for workers to go beyond outmoded guild and trade associations to form a universal union. Laura Strumingher, *The Odyssey of Flora Tristan* (New York: Peter Lang, 1988). See also Joyce Anne Schneider, *Flora Tristan: Feminist, Socialist, Free Spirit* (New York: William Morrow, 1980).

55. Flora Tristan, *L'Union ouvrière* (Paris: [chez tous les libraires], 1844), 5.

56. Flora Tristan, *Pérégrinations d'une paria (1833–1834)*, 2 vols. (Paris: Arthus Bertrand, 1838); *Méphis ou le prolétaire* (Paris: L'advocat, 1838); *Promenades dans Londres ou l'aristocratie et les prolétaires anglais* (Paris: H.-L. Delloye, 1840; new edition: Paris: Maspero, 1983); *L'Union ouvrière* (Paris: [chez tous le libraires], 1844).

57. Sandra Dijkstra, *Flora Tristan: Pioneer Feminist and Socialist* (Berkeley: Center for Socialist History, 1984), 24, 25.

58. Suzanne Voilquin analyzes extensively the Code in "La Justice des hommes," *Tribune des femmes* 1: 121–27. Reprinted here.

59. The possibility of Flora Tristan's lesbian sexuality, as suggested by some passages of *Peregrinations of a Pariah* and certain of her letters, remains a subject for investigation.

60. The concept of gendered symbolic economies was first developed in Luce Irigaray, *Speculum de l'autre femme*, and *Ce Sexe qui n'en est pas un*; and Hélène Cixous, "Le Rire de la Méduse." For an elaborated working out of the relation between sexual, symbolic, and capitalist economies, see Jean-Joseph Goux, *Freud, Marx: Economie et symbolique* (Paris: Seuil, 1973).

61. Alice Jardine, "Death Sentences: Writing Couples and Ideology," in *The Female Body in Western Culture*, ed. Susan Suleiman (Cambridge, MA: Harvard University Press, 1986), 84–98, 90.

62. *La Gazette des tribunaux*, 1 et 2 février, 1839, cited in Dominique Desanti, *Flora Tristan: Vie, oeuvres mêlées* (Paris: Union générale d'éditions, 1973), 64.

63. Flora Tristan, *Les Pérégrinations d'une paria*, modern edition (Paris: Maspero, 1980), 128. Further references to this book will be cited in parentheses after the quotation.

64. See Jacques Derrida, *Glas: Que reste-t-il du savoir absolu?* (Paris: Denoel/Gonthier, 1981), and "The Double Session," in *Dissemination*, trans. Barbara Johnson (Chicago: University of Chicago Press, 1981), 173–286.

65. Avant-propos to *Pérégrinations*, 1838 edition, 198–200. Emphasis in original. This text is translated in this book in two parts: "foreword" and "preface." Fur-

ther references to this text will be cited in parentheses after the quotation and will be designated either as "foreword" or "preface."

66. Flora Tristan, *Le Tour de France*. Further references to this text will appear in parentheses after the quotation.

67. Phyllis Zuckerman, "Ideology and the Patriarchal Family: Nerval and Flora Tristan," *Sub-stance*, no. 15 (1976), 146–58.

68. Jean-Jacques Rousseau, *Les Confessions*, 1: 43.

69. Jean Starobinski, *Jean Jacques Rousseau: La transparence et l'obstacle*, 47, 59, 225–26, 247; E. S. Burt, "Developments in Character: Reading and Interpretation in 'The Children's Punishment' and 'The Broken Comb,' " 192–210.

70. Irigaray, *Ce Sexe*, 73–74.

71. Jacques Lacan, "The Function of Language in Psychoanalysis," in *Speech and Language in Psychoanalysis*, ed. and trans. Anthony Wilden (Baltimore: Johns Hopkins University Press, 1968), 9–88, 41; and Wilden, "Lacan and the Discourse of the Other," ibid., 157–312, 296.

72. Jeanne-Désirée [Veret], "Par mes oeuvres on saura mon nom," *Tribune des femmes* 1: 69–70, 70. Reprinted here.

73. "Pièce officielle: Madame Flora Tristan, femme Chazal, a adressé à monsieur le garde des sceaux sa demande en date du 4 février 1839, à l'effet d'être autorisée à quitter le nom de Chazal, et à le faire quitter à ses enfants, Ernest et Aline Chazal, pour adopter celui de Tristan père de la dite Dame." Tristan, *Lettres*, 95.

74. Jeanne Deroin, Profession de foi, Fonds Enfantin 7608, no. 39.

75. Sandra Caruso Mortola Gilbert and Susan Dreyfuss David Gubar, "Ceremonies of the Alphabet: Female Grandmatologies and the Female Authorgraph," in *The Female Autograph*, ed. Domna Stanton (New York: New York Literary Forum, 1984), 23–54, 33. See also Nancy K. Miller's discussion of the feminine signature in *Subject to Change*, 73–75. She also, in analyzing Germaine de Staël's *Corinne*, points out that "Corinne erases the name of the father and takes a single name" (177).

76. The name of the author of *Peregrinations*, as well as her book, which is now considered by some Peruvian scholars the deepest and most useful book on Peru written by a foreigner during the period, was repressed from Peruvian memory until 1949, when Magda Portal, now president of the National Association of Peruvian Writers and Artists, delivered a paper entitled "Flora Tristan: Precursor" to the first National Congress of Women of Santiago, Chile. According to Portal: "When curious travellers began to discover Flora and started coming to Arequipa to conduct research, they questioned the most prominent families and combed the libraries and church archives in vain. They encountered absolutely no memory or reference: the name of Flora had been erased." "Ma Découverte de Flora Tristan," in *Un Fabuleux Destin: Flora Tristan*, ed. Stéphane Michaud (Dijon: Editions universitaires de Dijon, 1984), 11–14, 12. According to this article, Tristan is now a sort of national heroine, and groups of homeless people in Peru who take over land have named their social action centers after her.

77. See *La Gazette des tribunaux*, Jan. 10, Feb. 1, 2, 4, March 2, 31, August 31, 1839; and *Le Journal des débats*, Feb. 1, 2, 13, 1839. See also Dominique Desanti, *Flora Tristan: La Femme révoltée*, 167–79; and Jules Puech, *La Vie et l'oeuvre de Flora Tristan*, 90–95.

78. Karl Marx, *Capital*, vol. 1 (New York: International Publishers, 1972); 65–70; see also Goux.

79. Denys Cuche, "Le Pérou de Flora Tristan: du rêve à la réalité," in Michaud, *Un Fabuleux Destin*, 19–37, 34.

80. Stéphane Michaud, Introduction, in Michaud, *Un Fabuleux Destin*, i–vi, i.

81. Cixous, "The Laugh of Medusa," 54.

82. For an explanation of Lacanian concepts in relation to the autobiographical subject, see Shari Benstock, "Authorizing the Autobiographical," in *The Private Self*, ed. Benstock, 10–33.

83. Tristan frequented the Saint-Simonians and heard Enfantin's sermons before she went to Peru. See Desanti, *Le Femme révoltée*, 38–48.

84. Dijkstra, 26.

85. Struminger, 111.

86. Talbot, 233. Talbot also says that "By September [1844], she was signing her letters to the workers' circle in Toulouse, "Votre Mere" (234). But in fact, there is only one letter so signed, and in it, Tristan also calls the workers "chers frères." As Talbot seems to suggest, if Tristan does cast herself in the mother role, it is with a great deal of distance, and in response to an image projected onto her.

87. Pierre Levêque, "Mission impossible? Flora Tristan en Bourgogne, vue par la presse locale," in Michaud, *Un Fabuleux Destin*, 65–81, 78.

88. Claire Démar, "Appel d'une femme au peuple sur l'affranchissement de la femme," in *Ma Loi d'avenir*, 75–75, 71; and "Ma Loi d'avenir," ibid., 21–59, 24. For an analysis of this rhetoric in Démar's writing, see Rabine, "Ecriture féminine as Metaphor: Reading Claire Démar with Hélène Cixous," *Cultural Critique*, no. 8 (Winter 1987–88), 19–44.

89. Toni Morrison, *Beloved* (New York: Knopf, 1987).

90. Chodorow, *The Reproduction of Mothering*; Carol Gilligan, *In a Different Voice: Psychological Theory and Women's Development* (Cambridge, MA: Harvard University Press, 1982).

91. Temma F. Berg, Anna Shannon Elfenbein, Jeanne Larsen, and Elisa Kay Sparks, eds., *Engendering the Word: Feminist Essays in Psychosexual Poetics* (Urbana: University of Illinois Press, 1989); Teresa Brennan, ed., *Between Feminism and Psychoanalysis*; Richard Feldstein and Judith Roof, eds., *Feminism and Psychoanalysis*; Shirley Nelson Garner, Claire Kahane, and Madelon Sprengnether, eds., *The (M)other Tongue* (Ithaca: Cornell University Press, 1985); Marianne Hirsch, *The Mother/Daughter Plot*; Margaret Homans, *Bearing the Word*.

92. Carolyn Heilbrun, *Reinventing Womanhood* (New York: Norton, 1982), 93–124; Janice Haney-Peritz, "Engendering the Exemplary Daughter: The Deployment of Sexuality in Richardson's *Clarissa*," in *Daughters and Fathers*, ed. Linda E. Boose and Betty S. Flowers (Baltimore: Johns Hopkins University Press, 1989), 181–207; Katherine C. Hill-Miller, " 'The Skies and Trees of the Past': Anne Thackeray Ritchie and William Makepeace Thackeray," ibid., 261–383; Nancy K. Miller, "My Father's Penis," in *Refiguring the Father: New Feminist Readings in Patriarchy*, ed. Patricia Yaeger and Beth Kowaleski-Wallace (Carbondale: Southern Illinois University Press, 1989), 312–26; Elaine Showalter, *A Literature of Their Own: British Women Novelists from Brontë to Lessing* (Princeton: Princeton University Press, 1977), 61. See also Cheryl Herr, "Fathers, Daughters, Anxiety, and Fiction," in *Discontented Discourses: Feminism/Textual Intervention/Psychoanalysis*, ed. Marleen S. Barr and Richard Feldstein (Urbana: University of Illinois Press, 1989), 173–207.

93. Ana Castillo, *My Father Was a Toltec* (Novato, CA: West End Press, 1988). See especially the poem "Daddy with Chesterfields in a Rolled Up Sleeve," (10–14). Sandra Cisneros, *My Wicked Wicked Ways* (Bloomington: Third Woman Press, 1987); Adrienne Rich, *Your Native Land, Your Life* (New York: Norton, 1986).

BIBLIOGRAPHY

Manuscript Sources

The Saint-Simonian archives—the Fonds Enfantin—are housed at the Bibliothèque de l'Arsenal in Paris. Of special interest are the "prédications" (sermons) and other propaganda such as the "enseignements" (teachings), all of the Saint-Simonian newspapers, the personal correspondence (especially the letters of Claire Bazard, Claire Démar, Cécile Fournel, Clorinde Rogé, Pauline Roland, Aglaé Saint-Hilaire, Marie Talon, Suzanne Voilquin, and the "Correspondance du *Globe* [Dames]"), and the diaries of Charles Lambert from Egypt.

The Bibliothèque Thiers holds the Gustave d'Eichthal papers, which also include useful materials for a history of Saint-Simonianism. Of special interest is the correspondence between d'Eichthal and Claire Bazard from the 1860s.

Newspapers

Le Globe. 1830–32.
Tribune des femmes. 1832–34. (First published under other titles: *La Femme libre, La Femme d'avenir, La Femme nouvelle, Apostolat des femmes*, and *Affranchissement des femmes*.) Edited and published by Suzanne Voilquin for most of its existence.
Foi nouvelle: Livre des actes. 1833. Edited first by Cécile Fournel, then by Marie Talon.
Gazette des femmes. 1836–38. Edited and published by Frédéric de Mauchamps.
La Gazette des tribunaux. Jan. 10; Feb. 1, 2, 4; March 2, 31; August 31, 1839.
Le Journal des débats. Feb. 1, 2, 13, 1839.
Almanach des femmes. 1853–54. London. Edited and published by Jeanne Deroin in French and English.

Articles, Books, and Pamphlets

Adler, Laure. *A l'Aube du féminisime: Les Premières journalistes (1830–1850)*. Paris: Payot, 1979.
Albistur, Maïté, and Daniel Armogathe. *Histoire du féminisme français du moyen âge à nos jours*. 2 vols. Paris: Editions des femmes, 1977.
Alcoff, Linda. "Cultural Feminism versus Post-Structuralism: The Identity Crisis in Feminist Theory." *Signs: Journal of Women in Culture and Society* 13 (Spring 1988): 405–36.
Alexander, Sally. "Women, Class, and Sexual Difference in the 1830s and 1840s: Some Reflections on the Writing of a Feminist History." *History Workshop*, no. 17 (Spring 1984): 125–49.
Alexandriane, Sarane. *Les Libérateurs de l'amour*. Paris: Editions du Seuil, 1977.
Allemagne, Henry-René d'. *Les Saint-Simoniens, 1827–1837*. Paris, 1930.
Allen, Jeffner, and Iris Marion Young, eds. *The Thinking Muse: Feminism and Modern French Philosophy*. Bloomington: Indiana University Press, 1989.
Ariès, Philippe. *Centuries of Childhood: A Social History of Family Life*. Translated by Robert Baldick. New York: Vintage, 1962.
Armogathe, Daniel. "Pour un cent cinquantenaire: 1833: l'Appel de l'orient, les Saint-Simoniens à Marseille." In *Le Miroir égyptien*, edited by Robert Ilbert

and Philippe Joutard, 189–209. Marseille: Editions du Quai Jeanne Lafitte, 1984.

Aron, Jean-Paul, ed. *Misérable et Glorieuse: La Femme du XIXe siècle*. Paris: Fayard, 1980.

Auerbach, Judy, Linda Blum, Vicki Smith, and Christine Williams. "Commentary on Gilligan's *In a Different Voice*." *Feminist Studies* 11 (Spring 1985): 149–61.

Badinter, Elisabeth. *Mother Love: Myth and Reality*. New York: Macmillan, 1981.

Baelen, Jean. *La Vie de Flora Tristan: Socialisme et féminisme au 19e siècle*. Paris: Editions du Seuil, 1972.

Barrett, Michèle. "The Concept of 'Difference.' " *Feminist Review*, no. 26 (July 1987): 29–40.

Barthes, Roland. "To Write: An Intransitive Verb?" In *The Structuralist Controversy: The Languages of Criticism and the Science of Man*, edited by Richard Macksey and Eugenio Donato. Baltimore: Johns Hopkins University Press, 1970.

Bazard, P[almyre]. *Aux femmes sur leur mission religieuse dans la crise actuelle*. Rouen: Brière, n.d. [1831].

[Bazard, Saint-Amand]. *Religion Saint-Simonienne. Discussions morales, politiques, et religieuses qui ont amenées la séparation qui s'est effectuée au mois de novembre 1831, dans le sein de la société Saint-Simonienne. Première partie. Relations des hommes et des femmes, mariage, divorce*. Paris: Paulin, Delaunay, and Heideloff, 1832.

Beauvoir, Simone de. *Le Deuxième Sexe*. 2 vols. Paris: Gallimard, 1949.

———. *The Second Sex*. Translated by H. M. Parshley. New York: Bantam Books, 1961.

Beecher, Jonathon. *Charles Fourier: The Visionary and His World*. Berkeley: University of California Press, 1986.

Bell, Susan Groag, and Karen M. Offen. *Women, the Family, and Freedom: The Debate in Documents*. 2 vols. Stanford: Stanford University Press, 1983.

Bellanger, Claude, Jacques Godechot, Guiral Rerrer, and Terrou Fernand, eds. *Histoire générale de la presse française*. 4 vols. Paris: Presses universitaires de France, 1969.

Benjamin, Jessica. "A Desire of One's Own: Psychoanalytic Feminism and Intersubjective Space." In *Feminist Studies/Critical Studies*, edited by Teresa de Lauretis, 78–101. Bloomington: Indiana University Press, 1986.

Benstock, Shari. "Authorizing the Autobiographical." In *The Private Self: Theory and Practice of Women's Autobiographical Writings*, edited by Benstock, 10–33. Chapel Hill: University of North Carolina Press, 1988.

Benveniste, Emile. *Problèmes de linguistique générale*. Paris: Gallimard, 1966.

Berg, Temma F., Anna Shannon Elfenbein, Jeanne Larsen, and Elisa Kay Sparks, eds. *Engendering the Word: Feminist Essays in Psychosexual Poetics*. Urbana: University of Illinois Press, 1989.

Bergues, Hélène, et al. *Prévention des naissances dans la famille*. Paris: Presses Universitaires de France, 1960.

Blin-Sarde, Michèle. "L'Evolution du Concept de Différence dans le Mouvement de Libération des Femmes en France." *Contemporary French Civilization* (Fall-Winter 1982): 195–202.

Bock, Gisela. "Challenging Dichotomies: Perspectives on Women's History." In *Waiting Women's History: International Perspectives*, edited by Karen Offen, Ruth Roach Pierson, and Jane Rendall, 1–23. Bloomington: Indiana University Press, 1991.

———. "Women's History and Gender History: Aspects of an International Debate." *Gender and History* 1 (Spring 1989): 7–30.

Bonald, Louis de. *Du divorce considéré au XIXe siècle relativement à l'état domestique et à l'état public de société*. Paris: Adrien le Clerc, 1847.

Bouglé, G. Célestin Charles Alfred. "Le Féminisme saint-simonien." *La Revue de Paris* 25 (September 15, 1918): 371–99.

Boxer, Marilyn J., and Jean H. Quataert, eds. *Socialist Women: European Socialist Feminism in the Nineteenth and Early Twentieth Centuries.* New York: Elsevier, 1978.

Braidotti, Rosi. "The Politics of Ontological Difference." In *Between Feminism and Psychoanalysis,* edited by Teresa Brennan, 89–105. London: Routledge, 1989.

Brennan, Teresa, ed. *Between Feminism and Psychoanalysis.* London: Routledge, 1989.

Briscoe, James. B. "Enfantinism, Feminism, and the Crisis of Saint-Simonism." Paper delivered to the Society for French Historical Studies, University of Virginia, April 1984.

Brooks, Peter. *Reading for the Plot: Design and Intention in Narrative.* New York: Knopf, 1984.

Bulciolu, Maria Teresa. *L'Ecole Saint-simonienne et la Femme: Notes et documents pour une histoire du rôle de la femme dans la société saint-simonienne.* Pisa, Italy: Goliardica, 1980.

Burt, E. S. "Developments in Character: Reading and Interpretation in 'The Children's Punishment' and 'The Broken Comb.'" *Yale French Studies,* no. 69 (1985): 192–210.

———. "Poetic Conceit: The Self-Portrait and Mirrors of Ink." *Diacritics* 4 (1982): 17–39.

Busst, A. J. L. "The Image of the Androgyne in the Nineteenth Century." In *Romantic Mythologies,* edited by Ian Fletcher, 1–96. New York: Barnes & Noble, 1967.

Butler, Judith. *Gender Trouble: Feminism and the Subversion of Identity.* New York: Routledge, 1990.

Carlisle, Robert B. *The Proffered Crown: Saint-Simonianism and the Doctrine of Hope.* Baltimore: Johns Hopkins University Press, 1987.

Casaubon, E. A. *Le Nouveau contrat social ou place à la femme.* Paris: Dupuy, 1834.

Castillo, Ana. *My Father Was a Toltec.* Novato, CA: West End Press, 1988.

Cerati, Marie. "Elisa Lemonnier." In *Femmes extraordinaires,* 34–85. Paris: Editions de la Courtille, 1979.

Charléty, Sebastian. *Essai sur l'histoire du Saint-simonisme.* Paris: Hachette, 1896.

Chateaubriand, François-Auguste. *Mémoires d'outre-tombe.* 3 vols. Paris: Le Livre de poche, 1973.

———. *René.* Geneva: Droz, 1961.

Chevalier, Louis. *Classes laborieuses et classes dangereuses à Paris pendant la première moîtié du XIXᵉ siècle.* Paris: Plon, 1958.

Chodorow, Nancy. *The Reproduction of Mothering: Psychoanalysis and the Sociology of Gender.* Berkeley: University of California Press, 1978.

Cisneros, Sandra. *My Wicked Wicked Ways.* Bloomington: Third Woman Press, 1987.

Cixous, Hélène. "Castration or Decapitation." *Signs* 11 (Autumn 1981): 41–55.

———. "The Laugh of the Medusa." *Signs* 1 (Summer 1976): 875–93.

———. *The Newly Born Woman.* Translated by Betsy Wing. Minneapolis: University of Minnesota Press, 1986.

———. *With ou l'art de l'innocence.* Paris: des femmes, 1981.

———. *Souffles.* Paris: des femmes, 1975.

Collins, Irene. *The Government and the Newspaper Press in France, 1814–1881.* London: Oxford University Press, 1959.

Corbin, Alain. *Les Filles de noce: Misère sexuelle et prostitution (19ᵉ et 20ᵉ siècles).* Paris: Aubier Montaigne, 1978.

Cott, Nancy F. *The Bonds of Womanhood: "Woman's Sphere" in New England, 1780–1835.* New Haven: Yale University Press, 1977.

———. "Feminist Theory and Feminist Movements: The Past before Us." In *What Is Feminism: A Reexamination,* edited by Juliet Mitchell and Ann Oakley, 49–62. New York: Pantheon Books, 1986.

———. "Passionlessness: An Interpretation of Victorian Sexual Ideology, 1790–1850." *Signs: Journal of Women in Culture and Society* 4 (Winter 1978): 219–36.

Cuche, Denys. "Le Pérou de Flora Tristan: du rêve à la réalité." In *Un Fabuleux Destin: Flora Tristan,* edited by Stéphane Michaud, 19–37. Dijon: Editions Universitaires de Dijon, 1984.

Culler, Jonathan. "Criticism and Institutions: The American University." In *Poststructuralism and the Question of History,* edited by Derek Attridge, Geoff Bennington, and Robert Young, 82–100. Cambridge: Cambridge University Press, 1987.

Daly, Mary. *Gyn/Ecology: The Metaethics of Radical Feminism.* Boston: Beacon Press, 1978.

Darrow, Margaret H. "French Noblewomen and the New Domesticity, 1750–1850." *Feminist Studies* 5 (Spring 1979): 41–65.

Daumard, Adeline. *La Bourgeoisie parisienne de 1815 à 1848.* Paris: SEVPEN, 1963.

Dauphin, Cécile, Anette Farge, Geneviève Fraisse, Christiane Klapisch-Zuber, Rose-Marie Lagrave, Michelle Perrot, Pierrette Pfzerat, Yannick Ripa, Pauline Schmitt-Pantel, Danièle Voldman. "Women's Culture and Women's Power: An Attempt at Historiography." Comments by Karen Offen, Nell Irvin Painter, Hilda L. Smith, Lois W. Banner. *Journal of Women's History* 1 (Spring 1989): 63–107.

Davis, Natalie Zemon. " 'Women's History' in Transition: The European Case." *Feminist Studies* 3 (Spring-Summer 1976): 83–103.

Decaux, Alain. *Histoire des françaises.* 2 vols. Paris: Librairie Académique Perrin, 1972.

DeGroat, Judith A. "Women's Work Identity: Female Labor in the Transitional Manufacturing Economy of July Monarchy Paris." Paper presented to the 38th Annual Meeting of the Society for French Historical Studies, El Paso, Texas, March 1992.

Delaporte, François. *Disease and Civilization: The Cholera in Paris: 1832.* Translated by Arthur Goldhammer; foreword by Paul Rabinow. Cambridge, MA: MIT Press, 1986.

De Lauretis, Teresa. "Desire in Narrative." In *Alice Doesn't: Feminism, Semiotics, Cinema,* 103–87. Bloomington: Indiana University Press, 1984.

———. *Technologies of Gender: Essays on Theory, Film, and Fiction.* Bloomington: Indiana University Press, 1987.

de Man, Paul. *Allegories of Reading: Figural Language in Rousseau, Nietzsche, Rilke, and Proust.* New Haven: Yale University Press, 1979.

———. "Autobiography as Defacement." In *The Rhetoric of Romanticism,* 67–81. New York: Columbia University Press, 1984.

Démar, Claire. "Appel d'une femme au peuple sur l'affranchissement de la femme." In *Ma Loi d'avenir,* 61–75. Paris: Au Bureau de la *Tribune des femmes,* 1834.

———. *Ma Loi d'avenir.* Paris: Au Bureau de la *Tribune des femmes,* 1834.

———. *Textes sur l'affranchissement des femmes.* Followed by an explanation of Saint-Simonian symbolism and ideology by Valentin Pelosse. Paris: Payot, 1976.

Deniel, Raymond. *Une Image de la famille et de la société sous la restauration.* Paris: Les Editions ouvrières, 1965.

Deroin, Jeanne-Victoire. *Aux femmes*. Paris: Auffray, n.d. [August 1832]. Reprinted from *La Femme libre* (*Tribune des femmes* 1, no. 2).

Derré, J. R. *Regards sur le Saint-Simonisme et les Saint-Simoniens*. Lyon: Presses Universitaires de Lyon, 1986.

Derrida, Jacques. *Glas: Que reste-t-il du savoir absolu?* Paris: Denoel/Gonthier, 1981.

—. *De la Grammatologie*. Paris: Minuit, 1967.

—. "The Double Session." In *Dissemination*, trans. Barbara Johnson, 173–286. Chicago: University of Chicago Press, 1981.

—. *Spurs: Nietzsche's Styles/Eperons: Les styles de Nietzsche*. Translated by Barbara Harlow. Chicago: University of Chicago Press, 1979.

Desanti, Dominique. *Flora Tristan: La femme révoltée*. Paris: Hachette, 1972.

—. *Flora Tristan: Vie, oeuvres mêlées*. Paris: Union générale d'éditions, 1973.

—. *Les Socialistes de l'utopie*. Paris: Payot, 1979.

Devance, Louis. "Femme, famille, travail et morale sexuelle dans l'idéologie de 1848." *Romantisme*, nos. 13–14 (1976): 79–103.

de Vigny, Alfred. "La Maison du berger." In *Poésies choisies*, 71–85. Paris: Classiques Larousse, 1935.

Dijkstra, Sandra. *Flora Tristan: Pioneer Feminist and Socialist*. Berkeley: Center for Socialist History, 1984.

Doctrine de Saint-Simon: Exposition, première année, 1828–1829. Edited by C. Bouglé and E. Halévy. Paris: Rivière, 1924.

The Doctrine of Saint-Simon: An Exposition, First Year, 1828–1829. Translated by Georg G. Iggers. New York: Schocken Books, 1972.

DuBois, Ellen, Mari Jo Buhle, Temma Kaplan, Gerda Lerner, and Carroll Smith-Rosenberg. "Politics and Culture in Women's History: A Symposium." *Feminist Studies* 6 (Spring 1980): 26–64.

Duchen, Claire. *Feminism in France: From May '68 to Mitterand*. London: Routledge & Kegan Paul, 1986.

Duhet, Paule-Marie. *Les Femmes et la Révolution, 1789–1794*. Paris: Julliard, 1971.

Edwards, Anne. "The Sex/Gender Distinction: Has It Outlived Its Usefulness?" *Australian Feminist Studies* 10 (Summer 1989): 1–12.

Eisenstein, Hester, and Alice Jardine, eds. *The Future of Difference*. Boston: G. K. Hall, 1980.

Elhadad, Lydia. Introduction to *Souvenirs d'une fille du peuple: ou La Saint-simonienne en Egypte*, by Suzanne Voilquin. Paris: Maspero, 1978.

Elshtain, Jean Bethke. *Public Man, Private Woman: Women in Social and Political Thought*. Princeton: Princeton University Press, 1982.

Enfantin, Prosper, and Henri, comte de Saint-Simon. *Oeuvres de Saint-Simon et d'Enfantin*. Published by members of the committee set up by Enfantin for the execution of his last will. 47 vols. Paris: E. Dentu, Ernest Leroux, 1865–78.

—. *Réunion générale de la famille: Séances des 19 et 21 novembre 1831*. Paris: Bureau de *Globe*, 1832.

Engels, Frederick. *The Origin of the Family, Private Property, and the State*. Edited by Eleanor Burke Leacock. New York: International Publishers, 1972.

"The Essential Difference: Another Look at Essentialism." A special issue of *Differences* 1 (Summer 1989).

Evans, David Owen. *Social Romanticism in France, 1830–1848*. New York: Octagon Books, 1969.

Evans, Martha Noel. *Masks of Tradition: Women and the Politics of Writing in Twentieth-Century France*. Ithaca: Cornell University Press, 1987.

Faderman, Lillian. *Surpassing the Love of Men: Romantic Friendship and Love be-

tween Women from the Renaissance to the Present. New York: William Morrow, 1981.

Feldstein, Richard, and Judith Roof, eds. *Feminism and Psychoanalysis.* Ithaca: Cornell University Press, 1989.

Firestone, Shulamith. *The Dialectic of Sex: The Case for Feminist Revolution.* New York: Bantam Books, 1970.

Fish, Stanley. "Being Interdisciplinary Is So Very Hard to Do." In *Profession 89,* 4–14. New York: Modern Language Association, 1989.

Fletcher, Ian, ed. *Romantic Mythologies.* New York: Barnes & Noble, 1967.

Foucault, Michel. *The History of Sexuality: An Introduction.* Translated by Robert Hurley. New York: Pantheon Books, 1978.

———. "Qu'est-ce qu'un auteur." *Bulletin de la Société de Philosophie* 3 (1969): 75–104.

Fourier, François Marie Charles. *Le Nouveau monde amoureux.* Edited by Simone Debout-Oleskiewicz. Paris: Editions Anthropos, 1967.

———. *Le Nouveau monde industriel et sociétaire, ou invention du procédé d'industrie attrayant et naturelle distribuée en séries passionnées.* Paris: Flammarion, 1973.

———. *Oeuvres complètes.* 6 vols. Paris: Librairie sociétaire, 1843.

———. *Théorie des quatre mouvements et des déstinées générales: Prospectus et annonce de la découverte.* Paris: Jean-Jacques Pauvert, 1967.

———. *Traité de l'association domestique-agricole.* Paris: Edition Anthropos, 1966–67.

Fox-Genovese, Elizabeth. "My Statue, Myself: Autobiographical Writings of Afro-American Women." In *The Private Self: Theory and Practice of Women's Autobiographical Writings,* edited by Shari Benstock, 63–89. Chapel Hill: University of North Carolina Press, 1988.

———. "The Personal Is Not Political Enough." *Marxist Perspectives,* no. 8 (Winter 1979–80): 94–113.

Fraisse, Geneviève. *Muse de la raison: La démocratie exclusive et la différence des sexes.* Paris: Editions Alinéa, 1989.

———. "Natural Law and the Origins of Nineteenth-Century Feminist Thought in France." In *Women in Culture and Politics,* edited by Judith Friedlander, Blanche Wiesen Cook, Alice Kessler-Harris, and Carroll Smith-Rosenberg, 318–29. Bloomington: Indiana University Press, 1986.

Freud, Sigmund. "Negation." In *General Psychological Theory: Papers on Metapsychology,* 213–17. New York: Collier, 1963.

———. *Totem and Taboo: Some Resemblances between the Psychic Lives of Savages and Neurotics.* New York: W. W. Norton, 1950.

Friedman, Susan Stanford. "Women's Autobiographical Selves: Theory and Practice." In *The Private Self: Theory and Practice of Women's Autobiographical Writings,* edited by Shari Benstock, 34–62. Chapel Hill: University of North Carolina Press, 1988.

Gallop, Jane. "The Father's Seduction." In *The Daughter's Seduction: Feminism and Psychoanalysis.* Ithaca: Cornell University Press, 1982.

———. "French Theory and the Seduction of Feminism." In *Men in Feminism,* edited by Alice A. Jardine and Paul Smith. New York: Methuen, 1987.

———. *Reading Lacan.* Ithaca: Cornell University Press, 1985.

———. *Thinking through the Body.* New York: Columbia, 1988.

Garner, Shirley Nelson, Claire Kahane, and Madelon Sprengnether, eds. *The (M)other Tongue.* Ithaca: Cornell University Press, 1985.

Gattey, Charles Neilson. *Gauguin's Astonishing Grandmother: A Biography of Flora Tristan.* London: Femina Books, 1970.

Gatti de Gamond, Zoë Charlotte. *Fourier et son système.* 5th ed. Paris: Capelle, 1841–42.

Gilbert, Sandra Caruso Mortola, and Susan Dreyfuss David Gubar. "Ceremonies of the Alphabet: Female Grandmatologies and the Female Authorgraph." In *The Female Autograph*, edited by Domna Stanton, 23–54. New York: New York Literary Forum, 1984.

Gilligan, Carol. *In a Different Voice: Psychological Theory and Women's Development.* Cambridge, MA: Harvard University Press, 1982.

Girard, René. *Deceit, Desire, and the Novel: Self and Other in Literary Structure.* Baltimore: Johns Hopkins University Press, 1965.

———. *Violence and the Sacred.* Baltimore: Johns Hopkins University Press, 1977.

Glass, D. V., and D. E. C. Eversley, eds. *Population in History.* Chicago: Aldine, 1965.

Goldstein, Leslie F. "Early Feminist Themes in French Utopian Socialism: The St.-Simonians and Fourier." In *Race, Class, and Gender in 19th-Century Culture*, edited by Maryanne Cline Horowitz, 195–212. Rochester, N.Y.: University of Rochester Press, 1991. Originally published in the *Journal of the History of Ideas* 43 (1982): 91–108.

Gordon, Linda. "On 'Difference.'" In "Theorizing Nationality, Sexuality, and Race." A special issue of *Genders*, no. 10 (Spring 1991): 91–111.

———. "Voluntary Motherhood: The Beginnings of Feminist Birth Control Ideas in the United States." *Feminist Studies* 1 (Winter-Spring 1973): 5–22.

Gossman, Lionel. "The Innocent Art of Confession and Reverie." *Daedalus* 3 (1978): 59–78.

Goux, Jean-Joseph. *Freud, Marx: Economie et symbolique.* Paris: Seuil, 1973.

Grosz, Elizabeth. *Jacques Lacan: A Feminist Introduction.* London: Routledge, 1990.

———. "Sexual Difference and the Problem of Essentialism." *Inscriptions* 5 (1989): 86–101.

Hanagan, Michael. "Proletarian Families and Social Protest: Production and Reproduction as Issues of Social Conflict in Nineteenth-Century France." In *Work in France: Representations, Meaning, Organization, and Practice*, edited by Steven Laurence Kaplan and Cynthia J. Koepp, 418–56. Ithaca: Cornell University Press, 1986.

Haney-Peritz, Janice. "Engendering the Exemplary Daughter: The Deployment of Sexuality in Richardson's *Clarissa*." In *Daughters and Fathers*, edited by Linda E. Boose and Betty S. Flowers, 181–207. Baltimore: Johns Hopkins University Press, 1989.

Harlan, David. "Intellectual History and the Return of Literature." *American Historical Review* 94 (June 1989): 589–609.

Harsin, Jill. *Policing Prostitution in Nineteenth-Century Paris.* Princeton: Princeton University Press, 1985.

Heilbrun, Carolyn. *Reinventing Womanhood.* New York: Norton, 1982.

Hellerstein, Erna Olafson. "Women, Social Order, and the City: Rules for French Ladies, 1830–1870." Ph.D. dissertation, University of California, Berkeley, 1980.

Hellerstein, Erna Olafson, Leslie Parker Hume, and Karen Offen, eds. *Victorian Women: A Documentary Account of Women's Lives in Nineteenth-Century England, France, and the United States.* Stanford: Stanford University Press, 1981.

Herr, Cheryl. "Fathers, Daughters, Anxiety, and Fiction." In *Discontented Discourses: Feminism/Textual Intervention/Psychoanalysis*, edited by Marleen S. Barr and Richard Feldstein, 173–207. Urbana: University of Illinois Press, 1989.

Hewitt, Leah D. *Autobiographical Tightropes.* Lincoln: University of Nebraska Press, 1990.

Hewitt, Nancy A. "Beyond the Search for Sisterhood: American Women's History in the 1980s." In *Unequal Sisters: A Multicultural Reader in U.S. Women's History*, edited by Ellen Carol DuBois and Vicki Ruiz, 1–14. New York: Routledge, 1990.

Hewlitt, Sylvia Ann. *A Lesser Life: The Myth of Women's Liberation in America*. New York: William Morrow, 1986.

Hill-Miller, Katherine C. " 'The Skies and Trees of the Past': Anne Thackeray Ritchie and William Makepeace Thackeray." In *Daughters and Fathers*, edited by Linda E. Boose and Betty S. Flowers, 261–383. Baltimore: Johns Hopkins University Press, 1980.

Hirsch, Marianne. *The Mother/Daughter Plot: Narrative, Psychoanalysis, Feminism*. Bloomington: Indiana University Press, 1989.

Hollinger, David. "The Persistence of Historical Knowing." *American Historical Review* 94 (June 1989): 610–21.

Holmlund, Christine. "The Lesbian, the Mother, the Heterosexual Lover: Irigaray's Recodings of Difference." *Feminist Studies* 17 (Summer 1991): 283–308.

Homans, Margaret. *Bearing the Word: Language and Female Experience in Nineteenth-Century Women's Writing*. Chicago: University of Chicago Press, 1986.

———. " 'Her Very Own Howl': The Ambiguities of Representation in Recent Women's Fiction." *Signs* 9 (Winter 1983): 186–205.

Hunt, Lynn. "The Many Bodies of Marie Antoinette: Political Pornography and the Problem of the Feminine in the French Revolution." In *Eroticism and the Body Politic*, edited by Lynn Hunt, 108–30. Baltimore: Johns Hopkins University Press, 1991.

Irigaray, Luce. *Le Corps-à-corps avec la mère*. Ottawa: Editions de la pleine lune, 1981.

———. *Ce Sexe qui n'en est pas un*. Paris: Minuit, 1977.

———. *Ethique de la différence sexuelle*. Paris: Editions de Minuit, 1984.

———. *Et l'Une ne bouge pas sans l'autre*. Paris: Minuit, 1979.

———. "The Gesture in Psychoanalysis." In *Between Feminism and Psychoanalysis*, edited by Teresa Brennan, 127–38. London: Routledge, 1989.

———. *Speculum de l'autre femme*. Paris: Minuit, 1974.

Ivray, Jehan d'. *L'Aventure saint-simonienne et les femmes*. Paris, Librairie Félix Alcan, 1930.

Janeway, Elizabeth. *Man's World, Woman's Place: A Study in Social Mythology*. New York: Dell Publishing, 1971.

Jardine, Alice A. "Death Sentences: Writing Couples and Ideology." In *The Female Body in Western Culture*, edited by Susan Suleiman, 84–98. Cambridge, MA: Harvard University Press, 1986.

———. *Gynesis: Configurations of Woman and Modernity*. Ithaca: Cornell University Press, 1985.

Jardine, Alice A., and Anne M. Menke, eds. *Shifting Scenes: Interviews on Women, Waiting, and Politics in Post-68 France*. New York: Columbia University Press, 1991.

Jelinek, Estelle C. *The Tradition of Women's Autobiography: From Antiquity to the Present*. Boston: Twayne, 1986.

Johnson, Barbara. *Worlds of Difference*. Baltimore: Johns Hopkins University Press, 1987.

Jones, Ann Rosalind. "Writing the Body: Toward an Understanding of *l'Ecriture féminine*." *Feminist Studies* 7 (Summer 1981): 247–63.

Kaplan, Steven Laurence, and Cynthia J. Koepp, eds. *Work in France: Representations, Meaning, Organization, and Practice*. Ithaca: Cornell University Press, 1986.

Kelly-Gadol, Joan. "The Social Relation of the Sexes: Methodological Implications of Women's History." *Signs: Journal of Women in Culture and Society* 1 (Summer 1976): 809–23.

Kerber, Linda, Catherine G. Greeno and Eleanor E. Maccoby, Zella Luria, Carol B. Stack, and Carol Gilligan. "On *In a Different Voice*: An Interdisciplinary Forum." *Signs: Journal of Women in Culture and Society* 11 (Winter 1986): 304–33.

Kofman, Sarah. *Le Respect des femmes (Kant et Rousseau)*. Paris: Galilée, 1982.

Kraditor, Aileen S. *The Ideas of the Woman Suffrage Movement, 1890–1920*. New York: Columbia University Press, 1965.

Kristeva, Julia. "Un nouveau type d'intellectuel." *Tel Quel*, no. 74 (1977): 3–8.

———. *The Powers of Horror: An Essay on Abjection*. Translated by Leon S. Roudiez. New York: Columbia University Press, 1982.

———. *Revolution in Poetic Language*. Translated by Margaret Waller. New York: Columbia University Press, 1984.

———. "Women's Time." In *Feminist Theory: A Critique of Ideology*, edited by Nannerl O. Keohane, Michelle Z. Rosaldo, and Barbara C. Gelpi, 31–54. Chicago: University of Chicago Press, 1981.

Lacan, Jacques. *Ecrits*. 2 vols. Paris: Points, 1971.

———. "The Function of Language in Psychoanalysis." In *Speech and Language in Psychoanalysis*, edited and translated by Anthony Wilden, 9–88. Baltimore: Johns Hopkins University Press, 1968.

———. "God and the *Jouissance* of the Woman." In *Feminine Sexuality*, edited by Juliet Mitchell and Jacqueline Rose, 137–48. Translated by Jacqueline Rose. New York: Norton, 1983.

Landes, Joan B. *Women and the Public Sphere in the Age of the French Revolution*. Ithaca: Cornell University Press, 1988.

Lang, Candace. "Autobiography in the Aftermath of Romanticism." *Diacritics* 4 (1982): 2–16.

Laqueur, Thomas. "Orgasm, Generation, and the Politics of Reproductive Biology." In *The Making of the Modern Body: Sexuality and Society in the Nineteenth Century*, edited by Catherine Gallagher and Thomas Laqueur, 1–41. Berkeley, University of California Press, 1987.

Lebassu, Joséphine. *La Saint-simonienne*. Paris: L. Tenré, 1833.

Lejeune, Philippe. *Le Pacte autobiographique*. Paris: Seuil, 1975.

———. "Le Peigne cassé." *Poétique*, no. 25 (1976): 1–29.

Lemonnier, Charles. *Elisa Lemmonier, fondatrice de la Société pour l'Enseignement Professional des Femmes*. Saint-Germain: L. Toinon, 1866.

Leprohon, Pierre. *Flora Tristan*. Antony, France: Editions Corymbe, 1979.

Levèque, Pierre. "Mission impossible? Flora Tristan en Bourgogne, vue par la presse locale." In *Un Fabuleux Destin: Flora Tristan*, edited by Stéphane Michaud, 65–81. Dijon: Editions universitaires de Dijon, 1984.

Lévi-Strauss, Claude. *Les Structures élémentaires de la parenté*. Paris: Mouton, 1967.

Levy, Darline Gay, Harriet Branson Applewhite, and Mary Durham Johnson. *Women in Revolutionary Paris, 1789–1795: Selected Documents Translated with Notes and Commentary*. Urbana: University of Illinois Press, 1979.

Lichtheim, George. *The Origins of Socialism*. New York: Frederick A. Praeger, 1969.

Lionnet, Françoise. *Autobiographical Voices: Race, Gender, Self-portraiture*. Ithaca: Cornell University Press, 1989.

Lloyd, Genevieve. "Woman as Other: Sex, Gender, and Subjectivity." *Australian Feminist Studies* 10 (Summer 1989): 13–22.

Locke, Ralph P. *Music, Musicians, and the Saint-Simonians*. Chicago: University of Chicago Press, 1986.

McBride, Theresa. *The Domestic Revolution: The Modernization of Household Service in England and France, 1820–1920.* New York: Holmes & Meier, 1976.

McLaren, Angus. "Abortion in France: Women and the Regulation of Family Size, 1800–1914." *French Historical Studies* 10 (Spring 1978): 461–85.

———. "Doctor in the House: Medicine and Private Morality in France, 1800–1850." *Feminist Studies* 2 (1975): 39–45.

———. "Sex and Socialism: The Opposition of the French Left to Birth Control in the Nineteenth Century." *Journal of the History of Ideas* 27 (1976): 475–92.

———. "Some Secular Attitudes toward Sexual Behavior in France: 1760–1860." *French Historical Studies* 8 (Fall 1974): 604–25.

Makward, Christiane. "To Be or Not to Be . . . A Feminist Speaker." In *The Future of Difference*, edited by Hester Eisenstein and Alice Jardine, 95–105. Boston: G. K. Hall, 1980.

Manuel, Frank. *The Prophets of Paris.* New York: Harper & Row, 1965.

Marks, Elaine, and Isabelle de Courtivron, eds. *New French Feminisms: An Anthology.* Amherst: University of Massachusetts Press, 1980.

Marx, Karl. *Capital,* Vol. 1. New York: International Publishers, 1972.

Mason, Mary Grimley, and Carol Hurd Green, eds. *Journeys: Autobiographical Writings by Women.* Boston, G. K. Hall, 1979.

Mayeur, Françoise. *L'Education des filles en France au XIXe siècle.* Paris: Hachette, 1979.

Maynes, Mary Jo. "Gender and Narrative Form in French and German Working-Class Autobiographies." In *Interpreting Women's Lives: Feminist Theory and Personal Narratives*, edited by the Personal Narratives Group, 103–17. Bloomington: Indiana University Press, 1989.

Maza, Sara. "The Diamond Necklace Affair Revisited (1785–1786): The Case of the Missing Queen." In *Eroticism and the Body Politic*, edited by Lynn Hunt, 63–89. Baltimore: Johns Hopkins University Press, 1991.

Merriman, John M., ed. *Consciousness and Class Experience in Nineteenth-Century Europe.* New York: Holmes & Meier, 1979.

———. *1830 in France.* New York: Franklin Watts, 1975.

Michaud, Stéphane. Introduction to *Un Fabuleux Destin: Flora Tristan*, edited by Stéphane Michaud. Dijon: Editions Universitaires de Dijon, 1984.

Miller, Nancy K. *Subject to Change: Reading Feminist Writing.* New York: Columbia University Press, 1988.

Millet, Kate. *Sexual Politics.* New York: Avon Books, 1970.

Mitchell, Juliet, and Ann Oakley, eds. *What Is Feminism? A Reexamination.* New York: Pantheon Books, 1986.

Modleski, Tania. *Feminism without Women: Culture and Criticism in a "Post-feminist" Age.* New York: Routledge, 1991.

Moi, Toril. *Sexual/Textual Politics.* New York: Methuen, 1985.

Moon, S. Joan. "The Saint-Simoniennes and the Moral Revolution." *Proceedings of the Consortium on Revolutionary Europe* (1976): 162–74.

———. "The Saint-Simonian Association of Working-Class Women, 1830–50." In *Proceedings of the Fifth Annual Meeting of the Western Society for French History, Las Cruces, New Mexico,* 274–81. Santa Barbara, CA, 1978.

Morrison, Toni. *Beloved.* New York: Knopf, 1987.

Moses, Claire Goldberg. *French Feminism in the Nineteenth Century.* Albany: State University of New York Press, 1984.

———. "Saint-Simonian Men/Saint Simonian Women: The Transformation of Feminist Thought in 1830s' France." *Journal of Modern History* 54 (June 1982): 240–67.

———. " 'Equality' and 'Difference' in Historical Perspective: A Comparative Examination of the Feminisms of French Revolutionaries and Utopian Socialists." In *Rebel Daughters: Women and the French Revolution*, edited by Sara E. Melzer and Leslie W. Rabine. New York: Oxford University Press, 1992.

———. "Debating the Present, Writing the Past: 'Feminism' in French History and Historiography." *Radical History Review*, no. 52 (Winter 1992): 79–94.

Nancy, Jean-Luc, and Philippe Lacoue-Labarthe. *L'absolu littéraire: Théorie de la littérature du romantisme allemand*. Paris: Seuil, 1978.

Offen, Karen. "Defining Feminism: A Comparative Historical Approach." *Signs* 14 (Autumn 1988): 119–57.

Ostriker, Alicia. "Comment on Homans's 'Her Very Own Howl': The Ambiguities of Representation in Recent Women's Fiction." *Signs* 10 (Spring 1985): 597–600.

Parent-Duchâtelet, A.-J.-B. *De la prostitution dans la ville de Paris*. 2 vols. Paris: Chez Baillière, 1836.

Parish, William, Jr., and Moshe Schwartz. "Household Complexity in Nineteenth-Century France." *American Sociological Review* 37 (April 1972): 154–73.

Perrot, Michelle. "L'Eloge de la ménagère dans le discours des ouvriers français au XIXe siècle." *Romantisme*, nos. 13–14 (1976): 105–21.

Phillips, Roderick. *Putting Asunder: A History of Divorce in Western Society*. Cambridge: Cambridge University Press, 1988.

Picard, Roger. *Le Romantisme social*. New York: Brentano's, 1944.

Pierson, Ruth Roach. "Experience, Difference, Dominance, and Voice in the Writing of Canadian Women's History." In *Writing Women's History: International Perspectives*, edited by Karen Offen, Ruth Roach Pierson, and Jane Rendall, 79–106. Bloomington: Indiana University Press, 1991.

Pinckney, David. *The French Revolution of 1830*. Princeton: Princeton University Press, 1972.

Planté, Christine. "Les Féministes saint-simoniennes: Possibilités et limites d'un mouvement féministe en France au lendemain de 1830." In *Regards sur le Saint-Simonisme et les Saint-Simoniens*, edited by J. R. Derre, 73–102. Lyon: Presses Universitaires de Lyon, 1986.

———. *La Petite Soeur de Balzac*. Paris: Editions du Seuil, 1989.

———. "Les Saint-Simoniennes." In *Femmes et contre-pouvoirs*, edited by Yolande Cohen, 81–100. Montréal: Editions du Boréal, 1987.

———. *Les Saint-Simoniennes, ou la quête d'une identité à travers l'écriture à la première personne*. Thèse du troisième cycle: Littérature française. Paris: Université de Paris 3, 1983.

Portal, Magda. "Ma Découverte de Flora Tristan." In *Un Fabuleux Destin: Flora Tristan*, edited by Stéphane Michaud, 11–14. Dijon: Editions universitaires de Dijon, 1984.

Poster, Mark. *Critical Theory of the Family*. New York: Seabury Press, 1978.

———. *The Utopian Thought of Restif de la Bretonne*. New York: New York University Press, 1971.

Price, Roger. *The Economic Modernisation of France*. New York: John Wiley & Sons, 1975.

Puech, Jules. *La Vie et l'Oeuvre de Flora Tristan, 1803–1844*. Paris: Marcel Rivière, 1925.

Puech, Marie-Louise. "Une supercherie littéraire: Le véritable rédacteur de la *Gazette des Femmes* (1836–1838)." *La Révolution de 1848* 32 (June-August 1935): 303–12.

Rabaut, Jean. *Histoire des féminismes français*. Paris: Editions Stock, 1978.

Rabine, Leslie W. "*Ecriture féminine* as Metaphor: Reading Claire Démar with Hélène Cixous." *Cultural Critique*, no. 8 (Winter 1987–88): 19–44.

———. "Essentialism and Its Contexts: Saint-Simonian and Post-Structuralist Feminists." *Differences* 1 (Summer 1989): 105–23.

————. "George Sand and the Myth of Femininity." *Women and Literature* 4, no. 2 (Fall 1976): 2–17.

————. *Reading the Romantic Heroine: Text, History, Ideology.* Ann Arbor: University of Michigan Press, 1985.

Rachid, Amina. "Regards croisés sur la France et l'Egypte: Riaa al Tahtawi et Suzanne Voilquin: Idéologie et conscience de classe." In *Le Miroir égyptien,* edited by Robert Ilbert and Philippe Joutard, 225–38. Marseille: Éditions du Quai Jeanne Lafitte, 1984.

Racz, Elizabeth. "The Women's Rights Movement in the French Revolution." *Science and Society* 16 (1952): 151–74.

Ragland-Sullivan, Ellie. "The Third Term: Desire, the Phallus, and the Materiality of Language." In *Feminism and Psychoanalysis,* edited by Richard Feldstein and Judith Roof, 40–64. Ithaca: Cornell University Press, 1989.

Rancière, Jacques. *La Nuit des prolétaires.* Paris: Librairie Arthème Fayard, 1981.

Ranum, Orest, and Patricia Ranum, eds. *Popular Attitudes towards Birth Control in Preindustrial France and England.* New York: Harper & Row, 1972.

Ranvier, Adrien. "Une féministe de 1848: Jeanne Deroin." *La Révolution de 1848* 4 (1907–8): 317–55, 421–30, 480–98.

Ratcliffe, Barrie. "Saint-Simonism and Messianism: The Case of Gustave d'Eichthal." *French Historical Studies* 9 (Spring 1976): 484–502.

Reed, Arden, ed. *Romanticism and Language.* Ithaca: Cornell University Press, 1984.

Religion Saint-Simonienne: Cérémonie du 27 novembre. Paris: Guiraudet, 1831.

Religion Saint-Simonienne: Morale. . . . Paris: Everat, [April] 1832.

Reynolds, Siân, ed. *Women, State, and Revolution: Essays on Power and Gender in Europe since 1789.* Amherst: University of Massachusetts Press, 1987.

Riasanovsky, Nicholas. *The Teachings of Charles Fourier.* Berkeley: University of California Press, 1969.

Rich, Adrienne. *Of Woman Born: Motherhood as Experience and Institution.* New York: W. W. Norton, 1976.

————. *Your Native Land, Your Life: Poems.* New York: W. W. Norton, 1986.

Richardson, Alan. "Romanticism and the Colonization of the Feminine." In *Romanticism and Feminism,* edited by Anne K. Mellor, 13–25. Bloomington: Indiana University Press, 1988.

Riley, Denise. *"Am I That Name?" Feminism and the Category of "Women" in History.* Minneapolis: University of Minnesota Press, 1988.

Robertson, Priscilla. *An Experience of Women: Pattern and Change in Nineteenth-Century Europe.* Philadelphia: Temple University Press, 1982.

Rodriques, O[linde]. *Réunion générale de la famille . . . 19 et 20 nov. Note sur le mariage et la divorce.* Paris: n.p., 1831.

Rosenfelt, Deborah, and Judith Stacey. "Second Thoughts on the Second Wave." *Feminist Studies* 13 (Summer 1987): 341–61.

Ross, Marlon B. "Romantic Quest and Conquest: Troping Masculine Power in the Crisis of Poetic Identity." In *Romanticism and Feminism,* edited by Anne K. Mellor, 26–51. Bloomington: Indiana University Press, 1988.

Rousseau, Jean-Jacques. *Emile.* Translated by Barbara Foxley. New York: Dutton, 1933.

————. *La Nouvelle Héloïse.* Translated by Judith H. McDowell. University Park: Pennsylvania State University Press, 1968.

————. *Les Confessions.* 2 vols. Paris: Garnier-Flammarion, 1968.

Rover, Constance. *Love, Morals, and the Feminists.* London: Routledge & Kegan Paul, 1970.

Rubin, Gayle. "The Traffic in Women: Notes on the 'Political Economy' of Sex."

In *Toward an Anthropology of Women*, edited by Rayna R[app] Reiter, 157–210. New York: Monthly Review Press, 1975.

Saint-Amand, A[dèle]. *Proclamation aux femmes*. Paris: H. Fournier, n.d.

Schiebinger, Londa. "Skeletons in the Closet: The First Illustrations of the Female Skeleton in Eighteenth-Century Anatomy." In *The Making of the Modern Body: Sexuality and Society in the Nineteenth Century*, edited by Catherine Gallagher and Thomas Laqueur, 42–84. Berkeley: University of California Press, 1987.

Schneider, Joyce Anne. *Flora Tristan: Feminist, Socialist, Free Spirit*. New York: William Morrow, 1980.

Scott, Joan W. "Deconstructing Equality-versus-Difference: Or, the Uses of Poststructuralist Theory for Feminism." *Feminist Studies* 14 (Spring 1988): 33–50.

———. "The Evidence of Experience." *Critical Inquiry* 17 (Summer 1991): 773–97.

———. *Gender and the Politics of History*. New York: Columbia University Press, 1988.

———. "Jeanne Deroin." Paper presented at the Annual Meeting of the American Historical Association, New York City, December 1990.

———. "The Problem of Invisibility." In *Retrieving Women's History: Changing Perceptions of the Role of Women in Politics and Society*, edited by S. Jay Kleinberg, 5–29. Oxford: Berg Publishers, 1988.

Scott, Joan, and Louise Tilly. "Women's Work and the Family in Nineteenth-Century Europe." *Comparative Studies in Society and History* 17 (1975): 36–64.

Sedgwick, Eve Kosofsky. *Between Men: English Literature and Male Homosocial Desire*. New York: Columbia University Press, 1985.

Segal, Naomi. *Narcissus and Echo: Women in the French Récit*. Manchester: Manchester University Press, 1988.

Sellers, Susan, ed. *Writing Differences: Readings from the Seminar of Hélène Cixous*. Stony Stratford, England: Open University Press, 1988.

Sewell, William H. "Property, Labor, and the Emergence of Socialism in France, 1789–1848." In *Consciousness and Class Experience in Nineteenth-Century Europe*, edited by John Merriman. New York: Holmes & Meier, 1979.

Shorter, Edward. "Female Emancipation, Birth Control, and Fertility." *American Historical Review* 78 (1973): 605–40.

———. "Illegitimacy, Sexual Revolution, and Social Change in Modern Europe." *Journal of Interdisciplinary History* 2 (Autumn 1971): 237–72.

———. *The Making of the Modern Family*. New York: Basic Books, 1975.

Showalter, Elaine. *A Literature of Their Own: British Women Novelists from Brontë to Lessing*. Princeton: Princeton University Press, 1977.

Smith, Bonnie G. *Ladies of the Leisure Class: The Bourgeoises of Northern France in the Nineteenth Century*. Princeton: Princeton University Press, 1981.

Smith, Sidonie. *A Poetics of Women's Autobiography: Marginality and the Fictions of Self-Representation*. Bloomington: Indiana University Press, 1987.

Smith-Rosenberg, Carroll. "The Female World of Love and Ritual: Relations between Women in Nineteenth-Century America." *Signs: Journal of Women in Culture and Society* 1 (Fall 1975): 1–29.

Sowerwine, Charles. *Sisters or Citizens? Women and Socialism in France since 1876*. Cambridge: Cambridge University Press, 1982.

Spivak, Gayatri Chakravorty. "Displacement and the Discourse of Woman." In *Displacement: Derrida and After*, edited by Mark Krupnick, 169–99. Bloomington: Indiana University Press, 1983.

———. "Feminism and Deconstruction, Again: Negotiating with Unacknowledged Masculinism." *Between Feminism and Psychoanalysis*, edited by Teresa Brennan, 206–24. London: Routledge, 1989.

Stacey, Judith. "The New Conservative Feminism." *Feminist Studies* 9 (Fall 1983): 559–83.

Stanton, Domna C. "Autogynography: Is the Subject Different?" In *The Female Autograph*, edited by Domna Stanton, 5–22. New York: New York Literary Forum, 1984.

———. "Difference on Trial: A Critique of the Maternal Metaphor in Cixous, Irigaray, and Kristeva." In *The Poetics of Gender*, edited by Nancy K. Miller, 157–82. New York: Columbia University Press, 1986.

Starobinski, Jean. *Jean-Jacques Rousseau: La Transparence et l'obstacle*. Paris: Plon, 1957.

Stone, Lawrence. *The Family, Sex, and Marriage in England, 1500–1800*. Abridged edition, New York: Harper and Row, 1979.

Struminger, Laura. *The Odyssey of Flora Tristan*. New York: Peter Lang, 1988.

———. *Women and the Making of the Working Class: Lyon, 1830–1870*. St. Alban's, VT: Eden Press Women's Publications, 1979.

Sullerot, Evelyne. *Histoire de la presse féminine en France, des origines à 1848*. Paris: Armand Colin, 1966.

Sussman, George D. "The Wet-Nursing Business in Nineteenth-Century France." *French Historical Studies* 9 (Fall 1975): 304–28.

Talbot, Margaret. "An Emancipated Voice: Flora Tristan and Utopian Allegory." *Feminist Studies* 17 (Summer 1991): 219–40.

Taylor, Barbara. *Eve and the New Jerusalem: Socialism and Feminism in the Nineteenth Century*. New York: Pantheon, 1983.

Terdiman, Richard. *Discourse/Counter-Discourse: The Theory and Practice of Symbolic Resistance in Nineteenth-Century France*. Ithaca: Cornell University Press, 1985.

Tetu, J. F. "Remarques sur le statut juridique de la femme au XIXe siècle." In *La Femme au XIXe siècle: Littérature et idéologie*, edited by R. Bellet, 5–18. Lyon: Presses universitaires de Lyon, 1979.

Thibert, Marguerite. "Une Apôtre socialiste de 1848: Pauline Roland." *La Révolution de 1848* 22 (1925–26): 478–502, 524–40.

———. *Le Féminisme dans le socialisme français de 1830 à 1850*. Paris: M. Giard, 1926.

Thomas, Edith. *Pauline Roland: Socialisme et féminisme au XIXe siècle*. Paris: Marcel Rivière, 1956.

Thompson, Denise. "The 'Sex/Gender' Distinction: A Reconsideration." *Australian Feminist Studies* 10 (Summer 1989): 23–31.

Tilly, Louise, and Joan W. Scott. *Women, Work, and Family*. New York: Holt, Rinehart & Winston, 1978.

Tilly, Louise, Joan Scott, and Miriam Cohen. "Women's Work and European Fertility Patterns." *Journal of Interdisciplinary History* 6 (Winter 1976): 447–76.

Toews, John E. "Intellectual History after the Linguistic Turn: The Autonomy of Meaning and the Irreducibility of Experience." *American Historical Review* 92 (October 1987): 879–907.

Tristan y Moscozo, Flore Célestine Thérèse Henriette [Flora Tristan]. *L'Emancipation de la femme ou le testament de la paria*. Completed after her notes and therefore attributed to her, by Alphonse Constant. Paris: n.p., 1845.

———. *Lettres*. Edited by Stéphane Michaud. Paris: Editions du Seuil, 1980.

———. *Méphis ou le prolétaire*. 2 vols. Paris: L'advocat, 1838.

———. *Nécessité de faire un bon accueil aux femmes étrangères*. Paris: Dalauney, 1836.

———. *Pérégrinations d'une paria (1833–1834): Dieu, franchise, liberté*. 2 vols. Paris: Arthur Bertrand, 1838. Reprint edition, Paris: Maspero, 1980.

————. *Promenades dans Londres ou l'aristocratie & les prolétaires anglais*. Paris: H.-L. Delloye, 1840. Reprint edition, Paris: Maspero, 1983.

————. *Le Tour de France, journal 1843–1844*. 2d ed. 2 vols. Text and notes by Jules Puech, preface by Michel Collinet, and a new introduction by Stéphane Michaud. Paris: Maspero. 1980.

————. *L'Union ouvrière*. 1843. 3rd edition. Paris, 1844. Reprint edition, Paris: Editions d'Histoire Sociale, 1967.

Van de Walle, Etienne. "Alone in Europe: The French Fertility Decline until 1850." In *Historical Studies of Changing Fertility*, edited by Charles Tilly, 257–88. Princeton: Princeton University Press, 1978.

————. *The Female Population of France in the Nineteenth Century*. Princeton: Princeton University Press, 1974.

Vanier, Henrietta. *La Mode et ses métiers: Frivolités et luttes de classes, 1830–1870*. Paris: A. Colin, 1960.

Vicinus, Martha. " 'They Wonder to Which Sex I Belong': The Historical Roots of the Modern Lesbian Identity." *Feminist Studies* 18 (Fall 1992).

Vidalenc, Jean. "Les Techniques de la propagande saint-simonienne à la fin de 1831." *Archives de la Sociologie des religions* 10 (July–December 1960): 3–21.

Voilquin, Suzanne. *Mémoires d'une Saint-Simonienne en Russie*. Paris: Editions des femmes, 1977.

————. *Souvenirs d'une fille du people ou la Saint-Simonienne en Egypte*. Paris: Chez E. Sauzet, 1866.

————. *Souvenirs d'une fille du people ou la Saint-simonienne en Egypte*. Introduction by Lydia Elhadad. Reprint edition, Paris: François Maspero, 1978.

Voloshinov, V. N. *Marxism and the Philosophy of Language*. Translated by Ladislav Matejka and I. R. Titunik. Cambridge, MA: Harvard University Press, 1973.

Walch, Jean. *Bibliographie de Saint-Simonisme*. Paris: J. Vrin, 1967.

Waller, Margaret. "Being René, Buying Atala: Literary Production and Cultural Reproduction in Post-Revolutionary France." In *Rebel Daughters: Women and the French Revolution*, edited by Sara E. Melzer and Leslie W. Rabine. New York: Oxford University Press, 1992.

————. "*Cherchez la femme*: Male Malady and Narrative Politics in the French Romantic Novel." *PMLA* 104 (March 1989): 141–51.

Weill, Georges. "Le Saint-Simonisme hors de France." *Revue d'histoire économique et sociale* 9 (1921): 103–14.

Weitzman, Lenore. *The Divorce Revolution: The Unexpected Social and Economic Consequences for Women and Children*. New York: Free Press, 1985.

Welter, Barbara. "The Cult of True Womanhood, 1820–1860." *American Quarterly* 18 (Summer 1966): 131–75.

Wenzel, Hélène Vivienne. "The Text as Body/Politics: An Appreciation of Monique Wittig's Writings in Context." *Feminist Studies* 7 (Summer 1981): 264–87.

Wheaton, Robert, and Tamara K. Hareven, eds. *Family and Sexuality in French History*. Philadelphia: University of Pennsylvania Press, 1980.

Whitford, Margaret. *Luce Irigaray: Philosophy in the Feminine*. London: Routledge, 1991.

Wilden, Anthony. "Lacan and the Discourse of the Other." In *Speech and Language in Psychoanalysis*, edited and translated by Wilden, 157–312. Baltimore: Johns Hopkins University Press, 1968.

Yaeger, Patricia, and Beth Kowaleski-Wallace. *Refiguring the Father: New Feminist Readings in Patriarchy*. Carbondale: Southern Illinois University Press, 1989.

Zeldin, Theodore, ed. *Conflicts in French Morality*. London: George Allen &
    Unwin, 1970.
———. *France. 1848–1945*. 2 vols. Oxford: Clarendon Press, 1973–77.
Zuckerman, Phyllis. "Ideology and the Patriarchal Family: Nerval and Flora
    Tristan." *Sub-stance* 15 (1976): 146–58.

INDEX

CLAIRE GOLDBERG MOSES is Professor and Director of Women's Studies at the University of Maryland, College Park, and editor and manager of *Feminist Studies*. She is author of *French Feminism in the Nineteenth Century*, which won the Joan Kelly Memorial Prize in 1985.

LESLIE WAHL RABINE is Professor of French and Director of Women's Studies at the University of California, Irvine. She is author of *Reading the Romantic Heroine: Text, History, Ideology*, which won the Alice and Edith Hamilton Prize in 1985, and co-editor with Sara E. Melzer of *Rebel Daughters: Women and the French Revolution*.